BORN 1900

BORN 1900

*A Human History of
the Twentieth Century –
For Everyone Who Was There*

HUNTER DAVIES

LITTLE, BROWN AND COMPANY

A *Little, Brown* Book

First published in Great Britain in 1998
by Little, Brown and Company

Copyright © 1998 by Hunter Davies

The moral right of the author has been asserted.

*All photographs are from private collections
apart from those on: p. 35 (Popperfoto); p. 136 (Hulton Getty);
p. 143 (Hulton Getty); p. 272 (Associated Press);
p. 318 (Hulton Getty); p. 359 (Hulton Getty).*

A CIP catalogue record for this book
is available from the British Library.

ISBN: 0 316 64471 4

Typeset in Adobe Garamond by M Rules
Printed and bound in Great Britain
by Clays Ltd, St Ives plc

Little, Brown and Company (UK)
Brettenham House
Lancaster Place
London WC2E 7EN

For Jake and Rosa,
wishing them well in the twenty-first century.

CONTENTS

ACKNOWLEDGEMENTS

I am grateful to all those people born in 1900, and their families, who agreed to be interviewed, allowing me to share their memories and their memorabilia, along with five who were not included in the final book – Cecil Foster, Gwen McIntyre, Beatrice Blair, William Jenner and Lily Spark. To the British Legion, Help the Aged and other organisations who passed on names and contacts. To those officials at the *Daily Express*, Birmingham University, Mercedes-Benz, West Ham United, the Freud Museum, McDonald's, the Labour Party and the Queen Mother's Household who helped me along the way.

INTRODUCTION

Arthur Forster in 1926, aged 26

It was Arthur Forster, my father-in-law, who set me off. He was born in 1900 and I have always envied him the neatness of knowing he was the same age as the century. I have also envied his capacity for beer, his appalling fry-up breakfasts, his strength of mind and body, his skills in the garden and the house and, of course, his memories, such as knowing precisely where he was when the First World War broke out.

I had been thinking of a millennium book, full of historical facts and figures, surveys and reports, but then it occurred to me that the best way to look back at the century would be with the people who were there, through human eyes and ears, memories and emotions. Could I possibly find other people like Arthur who were born in 1900? They'd have to be fit enough mentally and physically to put up with me for at least two hours, for I can be rather tiring.

Arthur is a fairly unusual case, but then most people are, once you look into their lives and their thoughts. As I write, he is in a nursing home in Carlisle, mentally alert at the age of ninety-six, bossing the nurses around, making personal remarks about their hairstyles or any spots they might have. Until a year ago he was in his own bungalow, living on his own as he had since his wife Lily died in 1981, doing all his cooking, cleaning, painting and gardening; it was after one or two falls that it was decided he needed proper attention. He has his own room in the nursing home, filled with bits of his own furniture and personal items. There are photographs of his three children, six grand-children and two great-grandchildren. He also insisted on having his tools with him, his hammer and chisels, for which he will never again have any use – unless in the next life God, or similar, is in need of a good mechanic.

Arthur is unusual in that he has spent the whole of his life within two miles of his birthplace. He has never lived or worked elsewhere and only once been on a plane for a foreign holiday, when he came to visit us in Malta in 1968. He has never owned a car – though he always had a motorbike in his youth – nor his own house. He was in a council house until Margaret, his elder daughter, bought the bunga-low.

He left school in Carlisle at thirteen and became an apprentice fitter in a factory. A few years later he joined a local garage and became a motor mechanic. Today, while visiting him, I asked why he hadn't become a mechanic earlier, and he looked at me as if I was a total idiot: 'There were no bloomin' cars.' After that, he refused to answer any more of my barmy questions. That's one reason I have not included him in the main part of this book. It is hard to ask questions of someone when you know so much about them, or think you do.

Arthur was on holiday with his parents in a guest-house in Port Carlisle on the Solway coast when the First World War was declared. He still points out the exact house every time we go past. Naturally he wanted to join up, as all young men did in 1914. When he was sixteen he ran off to Newcastle, lied about his age and was filling in the forms, about to have his medical, when his father arrived from Carlisle. He was then dragged home. His date of birth is 4 December 1900, so the war was over by the time he reached eighteen. Many people born in 1900 did manage to serve, by being better liars and a few months older. I hoped to find some of them.

Like all those born in 1900, Arthur has followed the progress of the Queen Mother, comparing her health with his own. Today he handed me the *Daily Express*, which he has read all his life, starting with the sports pages for the horse-racing, and pointed to a photograph of the Queen Mother. I couldn't see anything unusual. 'She's wearing a plaster,' he said, pointing to her left leg.

Until he was ninety, Arthur had never been in hospital. When he went to his GP after his first fall, they couldn't find any notes on him. I am some thirty-six years younger than he is, but I have doctors' files big enough to fill a whole shelf, in both London and Cumbria, but then I do like to spread my medical symptoms around.

He did smoke, when he was younger, though he now denies it, despite the fact we have photographs to prove it. He has always been a beer drinker – followed by a Scotch, if he had the money. His diet, in theory, has been appalling, with fried eggs, bacon and sausages for breakfast all his life. He has never cared for green vegetables, although he has spent much of his spare time growing some magnificent specimens. Hard to believe his diet is typical of most people who get into their late nineties.

He never moans or groans, about his state of health, or about the world in general, or even about the all-pervasive sex and violence of today which so upsets many of the elderly. He seems to have been cynically amused all his life, always seeing through every politician, condemning most news items as gimmicks or stunts. His personal aim appears to have been to keep his head down and his nose clean, never drawing attention to himself, not speaking to strangers or revealing anything personal. As a little girl, my wife Margaret would ask why she couldn't talk to people or give her opinions. 'That's how Hitler found out things,' he said.

I asked him for the secret of his long life, a fairly dopey thing to say, but I wanted to see his reaction before I tried out the question on other people. I expected a grunt, or silence, or that he'd turn on his TV to watch the racing. 'Keep your bowels open and trust in the Lord,' he said with a smirk. Then he turned on the telly. He has no religious beliefs, and dislikes all clerics, so it was partly a silly answer to what he considered a pretty silly question. Would I have more success with other people born in 1900?

I hoped to find around ten suitable people, and at first I had trouble finding anyone, endlessly ringing up Help the Aged societies, old-soldier clubs and alumni organisations, but they didn't seem to have proper age records, or none into which they could hack easily. Then I did what I should have done in the beginning: I sent a letter to the editors of a selection of leading provincial newspapers, and also to the *Oldie* magazine, asking for people born in 1900. Suddenly, responses were flooding in.

There are, of course, more real oldies out there than ever before in our history. In 1951, for example, there were only 271 people over the age of 100 in Britain. By 1971, this had risen to 1,185. In 1991 it was 4,400. I estimate that in the year 2000 there will be at least 5,000 people still alive who were born in 1900. They will include, I hope, many of the people I met.

I tried to balance my selection by region, occupation and sex, though in the latter I was distorting the national average as there are about twice as many women as men over ninety. Two world wars thinned out the men. But I wanted as many male as female views of the century.

Now that I look down my list, I see I have ended up with five people out of the twenty who went to university, which is a huge exaggeration of the national average. (In 1900, only one in 2,000 went to university compared with one in three today.) I found several men who had seen active service in both wars – and a woman who had been a founder member of the RAF.

I tried to have a member of each interviewee's family present, or at least on hand, while I was talking to them, to help out or reassure. I also asked them to dig out in advance any photographic albums or other memorabilia. I would have loved to have produced a whole book just on this material, but my publisher was not quite so keen.

As with Arthur, my subjects' memories were best on their early years, and they delighted themselves with detailed stories of people and things now gone. I attempted to check their memories with their families or known facts, but did not always succeed. People's memories are true to them, whatever they have chosen to remember, and have to be accepted as such.

I always finished by asking them, as I asked Arthur, to explain how they had got to this great age, then to sum up and look back, to decide

Arthur aged 94

whether it had been a happy life, a fulfilled life, to tell me what regrets they had, if any, what they thought of the so-called modern world, and asked if they would go through it all again.

In the book, I have also included Things Begun in 1900. I thought I should balance the people with topics or institutions which also began this century. I started off with a long list but then whittled it down, partly because the People Born in 1900 proved so interesting and also because I decided I wanted things which have not only survived the century, but have grown with it, which have a story to tell, as the humans did. I have tried to link them where possible, looking out for internal connections between the People Born and the Things Begun in 1900, so the story of the century builds up as we go along. It was, however, pure luck that I found a woman born in 1900 who had gone to a university also born in 1900.

Some important medical and scientific inventions date from 1900, but on reflection, they didn't have a progression, a history, quite as world-wide or influential as, for example, the humble hamburger. The opera *Tosca* was given its première in 1900, and it would have been fun to chart from that the changes in cultural appreciation, but I feared it would have been of limited interest and provide few links with the real lives I was examining. The *Daily Express*, born in 1900, gave me a chance not just to look at Arthur's favourite newspaper but at the development of the mass media, a cultural experience we have all witnessed. I could have chosen a nice novel to follow, such as *Lord Jim*, but I chose non-fiction, Sigmund Freud's *The Interpretation of Dreams*. Through that, I could look at the history of psychoanalysis, one of the true wonders of the twentieth century – even if some people still wonder if it really works.

The object, with all the People and the Things, was to recall the flavour, the nature and concerns of this century, to remember inventions and events that have affected almost all our lives. I hope it will prove of interest, perhaps even a record of the twentieth century, for everyone who was there.

'When they launched the R-33 and R-34, they had all of us hanging on to the ropes. To keep it down, you see. The gas would have taken it up before they were ready to go, so all of us on the base, men and women, were hanging on the ropes to keep it on the ground. There were people shouting out orders at us, "*Heave starboard! Heave port!*" Oh, it was verra exciting.'

And what exactly did you do on the base as a member of the Royal Flying Corps? 'I was a waitress. Well, that's what it came down to, really. I was officially an Officer's Mess Orderly. I served in the Mess. Lady officers, mind you. Not men. We were all separated, men and women, on different parts of the base. No, I don't remember any romances, girls going out with the men. None of that. I got twelve shillings and sixpence a week. I lived on what we called the Mess Deck, with the other girls.

'One day we were told we were going into blue uniform. It turned out the RAF had been formed. So I was a founder member of the RAF. The new uniform was very nice as well. I never flew in an aeroplane myself, like, or an airship, but I used to walk inside the airships, right up and down, when they were in their hangars.

'It seemed like nothing at the time, being in the Royal Flying Corps or the RAF. We hardly took any heed of what was going on. We just did what we did. But, looking back now, it's history, isn't it? Oh, aye. Funny, really.

'I was the only northern girl on the base. Well, except for a Scottish girl from Portobello. They used to laugh at my accent and call me a Geordie. I would say I'm not a Geordie, I'm Northumbrian. They laughed at me when I said "divvent". A lot of people thought I must be Scandinavian or Danish, not English. They couldn't understand half of what I said. No, I didn't mind. Didn't upset me. I liked them all.

'Before the war had finally finished, they asked for women to volunteer to go over to France. They were running short of men on the front. I volunteered, of course, but then I was told you couldn't go unless you were twenty. I wasn't twenty, just coming up for nineteen. Then it came out you could go if your parents agreed. They contacted my parents – and they said no. They thought it was too dangerous. Aye, I was disappointed. I was dying to go. I loved it. Loved it all.

Jane's demob paper, 1919

'In 1919, when it was all over and there was peace, they said to us, "That's it, we don't want you any more, cheerio." They just discharged you and sent you home. There was nothing else I could do. I had to go home to Amble and become a maid again and get used to civilian things. Oh, aye. If I'd been allowed to stay on I would have done. Certainly.'

For the next four years, Jane worked as a maid, mainly with a Mr and Mrs Urwin who lived locally. 'She was called Jean Stray Urwin and she was an artist. She was a BA, oh yes, very well qualified. She had me in cloche hat standing on the beach for hours, sketching me standing there. I thought my face looked awful. I have some of her sketches somewhere. Then she got off landscapes and did portraits in her studio. I'd have to sit and pose for her. Oh, I liked it, liked it fine.'

There lived next door a young man called Albert Barrett, known as Butty, who worked as a fireman on the railway. He started walking out with Jane and they eventually got engaged. 'I think he was my first boyfriend. Oh, I liked the lads enough, but I wasn't really bothered much.

'His father was a bit of a bad beast. I don't mean a bad man, or a beast, in fact he was practically paralysed with war wounds. He'd been a regimental sergeant-major in the Boer War, in the Percy Artillery. He was just fierce. And I was pretty frightened of him.'

Working on the railway was thought to be a good job in those days, so was Butty considered a good catch? Jane thought for a moment, while Ann, her daughter, waited, wondering what the reply would be. 'No, not really,' said Jane at last. 'I could have done better.' Ann laughed.

They got married on 30 August 1924, at Amble parish church. 'We had no money so we couldn't afford a proper affair. There were no frills. I wore a nice costume, mind, with a black picture hat, which had a red rose on the side. The vicar did say to me I looked lovely. But we couldn't afford a photographer and no one had a camera so we had no wedding photographs. We had a short honeymoon at me auntie's house in Newcastle, and that was it.'

They moved into furnished rooms, then a one-bedroom cottage, before moving a few doors into the house Jane still lives in, where all her children were born. In 1925, she had twins, a boy and a girl, born at seven months, but neither survived. The little girl lived for an hour and the boy for nine days. In 1926, Howard arrived, followed by Bill in 1931 and Bradley in 1937. Then came a long gap, of almost ten years; Ann was born in 1946, by which time Jane was forty-six.

'Oh, aye, I was shocked,' she said. 'We had a river at the back of our house, and I said to the nurse when the baby was due, "If this is another boy, it's straight in the river. Ah divvent want him." Then the nurse said, "Oh, Mrs Barrett, it's a little girl."

'It was all meant. She was sent for a purpose. I couldn't have had a better daughter.' Ann made a face and raised her eyebrows.

Howard passed for the grammar school at Alnwick, then went on to Loughborough College of Technology. In the Second World War, he joined the army and became a captain, then left to go into the RAF, much to his mother's pleasure. 'I don't think it was anything to do with me, but I was verra pleased when he went into the RAF.' He rose to become a squadron-leader, ending at the Ministry of Defence in London. He has now retired and lives in Hertfordshire.

Bill went into the police and became a sergeant in Berwick, where he still lives. He, too, is retired. Bradley, always known as Brad, became a miner, like his grandfather, and retired from the pit at fifty. He lives near his mother. Ann worked in a chemist's shop after school, then at a hospital. Now she has the boarding kennels. All Jane's four children are married and she has eight grandchildren and four great-grandchildren.

Her husband Butty rose from fireman on the railway to engine driver on one of the earliest diesel locomotives on British Rail. He died in 1957, six miles away from home, at Widdrington, as he was taking the early-morning commuter train from Alnmouth to Newcastle. It was travelling at high speed when it went into a brick lorry on an unmanned level crossing. Butty was killed instantly. The driver of the brick lorry was uninjured.

'The first I knew was when a lady clerk from Alnmouth station came to our house. She said, "There's been a train crash." We weren't on the phone, you see. Then the doctor came to say my husband was dead. That was about all that happened, all I heard. I did get a bit of sympathy. People from the lorry-driver's side wrote to say they were sorry. There was also a letter of sympathy from a passenger on the train. The train was full that morning, but none of them were injured. It was a titled man who wrote. Lord Grey, was it, Ann?'

'I can't remember, Mother,' said Ann. 'I was at school that day. I was only eleven.'

Eventually Jane was awarded compensation of three thousand pounds. 'What I did with it was pay the house off. We'd already started to buy it. I thought, whatever happens to me now, I'll at least have a house.'

Jane had never flown in her RAF career, but when she was seventy-two her son Howard, then serving in the RAF on secondment in the USA, sent her a plane ticket. 'I went on my own, to Dayton, Ohio. Howard arranged it – oh, he's a brilliant lad, a canny lad. All the time in Dayton I was a VIP. It was functions night and day, functions all the way, visiting people and museums. I saw the world's biggest plane at the time, can't remember the type, and we went to the grave of the Wright brothers, you know, the ones who began planes.

'Then on my ninetieth birthday, I got a really big surprise. Howard had said he would pick me up and we'd go to Warkworth Castle and have a picnic. Well, when we got there, there was a helicopter in the middle of the castle grounds. Howard had got special permission from English Heritage to land it there. They'd cleared away the visitors so we could take off. We were up in the air for about half an hour, right up the coast to Berwick, over Bamburgh and Seahouses, oh, everywhere. The pilot said, "We'll dip down and look at your house," so we did, twice, to have a good look. It was champion, really nice. I was in the local paper.'

She has no intention of giving up her house in Warkworth, even though she was recently burgled. Two lads came to her front door, and while one engaged her in conversation, the other went round to the back and broke in. All they got was her purse containing three pounds. The police and local authorities were alarmed to realise that a vulnerable 96-year-old woman was living alone without a phone – and, of course, her own family were horrified. 'I think we were more worried than she was,' said Ann. 'She seemed to take it in her stride and hasn't dwelt on it. But she's now agreed we can put a phone in. It's being done when she gets back. She'll probably never use it. She hates anything technical or mechanical. That's why she won't have central heating. She had an open coal fire till recently. Now she's got an electric fire, but that's all she'll agree to.'

'No, I'm not leaving my house,' said Jane, defiantly. 'I'm not going into any of those places for old people. I'm going to die in my own house. So that's it.'

And probably perfectly made-up. Each morning, she not only dresses smartly but also puts on her make-up, whether she's going out or not. 'After I've washed my face, I put on my cream, my rouge, a bit of powder and lipstick. I use Oil of Ulay as well. Oh, that's very good for the complexion. I've always been smart, even when I had no money. "The smartest woman in Warkworth," that's what I've been called. I think people are a bit jealous of me because I look so smart and young. They can't believe I'm ninety-six. They say, "Turn it around and we'll believe you're sixty-nine. That's more like it."'

So what's the secret?

'I divvent kna. No idea. I've always eaten anything, never bothered about diets or things like that. And I still smoke, fifteen to twenty cigarettes most days. Oh, aye, it's one of my few pleasures.' Ann made another face, knowing very well that her mother has many pleasures left.

'I didn't smoke at all till I went into the RAF, then I saw all these lasses puffing away. I was the odd one out, so I thought I'd join them – and I haven't stopped. I'm the only one in my family who smokes, mind. None of them smokes.'

Have they tried to discourage you? 'Not at all. Howard sends me them as presents. This packet of Berkeley Mild, he sent them to me. And I'll tell you this, no doctor in my whole life, when I've been to see them, has ever said, "Stop smoking, Mrs Barrett." So there you are.

'Mind you, I don't drink. Well, a port and lemon at Christmas, and perhaps an egg flip, but that's it.'

Is being bright and cheerful a help in old age?

'Oh, I wouldn't say I was. I'm a worrier. Just look at my nails. Bitten right down. I'm a worrying sort of person. I worry about the way the world is going. All this crime and violence. You're not safe to go out. The world isn't getting better, now is it? When Ann was very ill recently, well, I was really worried . . .'

'I think her real secret,' said Ann, 'is that my mother is very young in mind. That's why she still takes a pride in her appearance. She feels young inside.'

Jane today

'I never had much luck in life, you know,' said Jane. 'Folks often say to me, "Oh, you're lucky with your family." Well, that's true, but I had no luck for a long time. Once they were all up and off, that's when things got better. I'm verra lucky these days. Why, aye. And I can get me teeth done for free.'

At that moment, Ann's husband John, the dentist, came into the room, saying he was going off to his surgery.

'Yes, life's easy now,' continued Jane, when he'd gone, 'though I do worry about Ann getting ill again.'

Would she have it all over again?

'Oh, I'm not coming back. That's it.'

How would she change things if she did come back?

'I wouldn't marry this time. In the Second World War, if I'd been single then, I would have been up and away. But I wasn't. I was tied.'

She was only fifty-seven when her husband was killed. Was there ever a possibility that she might have married again?

'No. Never again. Oh, I'm not anti-men, don't get me wrong. I like men. I just wouldn't want to be married next time . . .'

So what would you do? I asked, as Ann rolled her eyes, wondering what was coming.

'Well, I'd stay a spinster. Then, let me think, I'd get a job on an ocean liner as a stewardess and spend my life going round the world. That's, of course, if I couldn't get back in the RAF again.'

Jane's Royal Flying Corps and then RAF service is possibly now unique; at least, she has never heard of any other woman still alive who was in both. Her service was recognised in 1967 during the fiftieth anniversary celebrations for the foundation of the RAF. She was invited by the Queen Mother to an ex-servicewomen's garden party at St James's Palace.

'Oh, it was lovely. I shook hands with the Queen Mother, Princess Alexandra and the Duchess of Gloucester. There was a lot of high-class top brass from the RAF there. I didn't know anybody. The Queen Mother and the other royals went down the line, shaking hands. The Duchess of Gloucester stopped and talked to me and asked me where I'd come from. "My," she said, "you've come a long way." "Aye," I said, "but it's been worth it."'

Naturally, she has kept an eye on the Queen Mother all these decades. That day she admired her frock, which was pink, and also noticed her legs. 'A lot of knotted bits. She obviously had varicose veins. I suppose she's had them done by now. But she's a marvellous woman. Oh, yes, I admire her. But she's had to suffer with her family. All those problems, splitting up and things. I'm not sure you can call them the Royal Family. They're not really royal any more, are they? Just an ordinary family.

'Well, that's me up to date. You're in the picture. That's what happened, up to now. I think I'll go outside and have a cigarette.'

2

RICHARD JOYCE

Londoner and printer of the Radio Times

Richard Joyce in 1918

Richard Joyce was wearing his bowler hat when I first met him, as he always did if going out and about. A bowler was commonplace in Britain at one time, but is now only seen in period films or foreign parodies of British life. It wasn't just City types who wore them but craftsmen with a bit of status, a sure sign of their rank and position.

The particular craft in which Richard served always had a bit more status than the craft which Arthur, my father-in-law, had practised. Richard was a printer, a trade which traditionally looked after its own, and he had risen to become a rather important figure in the printing world. Like Jane Barrett, but unlike Arthur, he had also seen military service.

He was living in his own comfortable, spacious, first-floor apartment in a private block of flats at Hatch End in London's northern suburbs, his home for the last twenty-five years. He does his own cooking, has his own social life, and even drives his own car. Most unusual, given his age.

He shares his home with his son, Ted. That's also unusual: a more common situation is that an aged parent ends up in the care of a spinster daughter. Richard and Ted, a bachelor, are equal co-habitants, supporting each other like a modern, if slightly more affluent and up-market, version of *Steptoe and Son*.

Richard was born on 14 April 1900, in Edward Square, Islington – 'between the two prisons, Holloway and Pentonville'. He had five sisters and two brothers. His printer father was often out of work and very hard up, and Richard has memories of constant midnight flits. 'The first was when I was aged three or four. About twelve o'clock one night we were all woken up and told to get dressed. We then got on to the back of this horse and cart, with all our belongings. It belonged to the local greengrocer, who was a friend of my dad's. We were off to a new place in Haringey.

'I never knew the reasons at the time, but I realised later what was going on, because it happened three or four times. My dad had fallen behind with his rent, been unable to pay, probably run up other debts as well. The only way out was to do a bunk. In those days, there was no mercy, no social security. At a certain stage, they would just arrive and take away everything you owned, every stick of furniture, everything, except the bed. Oh, yeah, they left the bed. That was the rule. Take everything but the bed.'

Richard went to school in Haringey, Woodlands Park, and then in Tottenham, Risley Avenue, which was a new school and seemed very smart. 'I liked chemistry, poetry and geography.' Despite his father's bouts of unemployment, he can recall no real poverty: 'We were always shod.'

He left school on his fourteenth birthday, hoping to follow his father into the print business, but at first he had to take a temporary job as a tea-boy for a firm of cabinet-makers, Levy's, in Tottenham, while waiting for an opening in print, which eventually came on 4 August 1914.

'My father had eventually got me a job with the Amalgamated Press in Lavington Street, Southwark. This was part of Lord Northcliffe's empire, Alfred Harmsworth as he was. I remember seeing him in the *Daily Mail* offices. He was pointed out to me. I didn't speak to him, of course. And no, he didn't speak to me.'

Richard gave a throaty laugh and stuck out his tongue like a school-boy. He looks tough and severe much of the time, a person not to be meddled with, used to telling working men what to do, but when he laughs his face and eyes light up.

Beside him, where he was sitting, was a cushion embroidered with the legend, 'To the Ogre. Love from Tich.' That's a family joke, him being called the Ogre. Tich is his affectionate name for Veronica, his granddaughter, now aged forty-two, who happens to be almost six feet tall.

'That first day, when I started proper work, 4 August, was the day war broke out. I remember the newsboys shouting, "War declared!" In the street when I arrived were some Territorial soldiers from the City of London Rifles. It so happened that the general manager of the Amalgamated Press was also the colonel of their regiment. By chance, they were about to go off for two weeks of manoeuvres. They went off – but never came back. They just went straight into the war.

'Oh, yes, there was great excitement. People rushed in their thousands to join up. It was the thing to do. Kitchener wanted a million by Christmas, and I think he got two million. Everyone wanted to join. I think one of the reasons there was reluctance to join up in the Second World War was because they'd heard stories from the First. At the time, I was very disappointed. I thought there's no chance for me. It'll be all over by the time I'm old enough.'

His apprenticeship as a printing engineer – learning about the machines, rather than handling the type – began on 1 January 1915 and was scheduled to last seven years. His wage was eight shillings a week. 'We had all sorts of printing machines – Linotype, Indotype, Monotype. We did rotary printing, flat-bed printing, photogravure, offset, everything, really. At Amalgamated Press we were printing *Answers*, *Home Chat*, *Comic Cuts*, *Chips*, *Puck*. I liked working on the comics. I loved all comics as a boy. *Magnet* and *Gem* were my favourite, with Harry Wharton and Bob Cherry.'

When he got to seventeen and a half, with the war still going on, he decided to join the navy. 'I didn't have to lie about my age. They were taking boys at seventeen and a half. I passed all the tests to become an ERA – Engine Room Artificer – and was told which day I had to join HMS *Vernon* at Portsmouth. Just before I was due to go, all recruitment to the navy was stopped. I was stuck. I'd given up my job, expecting I was off to be an engineer in a submarine. I went down to Whitehall to find out what was going on, and asked if I could join the army. They gave me and some other chaps various tests. We had to wait a bit, but then in April 1918, by which time I'd become eighteen, I joined the Bedfordshire Regiment.

'I spent six weeks square-bashing at Brockton Camp in Staffordshire. It was also a prisoner-of-war camp. While I was there, one of the chaps caught some infectious disease, dunno what it was, diphtheria perhaps, but we were all isolated for three weeks to stop it spreading.

'When the training finished I was sent to Norfolk, where we all waited, hoping to go abroad. That was part of the excitement of joining up, hoping to go abroad. But there was an outcry in the papers, about young boys being sent off as cannon fodder. So they stopped it, for chaps of my age. I didn't go abroad till later in the year. I suppose that must have been about November, around Armistice time.

'I joined the British Army on the Rhine at a little place called Hennef, dunno how you spell it, near a place called Ceaseburg [Siegburg]. There was a sort of fifty-mile neutral zone, a no-man's-land where people weren't supposed to go. We were guarding one side of it, checking documents and things. The local Germans were in a shocking state. We were billeted on a smallholding, so our food was quite good. I used to scrape up the leftovers from the Mess and give them to the local people. All they had was potatoes. They'd never seen things like chocolate or soap. No, there was no ill feeling from the Germans. They were all very friendly.

'I never saw any fighting. The only casualty we had was when one of our chaps walked round the back of a train – and went slap into an oncoming train. Stone dead, that was it. He was a bit older and had been in the war since about 1915, fighting in the trenches, surviving all that, then he walks into a train. Kemp. He was called Kemp. It's come back to me.

'I enjoyed the army, all of it. I was a first-class shot. I was the only one in our company of two hundred men who could fire a Lewis gun and hit the target six hundred yards away while wearing a gas mask.'

Suddenly Richard burst out laughing, as if he had only now realised how funny it must have looked, shooting in a gas mask.

'I got crossed guns on my arm and it entitled me to sixpence extra a day. In all, I got one and sixpence extra a day for shooting skills. My basic pay was ten and six a week – but it came to a guinea a week with the extras. I only got fourteen shillings a week in my hand because the rest went direct to my mother. If you agreed to let your mother have more than three and six a week from your pay, the army would double it. I think that was the system.'

Richard left the army in May 1920, and returned home to resume his apprenticeship. 'I'd done four years before the army, and had three to go, but because of being in the army, they cut it in half. So I only had to do another eighteen months to finish my apprenticeship.'

When he did, at the end of 1921, he was given the traditional printers' ceremony of 'banging out', which happened when printers were accepted into the trade or when they retired. 'At twelve o'clock, on my last day as an apprentice, I walked through the engineers' workshop and all the men banged on their machines. Then you got a few little presents from your friends.'

On becoming a qualified craftsman, and a member of the adult working fraternity, Richard went immediately into a bowler hat – not just for work but for all social occasions too.

He was wearing his bowler when he first met his wife, Ethel Mardell, in 1921, on the top of a tram. 'I was going out for the evening with a couple of chaps. I was living with my parents in Lordship Lane at the time. We were on the way to Wood Green Empire. I loved the music hall. Can't remember who was on that night, but it might have been George Robey. Ethel was on the tram with a girl, going to the same music hall. It just sort of developed from there. We went to lots of dances. That was the way you met girls. I didn't have any lessons. I just picked it up by going to dances. The valeta, the lancers, that sort of style, at the Tottenham Palace or the Municipal Hall.'

Ethel worked as a 'nippy' for Joe Lyons, then moved from serving at tables to the front desk and then to outside catering, at Ascot and the Oval.

'She once served Jack Hobbs,' interjected Ted, Richard's son. He hadn't spoken so far, letting his dad take centre stage. He'd been hovering in the background, bringing tea and biscuits or looking out photographs and letters to jog his father's memory.

Richard and Ethel got married on 11 November 1922 in Wood Green register office. A simple wedding, not a white one, no reception, no honeymoon and no photographs. 'We couldn't afford it.' They moved into two rooms at nine shillings a week in Wood Green. Kathleen, their first child, was born in 1923, followed by Ted. 'I was born in 1928,' Ted added. 'The same year as Mickey Mouse.'

Although Richard started off his married life with no money, he was soon trying to better himself. He left Amalgamated Press six months after he had finished his apprenticeship and moved to a better job with Intertype, a firm at King's Cross, then to Cassell's in Ludgate Circus. 'That was a good job, but when it closed during the General Strike of 1926 it never opened again. I was out of work for three months, the most I ever was.'

Next he got a job with a firm installing print machines, which led to an offer from a firm in Crystal Palace. 'I'd erected a machine for them which worked okay when I was there, no problems, but they couldn't get it to work on their own, so they invited me to join them.' The firm was called Samuel Stephen Ltd and it printed nine local papers. Richard was there for seventeen years, until the end of the Second World War, rising to be in charge of the machine room. In 1937 he joined the Masons and has been an active member ever since.

He bought his own house in Crystal Palace and moved in just in time to witness at first hand one of the great national events of the decade, the Crystal Palace fire of November 1936.

'I'd been to a printing exhibition at Earl's Court that evening. On the way home, I'd gone into a pub with some friends. I was playing darts when someone says the Crystal Palace is on fire. I said, "Don't be daft. It's made of glass and iron, it can't go on fire." Cor, when I got home, what a sight. Our house was about three miles away, but to get home, I had to trample over miles of hose pipes. From our house, you could feel the heat and see the sky transformed.'

During the Second World War, he was technically in a reserved occupation, and therefore not liable to be called up, but he joined the Civil Defence and became a senior fire guard. In uniform once again, this time he ended up with three stripes. Kathleen joined the WAAF. Ted, still a schoolboy, was evacuated to Devon.

'I went out on fire duty about three times a week, looking for fires. Unpaid. It was all voluntary. We carried a stirrup pump and we had little fire engines, but mostly I was instructing other fire guards what to

Richard in the Civil Defence, 1943

do. I worked in Croydon, which was one of the most heavily bombed areas of London. There wasn't a house that wasn't damaged, even if it just had the windows blown out. Our house was blasted three times. The worst was a V1 rocket . . .'

'No, the V1 wasn't so bad,' said Ted. 'They were sort of flying bombs, so you could see them coming. The V2 was worse. That was the sort that just dived straight down, to a great depth, and then exploded.'

'Okay, then, it was the V2,' said Richard. 'Anyway, the wife and I were at the pictures when we heard it go off. On the trolley bus home we could see great clods of earth. Our house was okay, except for the windows – they'd all been sucked out. Sucked out, not blown in. Very strange.'

Meanwhile, Ted the evacuee, aged fourteen, was having his own problems. He'd written to his parents, saying he wasn't very well, so they went down to see him – and in 1940 brought him back to London, despite the bombing.

'We found he'd got osteomylitis, which is inflammation of the bone marrow. They said at the time that it was caused by malnutrition.'

'It wasn't the fault of the people I was evacuated with,' said Ted. 'They were fine. It was my own fault, really. I'd always been a finnicky eater. I was supposed to eat school dinners, but I never did. I didn't like them, but nobody knew. I just used to exist on things like cakes. I was a bread-delivery boy, so I got lots of cakes at work.

'Anyway, I eventually had an operation for the osteomylitis, but over the years things got worse. I started my working life as a printer, like my father, but was often ill and depressed. When I got to the age of thirty, my leg was ulcerating so much they took it off. Well, they took off half the leg. It's been fine since. That seemed to cure things – well, settle that particular trouble . . .'

Ted's voice fell. He went off to find a photo of his father in his Civil Defence uniform, to prove he'd got three stripes. It was in an album labelled 'Father Wins the War – Again!'

After the war Richard got himself a new and better job, as general manager in charge of the printing of a well-known publication. 'I'd heard that the chap at the *Radio Times* had just died, so I wrote and asked for the job. And I got it. I'd always looked in life to take a step above. I considered myself reasonably intelligent, even though I hadn't been to any college or got degrees. That never worried me. I never met anyone in the print industry who did get ahead of me because of his education. That all happened much later, with the new technology.'

The printing of the *Radio Times* was done at Park Royal by Waterlow's and was one of the company's biggest contracts. The *Radio Times* was the largest selling publication of any sort in Britain, shifting nine million copies a week. Richard remained as general manager of the printing side for twenty-one years, until he retired in 1966.

'I enjoyed all my years at the *Radio Times*. I was responsible in 1964 for the change-over to colour. That was a big development. But I have to say that during all those years my biggest problems were with the unions. I seemed never to be free of union troubles.'

As an apprentice he had joined the Amalgamated Engineering Union (AEU). When he became a printer, he was in the National Society of Operative Printers and Assistants (NATSOPA), then later in the National Graphical Association. 'I'm still in the NGA. I got a pension from them when I retired, only a pound a week, mind you, till their money ran out.'

As a young man he had benefited from the traditional power of the unions in being allowed into a trade which was almost a closed shop, but when he rose to management status he saw it differently. 'They used their power too much, overplayed their hands. It became ridiculous. They would agree a staff ratio per machine. Let's say it was twenty people to look after one machine, but if for any reason only nineteen turned up one day, because of illness or whatever, they would all down tools, even though the nineteen of them could easily do it.'

'In the print industry, it always took two people to change a light-bulb,' said Ted. 'Because an electrician always had to have his mate with him . . .'

'There was this case at the *Daily Express* print room, just after the war,' continued Richard. 'All the rolls of paper were coming from Newfoundland and they had wooden batons at the end of them, to keep them in place. Fifteen men were needed to take the batons off before they could be used. Anyway, then they stopped getting the paper from Newfoundland. The new supplies arrived from Europe, without any batons – but the unions insisted those fifteen men had to be kept on. Year after year they were kept on, even though they had no work to do. So I wasn't really sorry when Rupert Murdoch got rid of the lot of them, when he moved to Wapping and did without them. They'd spoiled it for themselves.'

While at the *Radio Times,* Richard became active in various printing-trade benevolent organisations. On his walls are photos of him with the Duchess of Kent and other royals. He also became something of a big cheese in the Masons, rising to Grand Standard Bearer. Sounds impressive. 'I was in two lodges. At one time I was out on Masonic business two or three times a week.'

Didn't your wife get fed up? 'Oh, no, she didn't mind. She had her bridge.'

When he retired in 1965, his salary was £3,500 per year. He got a reasonable pension, but soon found he was bored, although he played a lot of golf, so he set himself up as a consultant, specialising in waste paper. He worked almost full-time for about twenty years, all of it from home. 'I did a bit of wheeling and dealing, buying and selling paper.'

He has always had a car, from pre-war days, and he and his wife always took good holidays. In Devon or Cornwall before the war, then afterwards they went to Europe, mostly Switzerland, by train and later by car.

His wife Ethel developed heart trouble and died on Christmas Day in 1978, after a long illness. 'The year my wife died, I had two-thirds of my stomach taken out. I'd had trouble with ulcers, but I think the stress of her being ill had a lot to do with it.'

In June 1979, he got a call from Paddington Station to say that Ted, his son, then aged fifty-one, had collapsed on the platform and narrowly escaped being run over by a train. Richard went at once by car to collect him and to give him a piece of his mind, thinking he'd just been stupid – only to find the real cause of Ted's problems.

'I'd become an alcoholic,' says Ted. 'It wasn't to do with Mum dying, though that didn't help. At least she never knew about it. Neither Mum or Dad had ever suspected what was happening in my life. It had gone on for years. I'd just lost my nerve. I felt hopeless and useless and depressed, unless I had a drink. So I'd have a drink – and make myself worse.

'At the time I fell at the station, I'd been off work sick for a year. It was my nerves officially, but it was the drink that was doing the damage. I looked upon drink as a medicine. I'd taken it to give myself confidence. I didn't actually drink such a great deal. I've always had a weak stomach, like my father, so a little had a big effect on me. By the time I fell at Paddington, I was probably drinking a bottle a day. Gin, usually. That day I don't think I'd had a lot to drink, I just felt so hot all over. Sweating like a pig. Then I passed out. Yes, I could easily have been killed.'

Ted was taken to a hospital to dry out, then he joined Alcoholics Anonymous, which he still attends. He'd been living on his own in a flat at the time of his collapse, but after his return from hospital, he moved in with his father and has lived with him ever since. 'I came home for Mum's funeral – and just never left.'

'Yeah, that year was bloody tricky,' Richard sighed.

Ted has written his own memoir of his fight against alcoholism – *This Too Shall Pass*, subtitled *The Story of an Alcoholic*. He has also written a book about cricket. He fetched copies of them, which I admired, but I didn't recognise the publisher. 'I paid for them,' said Ted. 'They said they'd tried to sell all the copies, but they didn't. You can have one if you like.'

Ted hasn't had a drink since 1979 but says that no one is ever totally recovered. His father always used to enjoy a drink, downing three or four pints in an evening after work, perhaps finishing with a Scotch. 'I was lucky, you might say. I had a weak stomach, so I was always sick if I drank more than my stomach could stand,' he said. 'But many's the time I've driven home the worse for drink. Luckily, I never got caught or had an accident.'

'I think the worst bit about driving drunk,' said Ted, 'is when you start seeing double . . . But I have to say that my dad was a hero in respect of my alcoholism. He was aged eighty at the time, but he spared no effort or expense to get me back to the land of the living. I am indebted to him for my new life.'

Richard drives only short distances these days, in his Renault 20, just two or three miles to the shops. I hadn't realised that driving was still allowed at his age, without any special tests. 'It's like any other form, your income tax form or whatever. When you have to fill it in, you sign at the end to say you've told the truth. I told the truth last time I got my licence. My eyes are fine for driving. I have no medical problems which stop me driving. My knees might not be as strong as they were, but that's about it. Apart, of course, from my stomach problems. Oh, and I had a prostate operation five years ago. But that's all.'

Until he was ninety-five, Richard played golf regularly at Grimsdyke Golf Club. At his best, his handicap was 12. When he gave up last year, it was 37. 'I've stopped playing, but I still have my own golf club.'

What? You own a golf course?

'No, just the Richard Joyce Golf Society.' Ted went to fetch some headed notepaper and a set of the rules, to let me see.

'It began about twenty years ago when I was a consultant for a waste-paper firm. I was discussing with them incentives, loyalty awards for staff. I suggested offering golfing weekends. The boss thought it a good idea and asked me to organise it. Then a new boss arrived, and didn't like his senior staff having so many days off. By then I was organising golfing weeks in Spain, which people loved. They said they'd still go, in their own holidays. So that's what happened. Every year, twenty-five of us go for a week's golf in Spain or Portugal. We stay in the best hotels, play the best courses, and I arranged it all until just recently. Flights, everything. We also have a day out at Selsdon Park, and a dinner. The society is all men. Oh, no women. It's still called after me, and going strong. I missed the April trip, as I didn't feel quite so good. I didn't want to flake out and be a nuisance. But if I feel as good as I do now, I'll go next year. I'm still secretary of the residents' association for this block. There are sixty-four families, all leaseholders. Oh, yes, I still keep myself busy.'

When I arrived, I noticed he'd been reading a Catherine Cookson novel in ordinary print. So his eyes *are* still good. He watches the news and sport on television.

'*Countdown* is his favourite programme,' said Ted, in a rather superior, literary way. His father laughed.

Do they have rows?

'Oh, not really,' said Ted. 'Well, everyone has a row now and again, but we get on fine, better than we did. He's not really an ogre.'

'That started during the last war,' said Richard. 'When Ted and his friends came round to the house, they would go straight to our larder. All food was rationed then. I'd get really mad and shout at them when they tried to take anything.'

Ted does the shopping and provisioning for the two of them, but each does his own cooking and eats on his own.

'I have to be careful about what I eat,' said Ted. 'So does he. But we don't eat a lot, really. I do the household jobs, basically. But he pays for everything.'

Richard smoked cigarettes till he was sixty, then moved on to cigars, which he gave up five years ago. These days he is virtually teetotal. He finds he's lost the taste for drink. He has outlived all his brothers and

Richard today

sisters. Most managed to get to their eighties, and one to ninety. He doesn't know how he's managed it.

'Luck,' he said. 'That's all you can say. Bloody good luck. I suppose on the whole I've done things in moderation. I've had a good life. It hasn't been flowers all the way. I've had some bad times.' He paused. I thought he was going to say his wife's illness, or Ted's alcoholism. 'Being unemployed for three months, back in 1923. That was hard.'

'A lifetime of happiness,' mused Ted, clearly the philosopher in the family. 'No man could endure that.'

'What gets me,' said Richard, 'is all these buggers going on all the time today about stress. All this stress counselling. We didn't have any of that in the war, but we got through it. Look at Norway and Sweden, best social-welfare programme in the world, and they're all committing suicide. You can have too much help and guidance, if you ask me. You need a bit of stress in life or you go mad.'

Richard voted Labour for most of his working life, considering himself a working man despite his rise up the management ladder. 'That changed about fifteen years ago. The Winter of Discontent got me down. Then Labour's problems with the unions, and all the militants. I couldn't see any way Labour would sort out all those problems. Only Mrs Thatcher seemed to have the right idea. She was a good strong woman. She knocked the unions into shape.'

Has he now returned to Labour? 'No, I don't think so. I have liked some of their leaders in the past, such as Attlee and Herbert Morrison. They were good blokes. Tell you who I didn't like. The Chamberlains. I thought they were rubbish.'

He reads the *Express* and the *Daily Mail* each day, and the *Sunday Telegraph*, and considers himself up on most of the news.

'The world today is bloody awful. No one can deny that. The main problem is lack of discipline amongst the young. They're frightening, young people today. They just don't realise how lucky they are. That boy in today's paper, the one expelled from school. His parents are on the dole and they're "caught in the poverty trap". That's what it says. They don't know the meaning of the word. I saw his house on the telly. They've got a TV, a CD-player, fitted carpets, I noticed all of that – and a car! Yet both parents are on the dole, supported by the social services. That's not poverty. Poverty in my day meant nothing. No dole money, no nothing. And if you had anything, like a few sticks of furniture, they'd take that from you.

'But there's been a lot of good things since 1900, don't get me wrong. Medicine is much better. And the National Health Service. That's about the best thing in my lifetime. Quality of life is generally much better for everyone, even the poor.'

Ted thinks his father will get to 100 and see the next millennium. 'Oh, he will, the way he's going. He'll get to 2000.'

'I don't like to think about the future,' said Richard. 'But I won't be going into any home. I had a week in a rest home once, one of the Printers' Benevolent homes. It was okay, but I don't want to live in one. I want to stay here. But it's all in the lap of the gods . . .

'I would have to say, yes, I have had a happy life. Never had to worry about money. Not that I had a lot, but enough to live comfortably. I've got no regrets. None I can think of. There was one holiday I regretted missing, when my wife was first ill. We were booked up to go to South Africa. She couldn't make it. We both regretted missing that. That's about all, really.'

3

THE *DAILY EXPRESS*

THE ⛨ EXPRESS

Ludgate House 245 Blackfriars Road London SE1 9UX
0171 928 8000

The newspaper's letterhead today

The *Daily Express*, Arthur Forster's favourite paper, was born in 1900. Like many of those who entered the world that year, it has taken part in many battles, witnessed defeats and victories, experienced enormous technological advances, seen fortunes won and lost, been affected by great social changes, new habits and moral standards. Now, at the end of the century, it is not as strong on its feet, needs a helping hand, has not the influence it once enjoyed, but despite everything it is still with us. As we go to press.

Unlike the humans born in 1900, who were allowed time to get on their feet, the *Daily Express* arrived fighting, engaged in a battle that has gone on until this day, a war of words, but one that could well end in its death. And throughout its life, the battle has been against the same enemy: the *Daily Mail*. The *Mail* was founded by Alfred Harmsworth in 1896. The *Daily Express* was founded by Arthur Pearson – not by Lord Beaverbrook, as many believe.

Pearson was born in 1866, a year after Harmsworth, and had a similar, fairly impoverished middle-class background. His father was a hard-up curate, though his grandfather had achieved a degree of fame by writing 'Abide With Me'. The young Pearson got into Winchester, but left at sixteen when the family money ran out and became a freelance journalist.

In 1884, he saw a competition advertised in *Tit-Bits* magazine, some
130 questions to be answered over thirteen weeks with the winner
promised a job on the magazine at £100 a year. Arthur rushed to his
father's library to look up the answers, and when he couldn't find them,
he rode thirty miles on his bike to his nearest public library, which was
in Bedford. He won – and came to London, aged eighteen, to work as
a clerk on *Tit-Bits*, not as a journalist, and met the young Harmsworth,
who was writing stories for the paper. They were never close friends –
and, very quickly, became fierce rivals.

Pearson rose to become manager, but in 1890, aged twenty-four,
upset that George Newnes wasn't paying him enough, he followed the
example of Harmsworth and began his own magazine, which he called
Pearson's Weekly. It's interesting that young people with no capital, just
good ideas and energy – plus indulgent backers – managed to start their
own publications. Today, when modern technology has, in theory, made
publishing easier, it can take millions to start any sort of national magazine.

However, Pearson soon ran into financial problems. He was bailed
out by Sir William Ingrams, proprietor of the *Illustrated London News*,
who just happened to be an old Wykehamist. Such connections still
help today.

But it was a clever circulation-boosting competition that really made
him successful. All you had to do was guess the missing word in a verse
of poetry which had been written specially, so you couldn't look it up.
It was a shilling to enter – but the shillings were shared between all the
people who won. It was such an enormous success that by competition
number 53 there were half a million entries. Rival magazines pinched
the idea, until one was taken to court and prosecuted on the dubious
grounds of running a national lottery, which since 1826 had been
banned in Britain – until it returned with Camelot in 1995.

By 1899, aged only thirty-three, Pearson had made a great deal of
money, but his eyesight was failing and he was thinking of devoting his
life to good works – but his deadly rival Harmsworth's success with the
Daily Mail brought him back into the fray. In 1900, the *Mail*
announced the astounding news that it was selling one million copies a
day. Pearson was determined to grab some of those readers and beat his
rival. On 24 April the first issue of the *Daily Express* appeared.

It was the same price as the *Mail*, a ha'penny, the same size and shape, eight pages long. It boasted on the front page that orders for the first issue came to a million and a half but that they might not be able to satisfy this 'unprecedented and entirely unforeseen demand'. It was to be the organ of no political party but would be patriotic. 'Our policy is the British Empire.'

The *Express* was born at the height of the Boer War, when the country was high on patriotism. The first front page carried news of fighting at Bloemfontein. A few weeks later on 19 May there was even bigger news when they announced the relief of Mafeking. They doorstepped the family of the hero of the hour, Major-General Baden-Powell, and managed to get a few suitably restrained but emotional words from his sister.

The paper carried no photographs, just a few weedy line-drawings, and no screaming headlines. Everything was restrained and, to our modern eyes, unsensational. About the only things that made it different from the 'serious' press, such as *The Times*, were much shorter stories and a lack of classical quotations, which it was assumed the masses would not understand. But the masses, as Pearson and Harmsworth recognised, were being educated now in great numbers. 'Never forget the cabman's wife,' Pearson told his staff.

British newspapers kept in with the government in power. Pearson became a friend of Joseph Chamberlain, the colonial secretary, and was appointed chairman of the Tariff Reform League, which Chamberlain had launched. Chamberlain admired Pearson as an activist and called him 'the greatest hustler I have ever known'. It was meant, apparently, as a compliment.

The term 'tabloid' had been first used in 1900 by Alfred Harmsworth, when he designed and edited an experimental issue of the *New York World* for New Year's Day 1900. It was half the usual page size and was filled with short, easily digested stories. Until then, 'tabloid' referred to medicines sold in tablet or concentrated form. It is assumed that Harmsworth took the word from the tablets. Neither the Americans nor the British picked up the term until 1903, when Harmsworth himself founded what became the world's first tabloid, the *Daily Mirror*.

The *Mirror* started as a paper for gentlewomen. It didn't do very well at first, but with new developments in photographic reproduction, Harmsworth decided to fill it with large photographs – the first in a ha'penny newspaper. The second tabloid, the *Daily Sketch*, was founded by Sir Edward Hulton in Manchester in 1909.

Meanwhile, the *Daily Express* was thriving under its first editor, an American, Ralph Blumenfeld, who had been the London correspondent of the *New York Herald*. Blum, as he was known, was an original whiz kid, having whizzed over from the States full of the latest ideas and systems. Like many whiz kids, though, some of his ideas were not quite so hot: he predicted that London's Underground would not last, dismissed golf as a 'rubbidge' game that wouldn't last either, and was very suspicious of the new-fangled pneumatic tyres. But as an editor he was considered a genius, and by the time the First World War began, he had made a further fortune for Pearson.

Overnight the war reduced the size of all newspapers, put up costs and lowered their sales and influence. Most fell victim to various political intrigues, which provided the opportunity for a newcomer on the Fleet Street block: Max Aitken.

Aitken was born in Canada in 1879, one of ten children of a Presbyterian minister who had emigrated from Scotland. Young Max made a fortune in cement in Canada and then came to London in 1909. He backed his fellow Canadian and friend Andrew Bonar Law in his political ambitions and in 1910 became a Tory MP himself. He hoped for a ministerial post during the war, but Lloyd George, whom he had supported in a complicated manoeuvre to oust Asquith as Prime Minister, refused. He considered Aitken a 'little Canadian adventurer', but he did give him a peerage in 1916, which turned him into Lord Beaverbrook.

Beaverbrook needed a power base to fuel and fashion his various political intrigues and campaigns, and in 1916 he bought the *Daily Express* for £17,500, plus losses of around £40,000. He'd already helped it financially when it needed money. Lord Northcliffe, as Harmsworth had become, said Beaverbrook had made a terrible mistake, and that he would now lose all his fortune in Fleet Street. But it helped his national influence: in 1918 he finally got a government position when he was made Minister of Information.

During the war, the *Daily Express* was still using few photographs and modest headlines and was now being beaten for sales by the much live-lier *Daily Mirror*. Beaverbrook tried to buy the *Sunday Times*, but Lloyd George, who had taken over from Asquith as Prime Minister, would not allow this as Beaverbrook was a government minister. Instead, in December 1918, he founded another newspaper, the *Sunday Express*. It lost him £150,000 the first year, £300,000 in the second, but after that it reached a reasonable sale of 300,000 copies a week.

After the war, the *Daily Express* began to expand in sales and cover-age, thanks partly to its racing tips. In June 1922, the paper picked thirty-three winners in one month and the circulation jumped from 530,000 to 700,000. When the tips began to falter, so did the circula-tion. In 1929 Blumenfeld was replaced as editor by Beverley Baxter, a Canadian.

Beaverbrook made no secret of the fact that he was in newspapers to influence events. Modern media moguls, often from a similar colonial background, do much the same, though they are usually hoping to use their political influence for financial and business purposes. Beaverbrook later admitted to a Royal Commission that 'I run the paper for the purpose of making propaganda, and with no other motive.' But he was aware of the need to make money as well.

He was once upset to find his wife reading the *Daily Mail*. She said she took it for the drapers' adverts. At the time, the *Daily Express* didn't have any, so Beaverbrook contacted his American friend Gordon Selfridge, owner of the department store, and persuaded him to adver-tise in the *Express*. As a reward, Selfridge became one of the handful of people the *Express* empire was never allowed to criticise – allies worth having, as the empire had grown to three newspapers with the purchase of the London *Evening Standard* in 1923.

Arthur Christiansen is the editor most credited with the paper's success – a real working, inky journalist, as opposed to Pearson, Northcliffe and Beaverbrook, who were entrepreneurs or politicians. Christiansen was born in Wallasey in 1904. He worked on local papers in Liverpool, then joined the *Sunday Express* as a sub-editor in 1926. During the General Strike, he helped to produce a scab edition of the paper, aided by various un-inky society friends of Lord Beaverbrook, such as Edwina Mountbatten. He was then promoted to news editor on £12 a week.

In 1930, as an assistant editor, he was at home one Saturday evening, about to go on holiday next day, when news of the R101 airship disaster came through. He went straight back to the office – with his pyjamas on under his coat, it was later said – and set about producing a new edition, almost single-handed, hiring special trains to take it round the country.

Beaverbrook was most impressed, as were the deadly rivals over at the *Daily Mail* group. Lord Rothermere offered Christiansen £3,000 a year to edit the *Sunday Dispatch*. Christiansen, aged twenty-six, was then earning £2,000 and asked for time to consider, hoping that Lord Beaverbrook would hear, which he did. His salary was increased to the *Mail*'s offer. In this respect, little seems to have changed in journalism.

In 1933, aged twenty-nine, Christiansen became editor of the *Daily Express*, a position he held until 1958, during which time the *Express* became the dominant newspaper in British life. But not without a lot of expensive battles.

The 1930s was a time of give-aways: each paper competed to buy readers by offering them cheap or free presents. Some were excellent, such as encyclopaedias, atlases and dictionaries, which the papers often published specially and which were tailored to their readership. My parents were *Daily Express* readers, and when I was a boy during the last war, the only books we owned were *Daily Express* books – on gardening, medicine, the Royal Family. You can still find these cheaply produced pre-war editions in car-boot sales or dumped at the back of second-hand shops. Nobody wants them now.

But it wasn't only books. Newspapers went on to offer tea services, cutlery, watches and fountain pens, and then more abstract attractions such as insurance. Hard to understand how this was regulated, but the *Express* offered their readers free insurance policies, which they could get just by filling in a coupon. There are probably people still alive who are hoping to claim in due course.

The most lavish giver-away was not the *Express* but the *Daily Herald*, which had been bought in 1929 by Julius Elias, later Lord Southwood. He owned Odhams Brothers, the *People* and various magazines such as *Woman*, but he wasn't quite as powerful as the *Mail* or the *Express* owners. He was determined that the *Daily Herald* would become the number-one newspaper, even if it meant bribing readers with more and more expensive presents. The other proprietors asked for a ceasefire, saying that it was all getting out of hand and that some papers, if not all of them, would go bust.

Elias also fought on the journalism front, tempting away the leading hack of the day, Hannen Swaffer, who joined the *Herald* from the *Express* in 1929. Like most good journalists, then and now, he was not too bothered about the proprietor if the money and byline were big enough. The result was that the *Herald* soared ahead and in the early 1930s was the world's first paper to reach a circulation of 2 million.

The *Daily Express* fought back, and by 1937 went ahead again, reaching sales of 2,329,000, calling itself, on the front page, 'the world's greatest daily paper'. The *Herald* stuck at 2 million while the *Daily Mail* was at 1.5 million and the *News Chronicle* 1.3 million.

This newspaper war of the 1930s, according to Sir Emsley Carr of the *News of the World*, was verging on madness. 'We have given up selling newspapers – we give away mangles and ask people to accept the paper as a favour.' He estimated that the costs were running at £3.5 million a year when the total profits were little more than £2 million. Madness perhaps for the proprietors, but the readers got some bargains – and some excellent photographs as the papers competed to give the best pictorial coverage. It probably also explains why the British public, to this day, are among the most avid newspaper-readers in the world.

At the height of the newspaper war, on 17 July 1933, Beaverbrook's Red Crusader appeared with his sword on the mast-head of the *Daily Express*. Rather apt, as a war symbol, but it was simply to indicate Beaverbrook's pro-Empire sympathies. His personal dislikes ranged wide, but the readers weren't bothered and enjoyed the brightness of the paper's presentation and its aspirational values. Over at the *Daily Mirror*, Hugh Cudlipp felt it was too slick and empty, but he realised that the *Express* was appealing cleverly to its readers. Deep down, they wanted much the same thing – a car and a garage.

In 1936 King Edward VIII's romance with Mrs Simpson caused problems for every newspaper. The Americans had already run headlines saying 'KING WILL WED WALLY', but in Britain the press was deferential to royalty and didn't cover the story initially. The Establishment, and the public generally, was against the King marrying a divorced woman, but Beaverbrook supported Mrs Simpson, if just for devilment. Christiansen ran a headline saying, 'END OF CRISIS', which suggested that Mrs Simpson was willing to withdraw from the scene. He got it all wrong, of course. The King abdicated.

The *Express*, supporting Chamberlain's policy of appeasement, also got it wrong in September 1938 when its front page shrieked, 'PEACE'. Above was a statement saying, 'The *Daily Express* declares that Britain will not be involved in a European war this year, or next year either.' Many others got it wrong too, but it was a front page that Beaverbrook and Christiansen were never allowed to forget.

The real war had one good effect on newspapers: the circulation war between them came to a halt. The give-aways ceased and the *Daily Express*, like all newspapers, shrank in size, from twelve pages down to four. Beaverbrook, thanks to his friendship with Churchill, was given a job in the cabinet as Minister for Aircraft Production.

After the war, like most others, including Clement Attlee, he expected Churchill to be re-elected. His papers backed the Tories, suggesting that Labour and Attlee were 'National Socialists', that is, similar to the Nazis, a smear that backfired when Labour romped home.

Christiansen was sacked as editor in 1958. He'd had a heart attack, but it is thought Beaverbrook got rid of him because he was fed up with Christiansen continually being praised for the brilliance of the *Daily Express*. It was still, after the war, the dominant newspaper. Edward Pickering took over as editor – only the fourth in the paper's history.

Christiansen died in 1963 and Beaverbrook a year later. From the late 1960s, the power of the *Daily Express* slowly began to decline. For four decades it had been the newspaper on which most journalists would have liked to work: it led in design and presentation, news and features, in foreign coverage and cartoons – Rupert Bear, Giles, Osbert Lancaster and Beachcomber became household names just as much as Sefton Delmer.

The endless succession of editors, from the late 1960s to the present day, indicates that something went wrong – but what? Today there are many university journalism departments, some no doubt trying to work it out, but there's no single explanation. That Beaverbrook hung

Lord Beaverbrook

on too long, until he was eighty-five, was probably one reason. His son, Max Aitken, who took over aged fifty-four, had been a wartime fighter ace, but was not a businessman. And there were better, smarter rivals – but at first the opposition didn't come from the old enemy, the *Daily Mail.*

The *Daily Mirror*, under Hugh Cudlipp, appeared more in tune with the aspirations of working people. Then came the rise of the *Sunday Times*: in the 1960s, it began to take over from the *Daily Express* as the most exciting, innovative newspaper, the one journalists now wanted to work on.

The *Express* seemed to lose its way: it went upmarket for a while, then downmarket; it tried to attract young readers and hold on to its old Empire-loving, pre-war readers, unable to make up its mind as to where its future lay.

But there was another more serious problem facing all newspapers, not just the *Express*: the power of the print unions. Traditions had grown up in the good old highly profitable days and had now become embedded. There were 'Spanish customs', or downright fiddles and frauds, the management thought, in which wages were drawn in the names of non-existent workers. The unions dictated who worked where and when, and who was allowed to join their union in the first place.

It is generally accepted now that the print unions and their restrictive practices were draining the lifeblood from many newspapers, but there was also weak, short-sighted management – not to mention self-indulgent journalists, though they are rarely blamed for the death of the old regime.

I arrived in Fleet Street in 1960 when it was normal for better-paid journalists to have four-hour lunches, starting with champagne at El Vino's at twelve o'clock, then going on to a restaurant and ending up at an after-hours Fleet Street drinking club before staggering back to the office and managing somehow to knock out a few words, if only some fictional expenses for entertaining fictional contacts. Most features departments were grossly over-manned; writers who hadn't had a piece in the paper for weeks continued to draw large salaries and handsome expenses while moaning about bolshie unions causing shortfalls. This happened most evenings in the print-runs, losing millions for the paper.

When the *Daily Express* circulation started to fall, management took various economy measures: the Scottish edition was closed down and staff were laid off. In the 1970s there were even merger talks between Beaverbrook Newspapers and Associated Newspapers – deadly rivals for so many decades. It would have brought the *Daily Express* and the *Daily Mail* into the same bed, and probably resulted in the death of one, but the talks broke down. A deal was eventually done over their respective London evening papers, the *Evening Standard* and the *Evening News*, which killed off the *News*.

In early 1977, the *Daily Express* went tabloid, after seventy-seven years as a broadsheet. It was aping the *Daily Mail*, which had already gone tabloid, in the hope that this would revive its fortunes. It didn't. In July 1977, Beaverbrook Newspapers was sold for £13,690,000 to Trafalgar House, a mongrel company with no tradition in newspapers, whose main interests were in property, hotels and shipping. Victor Matthews, a poor boy from Islington who had done well in scaffolding, became boss of the *Daily Express*. In 1980, following a long tradition of governments keeping in with press barons, he became a real baron, Lord Matthews.

Trafalgar House soon gave up the *Daily Express* group, having done little to revive its fortunes. In 1985 it was taken over by United

Newspapers, led by David Stevens. He had slightly more media experience, and his company owned the failing *Punch* magazine, but essentially he was a financier. This didn't stop him in his turn becoming a press lord: he was created Baron Stevens of Ludgate in 1987.

Whatever might be said about Rupert Murdoch, and most things have been since he arrived from Australia in the late 1970s and gobbled up the *News of the World*, the *Sun* and *The Times* to become the dominant force in British newspapers, he has refused all offers of a peerage. Yet he has done most, for good or ill, depending on how you look at it, to create the national newspapers of today – just as Alfred Harmsworth did at the beginning of the century, and Lord Beaverbrook in the middle. It was Murdoch who finally cleared out the old and brought in the new. New technology, new attitudes, new nudes – well, girls with bare breasts – which we hadn't seen before in national papers.

He bought Times Newspapers in 1981. It had closed down completely for a whole year, 1978–79, when the management tried and failed to take back control from the unions. In 1985, he announced he was to start a new London evening newspaper, the *Post*. It seemed a good idea, long overdue, as only twenty-five years earlier London had had three evening papers. The new paper was to be printed at Wapping, in the East End of London, where a new plant with the latest printing machinery had lain idle because the management had failed to reach manning agreements. For some time, it had been realised that new technology would come in, but the problem was how and when. Basically, this meant that computers would replace hot metal: for about two hundred years, in and around Fleet Street, our national press had been put together by hand by printers using solid type. The system had hardly changed since Caxton set up his first printing press at Westminster in 1476, although quicker and better typesetting machines had been introduced.

We now know that the new evening paper was all a trick, a plot to hide his true intentions. No *Post* was being planned: it was a cover to explain why new machinery was being installed and tested. The print unions back in Fleet Street and Grays Inn Road, at the presses of Times Newspapers, were provoked into yet another dispute. They all walked out, confident that a deal would be reached to placate them and bring them back – only to find that the birds had flown. Overnight the golden goose had migrated to Wapping, where their papers were now being printed. On 25 January 1986 Rupert Murdoch pressed the button to start the Wapping plant – and an era of Fleet Street history was over. Some five hundred printers went on strike and were sacked, their jobs gone for good despite pickets and barricades.

The other newspapers soon followed suit, bringing in new technology and moving to new premises. Murdoch and his papers had had a flying start because he had ignored all the conventions and wisdoms of the old newspaper proprietors. He was concerned solely with the bottom line, making maximum profits. Nothing so soft as trying to make friends or influencing thinkers.

He was also determined to hammer the opposition papers, to take away their readers – perhaps even kill them off, which, of course, has always been the aim of most press barons. It was what Pearson had hoped to do when he founded the *Express* and started a war that still hasn't quite ended.

The give-away battles of the 1930s were replaced in the 1990s by a price war, thanks to Mr Murdoch. The *Sun* and *The Times* both lowered their price to well below the cost of production, in order to gain circulation. Received wisdom said that it wouldn't work – British newspaper readers wanted quality, not cheapness – but it did. Both papers saw spectacular increases.

Meanwhile, the *Express* lagged further behind: it did not have the resources to lower its price, but the real worry was the rise of the *Daily Mail*, which cleverly captured the middle ground of decent Middle England that the *Express* had held for so long.

In 1996 there was yet another change in ownership with mergers and restructuring that saw Lord Hollick emerge as the latest press baron, after a marriage between his MAI media group and United Newspapers. One of his first decisions was to kill off the *Sunday Express*. It disappeared as a separate paper, as did its editor, Sue Douglas, and became just another edition of a seven-days-a-week *Express*.

Sales had dropped from a peak of 4.3 million in 1964, the year Beaverbrook died, to around 1 million at the end of 1996. The *Daily Mail* had left it miles behind, selling almost twice as many copies. Yet in many ways newspapers were booming, with more sections, more pages, more advertising than at any other time in the century. The increase in size had started in the late 1960s with the arrival of the Sunday colour magazines. Then came separate sections, such as Style or Sport. In the 1990s it was the Saturday papers that started to explode, becoming as fat as the Sundays. Despite all its problems, the *Express* added a new magazine to its existing Saturday paper, offering 200 pages for only 35p. Where would it all end?

I went to find out. Not to Fleet Street – where for decades the *Express* had been located in one of the most distinctive buildings in London, a dark glass-covered box of a building known as the Black Lubyanka – but across Blackfriars Bridge to Ludgate House, where it moved in 1989. Now there are no national papers left in Fleet Street: they've gone east to Wapping and Canary Wharf, like *The Times* and the *Daily Telegraph*, or west to Kensington, like the *Daily Mail*. The *Express* is, at least roughly, still in the same central area.

The new building is rather handsome, glass and marble, with over-tones of its old architecture. The only dash of colour in its rather stark reception area was provided by Rupert Bear, a life-sized, or bear-sized, model, used by Muscular Dystrophy as a charity box. In a far corner I noticed an archaic hot-metal printing press, a reminder of ye ancient days.

Before I went round, I read the paper from cover to cover, something I hadn't done for years. I could find only three bylines that readers from pre-war years would recognise. William Hickey is still going strong at the gossip column, so are Beachcomber and Rupert Bear, although he appears only on Sundays. They tried to kill him off in one of the many recent upheavals, but readers complained. All three bylines are, of course, fictional – old generic names, hiding new authors.

The paper is now simply called the *Express*. I liked the lay-out, clean and attractive, more artistic than that of the *Mail*, and a lot more dig-nified than the *Sun* or the *Mirror*. The content seemed much the same as the *Mail*, aiming for the same sort of readers. I was impressed by their Sports pages, a separate daily section of between sixteen and thirty-two pages, and some pages at the end called Last Word, bits and pieces, little columns, did-you-know?-type information. It reminded me of 1900, the days of Answers and *Pearson's Weekly*. Some formulas, some topics, never change, just the way they are presented.

I was shown round the building that day by Jean Carr, deputy managing editor, though there wasn't a lot to see. When Express Newspapers first moved in they had all six floors. That day they were finishing off yet another cost-cutting exercise, which had resulted in the entire editorial staff of the *Express* being squeezed into one floor. Most of the other floors were now being let. Admittedly it is a large floor, open-plan, about a hundred yards long with facilities for 326 journalists. The total journalistic staff is 400, but they are not all in at the same time; as recently as the 1980s, there were 800 staff on the *Daily* and *Sunday Express* in London, Glasgow and Manchester.

Jean had been in charge of the move, and to make enough space for everyone she'd had to do a cupboard cull: people had had to remove their personal bits and pieces, ornaments, photos. These days, few journalists, except the top handful on any paper, have their own offices, but until recently each department tried to create its own territory, with its own flavour – yet even these simple demarcation lines had gone. It was impossible, walking through, to tell which department was which or who was the boss. In my day, every department head had his or her own office, as did the deputy, complete with secretary. Newspaper offices back then quickly became rabbit warrens.

Most people had a glazed, deadened expression as they stared trance-like at their screens. Those speaking on the phone did it quietly, staring into the air, equally trance-like. There was so little noise, so little life, so little activity, and certainly no sign of excitement. No more will editors scream, 'Hold the front page!' They did; oh, yes, they did. A lot of screaming and shouting went on. But these are modern newspapers, modern offices.

I noticed it seemed to be all men, mostly in their thirties, keen and fit and eager in white shirts and ties. I couldn't see one woman. 'Yes, we're ninety-six per cent male,' said Jean. 'At present, there are only two females – both sports reporters. We haven't even got a female sub, unlike most newspapers and magazines.'

I talked to Max Davidson, working on the letters page, who had been on the *Express* for thirty-five years, their longest-serving journalist. He clearly didn't think much of open-plan life. 'People don't talk to each other any more, which I think is valuable on a newspaper. Even worse, there is no laughter. In little offices, people could get together to gossip, to plan, to plot, or just let off steam. You can't do any of that now. In a room with three hundred people, you know you're being watched and observed. So everyone behaves and keeps quiet.'

As a young reporter Max worked under Lord Beaverbrook. What might the Beaver think today? 'One of his dictums, given to all staff, was that the only thing a politician responds to is a good kicking. So he'd have been horrified these last ten years, seeing the *Express* suck up to one particular party. Yes, he was Conservative, but he was just as likely to attack them on the front page one day, then praise them the next. He would also have put more emphasis on family values. He was a philanderer himself, but he did believe in the family.

'I also think things have got sloppier, with more mistakes. People think the new technology will do their spelling for them, but a computer can't understand meanings.

'When I began, the top writers were the kings. They were like film stars, and treated as such. When I first subbed Roddy Mann's column, I felt privileged just to be allowed to touch it. People outside would ask you, "What is Roddy Mann really like, or Logan Gourlay?" Those sort of stars have gone. The management, the admin people, they have all the power and status today.

'I hope we will make the year 2000, but I worry about all this contraction. We should be expanding, but we have been starved of investment for years. Our rivals have been able to spend money and have moved ahead.'

One of the present-day stars is Peter Hitchens. As an assistant editor, he is one of the few with his own office, which has a splendid view over the river. He has been on the paper twenty years and thinks he was hired by mistake, that perhaps the editor at the time mixed him up with his brother, Chris Hitchens, who is left-wing and radical, unlike Peter.

'I do miss the days when we worked in a living, breathing newspaper office. In the old Black Lubyanka, the sign saying *Daily Express* was illuminated at night and looked marvellous at dusk against the black glass. I also liked the rumbling in the evening, coming from the basement, when the printing presses roared into life. This feels like a dead building.'

The editor when I visited was Richard Addis. He had an equally good view from his office but rarely had time to enjoy it. His hours were so long, the pace so hectic. In effect he was running two newspapers, and was endlessly in meetings with management, owners, staff. He got into his office each day by eight-thirty and never left until eight at night. He had been known to be still in his office at four in the morning. In 1996, when the *Sunday Express* closed, he had to make eighty-five journalists redundant.

Aged forty, he was formerly features editor of the *Daily Mail.* He is known in Fleet Street – yes, the term still exists – for his casual pullovers, rarely ever being seen in a suit and tie, and for the fact that he used to be a monk. This had now taken on the status of a myth, and is often trotted out by *Private Eye* as a means of poking fun. Arthur Pearson was the son of a vicar, so there has been a clerical connection before, but is it true? 'Yes, I was a novice for over a year, from June 1974 to October 1975, at the Anglican Community of the Glorious Ascension at Cleeve Priory in Somerset. I gave up my novitiate after I went to Cambridge.'

On his walls were lots of photos. Most editors, when they have snaps on show, stick either to their own lovely family, which show what lovely family people they are, or they have snaps of themselves with famous people, such as the Prime Minister or royalty, which show how jolly important they are. On Richard's walls, it was mostly journalists, such as Geoffrey Wheatcroft and Craig Brown, friends rather than household faces. I also noted behind his desk a bookshelf filled with snowstorms – those plastic souvenirs you buy in corny gift-shops.

That day he was pleased that on Saturday they had sold 1.8 million copies, their biggest sale for ten years – at a special reduced price of 20p. The normal sale, on a normal day, appeared to have stabilised at around 1.2 million.

'My main object now is to show a consistent growth, however small, for the daily and the Sunday issues, and thus prove that Britain's first truly seven-day newspaper can really work.'

I asked if he felt under pressure from above – meaning his temporal bosses rather than spiritual. 'I would call it stimulus, not pressure, from having intelligent bosses. I've helped to plan and lead a complete revolution of the *Express*, turning it from an ailing giant into a new paper for the twenty-first century, intelligent and in touch.'

Alas, he himself did not survive, being succeeded in May 1998 by Rosie Boycott, the first woman editor of the *Daily Express*. What would Lord Beaverbrook have thought of that? But will she survive into the twenty-first century? And will the *Express*?

4

EMMA LOGAN

Manchester mill worker

Emma Logan in 1917

When Emma Logan was a worker, she didn't make it through to management level. But women then didn't have much of a chance, in a job at the bottom on the factory floor with only the basic education. Basic education, if you got it, did have one or two things to recommend it. It might not have lasted long, developed the potential, stretched the imagination or fulfilled the individual, but it did provide most people with jolly good handwriting and a clear command of English.

It was Emma herself who contacted me, not a friend or relation on her behalf, which was mostly the case. She sent me a letter in her immaculate hand 'to offer you my services'. She added that she had her original birth certificate, 'costing threepence', if I needed proof that she had indeed been born in 1900 – 1 December to be precise.

She lives in Droylsden, Manchester, in a flat on the second floor of a neat and tidy two-storey block. I rang her entryphone, to tell her I had arrived, then got into the lift where I met another elderly woman, rather nosy, who asked me who I'd come to see. So I told her. When I got out of the lift, I could see Emma waiting outside her flat, her door already open for me.

'This man's come to see you. He's writing a book . . .'

'I know,' said Emma, quickly but not rudely, letting me in and closing the door firmly.

She was dressed in a pretty two-piece summery costume and looked bright and lively. She has her own bedroom, sitting-room, kitchen and bathroom. She's in good health, with perfect hearing and eyesight, but there is a resident warden on the premises, just in case: the block is sheltered housing.

She made me tea, told me which chair to sit on, then got out her photo albums to take me through her life. She'd made notes, lists of things and events that she wanted to tell me about.

Her maiden name was Emma Mackay, and she was one of ten children – six boys, four girls – and her father was an overlooker in a cotton mill. He was originally from Edinburgh, very clever, said Emma, and he had progressed to the drawing office. They lived in a two-up two-down terrace house with no electricity or gas, though they later got penny-in-the-slot gas. In the backyard, they had a flush toilet, not a slops bucket unlike some of their neighbours. They were never poor, never went with bare feet, which many children did in her class at Johnson Street school. 'We always had food to eat, potato pot usually, and a roast on Sundays. We never wanted for food. But if the boys got a winter coat, we had to wait a year till it was our turn for a winter coat.'

She was good at school, enjoyed it, so she says, and left at fourteen to join her elder sister, Ethel, who was working as a shirt machinist at C. Begg's, off Oxford Road, Manchester.

'My father went to see Mr Begg about the job. He had to sign a form, bonding me to work for them for twelve months, whether I liked it or not. In seeing Mr Begg, he'd said I was good and reliable, and was also a good swimmer. I don't know why he said that, but Mr Begg replied, "Well, there'll be no swimming here." I was so annoyed with my dad for having said that to Mr Begg. So embarrassing.'

Emma started on piece-work, getting 1s. 11d. for every twelve shirts she sewed – not easy shirts either: they were double-breasted with awkward collars. In her best week, working from eight-thirty in the morning until six at night, with no breaks and eating her lunch-time sandwiches at her machine, she made eighteen shillings.

'I was just thirteen when the war began, still at school, but I remember the excitement. Lots of girls suddenly decided to get married. Their boyfriends were going off, so that was exciting in itself, but it was even more exciting, with so many weddings. No one even thought of the suffering to come.'

One of her brothers, Sidney, volunteered as soon as the war began and joined the Royal Scots Fusiliers. Her big sister Ethel was terribly patriotic and lined up all the brothers and sisters in the backyard and made them march up and down, singing patriotic songs. 'I can still remember them, word for word. Shall I sing one to you?' She sang me one called 'We Must All Fall In, If We Want To Win', which went on for several verses. It seemed to be mainly about doing one's duty for God and the country. She thinks she must have learned the words from some sheet music, perhaps handed out at the Metropole Theatre.

One day in 1915, when she and Ethel were coming home from work at the shirt factory, they saw some women had gathered at Mayfield railway station. They went over and heard a rumour that some wounded soldiers were expected, sent home from the front. Sidney was at the front, and they were a bit worried about him. Nothing had been heard from him for some time.

'As we were standing there, a new rumour went round – that it was German wounded. When the soldiers arrived, they *were* wounded, and they *were* German. Prisoners-of-war, I should think. When some old women in shawls saw they were Germans, they started booing. I said to one of them, "Don't boo, they're some woman's sons." One of them said I should be ashamed of myself, saying such a thing. Another turned round and gave me a clout. She really did. Then she asked if I was a German spy. She started telling the other women I was a German spy, so we had to run off in the end. When I got home, I told my father what had happened. He told me not to interfere in future.'

Some weeks afterwards, Emma and Ethel were again walking home from work together. 'It was a Friday, this time. We were walking over this place near our house we called the donkey common, a sort of bit of wasteground. I suppose there must have been donkeys on it at some time. There were some boys playing football. When they saw us, one of them shouted out, "Your Sid's been killed." We both screamed and started crying, and then we ran home as fast as we could.

'Sidney had been killed, in the Dardanelles, aged twenty-one. He was so clever. We always had fun with Sidney. The telegram had come that afternoon and my mother had already taken ill and had gone to her bed. She stayed there for days. I didn't know at first that she was pregnant. I then left work in order to look after her while she had the baby. I did all the shopping and cooking and looking after Mum. It was a baby boy, Stanley. We always called him the war baby.'

When her mother had recovered, Emma decided not to go back to the shirt factory. The two years had been very noisy and she hadn't been a very good machinist. In 1916 she got a better job in the purchasing department of an engineering firm, Crosley Brothers in Openshaw. She had to do a little test, to prove she could do sums. 'They were taking on girls in this department, which was unusual, because all the men were away at the war.'

It was there that she met Thomas Armstrong, chauffeur to Sir Kenneth Crosley. He used to stop in the street and give her a lift to work when he wasn't with Sir Kenneth. The car was an Armstrong Siddeley, she remembers, but there were others, whose names she can't remember. When Thomas wasn't driving Sir Kenneth, he would drive senior managers around or take visiting agents to the station. He was considered a good catch. He was twelve years older than Emma, which didn't worry her but it did worry her mother. They married in 1920.

'It was a church wedding, but we couldn't afford the full white wedding. I wore a fawn costume, in gaberdine.'

They moved straight in with his mother, and had their honeymoon six months later, in the Isle of Man, by which time they had found a house of their own to rent. 'This woman who helped us get it said I had to agree to organise a club. It was one of those clubs where everyone puts in so much a week, and then once a week you draw lots to see who is first to be able to buy something. The one who's last is never very pleased.'

Thomas had not served in the First World War because he had failed his medical. 'He was a very good chap, a good-living chap,' says Emma. They had some nice times together, going on holidays or days out to Blackpool or the Lake District. 'He knew all the firm's reps and if they were driving to Blackpool they would give us a lift there. We'd just have to pay for the train home.'

Thomas had a motorbike and side-car, which Emma never liked riding in – she was scared – but he eventually bought his own car, a Morris, through his brother-in-law in the motor trade. It was unusual for working-class couples before the Second World War to have their own car.

Their only child, Cyril, was born on 1 June 1924: 'I always wanted more, but it didn't happen.' If it had been 1994, not 1924, would she have taken fertility drugs? 'I don't believe in fertility treatment. It's not natural.' She paused. 'But I suppose if you were desperate, you might agree to take them. In the end, it was just as well . . .'

Thomas contracted cancer of the stomach and after a long illness died in 1945, aged fifty-six. Cyril was in the Royal Marines; he served from 1942 to 1946. 'I worried about him all the time. For weeks we never heard a word.'

In 1946, after the war was over, she was invited to a welcome-home tea party by a girl with whom she had once worked. The party was for her friend's brother George, returning home from a Japanese prisoner-of-war camp. He weighed only seven stone and was suffering from emphysema.

'I started going out with him and he asked me to marry him, but I had doubts. My son Cyril was still unmarried and unsettled. But friends of mine said go on, why don't you marry him?

'We went to the Isle of Man in the summer, six of us, three couples, and the other two couples were married. The next year we went to Bournemouth. He kept on saying, "I hope next year when we go on holiday we'll be married."'

So they were, in 1949. They had their honeymoon in Morecambe.

George Logan had had a trade before the war, as an engineer, but after his POW experience he wasn't fit enough to go back so he got a job as a caretaker for Manchester Liners. 'He didn't have any sort of war pension – he refused to apply for it.'

Emma herself has been working since 1941 when she took a wartime job running a machine for the English Steel factory at Openshaw. Then she worked at a towel mill before joining the cash office of a mail-order firm, where she worked until she retired at the age of sixty.

George's health began to deteriorate, despite his easier job, and the heavy medication he had to take made him somewhat bad-tempered. 'He could turn very nasty, but I knew it was the drugs doing it. He had suffered a great deal in that Japanese camp.' He died in 1975, while Emma was by his side, giving him oxygen. 'When you lose your husband, you lose your best friend.'

She never thought of marrying again. At least George had a pension from Manchester Liners: it was seven pounds a week when he died, but has increased since with inflation. (In 1997 it was twenty pounds a week.)

In 1975, after George died, Emma went to Canada to see one of her sisters. Then, in 1976, she went on a more surprising trip – to Russia.

'I had this friend from the mail-order company who was a member of the Anglo-Soviet Friendship Union. She said she was going on a trip to Russia, why didn't I come? I said I'd be frightened. I'd heard all these bad things about Russia. She said, "You'll be all right, you'll be with me." And she was right. They thought the world of her in Russia.'

Emma and her friend spent fifteen days visiting Moscow, Leningrad and Kiev. 'Leningrad was the best, seeing the Hermitage and the Palaces. They've got two, you know, the Summer and the Winter Palaces of the Tsars. Kiev wasn't so good, but the people were nice. Some schoolchildren gave us a loaf shaped like a cottage and a lump of salt for us to partake of. We also visited a lot of women working on

Emma with George Logan, Madrid, 1960

farms. They looked very dejected. But they were very friendly and gave us fruit.

'We went to people's homes, all arranged, and also to this lecture in English. At the end of it, the lecturer asked for any questions and so I stood up. I'd been impressed by all the schools and I asked if education was really free in Russia. He said yes it was, and asked me if it was free in England. "It depends on your circumstances," I said, "whether you pay or not." The lecturer loved this, saying how marvellous Russia was.

'So I then asked that if this was so, why did so many people defect? He said who, which people? I said Rudolf [Nureyev], that dancer. He said, "Ah, well, those sort of leading people, when they qualify and take their degrees and such, they are supposed to give back to the country, to train young people, give up their chances of making a lot of money. But some of them won't. Because some of them are greedy."

'I did love all that trip. Red Square was wonderful. We saw the haystack where Lenin hid, though I'm not sure he really did hide in it. I felt sorry for the women in Russia. They all live in apartments, you know, nobody has a house. Oh, one thing I did notice – such a lot of divorces.'

Was it the best experience of her life, going to Russia? Emma thought for a bit. 'I'd call it an education, not an experience. I learned such a lot.'

She has always voted Labour. Nothing that has happened in ninety-seven years has changed her view on that. 'I always liked Ramsay MacDonald. I thought he was a good man.' Was she influenced at all by her husbands and their politics? 'I never knew my first husband's vote,' she said, putting me in my place for making such a sexist suggestion.

Other major national events that made a big impression on her include the Crippen murder case. 'I remember the special editions of the papers as it all came out. I rushed to buy them.' Then there was the *Titanic* sinking in 1912 when she was still at school. She learned a long poem about it, which she can still recite.

> It was on the tenth of April
> A lovely summer's day
> In the busy town of Southampton
> I stood upon the quay . . .

She went through about five verses, pausing to say there were more to come, if I wanted to hear them all. I said thanks, but I'd prefer to hear more about her own personal experiences. She studied the notes she'd made about her life, to see what she hadn't mentioned so far.

'There is one story, but I'm not sure if you can use it. Hmm. Well, you can decide. See for yourself.' She cleared her throat, and then began. 'When I was young, we lived in Ardwick for a time, in Harcourt Street. It was a street with quite a few business people living there. Next door to my mother was this family called B———. Perhaps I won't give you the real name, at this stage.

'The father was in insurance, very comfortably off. They had a son called Frank. In 1914, at the same time as our Sidney, he went into the army – but he became a captain. I remember him coming home on leave. Oh, he looked marvellous. Anyway, the family eventually moved away from our street, but my mother remained friendly with his mother and she went to visit them.

'After the war, Frank moved to London and he got on in society. He was very gay.' Emma paused, with a slight smile. 'I mean, he lived a gay life, not how you mean it today. Lots of parties and dinners and things. Then, lo and behold, it came out that he was a co-respondent in a divorce case. He'd been, you know, with a very wealthy duke's daughter, the Duke of ———.

'Anyway, he was named in the case. The duke's daughter was divorced – and he did later marry her.

'He only came back to Manchester once, for a short visit to see his mother. Then he set sail for Africa, with his bride. On board ship, he got appendicitis and died.

'Oh, what a story it was at the time. It was in all the papers, all about his Manchester connections. Every time it was in the *Umpire* – yes, the *Umpire*, not the *Empire News*, that came later – I used to tell my friends at work that I knew him, that he lived in our street. They always said, "Go away, never!" In those days, any sort of divorce was a terrible thing, terrible scandal but, of course, a society divorce, with a duke's daughter, oh, everyone read about it.

'Well, that's the story. I leave you to decide whether to put in all the real names or not . . .'

She spelled out the full names of all concerned, but she still obviously

Emma today

felt a bit guilty about gossiping even though it all happened over seventy years ago, and all the people concerned are long dead. I assured her that I wouldn't name names. It was interesting that it had lodged in her mind all these years, with all the details and personalities still so clear.

Emma's memory is excellent, and so is her health. Both her parents died relatively young – her mother at fifty-nine, her father at sixty-two. She is the oldest remaining of their ten children, though one sister got to ninety-four and one brother to ninety-nine and a half. 'We had a big party for his ninety-ninth, just in case he never got to a hundred. If he had got to a hundred, the mayor had promised to come to his party. But he didn't make it.'

Will she? 'I don't know. I have looked after myself, which always helps. I've never neglected my food. I've never smoked, but every evening I have a drink.'

What of? 'Guinness, of course. When I was younger, going out with my husband to a club, I might drink one or two bottles of Guinness. Perhaps three at most. It didn't make me drunk, just merry. I was only ever drunk once. I was at this party and I'd mixed my drinks. I felt very poorly afterwards, so I thought, never again. Now I just have one bottle every night.'

Unlike many persons of her age, she doesn't seem to mind too much about the way the modern world is going, except for the violence. 'In the old days, your house was always safe. You could leave your door unlocked and walk down the street safely. There were no muggings and murders.'

Er, what about your Dr Crippen?

'Oh, well, that was years later. I meant when I was young, before the First World War. Things were safe then.'

She could think of no regrets, things she wishes she had seen, things she would like to have done. 'Except one thing. I would like to have written a book.'

She thinks, on the whole, she's had a happy life. But fairly tragic, I suggested, losing two husbands and a brother, killed so young?

'Yes, I suppose you'd have to say it's been a happy and a tragic life, but that's an education in itself, don't you think?'

5

KENNETH CUMMINS

Captain of an ocean liner

Ken Cummins, with his mother in 1917

Captain Cummins certainly made it, achieving most of the things to which most ordinary people aspire in their lives. He lives in an attractive detached house in the Wiltshire village of Bedwyn and, at ninety-six, he looked fit and strong in mind and body. That morning, he'd been to Marlborough to see his personal trainer. I thought I'd misheard at first. You mean he works out, at his age, like a film star or model? Not quite, said his wife, Rosemary. He used the Marlborough sports centre to build up his knees because he'd recently had a hip replacement. So, not quite as physically perfect as he first appeared but, goodness, there was no doubt about his mental and intellectual strength. I was put in my place quite a few times, and so was his wife. When she happened to correct or add something, she was told firmly to keep out of this, she knew nothing, this was his story. Later, she said that one of the things that first attracted her to him was his rudeness.

Kenneth Cummins was born in Richmond, Surrey, on 6 March 1900, the oldest of two brothers and one sister, the son of, well, his father. That was the first time I came up against his obstinacy. He wouldn't tell me his father's name. 'That's personal,' he said. I explained I'd come to ask personal questions, about his life. Must be some misunderstanding, he said. He thought I'd come to ask about his philosophy of life, his views on the century. Oh, all of that, I said, but first I need to know who you are, what you've done, before we can look back on it all and come to some conclusions, if any.

'Oh, well,' he said, 'fire away.' So what did your father do? 'I'm not telling you. Didn't you hear me?'

I told him it gave a shorthand picture of someone's background, social class and all that, to have a few details of their father. No, he still wasn't revealing anything about his father, except to say that as a family they moved around a bit. By the time Kenneth started public school, at Merchant Taylor's in Liverpool, they were living in Southport.

One of his clearest memories as a boy was going with some schoolfriends on a Saturday afternoon to Blundell Sands, about half an hour's walk from school. 'This must have been around 1911. We were going to see Goarham White take off from the sands in his single-engine biplane. He kept it on the sands, which were very hard and extensive. It was attached to a rope and anchored to a large stake in the ground. The plane was started, and when it had got up enough speed and pressure, the rope was released and it automatically took off. We boys were given the job of holding on to the rope, till the pilot was ready to take off. Which he did.

'There was a phrase in my time, I'm not sure if it's still in use today, "Pigs might fly." Well, one day, Goarham White took up a live pig on his plane and flew it all over Liverpool.'

From about the age of eight, while living in Southport, he still has a clear memory of muffinmen selling muffins, a barrel-organ with a monkey, a German band marching, a Russian bear dancing, all of them regular sights in the street.

He also has a memory of going to the Pier Head at Liverpool, during the First World War, and watching the bodies of American troops being unloaded. 'They had been killed by the influenza epidemic which swept the whole country, probably the States as well, unless they had caught the bug on board. It was a terrible sight. I was told that one third of the troops on board had died.'

At school, he joined the OTC and was on manoeuvres when war broke out, training with the King's Liverpool Rifles. 'All we did was follow after them, carrying our wooden rifles. I don't remember the war having much effect on us, not on the general population of Southport. The bands still played. Horses still played football on the front. They had huge balls, which came up to the chins of the horses, which they pushed around.'

At fifteen, he applied to P & O, the shipping line, hoping to win one of their scholarships to become a naval cadet. 'Hundreds applied, so I was told, then fifty of us were invited to London and given a grand dinner, with servants in livery and masses of silver. I suppose they were watching to see who used the correct knives and forks.' He was accepted and went to HMS *Worcester*, where he met Angus Macmillan, of Chapter Nine, who was a naval cadet at exactly the same time. They were together for two years, then never saw or heard of each other again until 1995, almost eighty years later, when both turned up at an HMS *Worcester* old boys' gathering, each a bit surprised to find someone else still alive from the 1915–17 vintage.

'I was at HMS *Worcester*, moored on the Thames, when I saw my first Zeppelin. I think it was the one shot down over Cuffley in Essex. I stood on the deck and could see it quite clearly. No, I didn't see the flames when it landed but I remember reading newspapers afterwards. From memory, a Flight-Lieutenant Robinson got the VC for shooting it down. His name has always stuck in my mind, for some reason.'

In 1917, he joined the Royal Naval Reserve as a midshipman and after training on HMS *Vivid*, was posted to HMS *Morea* where he served till the war ended. It was an armoured cruiser and its job was to escort merchant ships going from Britain to Freetown in Sierra Leone.

'There were various alarms, but we were never shot at or attacked by submarines. I had to look after a six-inch gun, under the supervision of a lieutenant. At eighteen, you have no responsibility so you can take things lightly. I enjoyed the First World War very much.'

In 1919, he was demobbed and went straight into P & O, which was the arrangement as they had paid half his cadet fees. And there he stayed, he said, for the rest of his working life, going from fourth officer through the grades to chief officer, and finally captain. 'That was about it, really.'

He then paused, as if waiting for me to get on to some philosophical questions, about life and the universe and all that, but I said, 'Hold on, what about the Second World War? Were you called up again, or what?' Rosemary, his wife, had already told me he always understates everything, whereas she, he maintains, is a terrible exaggerator.

Yes, well, the Second World War. Just before it began, he was chief officer on the *Ile de France*, one of the classiest in the P & O fleet. It was known as one of the Five Monsters, with the *Queen Mary*, the *Queen Elizabeth* and the *Mauretania*.

As soon as war started, many of the larger liners were taken over by the Admiralty and converted to troop carriers. Kenneth had to spend nine months in New York while the work was being done. That must have been a pleasant way to start the war. 'Oh, it was. We were put up in a hotel, though I can't remember which, but New York was expensive.'

Once the *Ile de France* was ready for its new life, equipped to carry some 10,000 troops, he made several voyages taking Allied troops to England and elsewhere. Did that make them a target for the Germans? 'Oh, there wasn't much danger. We could do 25 knots, faster than any German submarine. Don't forget, they didn't have any destroyers in the Second World War. We trapped their fleet. Only *Tirpitz* got out, and then it was sunk. There were German bombers, but they were very high overhead and didn't do much damage. As troop ships, we were, of course, very well protected by our armed destroyers.'

He then transferred to another liner, which had also been converted into a troop carrier, the *Viceroy of India*. 'She was very well equipped, very luxurious. She was turbo-electric, which meant there was no vibration. That was my favourite ship of all the ones I sailed on. A shame we lost her . . .'

Again he'd been giving the suggestion that life at sea in the Second World War was ever so safe and straightforward, till that last remark, almost in passing. So what happened?

In November 1942, she was part of a massive fleet of some twenty ships that set sail for North Africa, carrying troops for Montgomery's desert war. He went to get some photographs, to show me the ships going through the Straits of Gibraltar.

'Look at those ships. Oh, it was a magnificent show.'

The troops were successfully transported, with the *Viceroy of India* landing 2,000 men in Algiers. Then each ship set sail for home. On the way there, they had been in a fleet, and heavily guarded. Now, they had to make their own way home. Travelling back empty, it was felt they were less of a target.

'We were forty miles off the coast of Africa, and it was five past four in the morning. I had just arrived on the bridge. I hadn't even had time for my coffee when there was the most enormous explosion in the engine room and we started filling up with water. A submarine had hit us. It was dark, of course, and we were carrying no lights, which we were not allowed during the war. I suspect the submarine had been on the surface about a mile away, recharging her batteries, and had suddenly seen or heard us approaching. We did have six-inch guns, and anti-aircraft guns, but we didn't use them as we didn't know she was there.

'The engine room is the worst place to be hit, but it was also right in the middle of the bulkhead, which meant we started filling up with water and going arse end up. I knew it would take us about four hours to sink.

'At seven o'clock, the captain gave the order to abandon ship. Some sailors appeared on deck with cases, but they were told to leave them. As chief officer, I went back to my cabin and changed into my best uniform. No, of course I didn't take any personal possessions. But my cabin was full of them. That was my home, after all.

Ken (seated, centre) on the Viceroy of India, *1934*

'There were only about a hundred crew members and we all got safely into the lifeboats. The ship finally sank at eight o'clock. We were in the water just over an hour before we were rescued. HMS . . . now what was it? Did it have a Greek-sounding name? Hold on, it's coming – HMS *Boudicea*.

'We lost only four people – all killed in the engine room when we were first hit, two Europeans and two Indians.

'No, there was never any panic. Everyone knew the drill. We just had a job to do. It was 11 November 1942, Armistice Day. But it was most unfortunate. She was a lovely ship, very well built – 19,000 tons and could do nineteen knots.

'On one occasion, earlier in the war, we had done the rescuing ourselves when two ships collided west of Cape Town. That was most unusual. You don't normally get ships colliding out at sea but, of course, they were travelling without lights. It was a dark, hazy, drizzling night. The *Ceramic* and the *Atlas*, those were the names, both troop ships. We rescued about two hundred from the sea.'

In 1945, he was promoted to captain and took command of the *Maloja*, 19,000 tons. His first voyage was taking Italian prisoners-of-war back to Italy. He was not overly impressed by their sense of discipline or hygiene. 'Not compared with the Zulus. I had to take some of them home after the war. What a fine class of men they were, big, cheerful, well disciplined and very clean.'

After the war was over, Captain Cummins returned to his normal P & O duties, carrying the affluent, and sometimes the not so affluent, if they were on cheapo immigrant fares, back and forth across the world's oceans. I happened to use the word cruise liners, and was quickly reprimanded. His P & O ships were ocean liners, on service, on scheduled voyages from A to B, not footling around some Caribbean islands.

Before the war, Prince Farouk of Egypt had been one of his passengers. They dropped him off first in the South of France, where he went about his normal pleasure-loving life. 'While he was there, his father died, and that's when he became King. By chance, we also carried him back to Egypt, as King. This must have been 1936. On the way back, we had a Royal Navy destroyer sailing with us. We had the King on board and the British government was keeping in with Egypt.

As a junior officer, he was on the ship that brought home Lord

Carnarvon, discoverer of the tomb of Tutankhamen. 'He was dead at the time. We brought back his body in a coffin which weighed five tons. This was on the *Macedonia*, around 1926. He died from a mosquito bite in Port Said, but everyone said it was the Curse of the Pharaohs. Another time we transported an Indian prince who actually died on board. There was then going to be a special burial ceremony, back in India, so his body had to be preserved as it was. The ship's doctor, a very good doctor, got round this problem by putting the body in an ice-box bath.'

Captain Cummins's final command was the *Stratheden*, a liner of some 24,000 tons, the biggest he had been in charge of. It had a crew of 550 and carried around a thousand passengers. He took it over in 1955. The same year, he said, that he got married.

Hmm, so you were then aged fifty-five. What took you so long?

'I'm not discussing that. It's personal.'

Were you married before?

'Of course not.'

Did you have girlfriends? 'I'm not discussing that.'

I suppose it was difficult, spending a lifetime on ships, to have proper relationships? He thought about this question, which, of course, could have been a trick, before he eventually replied.

'No, not really. Most officers were married by the age of fifty-five.'

Was it because in your case the right person didn't come along, or that you simply didn't want to get married?

Again, he wouldn't elaborate. I knew that Rosemary was his wife, I had been introduced to her as such, so I turned and asked her how she had met him. Surely he couldn't object to that.

'It was in 1953, Coronation year,' said Rosemary. 'I was sailing on the *Chitral*, of which Kenneth was captain. I was in my early twenties, coming from Australia, my home country, to live in England. One day on board this man stopped me going up some steps and said, "You can't walk up those steps. Can't you read?" I didn't know he was the captain. He just struck me as an extremely rude person.'

'She was on a cheap trip,' interrupted Kenneth, which she had not been allowed to do during his stories. 'One of those cheap fares.'

'So what if it was?' continued Rosemary. 'There was no need to be rude. Anyway, I met him a few more times during that voyage, and he was equally rude and off-hand. But at the end of the voyage, he did ask me what I was going to do in London. I explained I'd been on the *Sydney Morning Herald* in Australia and I was hoping to get a job on the London *Evening Standard.* I hadn't a chance, he said, that was Fleet Street, no chance for someone like me. But he gave me his card and said look him up in London some time, if I ever did manage to get a job in London.

'Well, I did. I worked on the *Standard* for a couple of years, under my maiden name, Rosemary Byers. I was on the "London Last Night" column, which I loved. I almost met him on a story, when I was covering something on the *Chitral.* I wanted a quote from the captain, but the ship's doctor said there was no chance, the captain wouldn't speak to me. But later I did look him up and we met again. And that was it. In 1955 we got married.'

This took place in Sydney, with Kenneth in his number-one captain's uniform. They had four children in quick succession, two boys and two girls. When he retired in 1960, they built their own house at Bedwyn, the one they still live in. One daughter is a barrister, one son an accountant, one son in hospital management and the other daughter is married with children.

He was happy enough to retire, aged sixty. He had been at sea for forty-two years and had served in two world wars. His life as a P & O officer had been glamorous and adventurous enough, but the hours had been long. 'And you only ever got two weeks' leave a year in my time, until you became a captain. Now, I understand, everyone gets three months off every year.'

So have you regrets about your chosen career?

'What a silly question.'

Sorry about that. Right, some less personal questions at last. What are your views on the times in which you have lived?

'Since the First World War, England has not prospered. We have lost an empire and suffered because of this. Overall, I find it hard to think of any advances.'

Well, for example, what about the position of women?

'Oh, yes, and their supposed advances. They did nothing, pre the First World War. Now look at them.'

Aren't you proud your daughter is a barrister, that she is able to fulfil herself?

'Of course I am proud of her. I encouraged all my children to do what they want to do in life – but I am not talking personally. I am talking about the world in general. I still believe that women are born to do a job, which is have children and run a house, and men are born to work and earn money to support them. Yes, it might be old-fashioned but that is what I believe.

'Noise, that's another thing I don't approve of. The world was a quiet place when I was young, a pleasant place.

'The Church of England – that has certainly deteriorated. Now we have women priests, lesbian priests, sodomist priests. And the Church can't even manage its own finances. Yes, my outlook is old-fashioned, that's what my sons tell me all the time.'

Presumably you are against present-day morals, with people living and sleeping together before marriage?

'It is an impossible question to answer, whether morals have got worse or not. Noise is easy. There is no argument there. With morals, every generation has its own morals, its own codes. Mine are those of 1914, not of today. But whether more people now break the moral codes of their own time, well, who can say? It seems to be that the eleventh Commandment is still probably the most important – "Thou shalt not be found out." If you get found out, it's wrong. If you don't get found out, then fine.'

How about all the advances in science and medicine?

'What about them? We can now travel supersonic, but what's the use of that? We can get to the moon or Mars. So what? We had candles in my day, not electric light. There was nothing wrong with that. You just went to bed earlier. Yes, modern hygiene is better, but I'm not convinced all medical improvements are for the better. People are kept alive when they are cabbages. Is that any better for them, or for us? In my day, they died off.'

In his own personal case, with his hip replacement, he admits he is indebted to modern medicine. 'They did an excellent job. I have also had marvellous work done on my eyes. For three months recently, I lost my sight completely. Now I have the sight back in one eye. The other is not so good, but I can now read *The Times* again every morning. I didn't think I would do that again.

'I'm doing better than the Queen Mother. She had the same hip

Ken today

operation but is still using two sticks, so I've noticed. I just need one. I suppose I have been luckier.'

So has it been luck that has got him to ninety-seven?

'Love, I would say. Love is the most important element in human happiness. Not sex, though sex is part of love. Love brings contentment, which brings good health. Misery and unhappiness lead to ill-health. That's what I believe.'

But what about happy, cheerful people who then get struck down? 'Yes, you can be happy, yet still have bad health. I think people who then have to suffer bad health are very brave.

'But I'm not just talking about love of wife or husband being the most important element in life, but love of one's children, one's family, love of one's mother . . .'

Rosemary wheeled in an excellent lunch, with wine, which we all enjoyed. When I left, I thanked him for his time, hoped I hadn't been too tiring, though I felt I had been the one being tested.

On the train home, I thought about his passing remark about 'love of one's mother' and wondered if that was a clue to his strange reluctance to talk about his father.

I later discovered that his parents had apparently separated. As the oldest of the four children, Kenneth had seen it as his duty to provide for his mother, which he did, faithfully, until his help was no longer needed. That also explains why he never contemplated marriage until relatively late in life, when his duty was done.

And when, of course, Rosemary talked about admiring his rudeness, she really meant his directness, his honesty, his clear-sighted way of looking at the world and himself. Not many of us can do that, at any age.

6

DOROTHY ELLIS

Quaker and early university student

Dorothy Ellis in 1900, on her mother's knee

Education is an education in itself. And it did happen, though very rarely, that women born in 1900, even those from relatively humble homes, experienced university. Dorothy Mary Robson, born on 30 January 1900, was one of the unusual ones.

Before she was a year old she had had her first unusual experience. Her photograph made the front page of a national publication, not for doing anything particularly newsworthy, just for being born, really. She was photographed, sitting on her mother's knee, with her grandmother and her great-grandmother in the January 1901 edition of *Wings*.

This wasn't a leading magazine of the day, but it was read nationally, in homes where someone was either teetotal, female or Quaker: it was the official organ of the Women's Total Abstinence Union. The headline over the photograph said, 'Four Generations of Total Abstainers'. The *Daily Express*, even then, would probably have thought up a wittier, sharper headline, but at least it was true, all true.

Dorothy's grandmother and great-grandmother had all served the cause of abstinence by doing their bit as secretary of the Kelvedon branch of the WTAU. Her mother was also very active. 'And Dorothy, little Dorothy Mary, what can we say of her?' asked the unnamed writer in *Wings*. 'The time has not yet come to tell her life's story, or even to interview her for *Wings*. We must just pray that she may follow in the footsteps of her mother, grandmother and great-grandmother and serve her day and generation according to the will of God as they are doing.'

So what did happen to little Dorothy? Ninety-seven years later she got out the original photograph and the copy of *Wings* to let me see it. Beside her in her room was a box of files and folders. On the walls were paintings done just the week before by her own great-grandchildren.

I asked her for the exact names of the people in the photograph taken in 1900. Well, her mother was Mary Jesup Robson, née Barratt. Her grandmother was Sarah Barratt and her great-grandmother was called Docwra, always known as Mrs Docwra – she couldn't remember her great-grandmother's Christian name. 'Don't worry,' I said, 'it will come to you.' But her brow furrowed, upset at this minor lapse in what is a remarkable memory. She had dictated to me the spelling of Docwra, a most unusual name. I then checked the spelling of Barratt, just in case I'd got it wrong.

Two As, two Rs, two Ts and a B,
Put them together and spell them to me.

Her face brightened at the sudden arrival in her mind, after all these decades, of this bit of family doggerel her grandfather had taught her, so that she would go through life able to spell his family name.

Dorothy was born into a staunch Quaker family. There were many abstainers in the nineteenth and early twentieth century, people who made abstinence their life's endeavour, seeing drink as the single greatest scourge of the working man and his family, but traditionally the Quakers had been leaders of most temperance movements in Britain.

The Quakers began in the seventeenth century and were followers of George Fox, found mainly in the north of England at first, then all over Britain and America, determined to reinstate primitive Christianity, cut out all vanity, show and loose living. They swore no allegiances, refused all oaths, which meant they could not serve in the army or enter the universities or Parliament. They rejected feasting and similar indulgences. They avoided games, sport and even music – anything, in fact, that might 'arouse the emotions'.

Making money was not banned, but their commercial avenues were limited. They couldn't, for example, own a theatre. If they made money, they had to spend it wisely and care for their workers and the community, not their own selfish pleasures. They were particularly strong in food, as this was an essential industry, not a frippery: the Cadbury, Fry and Rowntree families were all Quakers and became leaders of the industry. They were also strong in banking: Barclays and Lloyds were both originally Quaker foundations.

Dorothy's family was not one of the rich or well-known ones, but they had some good connections, as all Quakers did. Nor, when Dorothy was born, were they particularly hidebound or strict, compared with the Quakers of a hundred years earlier. Dorothy's father played the violin and Dorothy herself had piano lessons. As a child, she was allowed to play cards, though she had to use a pack that was theologically sound and showed images of Noah and Lot.

'We didn't say "thee" or "thou", as all Quakers had in the old days, but I remember some of my aunts did when I went to visit them.'

Dorothy was the first of three sisters. After her came Alice and Kathleen. She was born at Audley Villas, Audley Road, in Saffron Walden. Her father ran the family grocer's in Saffron Walden, which his family had before him. Both her grandfather and great-grandfather had been mayors of the town.

Her earliest memory is of a tea party on the village green when she was about two years old, given by her grandfather, then the mayor. She also remembers being taken into the back garden in 1907 to watch Halley's Comet. 'This might be a real memory, or one I've been told about, but it is very likely, as my father had a scientific bent.'

They then moved to the nearby village of Elsenham, where she went to the village school. At around twelve, she started at the Friends' School in Saffron Walden – a Quaker school for boys and girls.

The main dramatic event in her early family life was a fire in her father's shop. He lost most of his money but through Quaker friends he got a job as an accountant. He had always been good at sums and, of course, as a Quaker, he was trusted. By a sequence of events, he became an expert at auditing the books of the brand new film industry. From 1900 there were many little film companies in London and Manchester, and her father went round the country, doing their books.

The person he mainly worked for was a founder of Price Waterhouse, Dorothy believes, and the work was in London so they moved to Woking. According to family legend her father once had lunch with Douglas Fairbanks Senior. Later on, changes in the firm decreed that as he was not a professionally qualified accountant he could not look after such important clients any more. He retired early, on half pay.

Dorothy was excellent at school, top in most subjects but best of all at maths. 'I remember getting ninety-eight per cent in an exam and being very upset because I'd made one mistake. Otherwise I would have got a hundred per cent.'

At her school, it was possible to take matriculation – the leaving exam around seventeen, the equivalent of A-levels, which paved the way for the professions or the universities – but only a couple of boys a year ever took it, never any girls. In the autumn term of 1915, aged fifteen, Dorothy moved to a much more academic and distinguished school: the Mount School, York, still one of the country's leading girls' schools (now called Mount College).

The Mount was founded in 1831, a sister school for the boys at Bootham. Joseph Rowntree, and the other founding fathers, were keen that Quaker girls should be educated, especially those 'not in affluence'. They were taught to make collars and shirts for their brothers, to sweep rooms, make beds and other useful jobs, discouraged from anything that might smack of self-adornment, but they learned Latin, maths and chemistry, which girls then were rarely allowed to study. By the 1860s, it was among the best schools for girls in England. The narrowness of the curriculum, which still did not include music or other frivolities, meant more time for academic subjects.

Dorothy felt a bit out of it at first. Most girls had been there since eleven but, early on, she was invited to take tea at Bootham, which gave her instant status: 'I was invited by one of the masters at Bootham. His secretary happened to have been a scholar at Walden, and she'd heard I was coming. Miss Winifred Sturge, the headmistress of the Mount, said I could go – as long as the secretary was present during the tea.'

Among her contemporaries at the Mount were several daughters of the Quaker establishment. 'We had a Dorothy and a Geraldine Cadbury and two of the Carrs from Carlisle, Rosalind and Betty. I don't think they had much to do with each other. I think they were daughters of Carr brothers who hadn't got on. On the staff, we had a Miss Dorothea Fry. I also got to know Arnold Rowntree.

'One day, on York railway station, I was coming home from school, and the guard put me and another Mount girl in a compartment full of young soldiers, going off to the front. Arnold Rowntree was on the platform and must have seen what had happened. He found the senior guard and said, "These girls must be put in another carriage – not with the soldiers."'

Her three years at the Mount, from 1915 to 1918, were all war years. Many of the school buildings were being used as a military hospital. 'Because of the war, we didn't get much food. Everything we were given was counted. Loaves were cut up into pieces and one day you were allowed eight pieces for the day, and the next day it was seven pieces.'

Another time coming home on the train from school, she remembers hearing a group of young men talking about the war: 'They were all saying they supposed they'd be joining up soon. I butted in to say they didn't have to, if they didn't want to. "Oh, I must go," said one of the boys. I was horrified.'

She has clear memories of many of her teachers at the Mount, particularly Miss Williamson, known as Billy, who was head of maths, Miss Eddington and Miss Grubb. 'She was the daughter of Edward Grubb. Surely you've heard of him.' She enjoyed the lessons but hated having to play cricket.

At the time, she wasn't aware that many of the girls came from much wealthier homes than she did, but it struck her later. 'After I left, I went back to an old girls' reunion. I found myself sharing with a girl who brought this enormous trunk full of different clothes for the weekend. I was rather shocked. I didn't go to the Mount reunion after that. I preferred the Walden reunions. The girls were more like myself.'

In her third year at the Mount, by which time she had been awarded a scholarship, Dorothy opted to take mechanics as an extra subject, one

of only two girls. They had to go to Bootham for their lessons. 'The
other girl became very keen on one of the boys. From then on, she
planned all her walks so she would walk into him. By mistake, of
course.'

Did you, er, become interested in any of the boys?

'Oh, no. I was always a very good girl.'

She was one of eight girls in her year who sat matriculation. 'We took
the actual exam at Bootham. When we went over there, the French
teacher said to us, "Oh, the last time there were eight girls from the
Mount, they all failed." That wasn't very reassuring, was it? But we all
passed. We had to go over again when our results came out. I remember the headmaster announcing the first hymn in morning service. It
was "Now Thank We All Our God". We sang that most enthusiasti-
cally.'

At eighteen, Dorothy returned to the Walden school and spent the
next year as a pupil-teacher, unpaid except for her keep. 'It was the time
of that terrible flu epidemic all over the country. I remember taking
orange juice round the houses of people who were very ill. The school
was worried about this, that I might bring back the infection. I had to
have a letter stating that I hadn't actually had contact with any of the
dying.'

She planned to become a teacher, for which her matriculation exam
was sufficient qualification, but she then decided to try for university,
though the choice was limited, especially for girls. She applied to
Westfield College, London. One of her fellow student teachers, a boy,
said she would definitely get in. 'He even bet me I would – and I took
his bet, the first and last time in my life I ever bet on anything. I didn't
get in, but I did win the bet. He had to pay me threepence.'

She then applied to Birmingham University and was accepted to
read for a degree in maths. 'I had to take chemistry as a subsidiary,
which I had to learn from scratch. I could have taken biology, but I had
always been against the idea of killing any living creatures. While at
Walden, as a student teacher, I'd become a vegetarian. I think I'd come
under the influence of one of the masters. My father wasn't very pleased.
It was simply because I couldn't bear to think of animals being killed.'

She went up to Birmingham University in 1919. She can't quite
remember who paid her fees or maintenance, but thinks some of her

better-off relations contributed because by then her father had retired. She lived in University Hall; a Miss Orange was in charge with a Lucy Burt as her assistant, who happened to be a Quaker. In Dorothy's year forty students were reading maths, only six of whom were girls.

'There was still a lot of building work going on. We had to walk in the open between the various departments and faculties. After I left, I think they completed a lot more covered walkways.'

While at Birmingham, she attended a lecture given by Albert Schweitzer, which was held in Cadbury Hall. 'I remember not agreeing with his theology, but that might have been the arrogance of youth, or my Quaker upbringing.'

She joined various Quaker student societies, mostly of an evangelical nature. 'Some of my older relations were very evangelical, which I wasn't, really. They used to bellow at me, "Are you saved?" I was too frightened to say no, so I always said yes. I presumed I was, anyway, according to my own definitions. I believed Jesus had died on the Cross to save us, so I was saved in that sense.

'There were some very good lecturers and professors when I was there. Elton Trueblood was professor of psychology. He was a Friend, and so was John Harvey, a very good psychologist.'

It was while she was at Birmingham that she first met Tom Ellis, a young Manchester Quaker. He was not a Birmingham undergraduate but a young working man, employed for a time by the Manchester Ship Canal company and then in a warehouse, who had been sent on a Quaker course in Birmingham.

'We met at the railway station at Selly Oak, when we were both getting a train to Birmingham. There was a big crowd, and the ticket man had run out of change. Tom paid for my ticket, sixpence ha'penny, it was, saying I could pay him back. So later I sent him the money and we started a correspondence.'

This developed into a close friendship – and then an engagement. Dorothy's father was not terribly keen. It wasn't just that Tom was not as well-educated as Dorothy – he had left school at fourteen – he worried that Tom, with his relatively humble clerking job, would not be able to support her.

Dorothy got through her first-year exams, then her second-year exams. Alas, she failed a vital part of her finals: 'It was the calculus part that did it. I just couldn't get the hang of it – though I gather today that school students now study calculus. I also couldn't understand scientific German. It was full of very hard words I couldn't follow.'

So Dorothy was not awarded her degree, which must have been pretty devastating. 'I can't remember now exactly how I felt. I suppose I must have been very disappointed. I think my father was more upset that I was.'

Did he blame Tom?

'No, he blamed vegetarianism. He said that was the real problem. Eating all that silly stuff, and not enough real food. That's what had left me too weak to study.'

All the same, she managed to get a teaching job, which had always been her aim, at a girls' school in Ashford, Kent. 'Miss Brake's School. I remember some of the girls being very posh. I wasn't very good at it. I couldn't seem to keep order. It was all my fault, really, though I think some of the girls had ganged up against me, being the new teacher. Anyway, Miss Brake paid me off after only six weeks. She gave me thirty pounds, which was very good of her, and I went home. My father said I could keep the thirty pounds, as we were saving up to get married.'

Dorothy stayed at home until she was married: her mother had fallen ill with TB and needed help in the new house they had moved

Marriage to Tom, 1925

to, which was still in the Woking area. She and Tom were married on 11 April 1925, at the Friends' Meeting House in Guildford, and had their honeymoon in the Isle of Wight. Dorothy moved to Manchester, where Tom worked, and they bought a house in Didsbury. 'A very kind aunt sent me a cheque, which helped us to pay the deposit of fifty pounds.'

Eventually Tom got a job working as a Quaker official, becoming in effect the secretary of the Manchester Quakers. He wrote letters, organised meetings and took the minutes. As the work grew, a secretary was employed to help him.

Their first child, Margery, was born in 1926 and their second, Michael, in 1930. Both went to local elementary schools in Manchester and then to Quaker boarding schools. Margery became a teacher and later the bursar at a Manchester University hall of residence. Michael qualified as an accountant.

During the First World War, Tom had worked with the Friends' Ambulance Unit in France. Quakers were conscientious objectors, opposed to all fighting. 'He had an absolute harridan in charge of his unit in France. It was made worse by the fact that he was based on a barge for a time so there was no escape for him.' Michael served in the Friends' Ambulance Unit from 1948 to 1950.

In 1949, Dorothy went on her one and only foreign trip, when she accompanied Tom to Australia: 'He had to go on Quaker business. I think the London Friends were asked to send someone out, to go round the Australian Friends, and they passed the invitation on to Manchester. The London Friends paid for it, but contributions were invited. George Cadbury sent a contribution of five hundred pounds, which meant the tour made a profit.'

They were away for eight months. 'We went by sea. I was dreadfully sick the minute we hit the Channel.'

There were only five hundred Quakers in Australia, scattered throughout the continent, so it meant enormous journeys just to see a handful of people. 'It was normal for Friends in Australia, when going to their nearest monthly meeting, to have to travel three days and nights. We did a lot of that, mostly by train. We usually had to sleep separately, sharing with strangers, as the sleeping berths were either for men or for women. I hardly slept with Tom on that tour.

'It was very exhausting for him. Some of the houses we stayed in were very primitive, with no internal doors. At one place, a woman got very upset that Tom was addressing their meeting when her brother had never been asked to address them. Oh dear. Tom developed an ulcer so that tour didn't really do him much good.'

He died in 1961. 'Yes.' She sighed. 'It does seem a lifetime ago.' He had had polio as a child, which had left him physically very weak. Later, he developed bronchitis and emphysema. 'Altogether he had a rotten time.'

For many years Dorothy lived alone, then eventually came to live beside her daughter Margery at Allonby, on the west coast of Cumberland. Margery married relatively late in life and has no children. Michael has a daughter, who is married and has two boys and a girl.

About five years ago, Margery fell ill and went into sheltered housing, and Dorothy moved into a nursing home in Silloth on the Solway Firth, which is where I met her. It's a handsome building, situated behind a golf course with splendid views across the sands to Scotland. It was purpose-built as a convalescent home and sanatorium in 1862 for people requiring 'unequalled salubrity'.

Dorothy has her own room, filled with some of her treasures, and is mentally very active. She was watching snooker on television when I arrived, with the sound turned down. Beside her bed was a thriller by Reginald Hill, *Deadhead.* She keeps all her own accounts and correspondence. Physically, she is not as sprightly as she was. She had a heart attack some twenty years ago, from which she recovered, but she takes medication for angina.

She had recently been researching into the Penn Club, a residential Quaker club in London, helping to produce a booklet on their history. She is still a Quaker, and has never lost her faith. 'Mind you, I don't agree with some of the modern Quakers.'

Why not? 'I don't want to go into that, if you don't mind.'

She agrees that the curse of alcohol is not quite what it was – but on the other hand, mankind has acquired even more curses.

'I remember as a young girl in Elsenham, watching the men on Saturday evenings. They would come rolling drunk out of the village pub, having spent all their week's wages, leaving nothing for their poor wives and children.

'Thirty years later, when I was first married, and living in Manchester, the curse then was betting. Men wasted their money on horses instead of their families.'

So what is it today – drugs? 'I don't know about that. I would say today's curse is the National Lottery.'

Politically, she was brought up a Liberal. 'My father was the Liberal agent in Saffron Walden for Arthur Pease. I'm not sure which year it was, but he carried me in his arms at one election. He got in that time, but not at the next election.

'When I grew up, I always voted Labour – except once. This was when we were living in Cheshire and I voted for Bromley Davenport. What a mistake. I bitterly regretted that.'

She has mostly been a *Guardian* reader. 'It started when they did a special cheap rate for ministers of religion. Tom wasn't, of course, but they let him have it, as a Quaker official. I later took the *Telegraph* for the crossword.'

She is not quite sure how to explain her longevity. 'I get asked that periodically. I've never drunk or smoked, though when I was at Birmingham University I had a cousin there who tried awfully hard to get me to smoke. But I always refused. So I suppose that's one reason. The second is being relaxed. I've tried in life never to get in a tizzy. I've

Dorothy today

had a lot of things to worry about, but I've tried hard to relax and just get on with life.

'I never expected, of course, to get to ninety-seven. It is a surprise.'

A pleasant surprise?

'No, I wouldn't say that,' she said, after a pause. 'It is not very pleasant to realise that the longer I'm here the less I'll have to leave to my family. I'm using up almost all the money I had hoped to leave to them. I am now getting to the end of my savings. Recently I had to sell some shares.'

How long to go before the money runs out?

'Ah, that would be telling, wouldn't it? But at the rate it's going, it won't be long. This very morning I wrote out a cheque for over a thousand pounds – and that was just for the last four weeks. Living a long time is an expensive business . . .'

Recently she had a modern equivalent taken of that 1900 photograph, the one that showed her as a baby, along with her mother, grandmother and great-grandmother. In the modern version, she sits with her first great-grandchild, Christopher, on her knee, with her daughter Margery on the right, son Michael, behind, and her granddaughter, Sonia Cooper, with her husband, Ted. 'Nice snap,' I said, but it was not quite as professional or as posed and polished as the 1900 studio sitting.

That old photo contained four generations of Quaker teetotallers. In today's version, only Dorothy could be termed a teetotaller and a Quaker. According to Michael, her closest relative who is still teetotal and still a Quaker is her younger sister Kathleen, who lives in East Anglia.

There was one occasion in her long life on which Dorothy did have a drink. It took place on that trip to Australia, in 1949, on the boat out. Perhaps it was just as well that *Wings* and the Women's Total Abstinence Union were no more.

'It so happened that it was the Queen's birthday while we were on board. That evening, at dinner, we all had to drink the Loyal Toast. Tom and I had ordered a soft drink, of course, but we waited and waited and it never came. By this time we had to stand up to toast the Queen. We were forced to take a sip of the only thing available, which was some Australian wine.'

And what was it like?

'Absolutely horrid. That's why I've never had a drink since, at least voluntarily.'

How do you mean?

'Well, I presume in puddings, things like sherry trifles, I must have tasted alcohol without realising it. And I have had quite a few sherry trifles in my life . . .'

7

BIRMINGHAM UNIVERSITY

The university logo

The reason why Dorothy remembers so much construction work at Birmingham University in 1919 was because it was still being built. She didn't seem to be aware at the time that the university was exactly the same age as she was and still taking shape. As it is to this day.

Birmingham University was created in 1900. There's no argument about that: they have a Royal Charter dated May 1900 to prove it. 'One of our many distinctions,' said the university's archivist, Christine Penney, 'is that we are the only English university with a Victorian character.'

You have to analyse those words carefully. Birmingham slipped into the last year of Victoria's reign, thus beating some of their rival institutions, such as Manchester and Sheffield, whose history is just as old, but who didn't get their Royal Charters until a few years later. Durham and London, England's third and fourth oldest English universities, were founded earlier, in 1832 and 1836 respectively, and were therefore not Victorian. You must also note the word 'English', which eliminates the University of Wales from the competition. That's a federal university, combining University Colleges in Cardiff, Swansea, Aberystwyth and Bangor. It received its Charter in 1893, so it is older than Birmingham, and Victorian, but it is not English.

These things matter. All universities are jealous of their achievements and also of their history, especially in these competitive days when every university, however famous, has to fight for students and money. Having a good history means lots of anniversaries and commemorations – that is, lots of opportunities for fund-raising. The Committee of Vice-Chancellors, which today looks after British universities, used to publish a list of foundation dates of all our universities. 'It was so contentious, and caused us so much grief, that we've stopped doing it,' said Dr Ted Nield, their former spokesman. 'The trouble is, they all made up their own rules. I remember when Aberdeen University celebrated its five hundredth anniversary – just thirty-five years after celebrating its centenary . . .'

The basic facts, on which we all agree, are that the two oldest English universities are Oxford and Cambridge. Even then, there are minor quibbles about the exact dates, but most people agree that Oxford was founded in 1249 and Cambridge in 1284. In Scotland there are four ancient seats of learning: St Andrews, 1412; Glasgow, 1451; Aberdeen, 1495 (re-founded 1860, hence the two anniversary dates); and Edinburgh, 1582.

These six foundations were on their own until Durham and London joined them. Later in the nineteenth century, several provincial colleges, some of which had been offering University of London external degrees, claimed university status. Birmingham was the first of England's so-called civic universities – which is only as it should be. Birmingham is Britain's second biggest city, with a population of over a million. It is larger than Glasgow, Liverpool or Manchester. Unlike Glasgow or Liverpool, Bristol or London, though, Birmingham as a city is relatively modern. The simplest explanation for this is that it lacks one vital element: a decent river. Without water transport, it was cut off from medieval trade and development and remained a fairly small town until the end of the eighteenth century, when it suddenly exploded. A handful of local engineers, chemists and inventors pioneered new methods in engineering and technology and, boom-boom, Birmingham was transformed into the Workshop of the World.

It didn't have a suitable civic leader, able to focus all its energies, until 1869 when Joseph Chamberlain was elected to the council; he became mayor in 1873. He was, in fact, a Londoner, who hadn't arrived in the city till 1854, aged eighteen, when he was sent by his father, who had invested in a local screw-making firm and wanted someone to represent his interests. Joseph worked hard and succeeded so well that by the time he was mayor his fortune was sufficient for him to devote himself to good works and politics. In 1876 he entered Parliament as a Liberal. Then he fell out with Gladstone over Home Rule and became a Conservative.

In Birmingham, he was the leader of a powerful group of Nonconformist manufacturers who believed in the 'civic gospel' of improving the appalling social conditions of the industrial poor. This didn't stop him from living in some style, being autocratic or marrying three times. (His first two wives died in childbirth.) He was handsome and dynamic, and Beatrice Potter, later Beatrice Webb of the Fabian movement, was one of those who had fallen in love with him.

Birmingham had had a bad press for most of the nineteenth century. In *Emma* Jane Austen has one of her more snobbish characters saying, 'They came from Birmingham, which is not a place to promise much . . . one has not great hopes of Birmingham.' Chamberlain, and other civic leaders, worked hard to improve the city, clearing slums, installing a proper gas and water supply, building new parks and houses. In due course, he turned his attention from living conditions to education.

There were already two centres of higher education. Queen's College was a medical school, originally founded in 1825 by a local surgeon, William Sands Cox, who had started by offering anatomical demonstrations in his father's front room. By 1843, it was also teaching theology, thanks to a large donation from a local clergyman. The drawback was that students were expected to have been confirmed in the Church of England – a bit limiting for a Nonconformist city.

Mason College was named after Sir Josiah Mason, a self-made Victorian industrialist, long forgotten at a national level, who devoted his energies and wealth to local institutions. He was born in Kidderminster in 1795, the son of a carpet weaver, and started work at eight, selling cakes in the street. He came to Birmingham and made it big in pen-nibs, the steel sort, doing so well that he was credited with the demise of quill pens. He had no children, no dynasty to provide for, so set about helping the young by opening an orphanage, and then the elderly by setting up alms-houses. Then he looked after those in the middle, students, by providing £200,000 for a scientific college, opened in 1880, a purpose-built, red-brick block in the middle of the city, near the town hall. He died a few months later, aged eighty-five, just after the first students had moved in.

Mason College was a great success. Chamberlain became a trustee, all four of his daughters attended its art classes and his son Neville, later Prime Minister, studied applied science there, rather than following his half-brother Austen, later Foreign Secretary, to Cambridge. The teaching and facilities at Mason College were so much better than at Queen's that by 1892 it had taken over medicine and all science teaching from the latter, leaving it as a theological college (which it still is).

The development of further education in Birmingham was mirrored in Manchester, Leeds and Liverpool, but they appeared to have got ahead by grouping together in a northern federation called the Victoria University. To counter this, there was talk in Birmingham of merging its colleges with those in Nottingham and Bristol and forming some sort of Midlands University – until Joe Chamberlain took up the cause and wanted it done his way.

In 1896 he visited Glasgow University, as its rector, and came back convinced that Birmingham must go it alone. It had to have its own university, 'worthy of its wealth and intelligence'. Chamberlain was then colonial secretary, and had the Jameson Raid in the Transvaal to worry about, then the Boer War, but he found time to campaign for a university in Birmingham, arguing that the genius of its people, the importance of its industry, its size with almost two million people living in and around Birmingham, necessitated one. 'If it is not the University of Birmingham, I am out of it,' he told his fellow trustees at Mason College. When you are a big cheese nationally, you can afford to make such local threats. They all agreed with him and the campaign went forward. All that was lacking was money, but he was confident that the existing Mason College building was sufficient for the moment and he secured a donation of £50,000 from Andrew Carnegie, a Scottish industrialist who had made his fortune in the USA. Chamberlain said he would like the money invested to provide an income for teachers and staff.

In October 1900, the first students were enrolled at the University of Birmingham, all 678 absorbed seamlessly from Mason College. Overnight the professors received university Chairs and the students became undergraduates. The first principal was Oliver Lodge, later Sir Oliver, who had been professor of physics at Liverpool. Chamberlain was made Chancellor.

Carnegie, however, had his own ideas about how his money was to be spent. He knew about American universities, that they had proper campuses, and he also knew about the psychology of philanthropy: people who give like to see something solid for their money, not just an abstract concept. 'The money must be spent,' he told Chamberlain, 'or you will get nothing.'

There was an exchange of letters and Chamberlain, a smart politician, changed his position and said, 'Of course we must have new buildings, oh yes,' and Carnegie offered to pay for two of the new professors to visit some American universities to see what they looked like. Academics then, as now, were always keen on overseas jaunts – sorry, research projects – and jumped at the chance.

Then Chamberlain secured the gift of twenty-five acres at Edgbaston, some three miles outside the city centre, from his friend Lord Calthorpe, and the eminent London architects Sir Aston Webb and Ingress Bell, who had designed the Victoria & Albert Museum, were commissioned to plan Britain's first civic university. They incorporated American campus ideas, on the advice of Professors Poynting and Burstall, who had done the research. The idea of including a monumental tower on the new campus emerged in 1902. Chamberlain was keen and said it should be Italian in style. He and his wife had visited Siena in 1904 and were most impressed by the Mangia Tower. In 1905, he announced another large donation of £50,000, this time anonymous, which he said should go towards the cost of the tower. The donor was never identified and it might be that Chamberlain had arranged it so he could get his own way with the tower's design.

Someone proposed that the edifice should be called after Professor Poynting, which would have been fitting but would probably have led to endless jokes (a shame, really: the Poynting Tower of Birmingham would have been a nice rival to the Leaning Tower of Pisa). John Henry Poynting was the first professor of physics, one of Birmingham's many distinguished scientists, a medal winner at the Royal Society, known for his experiments with gravity or 'weighing the earth', as it was commonly described. In the event the tower was called the Chamberlain Tower, which was probably what Joe had hoped. It was one of the buildings that were opened officially by King Edward VII and Queen Alexandra at a grand ceremony on 9 July 1909. On the day, the tower's clock workings were not quite ready. During the ceremony, so it is said, the hands were slowly advanced by a young man using a crank handle – just in case His Majesty should think that time was going jolly slowly on his visit to Birmingham. Chamberlain himself didn't make it: he had a stroke in 1906 from which he had never fully recovered.

The completion of the building programme was interrupted by the First World War, during which the university was turned into a hospital. By the time young Dorothy Robson (later Ellis) arrived in 1919, the next stage of the building plans was just starting up. Gothic cathedrals had similar problems.

Birmingham has always been strong on science. Apart from Professor Poynting, another eminent scientist in the early days was Sir William Tilden, professor of chemistry, who helped to manufacture synthetic rubber. Later, in the 1930s, Professor Norman Haworth, a Nobel Prize-winner, along with Professor Maurice Stacey, developed synthetic ascorbic acid (Vitamin C), the world's first synthetic vitamin.

From the beginning there was also a sprinkling of people well-known in the arts: Edward Elgar was the first professor of music, appointed in 1904, while one of the earliest students was Francis Brett Young, who became a successful novelist, author of *My Brother Jonathan*. In 1906, aged twenty-two, he was studying medicine (as have many other novelists in early life, such as Somerset Maugham and A. J. Cronin) and the university's archives contain a letter from him, written in January 1906 during a surgery lecture by Sir Gilbert Barling. He is clearly not listening very hard as he is writing to his fiancée, Jessica. 'This is terribly disconnected, my darling, because Barling will lecture and I must post this before I go home.'

Birmingham's foundation brought the number of English universities to five, and the total number of university students in Great Britain was then around 20,000. A third were at Oxford and Cambridge, still by far the two biggest universities. By 1910, Birmingham had about a thousand students and by 1920 nearly two thousand.

Women students were in the minority, but in 1903, the professor of German was taken by surprise when the best candidate for the first

Harding Scholarship for modern languages turned out to be a woman. He accepted this, albeit reluctantly: 'Though I would rather have commenced work with a man, I felt that it would be unjust to pass over such a good and promising candidate.' When Dorothy arrived at Birmingham, 28 per cent of British university students were women, a higher number than might, perhaps, be expected.

The first women graduates anywhere in Britain were from London University in 1880. Until that year, women could study but were not allowed to sit degree examinations. At Cambridge, the all-women Girton College had existed since 1873, but admission to examinations was not permitted until 1881. Even then, women were not considered members of the university. By 1921, they could wear a cap and gown and call themselves Bachelors of Arts, but it wasn't until 1948 that Cambridge allowed women full membership of all university bodies. At Oxford, women were admitted fully from 1919.

All fees, for male and female students, had to be paid by themselves or their families, and the government contributed nothing. However, around half of all students were awarded some form of charitable grant or scholarship. This meant there was always a proportion of poor students, though the vast majority were from middle-class backgrounds.

Some interesting figures about the early decades of our universities appear in a 1930 book called *Universities in Great Britain* by Ernest Barker, professor of political science at Cambridge. By then there were seventeen universities: eleven were in England – the six new ones being Manchester and Liverpool, each founded in 1903, Leeds in 1904, Sheffield in 1905, Bristol in 1909 and Reading in 1926. There were the same four in Scotland and one in Wales, while Queen's University, Belfast, had been founded in 1909. The total student population in 1930 was 44,660, of whom around 31,000 were men; that year, 8,685 graduated. Professor Barker also gives us the ratio of students to the population as a whole in the appropriate age group: in England and Wales it was 1:1,150 while in Scotland it was 1:455, so almost three times as many people went to university in Scotland compared with England. Traditionally Scotland had always been keener on education, with proportionally more universities, lower fees and more generous scholarships. There was not enough graduate employment for

Scots at home so an export trade developed: many Scottish graduates came to London or went abroad to run the empire.

The government, in the form of the University Grants Committee, made a modest contribution towards the cost of the universities: in 1889 it was only £15,000, but by 1930 it had risen to £1.8 million out of a total cost of £5 million. There were then 750 professors earning an average of £1,100 a year.

Professor Barker makes the point that the universities, both old and new, were powerhouses for the nation's intellectuals, the main centres for research, whereas in the nineteenth century many leading intellectuals, such as Macaulay, J. S. Mill, Walter Bagehot and Charles Darwin, had operated as private scholars or in other activities. He also lists some of the new modern subjects that could be studied in 1930: textiles at Leeds, journalism at London, brewing and commerce at Birmingham. That surprised me: I had assumed that such subjects dated from the 1960s. In 1930 there were also Appointments Boards – probably no more useful or efficient than they are today.

In Germany, according to Barker, there were thirty universities with 90,000 students, giving a ratio of 1:690 – much better than England but not as good as Scotland. In the USA the ratio was best of all: 1:25. He doesn't give the exact number of US students or universities, except to say, rather sniffily, that many of them 'might not be classed as universities'.

He considered what might be the optimum student population and thought that England had it about right. Too many, he believed, would lead to 'mechanical mass production' and an 'inadequately employed intellectual proletariat' which would be 'the seed-bed of revolutionary movements, political and economic'. How true.

In 1930 London University, in its various colleges, had a total of 9,150 full-time students. Cambridge had 5,700 (500 women) while Oxford had 4,500 (800 women). Glasgow had 5,000 students, a lot of whom were home-based. No single English university, he said, which wasn't made up of separate colleges, should ever take more than 2,000 students, which was the size of Manchester and Birmingham. A warning, therefore, not to grow.

British universities still sent MPs to Parliament, which Barker admitted was an anomaly, dating back to James I who considered Oxford and Cambridge Universities as parliamentary boroughs. In 1930, Oxford and Cambridge returned two MPs each, Scotland had three, London, Wales and Belfast one each and the remaining English 'provincial' universities, as Barker called them, shared two MPs, making a total of twelve.

The breakdown of disciplines is interesting: over half the student population, 53 per cent, were studying for an arts degree, while 19 per cent were doing medicine, 17 per cent pure science and 11 per cent technical subjects. Fees per student were £70 a year at Oxbridge while at a provincial university it was £30 for arts students and up to £50 for scientists. There was no tradition at English universities, Barker noted, for students to support themselves by working during their studies.

The big change in British education came with the Butler Education Act of 1944, which greatly increased academic opportunities, making grammar schools free and open to all who could pass the entrance exam. It also introduced generous grants for university education. By 1950, the British student population had risen to 85,500. Five provincial colleges that had been under the umbrella of London University became universities in their own right – Nottingham in 1948, Southampton in 1952, Hull in 1954, Exeter in 1955 and Leicester in 1957.

In the late 1950s, when my wife and I went to university – to Oxford and to Durham – we felt surprisingly well-off. Coming from working-class homes, we both received maximum awards and my wife also had a scholarship. They were still, however, middle-class, male-dominated institutions. We wore gowns for all lectures and most students had college blazers, ties and scarves. My wife now denies she ever bought her college scarf but I have a photograph to prove she did. We didn't realise it at the time, but we were still part of an élite: only 2 per cent of the population went to university. In 1958 Durham had only 1,500 students.

The next, much bigger advance came in the 1960s. The Robbins Report of 1963 reinforced plans to expand the higher-education system and by now the government was automatically giving a grant to anyone who got a university place. Seven brand-new universities were built in England on green-field sites, with new ideas, new methods of teaching and organisation, offering degrees in new or a mixed range of subjects. Sussex was the first to be opened in 1961, followed by Keele in 1962,

East Anglia and York in 1963, Lancaster and Essex in 1964, Kent and Warwick in 1965, and Stirling in Scotland in 1967. In ten years the student population had more than doubled to 188,000.

The biggest and most dramatic change of all came in 1992, when at a stroke around thirty polytechnics became universities. In 1990, there had been 447,000 university students. By 1996, this had jumped to over a million, of whom 972,100 were doing first degrees and 134,000 postgraduate degrees. It was estimated that there were another 500,000 part-time students, including those at the Open University, founded in 1963.

There are now eighty-nine universities, or 115 university institutions if London and the Welsh colleges are classed individually, employing 102,700 full-time academic staff. The average professor earns £33,000, making him worse off proportionally than he was in 1930. The ratio of male to female students is almost equal – 51 per cent men to 49 per cent women. Socially, there have not been such dramatic changes: only 30 per cent of students are classified as working class, much the same as it has been over the last fifty years. And it won't change much, now that history is going backwards and students have to pay tuition fees, just as they did in 1900.

The target for the year 2000 was that one in three should go on to higher education, 33 per cent compared with just 0.1 per cent in 1900 – if, of course, the whole edifice does not collapse through overcrowding and lack of resources. Many universities, forced to keep increasing their numbers to qualify for government grants, have already run into debt. Total numbers might have gone up, but funding per student has dropped by 28 per cent in the last six years. Back in 1930, Professor Barker feared that when mass production arrived there might be revolution. In the event, the fear is bankruptcy. In 1996, I was appointed a Deputy Pro-Chancellor of Lancaster University, and at every meeting I attended the main subject was finance: how to cut corners, cut staff, raise or borrow more money. Yet Lancaster was generally graded as being in the top ten.

In 1997, Birmingham was graded 25th out of the 115 university institutions, using the grading system, based on research ratings, which of course not all universities agree with. Using other rankings, such as applications and difficulty of entry (you need A-level grades of ABB to read English, AAB for law, ABB for medicine), then Birmingham is also in the top ten. It is also one of the few not in serious financial danger. This is partly due to its history, going back to the days of Chamberlain, when it made great efforts to draw support from the local industrial community. It is also due, their head of public relations boasted – yes, all universities have PRs today – to being a well-run university. In 1993, a survey revealed that Birmingham was the best-managed university in Britain.

In the last few years, it has had to fight competition from several new universities in and around Birmingham, all trying to improve their research ratings. 'It's very like football teams,' said Birmingham's PR, 'trying to sign up the best players. Top professors do get tempted away with big money offers, special laboratories, lots of assistants, so that their departments will score well when the next research assessment is done.'

The growth and expansion at Birmingham has been as remarkable as that in the rest of the country. In 1960 there were 4,000 students. This rose gradually to 9,000 by 1990. In 1996 the total had shot up to 17,000. Over 4,000 of these, some 26 per cent of the total, are research students – the largest number in any British university, outside Oxbridge and London. There are now almost 2,000 members of staff – no Nobel Prize-winners at present, but they have eight professors who are Fellows of the Royal Society. The annual cost of running the place comes to around £200 million. In 1994 it made a surplus of £16 million.

What surprised me most on my visit was the campus. In my mind, before I had researched its history, I had lumped it with ten or so other red-brick universities and expected boring urban blocks. I had visited the city centre over the years, and it seemed just as ugly and unattractive as ever, despite the new roads and buildings. I had never been out to Edgbaston, though. It was positively bucolic, with the feeling of an American campus. The university is awash with trees and greenery, even a lake, and today covers 200 acres, much bigger than the original site.

Chamberlain's buildings, especially his tower – which is just as handsome as Siena's – and the Great Hall, are now accepted as important works of architecture, not just as seats of learning. The Barber Institute of Fine Arts, located at the East Gate to the campus, is one of the finest

Birmingham University today

but least-known picture galleries in Britain, with paintings by Canaletto, Guardi, Poussin, Murillo, Monet, Degas, Renoir and Van Gogh. Among its rare books and manuscripts is a collection of fifty-nine diaries and letters relating to Edward Elgar, their first professor of music.

Birmingham's better-known present-day staff and alumni include Victoria Wood, Desmond Morris, Terry Hands, Stephen Littlechild, Sir Alex Jarratt (now the university's Chancellor), Sir Austin Pierce of British Aerospace, Sir Peter Walters of BP and Dr D. M. Mutasa,

Speaker of the Zimbabwe Parliament. But perhaps the best-known is David Lodge, if only because he has put Birmingham University into so many of his novels, usually referring to it as Rummidge. At the same time as Lodge was using red-brick Birmingham, Malcolm Bradbury, a professor at East Anglia, was doing much the same for the new 1960s universities with *The History Man*. Both poke fun, but their work makes a change from a century of novels set ever-so-reverentially in Oxbridge quads.

David Lodge graduated from University College, London, and arrived in Birmingham as an assistant lecturer in 1960. 'It was chance, really. I was trying to get a job anywhere as an English lecturer. I originally failed to get the job, but the person who got it couldn't take it for a year, so they contacted me, offering me a position – but only for a year. I had a wife and a young baby, but we all decided to move up to Birmingham. I suppose it was a bit of a gamble. But at the end of the year, they kept me on – and I just never left.'

He became a professor in 1976, and then an honorary professor from 1987, when he retired to write full-time. Over the years, he was invited to apply for positions at other British universities, some in theory more distinguished. 'In the end, I had such a comfortable life, working only part-time as a professor, which is very rare, so I didn't want to leave. I still live in Edgbaston, very near the university.

'When I arrived in 1960, Birmingham as a city was pretty depressing and deeply provincial. Night life meant some Victorian pubs and a couple of Indian restaurants. The university was the only reason to be here and it was quite exciting, things were expanding, thanks to the Robbins Report. The English department had been in some old Victorian buildings in the town, part of the old Mason College, but we moved to the Edgbaston campus the year I came.

'As in all universities today, the working conditions are much harder for staff and students. There's no space to sit down in the library. Teaching small groups has gone. Birmingham has had to struggle to keep its head above water, but it's remained in the Ivy League. It still seems to be popular with students.

'The city itself is much more lively. It's like a British Frankfurt, with its international exhibition halls, world-class symphony orchestra. The quality of life is much better than when I arrived.'

Lodge first referred to Birmingham as Rummidge in his novel *Changing Places* in 1975. 'I suppose I was being a bit ironic and satirical, sending it up. No one objected. Birmingham people are not chauvinistic. They are affectionate towards their city, but they know its faults.

'I didn't think I'd be returning to it, as a fictional setting, but I have done – in *Small World, Nice Work, Therapy*. I now find myself describing it more realistically, more sympathetically. I suppose it's how I now feel. I almost love the place.'

A collection of Lodge's literary papers is held in the university, along with other relics, such as letters from Chamberlain, early scientific instruments and the chair used by Edward VII for the 1909 opening ceremony. They also have the inkstained pen with which he signed the visitors' book. This was used by the university's visitors until 1975 when the Queen declined it, preferring her own ballpoint.

In fact Lodge wasn't the first person to write about Birmingham University in fiction. Francis Brett Young did, about fifty years earlier, in his novel *Dr Bradley Remembers*, in which he describes the original Mason College, where Lodge lectured in the 1960s, as the 'new red-brick Gothic building'. The term red-brick caught on in 1943, with the publication of Bruce Truscott's *Red Brick University*. It was used as a generic adjective for all civic universities, as opposed to Oxbridge, often with slightly condescending overtones. That faded with the arrival of a third species of university, the New Universities. Today, the term is used with pride – it is even the title of Birmingham University's student newspaper.

'About three-quarters of the students in the 1960s were like myself – first-generation university students,' says Lodge. 'Some could be a bit difficult, let's say bolshie, as they were very political in the '60s. But they were interesting and rewarding to teach. Most of the brightest in my department wanted to go on and be university teachers.

'Today it's the reverse. Most are the children of graduates. It's just the normal thing for them, part of their career pattern, but now the brightest rarely think of becoming lecturers. They all want to be in the media.'

8

DAME ELIZABETH HILL

Cambridge University professor

Elizabeth Hill (right), aged 6, with sister Daisy

I met Dame Elizabeth Hill in Chiswick, West London, in a suburban house where she was convalescing with the help of some Russian friends. Her leg had been paralysed, she said, but she was now recovering, though I couldn't have guessed there was anything remotely wrong with her. She sat upright at a polished mahogany table and fixed me severely with a cool, intellectual stare, as if giving a tutorial to a particularly slow student. A Russian girl brought coffee when I arrived, but after that there were no interruptions. For four and a half hours Dame Elizabeth – known to her friends as Lisa – talked without a break, without a pause. Now and again, when I tried to ask a question or hurry her along, she lifted her hand and said, 'Wait, I'm coming to that.'

She was born in St Petersburg, Russia, on 24 October 1900, so it states in *Who's Who*. 'Not quite correct,' she replied. 'I was actually born on the eleventh of October, according to the Gregorian calendar.

You have to add on thirteen days in the English calendar for this century, so that's why I made it the twenty-fourth. When we get to the year 2001, I will change my birthdate to the twenty-fifth . . .'

She smiled, a thin, intellectual smile. She'd made a neat academic point, at the same time indicating that she expected to live into the next century.

Her father was British, and so is she, hence her clipped English accent. He came from a long line of Anglo-Russian businessmen, who had been in Russia for generations, attracted by the industrial and financial opportunities during the reigns of Peter and Catherine the Great. Hill & Whishaw, his firm was called, coal importers. Originally, Lisa's father's family had come from Scotland, eight generations earlier. He was sent to a British public school, as all the sons had been, and went to Lancing, but he had broken the mould by marrying a Russian woman and not another Russo-Brit, as was the family custom. His wife, Lisa's mother, was from Russian nobility and had brothers and uncles who were generals in the Tsar's army.

'My earliest memory is of when I was about three or four, hearing people talk about the war with Japan. The Russians were beaten and it was a national disgrace to be defeated by such a small country. All Russians were proud of their empire, just like the British, with complete confidence in their army.

'I can also remember the first Russian Revolution of 1905. My nurse was making remarks about how awful it was, but of course it was quickly squashed.'

She had three older brothers and two sisters and they lived in some comfort and affluence in St Petersburg, in a large apartment in Maryinsky Theatre Square, opposite the ballet. At one time, they had a staff of fourteen – cook, washer-up, laundress, ironer, housemaid, serving-maid, parlourmaid, lady's-maid, plus nurses and governesses. 'All were women. We had no male staff. The parlourmaid was always the best-looking, kept for my parents' dinner parties. I was never allowed to eat with my parents. Not until I was seventeen.'

As a young child, she had a Russian nurse, then a host of governesses from England or elsewhere in Europe. 'By the age of eight I was fluent in four languages. English and Russian, which I spoke with my father and mother, then French and German, which the governesses taught us.

No, I wouldn't say it was amazing. That was normal for an educated family of the time, interested in culture and the arts.'

They made regular trips to England, every year or so, travelling as a family. In 1912, while staying with some of her father's relatives, she found that her girl cousins were going to school, not being taught at home by governesses. Back in Russia, Lisa and her younger sister Daisy plagued their mother to let them follow suit. 'She said being educated at home was best, but we begged and begged till she gave in. She said it was on condition that the household went on as before, with our French and German governesses. And if she wanted to add to that, with, say, a history of art tutor, then school would have to be fitted in around it. So off we went. It was actually a German school, part of a Lutheran Church. Its education was excellent. But then all schools in Russia are good to this day, far better than in Britain.'

In 1914, her three older brothers, being British and public-school educated, volunteered to go off and fight for King and country. The eldest, Eric, joined the Black Watch. 'He became ADC to General Pool and was killed in Galicia on a military mission on the Russian front. I think he was the first British soldier to be killed in Russia, so we were told.'

The second, Alfred Ferdinand, was given up for dead at the Battle of the Somme, but somehow recovered, only to be captured on some secret mission with Bruce Lockhart to Russia and locked up in the Lubyanka prison. The third, George Edward, went on to serve in both world wars, and in the Indian Army in between, but was killed at Dunkirk. 'When I say killed, I mean vanished, because we never found out what happened to him.'

In 1917, while all her brothers were away fighting for Britain, there was more trouble at home in Russia. It was expected that, once again, the Tsar's army would put down any troublemakers – but this time it was different. This time it was the beginning of the Russian Revolution.

'I will tell you what happened. One day, my father called us all together and said we are going away to England for a few months, till all this nonsense was over. We could each take one case, and five pounds' worth of money, but nothing else. All my mother's jewellery was left behind. We didn't cheat. Nobody pinned precious things in the linings of their suitcase. Everything was left at home for the servants to look after till we returned. My father explained that the National Bank in Russia would transfer a certain amount every month to London from his account, so we would have more than enough to live on. It was just going to be an extra holiday, that was all.

'It is interesting to realise now that there are people all over the world, this very moment, who think they are in the know, who think they are in touch with what is going on in their country, but in fact have absolutely no idea. There could be a revolution tomorrow in England. Who is to say there won't be?'

She and her family made their way slowly to England, via Finland, Sweden, Norway, then in a boat to Aberdeen, on to London by train where they booked into a hotel. A top hotel, she said, so I asked if it was the Savoy or the Ritz.

'I don't want to name it, for reasons which will become apparent. But it was in the top five hotels in London and all five of us booked in. After a week, my father's money still hadn't come through. He told them the problem and they said, "Don't worry, it's quite all right, sir, stay another week." Which we did. After another week, the money still hadn't come. We then had to leave, er, hurriedly. We moved to a much cheaper place, waiting for the money, and when it still didn't arrive, we moved again, this time to a rented house in St John's Wood at five pounds a week.

'Meanwhile, Daisy, my sister, had started school at Francis Holland while I was registered at Bedford College, in Regent's Park, to study for my matriculation. At the end of the autumn term, 1917, Lenin had come to power. There was now no prospect of getting any money out, or any of our possessions. Daisy had to leave school, as my father couldn't pay the bills. So did I. We kept on changing addresses till we all ended up in a ghastly room at two pounds a week. What a comedown, how shaming, after all those servants.

'We were not ashamed of our poverty because we had been brought up not to boast about our wealth. Talking about money, either way, was vulgar. But it must have been terrible for my father. I don't know how he managed. I never asked him. I supposed he borrowed from friends, did little jobs here and there, won money at bridge. But, no, I don't remember my sisters and I feeling ashamed. We didn't go around telling people we'd once been rich. We just got on with it and readjusted. I remember thinking, I will stand on my own two feet. I will earn my living somehow. But what do you think I did? What would you have done?'

Er, well, I mumbled, assuming this was rhetorical, that I was not expected to reply, which was indeed the case.

'I was a cultivated, educated person,' she continued, 'able to speak four languages. I discovered an agency called Gabbitas & Thring and went along to see them about a teaching job. I told a secretary I spoke four languages, and she wrote it down, as if not believing me. I didn't say I was from Russia. British people don't like foreigners.

'I said I wanted to teach in a boarding school – that was because I wanted to be fed. She went through a list and there was one for a French ma'mselle at a girls' boarding school in Wales. I said, "I'll take that." She said, "Oh, no," looking at me as if I were a lunatic. "You'll have to write and apply." Anyway, I did, and got a telegram by return, offering me the job. It was at Penrhos College in Colwyn Bay. We imagine we run our own lives, but I think it was destiny, getting that job.

'I got only forty-five pounds a year, and worked very hard, from morning till night, but I didn't consider it exploitation. You don't when you're young. It was a magnificent school, with huge grounds, near the sea. I'd never seen such seagulls before. It had once been a hydro and most girls had their own bedroom.

'The first evening I arrived I was told, "Ma'mselle," for I was no longer Miss Hill, "Ma'mselle, tomorrow morning, you'll be taking this class for cricket. Here is your whistle." And that was it. I hadn't the slightest idea about cricket. I went to the *Encyclopaedia Britannica* and read eleven pages on cricket, but it was full of words I didn't understand. I did recognise the word umpire, so next morning, when I got my class on the cricket pitch, I said to the most responsible-looking girl, "Here's the whistle. It's about time you learned about umpiring." Every time I heard the word "over" I thought, Thank God, it's now over. Anyway, I soon picked it up. But I never got the hang of lacrosse. When that came up, I elected to take the wet walks along the seaside and look at the seagulls.

'I never told anyone about my life in Russia, about our fourteen ser-vants and that sort of thing. I'd always rather looked down upon our governesses, thinking they were poor things who had to earn their living. Now I knew what it was like. I soon found out that teachers who were graduates got a great deal more than me. If they had been to university, they felt superior to those who hadn't.

'They were all scared of the headmistress, but I wasn't at all. I just treated her like another human being. In social occasions, I have never just stood there like a dolt. I've always had something to say. I used to read to the headmistress in French after lunch until she fell asleep.

'I had no clothes, so things like chapel were a problem at first. You were supposed to wear a hat and coat, but the violin mistress helped me. She took me to a shop where I bought a black straw boater with a green ribbon. I felt like a clown, but I thanked her very much. I spent most of my spare time reading, because the school had a good library.

'I eventually became friendly with the geography teacher and let her know about my Russian background. She at least knew where Russia was. I went on lots of walks with her and she was the first person who said I should try to go to university. I had no money, hadn't passed matriculation, but she told me about this correspondence college which was frightfully cheap, so I started studying in my spare time.

'She then left the school, which was a shame, but she wrote to me one day and said she'd discovered a British War Fund, which was offering a hundred pounds a year to British girls whose education had been interrupted by the war. I was British, so I qualified on those grounds. My education had been interrupted by the Russian Revolution – but was that technically a war? The rules didn't actually say what sort of war. Anyway, I applied and I got the funding, on condition I passed my matric.

'I had to chaperone to Bangor three girls from the school who were taking their matriculation exam – and I sat mine with them. Then I gave in my notice, convinced I had passed. There was a farewell for me at the school and I was given a Swan fountain pen. I was at the school three and a half years and loved it.

'I went back to London, where my parents were living in sordid conditions in Earl's Court. My older sister had got a job with the War Graves Commission and Daisy was doing sewing, working in some basement. I think my father was door-to-door selling.

'To get your matric, you had to pass in five subjects – English, maths, a science and two others. I passed English, Russian, French, botany –

but I failed maths. So I failed the matric, despite being so confident and having given up my job.

'I decided to resit and spent a lot of time studying in Brompton Road library. I had no money to live on so I used to make little Russian cakes with Daisy and we'd take them to a Russian tea-shop in Kensington.

'The day the results were due, I couldn't face it. I told Daisy my number and sent her to find out while I sat on a bench in Kensington Gardens. After a long while, she came back and said my number wasn't on the board. I thought she was playing a joke, but she said, no, it wasn't there. So I went to look. I can still feel my legs shaking. At the top of this enormous list, there were just a few lines of people in the First Division. And there was my number! "Oh, I never thought of looking there," said Daisy.'

In 1921 Lisa entered University College, London, but half-way through her first term she was told she'd have to leave. 'The Dean called for me and said it had been discovered I hadn't offered Latin – and to study an arts subject at a university in those days you needed to have passed Latin. Nobody had told me. Nobody had explained the system. So, after all that hard work, my whole world had collapsed.

'I went for help to an Armenian who lectured in Russian at King's. He was just a carpet-dealer, really, but very smart, and he said, "Write a letter to your dean saying you will be passing the Latin exam in January." The Dean accepted this idea but it meant I had to learn Latin in a month and half. I studied twenty-four hours a day, sitting on buses, translating everything I saw into Latin. "That girl opposite has no spear . . . That old man has returned from the wars." I sat the exam – and failed.

'I thought, that's it, I must leave now, but the Armenian, who was very clever, said laws are made for people, not people for laws, so you must send another letter. He told me to ask to be allowed to sit my intermediate – the exam at the end of the first year – but they would store my marks, keep them on record, till I had passed my Latin. The next Latin exam, you see, was after my intermediate. If I then failed Latin, I would definitely leave. But if I passed, then my intermediate exam would count. Wasn't that clever?

'I think the Dean was staggered by the suggestion, but it had to go to a board this time. They thought, Why kill this girl off? Give her one more chance. And they did. And I passed both – the intermediate and the Latin.'

So at long last, Lisa was a proper living undergraduette, with a modest grant from the British War Fund. After her first year, she chose French as her speciality. She studied very hard, she said, with no time for pleasures or pastimes. Not even a boyfriend?

'I had abandoned the idea of marrying. That would have been my role in life in Russia, to marry someone suitable, but I had lost my motherland and felt dispossessed in my fatherland. In fact I felt I had been de-countrified. I didn't belong anywhere.

'Anyway, how could I meet people when I had no money? Think of the modern world. Students meet through sport or in bars or over coffee. I didn't play any sports. I had no money for tea. I couldn't even go on the tube. I walked everywhere. Public-school boys might try to pick you up, but for ulterior motives.' Tut tut, I said, shaking my head. Then she smiled.

'However, I did have one flirtation, my first love, Reginald. Which I will tell you about. He was a student in the year ahead, a few years older than me. Everyone said he was very clever and would get a first. He wore sandals and no socks, no tie, just a tennis shirt, which was most unusual for those days. He looked like he could be the son of an earl, though, of course, I didn't know what earls looked like. He had beautiful handwriting – always writing in between the lines, not on the lines.

'I happened to ask him what he had done in the war and I thought he said he'd been in Dartmouth. I'd heard of that, the naval college, so I presumed he must have been an officer. It came out later he'd said, "Dartmoor." He'd been breaking stones, as a conscientious objector.

'One day on the way to Liverpool Street station he kissed me in the street. I was rather shocked, believing that only servant girls kissed in the street. I'd realised by then that he was a bit eccentric. Instead of giving me a bunch of violets he once gave me a bunch of watercress. He was, of course, a vegetarian.

'He then invited me home to Sunday lunch to meet his mother. He said he lived out in the country, in Essex. I got the bus, as he directed, then I had to walk for a bit. I kept on expecting to come to green fields, as he'd said it was the country, with big gates leading to his home. Instead I came to a one-up and one-down in a terrace, like *Coronation Street*. His father was a porter and his mother was some sort of religious maniac who that afternoon was holding a prayer meeting in his house. You walked into the living room straight from the street, and there was linoleum, an aspidistra on a table and lots of chairs lined up along the walls for the prayer meeting. Reginald whispered to me that after lunch we would slip upstairs while his mother held her meeting. What does that mean? I thought.

'During lunch, his mother looked daggers at me, as if worried about losing her son to a bloody foreigner. For lunch we had cheese scones, roasted cheese, cheese on biscuits and lots of nuts. I munched my way through it all. Then his mother started arranging the chairs, so we slipped upstairs to his room.

'All he had in the room was a bed, one chair and lots of books, so we sat on the bed. He started embracing me, then he stopped and said, "I don't believe in sleeping with women." I didn't understand this and wondered if he was a homosexual.

'Next day, we met again and he said, "Let's go to the Natural History Museum." We sat on a bench and he said to me, "My mother approved of you. She thinks you will make a good wife. Will you marry me?"

'I think I muttered some reply like, "Oh, Reg, thank you for the honour," because I'd been reading lots of silly novels at the time, but I added that I had no intention of marrying. I had to get my degree, then help my parents, so it could be ten years before I would think of marrying.

'He was rather upset and said, "There are plenty of facets to a big diamond." I was never sure what that meant. That I was a diamond, showing one of my facets? Or that he was, and would easily find someone else?

'He did in the end. Reginald Blyth was his name. Have you heard of him? One of the greatest Japanese scholars of this century. He went off to Japan, got a job as tutor to the Emperor and translated sacred Japanese books into English. He married an English girl first, then a Japanese, but I think really he might have been homosexual as well.'

If he had asked to sleep with you, on the bed that time, what would you have done?

'I would have said no. I wouldn't have thrown myself away on such a chap. Besides, one didn't do that sort of thing. Not like today, where sex is a sport. In those days, sex was for breeding. Pleasure and sport didn't come into it. Women of all classes were for breeding, so peasants chose strong women to have strong peasant children, just as the nobility chose noblewomen. Women of all classes remained faithful. They didn't enquire what their husbands did, when they themselves were busy breeding. People in those days went to bed in the dark. Most people, men and women, had little idea what sex was all about.'

In her final year, she transferred from an honours degree in French to a degree in a brand-new subject, Slavonic studies. This was the result of the arrival from Liverpool of Bernard Pares, later Sir Bernard, as professor of Russian.

'He touted round the colleges at London University, telling people they would be pioneers. "You'll all end up professors." I had begun to think that with a French degree I'd just end up a French teacher, one of the many. Slavonic studies sounded more interesting, especially with my Russian background.

'I was one of his first students, along with Joshua Cooper and Phyllis Kemp. They were very well-connected, from well-known British families. Our lecturers included Prince Mirsky and Baron Meyendorf. They were both very grand and only shook hands with you once a year. Then there was Norman Jopson who was much more like a normal human being.'

As her finals got near, in 1924, she found herself becoming weaker and weaker through lack of food. 'I drank water from the wrong side of a glass, to spin it out. I used to go to the Holborn Restaurant and breathe in the roast-beef fumes coming from a grid in the basement. It made me feel full. The reason why chefs are fat is not because they eat a lot but because they breathe in fatty food all day long.

'I was getting at the end of my tether, with no money and no food, when a miracle arrived in the form of Doris Mudie.'

She was a well-off woman, just a few years older than Lisa, a member of the family that owned Mudie's Library, one of the best-known subscription libraries of the time. She had been doing charity work, helping war victims and refugees in Europe after the First World War.

'We met because she decided to do a journalism course at London University. One day she said to me she'd got a big house in Westminster, at 2 Vincent Square, and a maid. "Why don't you come and live with me there and do your studies? Don't worry, I'm not a lesbian."'

'It turned out she had been engaged. While travelling on a train one day, she'd opened her *Times* to see that her fiancé had got married to someone else, a millionaire widow. She had a nervous breakdown. It was after that, when she recovered, that she had decided to help others less fortunate than herself.'

Lisa moved in, studied hard in peace and comfort, and got a first. She then started work on a Ph.D. She paid a modest rent for the run of the house and the use of a maid, but was now able to make quite a bit of money by private tuition.

'I had tried in the past to give lessons to lazy children of the middle classes, trailing out to their homes in Islington or wherever, but now, with a grand address and a maid to open the door, I had people coming to me from very grand families – like the children of Sir Trenchard Cox, director of the V & A, the children of Sydney Jarrold, the publisher, the daughter of the Speaker of the House of Commons, and Veronica Wedgwood from the Wedgwood family. I also went out and gave lectures about Russia. Doris took a photo of me in Russian costume and printed leaflets, which she gave out, saying I could lecture to schools on Russian tales, charms and curses for five pounds a time. It gave me experience in lecturing and also a platform manner.'

She got her Ph.D. in 1928. Doris then decided they would set up together in a literary partnership. 'I translated books from the German or French, doing it orally, while she would write it out in English. We got lots of work from publishers such as Methuen, Jarrold's, Constable. We also wrote one original book of comic tales, which we called *For Readers Only*. The title was a reference to the British Museum rules. We did it anonymously as "J. Penn". It was published by Allen & Unwin, and became one of the books of the year. No one ever discovered we wrote it.

'One day, while in the Reading Room, a woman I didn't know came up to me and said, "Is your name Lisa?" She must have heard one of my friends calling me that. I said yes. She said that a famous spiritualist and clairvoyant called Hesther Dowden had given out a message for Lisa which said, "In a few years, her entire life will change and she will never look back." She wondered if I was the Lisa.'

Not long afterwards she heard that a lecturer in Slavonic studies was to be appointed by Cambridge University. 'It was a man's university, everyone knew that, so there was no point in a woman applying. I was discussing it with a friend, who pointed out that the advert didn't actually say women couldn't apply. It was obvious, though, that to apply you needed the backing of Sir Bernard Pares, who had started the first Slavonic studies department. I didn't have much respect for him – he'd started as a journalist and traveller, and wasn't really an academic. I went to see him, though I suspected he was already backing his own candidate. I asked if I could use his name as a reference – and he said, "Certainly not". I pointed out I'd been his star pupil. I'd got a first and a Ph.D. He said, "Yes – but you are a woman!" So that was it.

'I came home and told Doris. She said, "Blast that man! How many references do you need?" I said three – academic, social and clerical. That was the system then. I didn't know any Church of England clerics at all because I was Russian Orthodox. She said, "Get Norman Jopson for the academic, that will be easy, then I'll get you the Dean of St Paul's as a cleric." Hold on, I'm not sure if you should write that down. You see I really had never met him. Anyway, I put his name down. For social, she suggested Lady Wedgwood. Well, I did at least know her daughter, having given her lessons, and I'd once been invited to their house for dinner. I hadn't spat cherrystones on the floor or eaten peas off my knife, so that was sufficient really for a social reference. So I filled in my application and sent it off.

'After I'd done it, I thought, this is the moment to test destiny. So I went to see Hesther Dowden, the clairvoyant, in her house in Chelsea, where she charged all of three and a half guineas. She was a little Irishwoman who waddled across the room and sat on a divan, holding sheets of paper in her lap and a pen, saying she was being invaded by spirits from 1000 BC.

'All I'd told her was that I was called Miss Hill – nothing else. She started writing and the first message was, "You are going to Cambridge." She then asked if I was moving house. If so, I had to beware because Cambridge was very damp. I asked how long I was going for and she wrote down three and a half years. Now, this did seem non-sense. No job is for three and a half years, unless I was going to be thrown out for immorality or stealing or something. I said, "Why so short?" She replied, "I speak of events not yet born in the womb of time but in the vortex of politics." I wrote it down, word for word what she said, then I explained I wasn't interested in politics. She said, "I am never wrong." I handed over my three and a half guineas and left.'

Lisa was called to Cambridge for an interview. She arrived in a new hat, bought in France. It was canary yellow with an eye veil, which she worried might appear too frivolous. She passed the interview – and got the job.

So the clairvoyant had been right, I said, waiting for Lisa to laugh about it. I know that clairvoyancing used to be very fashionable, even among the most intelligent of women, such as Elizabeth Barrett Browning, who swore by it, but all the same, no one could really believe it. She'd just made a good guess. Lisa glared at me at the very suggestion.

Her only worry, having got the job, was that it might ruin her friend-ship with Doris. She had recently had another breakdown. 'But Doris said I had to take it – I would be made a fellow in time.'

Lisa arrived in Cambridge in the autumn of 1936 on a salary of £300 per annum and took a small flat. Then she tried to find out what her job would entail, but nobody seemed able to tell her. 'I rang the Appointments Board and said, "I have arrived – what do I do now?" Someone said, "The reporter will tell you," and hung up.

'The only person in Cambridge I knew was old Sydney Heffer, whom I'd met through Jarrold's, the publisher. I went to see him and asked him who or what the reporter was. He opened a drawer and pulled one out. It was a university publication which I didn't know existed. In it I found that Miss Hill would be giving six lectures in ML5. Note that it didn't say "Dr Hill". That upset me. I was proud of my Ph.D. But Cambridge only recognised their own degrees, not anyone else's, not even Oxford's.

'I had a terrible struggle finding out what ML5 was. In Cambridge none of the colleges has its name on because it's presumed everyone has been to Cambridge and knows which is which. Turned out ML stood for Mill Lane, but 5 was not number five, Mill Lane, as you might assume, but a lecture room.

'Oh, everything seemed so confusing and unwelcoming. It was only towards the end of the term that I met an American woman, a lecturer from Girton College, who said, "We haven't seen you in college." I had been given a note which said I was "attached to Girton" but didn't know what that meant. I assumed you had to be a fellow to actually go into colleges. No, she said, you have Dining Rights. Another phrase I didn't know – and it took an American to tell me. Anyway, in the end I gradually got the hang of things.'

She started with only three students, both third-years, who thought Slavonic studies sounded amusing, but they had little interest and didn't speak any of the relevant languages. 'When it came to the exams, I had to have an external examiner. I found someone at Oxford who was willing, but he was a complete fraud in that he didn't write or speak any Slav languages. Those early days of the department were a shambles.

'So what I did was open my lectures to anyone. It wasn't the done thing, but I was young and vigorous and unconventional. I didn't know the rules, so I just did things because I was fanatic for Slavonic studies. I got wives of dons turning up, and made them all sing songs in a chorus to get the rhythm of the Slav languages. I invited groups of twenty to my house and gave them Russian tea in samovars and we'd all sing Russian songs.'

Eventually she was joined in her Cambridge flat, at Croft Gardens, by Doris. She'd had yet another breakdown and was now relatively poor, having given away all her money to good causes. 'One of her family said she should go into a lunatic asylum, but I said, "Certainly not." I had lived with her for thirteen years. She had saved my life, so it was my turn to help her, now that I had a home and a proper job.'

Three and a half years after her appointment, the Second World War started: most departments at Cambridge University closed – and again the clairvoyant was proved right.

Lisa was moved to London as a Slavonic expert at the Ministry of Information. Her knowledge of Russia and the Russians was considered valuable for liaison with our Russian allies.

'One day I heard that the ministry was about to recruit Russian interpreters from a certain part of Canada. I knew all about these people. Yes, they were Russians who could speak English, but they were also religious fanatics, part of a sect who stripped naked in law courts when going on oath. I said they would cause problems. And, anyway, we didn't need to send all the way to Canada for Russian speakers. "Give me six months," I said, "and I'll provide you with two thousand Russian speakers from Cambridge."

'I got agreement from the ministry – but I had omitted to tell the Cambridge authorities. I just landed it upon them. Didn't ask the university's permission or anything, and suddenly there were all these people arriving to study Russian at Cambridge. I was told to remove them at once.

'I went back to the War Office. They got on to the police and the army, and some high-up was sent to the Vice-Chancellor's department, saying it was all hush-hush war work, so would they kindly pipe down. Anyway, they were placated. We were allowed to put the first students in a hotel, now part of St Catherine's College.'

And so began the famous intensive Russian-language courses at Cambridge. At first, it was mainly for young officer cadets, who but for the war would have been at some university anyway. Then after the war it was used by national servicemen, and others. With the coming of the Cold War, when it was believed that Russia was Britain's possible enemy rather than an ally, the courses continued to be considered of great importance for people going into diplomacy, the military and business, and many people who went on to become ambassadors, such as Sir Fitzroy Maclean and Sir Rodric Braithwaite, as well as professors, admirals, generals, MI5 and MI6 officials. There were also industrialists, like Sir John Harvey-Jones, writers such as Michael Frayn, and the spy George Blake.

'I worked fourteen hours a day when I began the courses. I had to find Russian teachers and organise all the students. Even when I became professor, I still rolled my sleeves up and got on with it, doing a lot of lecturing myself. You know, of course, that once you are a Cambridge professor you don't actually have to teach any students. You can just spend all day "looking after my subject . . ."'

She was appointed Professor of Slavonic Studies in 1948, one of Cambridge's first women professors, and held the position for twenty years. She retired officially in 1968, but then became a visiting professor at various American and European universities, picking up honorary degrees and other accolades along the way, including a fellowship at University College, London. In 1976, the Queen made her a Dame of the British Empire.

Doris Mudie, her friend and companion, died in 1970, having been paralysed and speechless for several years. 'She lived with me till she died, even when she couldn't feed herself.'

In 1985, to the surprise of most people who knew her, Lisa got married. She was then eighty-five. It was her first marriage. She lists it in *Who's Who*, so I asked for a few details.

Some of her stories so far had been rather complicated, filled with immense detail, not all of which I have given, but they made sense. However, I found the story of her marriage a bit difficult to follow and understand, given that she seemed such a clever, strong-minded woman, whom one would not expect to rush into what appeared to be an unusual union.

It all began during some lectures she was giving in Yugoslavia when she had become friendly with a very well-bred, English-educated, wealthy Serbian. 'I gathered he was descended from two royal families, had been to Oxford, inherited a huge mansion, but he had become a victim of Communism, which was why he was now living in near poverty.

Appointed Professor at Cambridge, 1948

'All right, then. Perhaps at first I had rather fancied him, though, really, he looked like a corpse, he was so ill. Looking back, it was compassion which brought us together, not love. I never made love to him, nor was I ever flirtatious, apart from writing "with love" at the end of letters. One does. I just felt sorry for him. Anyway, he fell really ill so I brought him over to London to a nursing home. He recovered – and proposed to me! Well, at eighty-four, I was not interested in sex any more. He was seventy-nine at the time. I thought a blessing in a church would be enough, but the Russian priest we went to said, "Why not get married? You can't have a boyfriend living with you at eighty-four." Why not? I thought. Oh, I can't explain it properly myself, but we did, we got married. The wedding was hysterical, with chaotic scenes, like something out of Tolstoy. He forgot to get himself a shirt before his own wedding.

'He never embraced me. There was no sex at all. He pretended he was potent, but I think that was all boasting. My friends, of course, thought it was wonderful – having a companion for my old age, how lovely for me, wasn't I lucky?

'But inside the marriage, I was spending all my money. He'd want a shirt, and insist it came from Harrods. I began to suspect some of the things about him. I looked up the Oxford University calendar to see if he had been at Pembroke, as he'd told me. He had – but never

Dame Elizabeth today

graduated. When I put this to him, he said he'd had to go home suddenly to settle the family affairs. He said he had no money – but I got someone to investigate and found estates worth about a million. He said it was all tied up. He couldn't get at it for legal reasons. I think it was because he was too mean to spend anything.

'We had endless arguments, furniture and things flying around. He fell ill and I had to look after him as he wouldn't go into a home. Then, last year, I had a stroke. That's why I have come here to Chiswick, to my Russian friends, to recuperate. It meant he went into a nursing home, at long last.

'Last week, we were officially divorced. Thank God. It is all over.

'When I have recovered, I will be going back to my home in Cambridge, to live on my own. When I arrived I couldn't move this leg. Every day I have it massaged with dandelion and spirits and now it is fine. The people here have been marvellous. It's a rest home, a charitable trust, for members of the Russian nobility. I plan to go home in another month, by which time I hope to be completely fit.'

She appeared perfectly fit already, considering her great age. How does she explain it? 'I believe in the spirit, the soul, which is always alive. Illness is only due to specific negative forces. Our present life determines our future life, just as we are part of our past life. Our genes come from the past and depend upon it. Life is like weaving a carpet. You don't know the pattern, the final shape, till the end.

'I am keeping myself alive in order to finish my memoirs. I have started to write them since I've been here. I have a title, *In Lisa's Mind's Eye*. Oh, I am sure I will find a publisher. I've also got some research I want to do. I want to prove that Alexander I did not die in 1825, which all the history books say, but became a hermit in Siberia where he lived for many years. I have ten cartons of material, which will prove it.

'I hope to live till I'm a hundred and six, but I don't expect to have my full mental powers for more than another three years. That will be enough, for my book and for my research.

'It has been a difficult life in a way, with lots of struggles. No, it's no use you asking if I would live it all again – because I won't. You don't come back to this world and live the same life. You live a different one.

'I have nothing really against this modern world. I was brought up in a noble family but this is the age of the common man, and the world is probably better for it. But I do think there has been a reduction in morals. People are mad about sex, these days. And the crime really is awful. But there are many wonderful people in this modern world. So we should be grateful for that . . .'

9

ANGUS MACMILLAN

Naval officer War One; RAF officer War Two

Angus Macmillan in 1924

Angus Macmillan's wife came to pick me up at Brockenhurst station, the other side of Southampton, in deepest Hampshire. She asked if I'd like the quickest way or the scenic way to their home. I said the quickest and she said, 'Hard luck, we're going the scenic.'

It was exceedingly scenic. We drove through beautiful heather- and bracken-covered moorland of the New Forest, past lots of ponies, roaming free. It was also very quick. 'Yes,' she said, 'I have in my time been warned about speeding in several continents.' She gave a huge, hearty laugh.

Like Captain Cummins, Angus Macmillan lives at home, his own home, with his wife. Most of those born 1900 live either alone, or with a son or daughter, or in some sort of home. Jeanne Macmillan is Angus's second wife, and a good deal younger, but all the same, it was unusual. Even those who have been married several times tend to outlive their partners, once they get into their nineties.

As she drove, Jeanne talked non-stop, about her life in Africa, in Australia, all over the world, in fact. For many years she had worked as a purser with Shaw Savill liners, hence all the travelling, though she was brought up and went to school in Essex. Suddenly she looked at her watch, put her fingers to her lips and said, 'It's eleven o'clock, no talking for the next two minutes.' I'd forgotten it was 11 November, Armistice Day. A memorable day in the life of her husband Angus, and in the lives of millions of others.

They have a pretty cottage with a good-sized garden quite near the sea, handy for popping over to the Isle of Wight. They'd recently been there for a week's holiday, an indication that Angus must be pretty fit. 'Oh, he is,' said Jeanne, but, alas, this last summer, for the first time, he hadn't quite managed to mow all the lawns himself.

Angus met us at the cottage door, wearing a tweed jacket, corduroy trousers, pullover and his RAF tie. He looked rather distinguished and officer class, which, of course, he is. We each had a generous dry sherry, then Jeanne disappeared into another room, saying she'd leave Angus to take me through his life story. From time to time, though, she bounced back into the drawing room to correct some fact or add a minor detail. There was then some good-natured husband-and-wife bickering, with him telling her to let him get on with it, it was his life story, after all.

Like Dame Elizabeth Hill, Angus comes from Scottish stock, and was also born abroad, in Brandon, Manitoba, in the depths of rural Canada, on 11 July 1900. His father and grandfather, both also called Angus Macmillan, were doctors.

At the mention of their names, Jeanne made her first appearance, bringing through a couple of ancient medical books written by Angus's grandfather. One was about an eye problem caused in the days when workmen smoked clay pipes. Apparently, by clenching their pipes to one side of their mouth, they often lost sight in that eye, as the eye was cooked. 'Oh, he doesn't want to know about all that,' said Angus. Jeanne then withdrew again.

Angus's father decided to give up medicine and left Scotland for Canada with his wife. They had a son and two daughters, one of whom died in infancy. His plan was to breed heavy horses, the sort used in farming, which had always been his real ambition. At first he did fairly well. 'Then, round about 1910, he could see that the arrival of motor-cars and tractors was going to mean the end of farm horses, at least in North America. He decided there were still possibilities for some decades to come in Australia and New Zealand, so when I was about twelve, he sold up in Canada and we headed for Australia.

'We stopped in England on the way. My mother, my sister and I visited relations but my father went on ahead to Australia, to look at possible farms to buy. While he was in the backwoods of Australia, he got appendicitis – and died. That was it. We were stuck in England, homeless and fatherless.'

Angus spent the next few years shuttling between four aunts and ended up living in Pocklington, Yorkshire, with his grandfather, who owned a small brewery. He was sent to the local public school, Pocklington. 'When I was thirteen, one of my aunts asked what I planned to do in life and I said, "Anything but sitting in a ruddy office." Her husband, my uncle, was a retired P & O captain and he said, "What about being a naval cadet?" If you passed a certain exam, P & O would pay half the fees. So that's what I did.'

In 1913, he joined HMS *Worcester*, a training ship for officer cadets, moored on the Thames. As the smallest cadet, he was made to shin up to the highest yard and, like all the cadets, was soundly reprimanded for the slightest mistake, and had to eat food that was less than adequate. At the outbreak of war in 1914, Angus was already in uniform as a cadet, and felt suitably proud and patriotic. 'I do remember white feathers being given out in the street, handed to any man of a certain age who wasn't in uniform. It was mainly middle-aged women who did it. My grandmother said that men who didn't serve their country deserved the white feather. But sometimes it was given out inappropri-ately. One man who was handed a white feather in the street said, "That's funny, that's the second thing I've been handed today." And out of his pocket he took a VC . . .'

At sixteen, Angus officially joined the navy as a midshipman on the battleship HMS *Neptune*, part of the Grand Fleet protecting Britain from German warships. He was known as a snotty, like all midshipmen. 'They were supposed to wipe their noses all the time on their cuff – which was why they had buttons on their cuffs to stop them.'

Lord Mountbatten, also born in 1900, was a midshipman about the same time. They didn't meet but Angus was interested to read his biography. 'He seems to have had a very hard time in the navy because of his connections, whereas I had a happy time, despite the war.'

He then moved to a small destroyer, HMS *Sybille*, of some 900 tons. 'We were under the command of Admiral Tirry. He was a fire-eater, like Admiral Beatty.' Their job was to escort merchant ships back and forth across the North Sea, from Harwich to Holland, which were taking food and supplies for the Allied troops in France. 'Almost the whole coast was in German hands so we came under fire all the time. There were Zeppelins above, coming to spy on us and pass on details of our movements. Then the German fighters would come and get us, or their submarines, which we had no means of detecting.

'We were once towing some flying-boats on a barge across the North Sea when the Zeppelins spotted us. They were out of range of our guns, and had no fear of the flying-boats, but one ship was also towing a fighter plane and had an experienced pilot on board. It was decided to set up some tracks, but they got in the way of his wheels and he went into the drink. Second time, we cleared the barge and the ship went full speed ahead, which was about thirty knots. He managed to take off in the fighter – the first time, I think, that was ever done. I mean, a plane taking off from a barge. He flew up in the air and, of course, caught the Zep totally by surprise. He wasn't expecting anything like this. He frantically tried to go higher and higher, but our fighter got above him and dropped bombs from above. He hit the Zeppelin, and down it came. We all stood on deck, cheering like mad.

'I can also remember some more amusing incidents. When we were once being fired upon by German destroyers, I was watching the ship's doctor trying to take cover. He was very young, probably just a second-year medic when the war began. Every time there was a flash, you knew there would be a fifty-second gap before the shell landed – either hitting you or not. What he did was rush behind a canvas screen which covered the entrance down to the Officers' Mess. On HMS *Sybille*, there were no corridors below deck. Access was through different hatches, down to each department. Anyway, after every flash, he disappeared behind this screen till the shell had exploded, then he'd come out again.

'I was on the bridge, working on an instrument which controlled our guns. The first lieutenant, who was beside me, turned to me and said,

"Look at the doc, Snotty, thinking that bit of canvas will save him. He doesn't bloody realise that if a shell hits us, the whole ship is finished."

'There was another amusing incident when we got a message saying, "You are being fired on by shore batteries." I was beside the captain, Captain A. A. Scott, who almost exploded. "Do they bloody think we don't know we're being fired on!" Anyway, we were going at full speed, but he turned the ship round and a damn great sea immediately came over all of us and the funnels sent out huge billows of smoke. The next day, the Germans claimed they had sunk us, thinking we had gone down.

'I was never injured. I lived a charmed life. God protected me. Everyone had the same philosophy – if a shell has your name on, that's it. If it hasn't got your name on, then you just got on with it. Most of the time it was pretty tedious, doing routine duties, till the attacks started. You have to remember it takes a hell of a lot of ammunition to be fired before there are any hits. In the Second World War, the ratio was even higher – it needed even more explosive to kill one man.'

In 1919 Angus was demobbed. He said farewell to HMS *Sybille*, which was due to be laid up, and also farewell to Captain Scott. 'He was always known as a lucky captain. I served with him for two years, on a fairly small ship, so even as a midshipman I knew him pretty well.'

Angus then joined P & O and on 1 April 1919 he set sail for Australia on the *Khyber*, taking home over two thousand Australian troops who had served in the First World War. 'It was the most incredible voyage I ever had. These two thousand Australian soldiers were the dregs of Australia. No discipline at all, their officers couldn't control them, and it became a gambling hell. Yes, I know they'd been brave heroes in the war, but first-class soldiers don't necessarily make first-class civilians.

'When we got into the Med, it turned out someone on board was suspected of having smallpox. The ship's doctor, who was a decrepit old doctor, God knows how old, had to inoculate everyone on board. That came to two and a half thousand, including crew. Once inoculated, we were in quarantine all the way to Australia. No one was allowed to get off at any port.

'Our first stop was Port Said. Now, you've probably been there. No? Oh, well. We moored in the harbour, getting ready to go down the Suez

Canal. The message went out, "No one goes ashore." Well, the Aussies went mad. Straight away someone put on a swimming costume, dived overboard and disappeared in the direction of Port Said. Others quickly followed him.

'Because no one was supposed to get off, there was no indication or warning about when we would leave. Not long after, we just quietly departed, heading down the canal, which as you know is dead straight across the desert. Well, we were pursued for several miles down the canal by half-naked Australians who had hired taxis or were speeding behind us in launches to catch us up. We didn't stop, but we let down gangways. The Australians had to dive into the water while sailors tried to pick them up. God knows how many Australians got left behind in Port Said. Some of them are probably still there.

'Next stop was Colombo in Ceylon, as it was then. This was a coaling stop, with coal barges coming back and forward to our ship. Once again no one was allowed ashore, but once again some of the Australians jumped on to the coal barges going into Colombo and disappeared. We left a few there as well.

'Our first stop in Australia was Fremantle. The problem there was that the local dockers were on strike and wouldn't let us dock. Our Australians from Fremantle, who were due to get off, ended up in pitched battles with the dockers.

'At Sydney, we arrived in pouring rain in the middle of their winter. All the soldiers disembarking there were told to go straight into quarantine and follow local regulations. Have you been to Sydney? Well, the quarantine place was up on the North Head. We could see it from the ship. Appalling-looking place. The soldiers from the Sydney area knew how primitive it was – and they refused to get off! Having endlessly jumped off illegally, they now wanted to stay on board.

'A general was called to the ship to talk to them. He lined them all up on deck and said, "One step forward any soldier who refuses orders to go ashore." Every bloomin' soldier stepped forward! In the end, a compromise was reached. They each had to have a disinfectant bath, then they were allowed home.'

Angus continued with P & O for the next few years. In 1923, he had shore leave in order to take his first mate's ticket and he happened to see an advertisement for RAF officers. They were looking for people who had been officers in either the army or the navy. He decided to resign from P & O and apply to the RAF.

'It was the advert that suddenly did it, but my P & O salary was going down all the time, not up, because of the post-war recession. But I had always been fascinated by aeroplanes. On board ship during the First World War I'd watched the flying-boats and thought they were marvellous. Even as a little boy I'd been fascinated by planes. I'd once waited weeks in a field in Yorkshire because there was a rumour that Colonel Coady or the Wright brothers were going to land in their little plane from America. Can't remember which, but neither arrived.'

Angus passed the RAF entrance exam and medical, and became a trainee pilot officer stationed at Shottick, near Chester, on the Dee estuary. 'We trained on Avros, Bristols and a DH 9A, which was a De Havilland.' He got his wings as a pilot officer and joined the 17th Flight Squadron at Hawkinge, near Folkestone. He did a lot of flying in Sopwith Snipes and met the Queen Mother, as Duchess of York, at a party for RAF officers. She has been his favourite royal ever since.

While he was stationed there, he became engaged to Doris. They had met earlier when she and her mother had been passengers on a P & O boat to Shanghai. As is the custom to this day, one of Angus's duties as a ship's officer had been to dine with passengers: 'We were always given the same instructions: "Officers must not linger over the wine and nuts."' However, he lingered long enough to get to know Doris, who lived in Shanghai where her father was a director of a British firm.

They got married in 1926, but it nearly didn't happen. 'The General Strike started a few days before. During the strike, as you know, servicemen were called on to carry the mail, drive vehicles and other duties, so immediately all leave was cancelled. I went to my CO and explained that the wedding was all planned, and the honeymoon. I said I just had to have my leave. He rang the Air Ministry. They said that was the rule, all leave was cancelled. But in the end, I was unofficially allowed the day off. We got married on the Saturday and I returned to base the next day – so we never had a honeymoon.'

All the same, it was a pretty impressive white wedding, with all the trimmings and lots of guests, as can be seen from the photographs. Angus and his best man were in RAF officer dress uniform, holding their plumed helmets (the same as the one worn by the Duke of York

Angus and Doris's wedding, 1926

when he married Lady Elizabeth Bowes-Lyon in 1923: he was then an RAF officer).

They couldn't live together at first, because he was too young to be allowed married quarters. 'The RAF did not officially recognise married officers till they were thirty. Then you got accommodation and a married allowance. Until then, you had to make your arrangements.'

He was then sent on a gunnery course, despite having trained as a pilot. 'That's what all the services do. They say, "Ah, that chap's a good navigator, let's put him into armaments."'

His commission in the RAF was for three years. When that finished, he decided to sign on for a permanent commission. This led to a posting in Hong Kong in early 1930. He went out on aircraft-carrier HMS *Hermes*. 'I was an RAF flying officer, but on board there were also naval flying officers. Several later went on to great distinction. One was Caspar John, son of Augustus John, the artist, who became an Admiral and Chief of the Defence Staff.

'When I got to Hong Kong, I sent for my wife and she joined me. I had to pay her fare out as I was still not thirty. She'd only just arrived when I was told I was being axed. The new government was making cuts all round. It was a Mr Geddes, whoever he was, some government minister, who announced it. I was one of those deemed dispensable because it was last in, first out.

'I then had to bring my wife home again, at my expense. We caught the same boat home from China as she'd come in – after only ten days.'

Fortunately Angus got a posting to the Air Ministry in London as an inspector of explosives. 'It was a bit like the modern bomb-disposal service, except we looked after our bombs not anyone else's. I went round RAF stations all over the country, checking their explosives were in order.'

They were just about to settle down at last to domestic married life when Angus was sent to Iraq for two years as an explosives expert. 'I could theoretically have taken my wife this time, but Iraq was considered too dangerous. No, my wife never complained during all these years. She realised my job was important. And that was it.'

In 1934, their first and only child was born – John, who was educated at a public school, King's, Canterbury. When the Second World War broke out, Angus was still working for the Air Ministry as an explosives expert. 'I was at an RAF station in Harrogate in 1940 when the call came out that an inspector of explosives was wanted by RAF HQ in France. Which one of you will go? I was the mutt who said I would.'

So in 1940 he was back in uniform, one of those who served in both world wars – and one of the few who served each time in a different service. First time, he had been a naval officer. Now he was an RAF squadron leader. 'And I'll tell you a very strange thing that happened. I was *en route* to Southampton to board my ship to France. I arrived an hour or so too early so I went to this hotel to put in the time. As I was going into the hotel, out of the door came someone I thought I recognised. It was Captain Scott, my captain from the First World War! Wasn't that a coincidence? I had neither seen nor heard a word about him since I'd been demobbed from the navy in 1919. He looked exactly the same, except he had four stripes on his naval uniform this time, not three. Of course I was in RAF uniform, so he didn't immediately recognise me.

'"Scott?" I said, just in case I'd got it wrong. He looked at me in astonishment, then said, "Good Lord, it's Mac!" Naturally he asked what I was doing in RAF uniform. I told him what had happened, and that I was off to France. We chatted for a few moments, then we shook hands and off he went – and off I went to France. I never saw him again, from that day to this . . .'

Angus was posted to RAF HQ at Colombier where he found they were under heavy German gunfire. 'In fact, we were retreating pretty soon, being chased across France until we got to Brest. I was supposed to be evacuated on the *Lancastria*, but by chance, I didn't go on it. I was waiting for transport when my CO happened to pass me in his staff car. He said, "Which boat are you on?" and I said the *Lancastria*. He said, "There's a spare seat here in my car. Come with me instead." So I went with him, and we caught a different boat. Funnily enough, I can't remember which boat that was. It was packed absolutely solid with humanity. The conditions were unbelievable, but we got safely home. I remember the name of the boat I didn't catch because it was the *Lancastria*. It went down with huge losses of about two thousand people . . .'

Angus returned to the Air Ministry, and was then back in uniform, this time as an RAF group captain, based at Woolwich, looking after armaments for the RAF. 'My career always has been a bit difficult to explain. I was serving under an army general, even though I was in the RAF. As my opposite numbers were colonels, I was promoted to group captain.'

After the war, he returned to the Air Ministry in Whitehall. 'That had lots of name changes as well. It was originally Aircraft Production, then Air Ministry, then Supply, then eventually Defence. I became head of the armaments division in the Aeronautical Inspectorate.'

He retired in 1960, having been more or less in uniform since the age of thirteen. The first thing he did was something he'd promised himself since 1912: he went to the wilds of Australia to find his father's grave.

'I went on my own as my wife had just been on a long trip to see her family. Finding the details of my father's grave was easy. I walked into the appropriate department in Sydney and quickly got his grave number. I travelled to the place without mishap, but the day I arrived there had been massive floods. All the grave numbers had been washed away. All I could do was stand roughly in the right area, probably within twenty yards of where he'd been buried. So I considered it was a worthwhile trip.'

John, his only son, did his national service in the RAF, which pleased his father. He got a history degree at Trinity College, Oxford, took a social sciences degree in London, then a degree in criminology at Reading. Today he is married, with no children, works as a lecturer in criminology at Middlesbrough, and is soon to retire.

Doris died in 1980. 'She'd had blackouts for some time, just falling in a heap. It was most peculiar.'

In 1985, he married Jeanne, whom he had known for some years. He had first met her when she was working on a Shaw Savill liner. This time he had been a passenger. Jeanne had never been married and was then aged fifty-seven. Which makes her twenty-eight years younger than Angus. Quite a gap.

'Oh, that didn't worry me,' said Jeanne, now back in the room, as Angus had finished his life story. 'He has always been remarkably fit. At sixty-five, he looked forty-five. At eighty-five he looked sixty-five.

'The only problem has been the generation gap, not the age gap. Angus was brought up always to have a stiff upper lip, putting up with things. Those were the unwritten rules, what one does. One accepts and obeys and does one's duty. I'm not like that at all. Oh no. If I don't agree, I won't put up with things, not if I think I can do something to improve them.'

'Jeanne has been a godsend,' said Angus. 'My guardian angel. I would be lost without her.'

At ninety-seven, he still looked fit, though recently his eyes had begun to fade a bit and television has become a blur. He can't remember having any operations in his life, except at thirteen in Yorkshire when he had appendicitis. 'The doctor came and cut it out on the kitchen table. He really did. I suppose I must have had chloroform or something, but I can't remember.'

How did he explain his longevity?

'Eating celery every day,' said Jeanne, guffawing.

'Look, I'll answer that question,' said Angus. 'I think it goes back to the time I first joined the RAF in 1924. To be a pilot you had to have spot-on health. They then gave you an annual medical and if anything was wrong that was it. You were grounded. So the moment I joined, I took very good care of myself. One of the first things I did was stop smoking. No one told you not to in those days, but I decided it couldn't be good for your health. I'd already given up sugar in the 1914–18 war.

It was rationed and very scarce, so I decided to do without, even in my tea. I've always been a keen walker. My first wife and I had many, many holidays in the Lake District. Our record was walking twenty-three miles in a day – over mountains most of the way.

'I do drink. A sherry at lunch-time and a gin or a whisky in the evening. Plus a beer now and again. We seldom drink wine. Of course, the vital element in all this is luck. I put everything down to luck . . .'

You mean your health or surviving, getting through alive after active service in two world wars?

'Oh, that was luck. I forgot to tell you I survived three plane crashes, two of them when I was flying the plane myself.'

Jeanne went off to find his photo albums. They show him flying a variety of very shaky, very primitive, very dodgy-looking planes.

His first crash was in 1924, when he was learning to fly in a DH 9A. He was about to land on a small airfield when he noticed that an Avro, a smaller plane, also with a trainee pilot, had somehow got underneath him and was about to land on the same spot.

'The aerodrome was flooded, and there was only room for one plane. I realised I could either kill two people or just kill myself, so I swung my plane over and crash-landed in the water. My plane landed on its nose and was about to go over. I would have been drowned, trapped under water with the plane on top of me but, for some reason, it just stuck there, vertically, on its nose. I was safe, though I had to wait for some

Angus and his wife Jeanne today

time to be rescued as the fire brigade and ambulance had to get through all the water.'

The second time he was landing his plane in bad weather, with high winds and fog, and couldn't see the landing lights, which consisted of paraffin flares. He flew straight into the ground and wrecked his plane. Miraculously, he suffered only concussion. 'Plus the embarrassment. I was an instructor at the time.'

In the third crash, in 1930, he was the passenger in a small plane that was taking him from Cairo to Nairobi when he was an Air Ministry inspector. 'We had to stop to refuel at a little aerodrome somewhere in Uganda. As we were landing we could see that the whole place was covered with storks. They make these enormous journeys, right across Africa, then suddenly they all flop down when they get tired. We could see little native boys frantically trying to chase them away with sticks. Anyway, we somehow managed to land safely.

'When we took off we managed that as well, but when we were about a thousand feet high we ran into more storks in the air. One of them went smack into our propeller and broke it off. At once we fell like a stone, straight to the ground. We hit the deck and our plane burst into flames. But, by the grace of God, each of us dived out just as we hit the ground before the fire started. All we suffered were a few bruises. You could just jump out of planes in those days. They all had open cockpits.'

During his long life Angus has always voted Tory, as one might expect of an officer and a gentleman. I asked if he wasn't tempted in any way by Mr Blair. This led to an unexpected burst of laughter. All his stories so far had been told solemnly, even the ones he said I might find amusing. So what was the joke this time? 'I'm laughing at the thought of anyone being tempted by Mr Blair.'

I suggested that perhaps his liking for the Tories was helped by his similarity to his namesake, Harold Macmillan, especially around the eyes.

'I used to look even more like him when I was younger. I did meet him once, when I was at the Air Ministry. He was invited to a dining club I was a member of. We got talking and tried to find relations in common but couldn't. His ancestors are from the Isle of Arran. Mine were from all over Scotland. But we agreed we were from the same tribe.'

Jeanne drove me back to the station, talking all the while, and said that while Angus might appear to have a totally stiff upper lip, having been brought up to control his feelings, he has started to betray more emotion in the last few years.

Despite being able to tell stories about his air crashes, all calm and matter-of-fact, and recall amusing incidents about silly naval doctors under fire, he has recently begun to have nightmares, imagining himself back in the First World War. In one recurring dream, he is in a destroyer that has been hit and all the lifeboats are missing. In another, he crashes into the desert, and this time he is trapped in his burning plane.

On the way home, I thought about all the ex-servicemen, from either of this century's two world wars, who must have suffered similar nightmares. Yet it was strange to experience them so many years later, when the horrors were long since over. But perhaps in his mind Angus is thinking forward, when his luck in battle will finally run out . . .

10

LEN VALE-ONSLOW

Birmingham's motorcycling ace

Len Vale-Onslow, aged 4, with sister Enid

Leonard Vale-Onslow, MBE, sounds like an officer-class person, perhaps a lordly type who rides to hounds. He is, in fact, a worker rather than a gentleman, with a broad Brummie accent, who has always preferred a motorbike to a horse. But he has a claim to distinction, even to fame, which no one else born in 1900 can boast. He was not just the only working person of his age I met but possibly the oldest in the United Kingdom.

He first acquired this accolade in 1994, when the newspapers described him as our oldest worker, beating a 92-year-old woman shop assistant from West Yorkshire. In recognition of this achievement, he was invited to London by the then minister for employment, Ann Widdecombe. What an honour. He is also the world's oldest motorcyclist, with a valid licence. Proof of that is a mention in the 1997 *Guinness Book of Records*. So it must be true.

When I visited him in 1997, he was, indeed, still working. He was doing eight hours a day, six days a week. So he said. And I believed him. He was sitting beside a calor-gas fire, wearing a Castrol Oil baseball cap and blue overalls with his pens and tools sticking out of his top pocket and a radio blaring away. Not exactly rushing around, but he was there, at work, in the back office of his motorcycle business in the middle of Birmingham. In one hand was a mug of tea while the other held the phone as he spoke to a customer.

The premises are large, stretching from 98 to 116 Stratford Road, Birmingham, but not all of the space is in use. He has a staff of seven and an impressive length of shop-front, but his business has clearly seen better days. It is now, alas, rather run-down, not to say chaotic, with bits of dead bikes all over the shops, but while I was there, customers arrived, mostly in their leathers, some almost as old and decaying as the motorbikes. Some of his rather elderly mechanics were wandering around, looking suitably oily but still active at their workbenches.

Vale-Onslow, as the shop is called, has been in existence for almost sixty years, a legend in Birmingham, a power in Midlands motorcycling circles. The street, like the shop, is not what it was, now that the centre of Birmingham has been redeveloped. The same has to be said for British motorcycles: once a power throughout the whole world, they have now been eclipsed.

Len himself has seen better days, proof of which are the fading photographs around his office that show him in his championship years as a demon scrambler. But, for his age, these are still good years. He has left all the human opposition behind, either gone to the great garage in the sky or staggering around at home on their zimmer frames. Len is bespectacled and rather portly, but he positively glows with health, is in control of all his faculties, and his business, answering queries from customers or telling his staff where things are. He still works on the bikes himself every day: he can fiddle and fix, restore and repair, make things spark and come to life, but he is not quite so nifty at tightening nuts. Younger, stronger men, striplings in their sixties, such as his two sons who work with him, check his work before the bikes leave the shop.

It does sound posh, Vale-Onslow, especially combined with his MBE, which he got in 1994 for services to motorbikes. As a boy, his mother told him they were related to the Earl of Onslow's family. 'A widow of a younger son got remarried to a Squire Vale of Handsworth. That's the part of the family we came from, so I was told. Mind you, it all happened a good few generations ago.'

Len was born on 2 May 1900 in Sutton Coldfield, at Laburnum House, Jockey Road, one of six brothers and two sisters. 'I wasn't born, I was hatched, that's what I always say.'

His father was a master-builder who specialised in factories. 'They were going up all over Birmingham as we started the Industrial Revolution. He was always in work. My mother worked as well – she ran a brass foundry, which produced brass trays. At one time, she had twenty girls working for her.

'I had a nanny when I was little, so we must have been doing OK, well, a sort of nurse who looked after me, Minnie Jason-Ward. Yes, she was double-barrelled as well. At two and a half I was sent to a private school run by the Misses Wells, two spinster ladies. This was in Birmingham, where we'd moved to.'

Len was the youngest of the six brothers, but not exactly spoiled and petted, more a plaything. 'They used to hang me out of a window when I was little, on a piece of sash cord, till people in the street would see me and call the police. All my brothers were mechanically minded and had their own motorbikes, which they put together. They'd give me rides and I'd fall off, or they'd sling me off going round bends. You have to remember there was no TV or radio in those days. We made our own amusements.

'In 1909, when I was eight or nine, they built their own aeroplane. Yes, they really did, out of bamboo and balloon fabric. Everyone was trying to make an aeroplane which would fly in those days. We'd heard of Bleriot getting across the Channel, and the Wright Brothers at Kitty Hawk. My brothers helped to found the Midlands Aero Club. They eventually got a plane which flew 250 yards at Castle Bromwich. Only twelve feet off the ground, mind you, but it did fly.

'Anyway, this home-made plane, when I was eight, had detachable wings so they could keep it in the shed at the bottom of our garden. One day they tied me under one of the wings and tied the plane to a long bit of rope, about fifty feet long, then they ran like hell, trying to get me airborne. I did get up in the air. I could see over the road towards Brook Vale reservoir. It's gone now. It's just Brook Vale park. I thought I was going to end up in the reservoir, but they stopped running. I fell to earth and lay there unconscious. They thought I was dead. They took me home and put me on a couch, as if I'd died of natural causes. Then they ran away. I was unconscious for fourteen days. Yes, it's a wonder they didn't bring about my early demise.'

When the war began, two of his brothers went to join up. 'They wanted to fight Kaiser Bill – and Little Willie. Do you remember Little Willie, the Kaiser's son? He was an imbecile, oh, we all knew that. The Germans were better prepared for the war than we were. Our forces were all outdated. It's a wonder we won – well, we didn't really. We won neither war. The Americans won it for us, both times, if you ask me. Mr Schickelgruber was in that first war, a tuppence ha'penny corporal and failed painter. I think that was his name. He later changed it to Hitler. Well, you couldn't have people saying, "Heil, Schickelgruber," could you? His big mistake was writing *Mein Kampf.* In it, he said he was going to take Russia. Well, he'd done a peace pact with Russia, hadn't he, so when they read that, they were on to him, weren't they?'

Your two brothers, Len, let's get back to what happened to them.

'Brother Percy became a motorbike despatch rider. He was killed at the Somme, after winning a medal. The other brother, Cecil, volunteered at fifteen, saying he was seventeen, but he was turned down on health grounds. He'd had rheumatic fever when young. The army doctors said he had valvular heart disease and wasn't long for this life, but you know what? He lived till he was ninety.'

Len left school at fourteen, determined to follow his brothers into the motor trade. 'My oldest brother, Gordon Henry, worked at the Wolseley company as a draughtsman, along with Herbert Austin, who was then works manager. My brother went with him when he left to start Austin Motors. Then he went back to Wolseley, taking a design for a light car, which would cost only a hundred pounds. He was hoping to get Austin's job, as works manager, but they turned down his design.'

All Len's memories and stories are full of names and facts rattled off quickly, plus his own observations and diversions. It was hard to capture every one, or check them, but what I really wanted was to bring him back to his own story.

'I could ride a motorbike at eight and drive a motor-car at fourteen, so I wanted a job that involved some sort of driving. I went to see Leonard King. Oh, he was a top engineer, but a fierce-looking man. When I went to see him, he had in his workshop a Racing Mercedes, the first racing-car Mercedes had built. It had the back axle amidships, very unusual. It could do 180 m.p.h. I'm pretty certain this was the exact car which went on to be raced on the sands in Wales by J. G. Parry-Thomas. Oh, the stories I could tell you. You could be here for days . . .

'Right, well, I didn't get a job with Mr King. Instead I went to work with my brother on their lorries. We had six lorries, doing war work, hauling munitions from the factories. My father wanted me to be one of the drivers, even though I was still only fourteen. He was very influential and it was war work, so he arranged for a local police sergeant to test me. You had to be sixteen to get a driving licence at the time, fourteen for a motorbike. Anyway, he tested me and agreed I was a hundred per cent.

'I drove a three-ton Garner lorry, made in Birmingham. I did that for about two years, till I was sixteen, when our garage literally collapsed. It had been stables but my father had turned it into a garage when lorries came along. It was midwinter, and there was about twenty tons of snow on the roof. The drivers had been using braziers to keep warm, chucking on petrol to make it burn, and the heat helped to bring the roof down. Six feet of bricks fell around me and I got a six-inch nail through my hat. I was knocked unconscious, but there was a doctor's opposite and they rushed me there and he put in thirty-six stitches.'

After the war, when munitions were no longer needed, Len gave up lorry-driving. He moved to Worcester and began working on tractors for local farms, using engines converted from Model T Fords. His main passion in life became motorbikes, entering motorbike competitions, building his own and doing tricks on them.

'It was in Hallow I met my wife, when I was twenty-six and she was sixteen. She came to our garage with her sister one Sunday evening, asking for a pump to blow up her bike tyres. I knew who she was as I'd seen her in our church, though she lived in Broad Heath. Her dad was the local baker and pig breeder.

'I was very active in the church in those days, in fact I ran the parish, driving people places, running the Sunday school, everything. Mind you, all of this might be my fantasy but that's how it seemed to me. Since then, I haven't bothered with the church. Oh, I'm still religious, but I don't go. I have my own religion. Do all the good things you can do and none of the bad things.

'Anyway, she came the following Sunday after church, this time wanting a new valve. That's when I noticed she was pretty. She knew me, of course. Oh, I was a local celebrity. I used to ride through the local villages on my motorbike, standing up on the seat with my arms out. Everyone knew me – including the local policeman. He was always trying to catch me at it. He did one day, but I said he hadn't got a witness so he couldn't get me. There were two girls sitting on a stile, who'd been watching me, but they said no, I hadn't been standing on the seat. Then he went to the local pub, hoping for witnesses. They said the same. He tried for years, that policeman, to get me for things like no lights, but he never did.'

He married Elizabeth in 1929, at the register office in Edmond Street, Birmingham. 'Only cost me twelve and six. My grandson got married last year and his wedding cost a fortune.'

Len's wife had worked with her father in his bakery business, and was a good businesswoman. She encouraged Len to develop his motorbike manufacturing. He had established his own make, Super Onslow Specials, which he shortened to SOS. I said that seemed a big jump, going from mending and building motorbikes to manufacturing them, but he said you could do that, in those days, on a small scale. He dug out from his desk drawers some advertisements from the motorcycling press of the 1920s and 1930s. In 1929, according to an advert in *Motor Cycling*, he was producing a 196cc Super Sports model 'for the discriminating rider', which was selling at thirty-five pounds. The paper reported that SOS Motors of Hallow, Worcester, was that year marketing six other models.

'I began manufacturing motorbikes in 1927 and at my height, around 1930, I was producing twenty-five a week. I was selling them all over the country, and all over the world. I sent a load to Durban, in South Africa, for the Durban Post Office, which I'd adapted with special big bags for carrying the post.

'The cheapest bike I produced sold for nineteen guineas. The best one was fifty-two pounds. At one time, I had ten staff working for me,

Advert for Super Onslow Specials, c. 1930

at our premises in Hallow. I gave it up in 1933. I sold the SOS business for two thousand pounds.

'Well, it wasn't really doing so well, but the main reason was that something else was doing better. When we moved into Birmingham, we bought a shop in Livery Street, which is the longest street in Birmingham without a pub – did you know that? We had a retail shop, selling bikes, which my wife ran. It got to the point when the profit on each bike I made was two pounds, whereas she was making fourteen pounds on every bike she sold. That was when I gave up manufacturing. It seemed more sensible to concentrate on the retail and repair side.

'We also decided it was time for a family. She suddenly said to me, one day in 1932, "Right, Len, now's the time to start."' Len junior was born in 1933, Jean in 1936 and Peter in 1939.

Len moved to his present premises in 1956. He bought them from his brother Cecil. 'He was a much better businessman than me. He died a millionaire, which I won't do, but I've enjoyed myself and had some very good businesses. I used to have seven branches of this shop, in Walsall, Worcester, Handsworth, oh, everywhere. This shop alone used to have a hundred new bikes in the window. Now we don't sell any new bikes. None at all.

'Oh, I know the reasons. I've analysed them. Firstly, Birmingham was the motorbike capital of the world at one time, you'll know that. They all came from here. But it's not the Japanese that really finished us off, it's affluence. Everyone is affluent now. At one time, there were poor Jews round here, doing their tailoring, and lots of synagogues. Then it was Indians, and lots of Indian shops. But now they're all well off, like everyone else. They can all afford a motor-car. They don't want a motorbike.'

Len has not done too badly, these last thirty years, despite all the changes. He still has his business and he's managed to have a couple of rather expensive holidays. 'In 1980, my wife said to me she fancies the USA, so I said, "Right you are, sweetheart." We'd been all round the Med, the Canaries, *QEII* and all that, but we hadn't done the States. We took four of our grandchildren with us and we flew on Concorde to Washington. No, not cheap, but you haven't heard the half of it. We went to Las Vegas, stayed at Caesar's Palace. Did the Grand Canyon and ended in Orlando at Disneyland. The twenty-four days cost us a lot of money. It was my wife's seventieth birthday, that was the reason.

'In Miami, at the end of the holiday, I was taking her photo, sitting on a seat, and I said, "Sweetheart, you're looking a bit yellow, you're not catching jaundice, are you?" Well, she'd never been ill in her life. The minute we got home, I took her to the doctor and he sent her straight to a nursing home in Edgbaston. And they said she had cancer of the liver. From me taking that photo of her to the end, she only lasted eight weeks. No pain, no suffering, even at the very end. She just shut her eyes and said, "I'm fed up."

'I died for the next two years. Really, I was hallucinating. I didn't know anything. She'd been everything to me, everything. We'd gone scrambling together. Then we'd watched all our grandchildren start to ride motorbikes and do their scrambling.

'That's really when this business went right down. I couldn't be bothered with anything. Then one day I went out and bought a Yamaha organ. I couldn't play a note of anything, or read music. I'd just decided I wanted to play, so I went and got a teacher. He taught me to play. At the end of the two years, when I'd learned eighty tunes, I gave up. I gave the organ away. But it had done the trick. I'd come back to living. Life has to go on, hasn't it? Unfortunately—'

Len had to see to a customer, so I talked to his son Peter. All three of his children work in the business with him. Young Len does the stores, Jean the paperwork, Peter the repair side. Peter said it was true the business went down when his mother died and not just because his father was devastated: his mother had been the brains behind it. 'She was the gaffer. We couldn't keep up with her. She knew where everything was.

She made sure everything got done properly. My dad's too soft, really. He'd never tell people off. Today we do survive, but only just. Our main business is supplying spares.'

Len still lives alone, in the flat above the premises. It means he doesn't have far to travel to work every day.

'I live in a slum,' said Len, when he returned. 'I'm not going to let you see it. All my children live in Buckingham Palace, compared with me.'

'Yeah, but it's only a slum because of you,' said Peter. 'He has twenty-eight headlamps by the side of his bed. It's not a joke. I counted them the other day.'

Len smiled, quite pleased with this image of himself, his devotion to work and his beloved motorbikes. Each morning he makes his own breakfast. In the evening he has a hot meal, which Jean brings to work ready made for him to pop in his microwave in the evening.

He is still therefore self-reliant, even at ninety-seven. In December 1994, he went on his own to South Africa and travelled two thousand miles round the country.

'What happened was that one day a bloke came into this shop and he noticed I was repairing someone's SOS. That was the bike I used to make. He says, "Oh, I saw five of them the other day." Well, I didn't believe him. You don't see SOSs these days. If you do, they belong to collectors and could cost you fifteen thousand.

'He said he definitely saw five. I says, "Where?" and he says, "In the back of a garage in Durban." He'd bought an old Bentley out there, so he said, for seven thousand pounds, come back and sold it for thirty thousand.

'Well, I knew I'd sold some to Durban, all those years ago, which he didn't know. So I decided to go and see for myself. I booked it all up, with the help of a niece who works in a travel agent. I went first to Johannesburg, Pretoria, then Durban, travelling all on my own, even though it was 105 degrees. I saw the whole country, the wine areas, Mandela's palace, everything – but I didn't find one SOS. I searched every garage in Durban. Not a sausage.

'But I had a good trip, enjoyed myself. Except while I was out there my back went. I'd had this accident when I was ninety, a motorbike accident when I was scrambling, but I got over that, thanks to some laser treatment. When it went again in South Africa, I spent fifty pounds on an osteopath, which was fifty pounds down the drain as it did no bloomin' good. I even tried a witch-doctor. He gave me little green pills. No good either. I think it was the sixteen hours sitting on the plane that did it. Anyway, when I got back home, I did three sessions with the local osteopath, and now it's fine. No problems. I'm as right as rain.'

Which means he is back to riding his motorbike and still driving his car. He has a 2-litre Sierra and was going off that afternoon, driving himself to Tewkesbury, to pick up some parts.

'I have to have a medical every year. It's not to get my licence but for insurance purposes. Every year the doctor shakes his head when he checks my age and I say, "Am I ready to be put down yet?" But he still says I have the blood pressure, the eyesight and the heart of a forty-year-old. He thinks I could have another fifteen years to go. I say getting to a hundred will do me. Then I'll take the euthanasia pill. He says he's not allowed to give them. I say, "OK, then, I'll take a bottle of whisky."'

So what's the secret? 'I've only ever eaten to live, not lived to eat. That might have helped. I haven't smoked for forty years and I don't drink. Both my parents lived till ninety. I hardly sleep. Two hours a night sometimes. Probably not enough. When I'm filing away at that bench, I often find my head going to sleep.'

His son Peter agreed he was in good fettle, still able to do many repair

Len today

jobs, and drive his car. 'He's only had one little accident and it wasn't his fault. It was last year and this woman in a Golf stopped suddenly in the middle of the road. She was about to turn, but she hadn't indicated. Dad went into the back of her. He's gone through life telling us about the accidents he's seen happening around him but he's never been in one, till that one.

'Anyway, because of it, they said they weren't going to give him any insurance cover for this year. I contacted them and told them he'd die if they stopped him driving. That would really be the end of him. They finally agreed to give him third-party cover only, with a £2,500 excess. So he still drives, all over Birmingham, but he doesn't go on the motorways any more. Going to Tewkesbury this afternoon he'll use the side-roads.'

'When I get to a hundred,' said Len, 'I'm going to ride to London on my motorbike. I'm going to Buckingham Palace myself, to pick up my telegram.'

11

MERCEDES

Karl Benz

There have been lots of people like Len during this century, tinkering around with the new-fangled motor machines, developing and adapting, producing their own versions or converting someone else's. Almost all have now gone, given up long ago, as the world's motor manufacturers have been reduced to a mere handful. On the other hand, as Len observed, the motor-car has taken over the world. We are all drivers now. This has been the century of the internal combustion engine.

When and where did it all begin? Like so many inventions and creations we take for granted, it evolved over many years, with many hands, some known, some unknown, contributing along the way, like a baton being passed in a relay race. The vital breakthrough in what we now call the internal combustion engine, in which petrol not gas was used, came around the year 1886. It was the work of two engineers – both German, Gottlieb Daimler and Karl Benz – working within sixty miles of each other, in the Neckar valley, but independently. Even more remarkable, they never met. Since their deaths, their names, and their motor-cars, have become linked for ever.

By the 1890s, several early models of the motor-cars made by Daimler, Benz and others had been imported into Britain by wealthy enthusiasts. It was illegal to run them at speeds over 4 m.p.h., but a campaign to repeal the 'Red Flag' laws, led by a new magazine, *Autocar*, changed that: in 1896, the speed limit went up to 12 m.p.h. To celebrate, the first Brighton-to-London run took place. One of the entrants was Gottlieb Daimler, who came over from Germany and drove one of his own cars.

The change in the British laws immediately inspired a new industry, and the first firm to start producing motor-cars here was the Daimler Motor Company in Coventry. Despite its name, it was a British firm. Back in 1890, Frederick Simms had acquired the British rights to import Daimler engines and had successfully used one in a boat, which he demonstrated on the Thames in 1891 – thus creating the world's first motor-boat. When motor-cars became legal, Simms decided to use the name Daimler for his factory.

Meanwhile, in Germany Daimler had got himself a proper factory and was producing more powerful, sporty cars, in small numbers, of course, a handful at a time. They were bought mainly by wealthy individuals to race against each other. There were nasty accidents, some fatal, as they raced from town to town, so very often they raced under pseudonyms – Don Pascal, for example, was Baron Rothschild.

In Nice, in 1899, a wealthy gentleman called Emil Jellinek entered a motor-race under the name of his daughter. He had done well in insurance and banking and had become a diplomat, acting as Austro-Hungarian consul in Nice. His wife was French, he was Austrian, but they had given their daughter, born in 1889, a Spanish Christian name: Mercedes.

Jellinek had bought his first car from Mr Daimler in 1893 and had travelled up to Stuttgart to collect it. He was a bit disappointed with it as it did only 20 m.p.h. But the one he entered in the race in 1899, using his daughter's name, won the race, much to his pleasure. He visited Daimler's factory again and talked to the chief designer, Wilhelm Maybach. This time he wanted a much bigger, more powerful car, with a 36-horse-power engine. If they could produce one to his specifications, he would order thirty-six. This was a massive order for a small factory producing only around 120 cars a year. He also laid down two other conditions: he must have the exclusive rights to sell these new models in Austria, France and the USA; and they had to be called Mercedes, after his daughter. Daimler agreed at once and received 550,000 marks for the thirty-six cars.

Six were delivered and tested by the end of 1900. Jellinek raced one in Nice where it reached 53 m.p.h. and was considered a sensation by the local press. He announced that chauffeurs were invited to test them. The word 'chauffeur' was coined by the French, from the verb *chauffer*, meaning to heat or warm up, and that's what early chauffeurs had to do for their masters, crank the car and warm it up.

So the Mercedes was born, the first and oldest 'marque' of car in the world (another French word, showing that while the Germans might have been the car pioneers, the French were the first enthusiasts).

That first Mercedes was itself a pioneer. Its rakish design with a long, low, enclosed bonnet and a radiator grille at the front, as well as its enormous power, transformed the nature of motor-cars: until then, their shape had resembled a horseless carriage. From 1900, they looked much as they do today.

In 1902, the German Daimler company registered the name Mercedes. Mr Jellinek joined the board and changed his name to Jellinek-Mercedes – the first time in history that a man changed his name to his daughter's? He died in 1918. Mercedes herself went on to marry twice, both times to German barons. She died in 1929, aged forty. Gottlieb Daimler had died in 1900, aged sixty-six, leaving his two sons to run the firm.

In 1909, they registered a three-pointed star as the company logo. This had its origin in a postcard their father had once sent to their mother. On it he drew a three-pointed star over their house, which he said one day would rise over their factory. The three points represented land, sea and air, the three elements he hoped his engines would eventually conquer.

Mercedes cars were known for speed and sport, while Benz were known for comfort, but from the beginning, both were exclusive vehicles, large and luxurious, aimed at quality. In 1905 Benz listed the names of its royal and aristocratic customers. Mercedes boasted about all the races it had won. In 1903, a Mercedes reached 75 m.p.h. and won races all over Europe and America: Len Vale-Onslow in Birmingham was correct in remembering a racing Mercedes on its way to attempt another speed record.

Apart from Mercedes and Benz, many of the manufacturers of early sporting cars are still known to this day – Fiat, Ferrari, Alfa-Romeo,

Renault, Peugeot. Developments and advances in motor-racing, for better, faster cars, were slowly incorporated into ordinary models for ordinary use. The 1914 Grand Prix was held in France: forty-seven cars from six different countries entered and Mercedes took the first three places.

The First World War brought a halt to motor-races and motor-manufacturing in Europe, except for military purposes. After the war, the German companies had to start again from scratch in a faltering economy. In 1926, Mercedes and Benz decided to join forces. The new company, Mercedes-Benz, incorporated Gottlieb Daimler's three-pointed star as its logo, set inside a wreath, which was the Benz symbol.

The war in Europe allowed the USA to catch up in motor-car production. As in Britain, many Daimler engines had been imported, but local engineers soon started to develop their own variations. By 1898 there were fifty American makers of automobiles, though the term had not yet been universally accepted. Early models were billed as an oleo-locomotive, or an automaton or a motor fly, and in 1900, they were still mostly steam-driven cars. The first commercially successful automobile manufacturer in the USA, producing petrol-driven cars, was Ranson Eli Olds with his Oldsmobile in 1901. But what revolutionised the world of mass motoring, of course, was the arrival of Henry Ford.

Ford, the son of Irish immigrants, started work at fifteen as a machinist's assistant in Detroit. He worked for the Edison Electrical Company, then became interested in building racing-cars. In 1903, aged forty, he set up the Ford Company, with several partners, to build cars for ordinary people. In his first full year of operation he produced 1,700 cars, but it wasn't until the arrival of the Model T Ford in 1908 that the transformation was complete. This was the ninth of his models, each named after a letter: he started with A, B and C, moved on to F, K and N, then R, S and T. His aim was to produce a cheap, durable car, available to everyone, not just for the wealthy or sporting classes. Once he'd got the right model, he went into mass production. He built moving conveyor belts, with workers standing at each stage, doing repetitive jobs, producing identical cars with no frills, no variations, no choice of style, available in only one colour – black. Between 1908 and 1927, fifteen million Model T Fords were sold. The price came down dramatically from $950 to $290, by which time Ford was producing half the motor-cars in the world.

In 1911 the Ford Company started production in Britain, in Manchester. That year a Model T Ford was driven up Ben Nevis to show what it could do. Once it was being produced here, the British price also dropped dramatically, from £225 in 1909, when it was first imported, to £135 in 1914.

The Europeans, for all their inventive genius, had not envisaged the motor-car for ordinary people, capable of transforming ordinary lives, or a way of producing them at a price that ordinary people could afford. In 1908 an interesting demonstration took place in London at the Royal Automobile Club: the Cadillac Company brought over three of its cars, and separated each one into its hundreds of parts. The parts were then mixed up and the three cars reassembled, containing parts that had originally been in the others. Each was then driven off, and travelled five hundred miles. Nothing amazing about that to us today, but then a motor-car was still seen as an individual, exclusive piece of work, hand-tooled by craftsmen, for an individual owner.

America created the system of mass production and continued to develop cars, while Europe fell behind, during and after the First World War. Electric self-starting replaced the need for cars to be hand-cranked, and enabled women to drive with ease. Electric lighting, for inside and outside a car, was an optional extra for European cars until after the war, but was standard in America. Pneumatic tyres had been perfected by Michelin in 1897, but Mercedes were still treating them as an extra at the outbreak of the First World War. Until the 1920s, most cars were still open but by the 1930s they were enclosed, which allowed them to be used in all weathers. The Americans pioneered most of these refinements and changed the lives of ordinary people. The motor industry also transformed the American economy and it became the biggest single employer.

By the 1930s Mercedes-Benz had been revitalised and returned to the motor-racing scene, with many triumphs at Le Mans and elsewhere. It continued with its exclusive luxury and sporting cars, ignoring the humble Ford cars, or the modest Morris and Austin vehicles produced in Britain from the 1920s.

When Hitler came to power, he provided government grants for Mercedes-Benz and encouraged it to produce the world's best racing-cars, seeing their victories as a source of national pride. He also wanted them to dominate the top end of the luxury car market, so that Rolls-Royce, founded in 1906, could no longer boast that its Silver Ghost was the best in the world.

Hitler himself took delivery of a Mercedes Grosser, perhaps the most grandiose car ever produced. It appeared in 1930 and was greeted by the German press as a '*Prunkwagen*', for statesmen and party leaders. *Prunk* meaning pomp. It was not particularly innovative, but it was massive – some nineteen feet long and weighing three tons – and offered every known accessory, including armour-plating. The Kaiser ordered one. Emperor Hirohito ordered six. Only 117 were made, between 1930 and 1937, so it wasn't a massive seller.

Although the company wasn't interested in mass-production, it did produce rather more modest cars, such as the 170 saloon, of which 14,000 were sold. In 1936, Mercedes-Benz built the world's first diesel-engine car, named after Rudolf Diesel who invented but never manufactured a new form of ignition that used a new sort of fuel. (Diesel fell to his death from a boat while crossing the North Sea from Germany to England.)

Once again, war destroyed the German motor-car industry. Mercedes designers had to watch Jaguar win Le Mans in 1951, but returned a year later to win it themselves with their 300 SL. Jaguar won again in 1955, 1956 and 1957, but by then Mercedes had given up motor-racing. Britain was the post-war leader in racing-cars and also the major exporter of ordinary cars.

Britain's first big post-war success was the Morris Minor, which appeared in 1948. By 1960 a million had been sold, making it the country's first million-selling car. This was beaten by the Mini, which arrived in 1959, and was Britain's most technically innovative car. It cost only £496, cheaper than the Ford Anglia by £77, and became a symbol of the Swinging Sixties. Over 5 million have been sold. Eventually Britain was overtaken as the world's leading exporter by the Germans, thanks to the success of the Volkswagen Beetle, and by the 1970s, its car industry was in decline after a series of strikes, industrial problems and political changes.

In the 1980s it was the Japanese who got ahead. The first Japanese cars, Daihatsu, were imported in 1965 and sold for £699 – £200 more than the Ford Anglia. The motoring press were fairly sniffy about them, not to say dismissive, considering the Japanese to be copyists, who could pinch ideas and make them cheaply, but with little hope of improving what had been a Euro-American invention.

In 1970, only 14 per cent of cars in Britain were imported. By 1985 this had jumped to 58 per cent. It has now stabilised to about 55 per cent, because Nissan cars made in Sunderland are now counted as British. But almost all British car manufacturers are, in fact, foreign. Ford, which has bought Jaguar, is American, and so is Vauxhall, owned by Chrysler. Rover, which still sounds terribly British, is owned by the German BMW. The next wave, following the Japanese, is already with us: Proton is made in Malaysia, and Hyundai and Daewoo in South Korea.

Gottlieb Daimler and Karl Benz would be astonished, but in a way it was happening in 1900: from the very beginning, motor-cars did not recognise national boundaries. They were sold and driven anywhere. Different countries and different manufacturers developed different variations. All car-manufacturing is now international. The number of companies is decreasing, as the business is strictly for the big boys, but the total number of cars on the planet is increasing all the time.

Perhaps the strangest thing about the motor-car, which has so dominated our century, is that basically it is still as it was in 1900, in design and content. It is also powered in much the same way that Mr Daimler and Mr Benz created. There seems little chance at present that a new formula, based perhaps on solar energy, or an old one, based on electricity, will revolutionise our transport in the next few years. Meanwhile, the Mercedes, and all other marques, will still be with us, getting ready for another century.

Mercedes-Benz is one of the few big boys not to have a manufacturing presence in Britain. Their British headquarters is in Milton Keynes, where they have a staff of six hundred in a spacious, open-plan red-brick building, exuding that air of hygienic efficiency we associate – or did associate – with Germany. These last few years, Germany has had more industrial and employment problems than the UK.

In their courtyard they had on display two cars: one was a vintage

Gottlieb Daimler

motor from 1899, the Benz Ideal, just to remind visitors of their distinguished history as the world's oldest continuous car-manufacturer; the other was modern, something called an SLK two-seater sports car, rather zippy and quite attractive, I thought, till I looked at the price – £29,000. Seemed a lot for a fairly small sports car, compared with some equally zippy and attractive-looking Japanese models.

In 1996, 35,000 Mercedes-Benz cars were sold in the UK, plus 19,000 trucks – a record year, following two record years, but before that, they had had three rotten years with sales down in 1993 to 20,000. This is the nature of the motor industry. Recessions are felt immediately, which is why car sales are often used by economists as a gauge of a nation's health and wealth. Perhaps they would have done better during those slump years if they had been manufacturing in the UK, as BMW now do. In 1993, Mercedes in Germany considered building a factory in the UK for their new model, the Mercedes A-class. Sites were considered in Scotland and the North East.

'It had become cheaper to build outside Germany,' admits John Evans, head of communications for Mercedes in the UK. 'The German unions had negotiated such good working hours and social benefits that it would have paid them to come to Britain. But it became a big national thing, the thought of two hundred thousand Mercedes cars a year being built elsewhere. All that investment going abroad, while Germany had rising unemployment. So there were big concessions, by the government and the workers, who agreed to more flexible hours. Things had to change. In Germany, working for Mercedes had been looked upon as a job for life. They had to be more flexible. In Britain we learned that earlier.'

People selling Mercedes cars have also had to learn new things, in the UK as well as Germany. 'Some Mercedes dealers had become very complacent. Traditionally we have always been an exclusive car. We don't, for example, go for the corporate market or sell large numbers to the car-rental firms. That's not our image, not our market. Because of that, our dealers became used to buyers just walking in and giving orders. Suddenly, Mercedes and its dealers had to actually sell.' If they didn't, buyers might go elsewhere, which many did. BMW, their deadly rival, now sells 50 per cent more cars in the UK than Mercedes.

The biggest fright to Mercedes, on a world scale, came in 1992. A report on the motor industry by the Massachusetts Institute of Technology revealed that Mercedes was probably the world's least efficient car-manufacturer. Nothing wrong with the quality of their cars or their reliability. The problem was that in man hours and costs per car Mercedes was miles behind. The Japanese came out best: roughly half their workers produced the same number of units as Mercedes for half the cost.

'This was devastating for everyone in Stuttgart. We were selling well enough with the highest retention rate in the industry. Around 92 per cent of people who buy a Mercedes stick to a Mercedes for their next car – figures we are very proud of. But the MIT report showed something was wrong, though it hadn't become apparent. It did in 1993. Sales everywhere began to drop.'

Mercedes-Benz hired a new president and chief executive, Helmut Werner, who originally came from Continental Tyres. He was not a career Mercedes man, which had been the traditional route up for top executives. He decided on a different strategy: to compete with a premium car in all the car markets, not just at the luxury, exclusive end.

They defined five new markets to enter, starting with the most important of all: the small car. That's what the new Mercedes A-class is aimed at. In the four-wheel-drive market, they hoped to challenge Range Rover with their Mercedes M-class. Then, there's a people-mover, following the enormous success of the Renault Espace, a small sports car, their SLK, the one I'd seen outside and lastly, a small estate car, an estate version of their existing C-class.

The big investment was in the Mercedes A-class, which is small but not cheap, intended to compete at the top end of the small-car range, against the VW Golf. After a hundred years in business, Mercedes was entering a new market.

John Evans had already spent a lot of time and money on market research for the Mercedes A. Thousands of people had been asked about their possible reaction to it – what they did and didn't like. The result had been quite surprising, at least to some people at Mercedes who had always assumed that their number-one selling point was, well, that they were Mercedes – that is, a brand name everyone admired.

'What we've been told is that we should announce it as a completely radical car, a new solution to the small-car problem. After that we should say, "Oh, incidentally, it's a Mercedes." The wrong way would be to simply present it as just a small Mercedes.'

'We now have to get the trade ready, all the Mercedes dealers, to handle a new sort of car for a new sort of public. Traditionally, the Mercedes has been bought by men – between 80 and 90 per cent. But the A car will be for a much wider audience.

'And also for the first time people will be coming in to do part-exchanges on cars we have never handled before, such as VW Polos or Ford Fiestas.' Shock horror. 'Yes, our dealers know little about how to sell used Fords. There is a lot of retraining to be done.'

And also some hasty rethinking since a Swedish car magazine reported that the new Mercedes was not quite so clever on sudden corners, which caused a lot of worry for the big bosses in Stuttgart.

Stuttgart, where it all began, is today a fairly featureless city of some half a million souls, situated on the river Neckar, about sixty miles from where it joins the Rhine. It's clean and orderly and prosperous enough, but the devastations of the Second World War ripped out its old heart and few ancient buildings remain.

From the airport I got a taxi into the centre and admired a splendid new dome-like roof on the main football stadium, the home of VFB Stuttgart. It had formerly been called the Neckar Stadium. Now, thanks to some useful financial sponsorship by guess who, it is called the Gottlieb Daimler Stadium.

Mr Daimler and Mr Benz have certainly not been forgotten in Germany, least of all in their home area. There is a Daimler Strasse, a Benz Strasse, a Mercedes Strasse, and 35,000 people are employed locally by the Mercedes-Benz company. Their administrative buildings are in the heart of Stuttgart, near where Mr Daimler set up his first works in the back garden of his summer house at Bad Cannstadt. It's a city within a city, with its own barriers at the entrances, but it is open to traffic and the public, which is just as well as it also contains the Mercedes-Benz Museum.

They attract over 500,000 visitors a year, a phenomenal number for a specialist museum devoted to just one make of car, but as it happens to be a marque whose origins go back to the beginning, it covers the whole history of motor-cars. It's also free. Always a great help with visitor numbers. Another attraction is that it's in a modern glass building, with lots of light and air and foliage, and there's a nice café. In my experience, motor museums tend to be in dark old warehouses and can be pretty depressing, unless you're a motor freak. Mercedes-Benz, of course, are partly doing a PR exercise, boasting about themselves.

There are some eighty-five cars and pieces of car on show, starting in 1885 with Daimler's first motorised carriage, next to Benz's first, his three-wheeler. The Daimler is the original. The Benz is a reproduction, which they keep relatively quiet. (The original Benz No. 1 is in Germany's national museum in Munich.)

So who was first, Benz or Daimler? There is some confusion on exact dates in almost all books on the history of motor-cars. Most books say that both cars were launched in 1886, but my guide Max said that Benz finished building his the year before, so he has to be called first. 'Benz, as you know, was essentially a car-maker, while Daimler was a motor-maker. Benz stuck to motor-cars and by the year 1900, he had produced 2,630.' That was a new one to add to my surfeit of motoring facts.

As we walked round, I was admiring the beautiful colours, the deep creams and rich reds you never see today on motor cars, however expensive, and also the artistic shapes, the sumptuous upholstery, while Max pointed out things I was missing, such as electric headlamps suddenly appearing in 1910, replacing gas ones. A whole section is devoted to racing-cars, with models so small, delicate and flimsy you can't imagine how they managed 140 miles an hour, back in 1910.

I stopped for a long time to examine the famous Grosser cars of 1930. They have two, one of which was made for the German Kaiser, the other for the Japanese Emperor. The furnishings in the Kaiser's looked rather stark, with lots of leather. The Emperor's was much more ornate, with masses of brocade and the rising sun emblem on the doors. I was even allowed to step inside, and found that each had an intercom system. This enabled the Emperor or the Kaiser, sitting on the back seat, to give orders to the chauffeur. He was just a few feet away, behind his partition, but socially on another planet. It worked like a TV remote control, with seven little buttons, each marked in German or Japanese with a different command – Fast, Slow, Right, Left, Reverse, Go Home, Stop. The appropriate command was then lit up on the chauffeur's dashboard. All very simple, and ever so neat.

We came to a stunning 1936 'Spezial Roadster' in a red so brilliant I had to shade my eyes. Max said it would fetch ten million US dollars today. Only thirty-five were ever made. I also examined Konrad Adenauer's Mercedes of 1959. He had had seat-belts installed, which few had at the time, plus a radio phone and a fan above his seat for hot weather. In 1959, Mercedes had not yet got round to air-conditioning.

Then I went to the main factory, twelve miles outside Stuttgart at Sindelfingen, and joined a factory tour. We were shown a film first, which was very boring, the sort of instructional film I haven't seen since school and hoped never to see again – heavy with portentous music and moody shots of blokes in white coats looking sincere. The actual tour was fascinating. We went in an articulated bus that trundled in and out of the main parts of the plant. An excellent guide, speaking English and German, gave us each a head-set so we could hear every word, no matter how far away we were. The automatons were awesome – massive heads and limbs, bending into impossible shapes, programmed to pick up a whole dashboard, take it to the moving conveyor belt, identify which car body was next, estimate the correct position, fix it exactly in place, then bend out again and start afresh.

I wondered where all the people were, the 35,000 workers. On the tour, I saw no more than five hundred, mainly attending the conveyor belts, but the tour was round the more dramatic, automated parts, of course, not the offices. They have their own school, with 1,100 trainees at any one time. Proportionally, it would look as if they still have more staff than in Britain or Japan because all German workers are on a thirty-five-hour week, with an average wage of £22,000.

I also wondered why there is such a waiting list. In that Mercedes factory, one of twelve plants in Germany, they were producing 1,900 cars a day, yet you can still wait up to two years for a certain model. I never understood the answer to that, except that the longest waiting lists are for cars with the smallest production numbers.

Every day, around six hundred people who can't wait, and want the fun of a factory tour, pick up their new Mercedes in person. This is a special feature of Mercedes. Almost all the customers come from inside Germany, the rest from abroad. The day I was there fourteen people had come from Britain, followed by four from France, two each from Austria, Italy and the USA.

The reason for the high number of Brits is that Mercedes-Benz UK offers a unique package of attractions: a free flight, free hotel, free Cross Channel trip back, if you pick up your own car. The price is exactly the same, £425, as the delivery charge for collecting your car from your local dealer. They lose money on the offer, but consider it's worth it for the goodwill. Most Brits turn it into a holiday, driving back slowly through Germany and France in their new car.

It's proved so popular, for Germans and foreigners, that Mercedes has made it into an event in itself, with a special customer delivery centre, fitted and furnished like a posh hotel, complete with restaurant, bar, boutique and excitements like the film, factory tour and a gape at the automatons. Not so much a car pick-up point, more a Disney experience.

It was there that I met Bob and Julie Knappett, from Newmarket in Suffolk, where they run a roofing company employing seven workers. They had come to pick up their new SLK. They had ordered it two and half years earlier, after they'd seen a design version at the Birmingham Motor Show.

'We chose it in silver,' said Bob, 'with a few extras such as a CD player and a pop-out cup holder, which Julie is very keen on. The basic price is £29,500 but it comes to £33,000 with extras.'

'It started as a dream,' said Julie. 'It only became a reality very slowly. We got three photos of it. I kept one in my office and two in Bob's, and we looked at them every day. For Christmas I bought Bob an SLK lighter and an SLK key-ring. It's made presents very easy, these last two years.

'Countdown began six weeks ago. We planned to keep the date secret, as our little treat for ourselves, but our foreman took a call a week ago, so our trip to Stuttgart came out.'

'I'd say there's no one within a radius of twenty miles of Newmarket who doesn't know we're here today,' said Bob.

Just before they left, a man offered them £50,000 in cash for their car before they'd even paid for it. 'I think it's these yuppies in the City, who have just got their huge bonuses. They decide they want the latest car and can't wait two years for it as we've done. I refused, of course. It's only a car, I know, but it's our dream.'

There was an air of expectancy, like sitting outside a maternity ward, when it finally arrived. It was the only SLK in sight so everyone crowded round to admire it. Bob was soon fussing with the bodywork, maintaining he had spotted a bit of dust in the paintwork, which was causing a blemish. Julie couldn't see it, I couldn't see it, but he made the Mercedes engineer do a bit more polishing till he was satisfied.

Then there was some consternation when they tried to pack their two slim cases into the boot. Part of their fantasy had been to drive out of the Mercedes factory with the hood down: they'd forgotten that the electrically operated metal roof folds down into the boot, and halves the space.

'Let's just drive her with the roof up, till we repack the cases,' said Julie. Bob got the CD working and put in Shirley Bassey singing 'Big Spender'. And off they zoomed in their new car, taking her for a spin across Europe.

Jellinek picked up his original car himself from Stuttgart in 1900. And all cars are still feminine, not just the one he named after his daughter.

12

Anne Westman

German-born, regular Savoy luncher

Anne Westman in 1941

Anne Westman also comes from Germany. Even today she has the look of a sleek, exclusive model: blonde and blue-eyed, incredibly stylish, very well-dressed, exuding grace and affluence. Every day she eats out at a fashionable London hotel. Seven days a week, she gets a taxi on her own, goes off to the West End and has lunch on her own. Just going out into a busy London street and calling a taxi is unusual enough for someone in their nineties. Of all those born in 1900 whom I met, her lifestyle today was the most remarkable.

She lives alone in an expensive apartment block in St John's Wood, London. On the telephone, giving me directions, she said she'd arrange a resident's parking space. When I parked my car, I noticed there was a white Rolls-Royce in the next bay. Not hers. She doesn't drive now that she's almost ninety-seven. Hence the taxis. Every day, at around twelve o'clock, she leaves her first-floor apartment, goes down in the lift, through the front hall, past the porter's lodge, out into the courtyard, under the entrance arch and out into the street where she flags down a black cab and asks for the Savoy, Claridge's or the Churchill in Portman Square. That day she'd had lunch at Claridge's. Just a simple meal. Smoked salmon followed by *pâté de foie gras*.

She'd made our appointment for three-thirty, giving her time to get a cab home from lunch. She opened the triple locks on her front door looking immaculate, fresh and composed, not a hair out of place, as cool and elegant as Marlene Dietrich. Hard to believe she'd been up west. When I come home, having struggled through London traffic, all I want to do is collapse.

She was born Anna Perschmann in Berlin on 27 March 1900, and baptised in a Lutheran Church with water from the river Spree. Traditionally, so she said, this was the mark of a true Berliner. She and her younger sister, Charlotte, were brought up in some comfort with a nanny to look after them. 'I suppose you would say we were upper-middle class.' Her father was a senior civil servant in the German Post Office. 'Germany had won the Franco-German War in 1871, so it was a period of prosperity and well-being in Germany.'

Her earliest memory is of starting school when she was six. 'My teacher's name was Miss Henning and she was very pleased with my behaviour.' Did you get a star, a stripe, some reward for this good behaviour? 'Oh, I can't remember that. Ha ha ha.' She tilted her delicate chin as she laughed prettily, her blue eyes sparkling. Her English is fluent but she still has a pronounced German accent and a certain German stiffness.

At the age of thirteen she was one of a handful of Berlin school-children chosen to meet the Kaiser. Which Kaiser? I asked, and was immediately given a short history lesson.

'People born in England in 1900 were born in the reign of Queen Victoria, so they can call themselves Victorian. I was born in the reign of Kaiser Wilhelm I. In the year 1888 there had been three Kaisers. Wilhelm I died, Kaiser Frederick took over, but he lasted only ninety-nine days, then was succeeded by Kaiser Wilhelm II. So in 1913, when I was thirteen, it was twenty-five years since he had been Kaiser. There were jubilee celebrations throughout Germany. I and some school-friends were chosen to go to the Royal Palace and sing some hymns and hand over some flowers. The Royal Palace was beautiful. I can still see the corridors, filled with flowers.'

She picked up a photograph of the Kaiser and pointed to his left arm. 'You can't see it in this photograph, but he had a withered arm. Oh, everyone knew about it. He didn't try to hide it. It happened when he was born. Poor obstetrics.'

What did you wear? 'My first ever long dress, which I had got for my confirmation. My parents were Lutheran, but not extreme. We celebrated all the usual things, like Easter and Christmas. On Christmas Eve, we could go to church then come home and I would recite a poem. Then I would get my Christmas presents. Always on Christmas Eve, not Christmas Day. Oh, just the obvious things. Dolls, toys, books, games. No, we didn't have a stocking. We did have a Christmas tree, a real Christmas tree, with real candles. Everyone did that. There was always one house every year which went on fire. But not our house.'

She can't quite remember what she was doing the day the First World War broke out, apart from being at school. But she remembers that all young people thought it was a big adventure. She was excited by the sight of her first Zeppelin, which she watched landing at Friedrichshafen on the Bodensee, the German name for Lake Constance.

As the war progressed, Berlin was soon filled with wounded soldiers. 'That was terrible. The hospitals couldn't cope.' She had two uncles in the army, who ended up on the Russian front. Her father was too old to serve but he died during the war, in 1913 aged fifty-one. Her mother was left with an ample pension but had to struggle alone during the blockade of Berlin, through rationing and endless shortages. 'I remember going with my mother to a soup kitchen and all we were given to eat was horseflesh. My sister and I said we would rather eat nothing than eat horseflesh. I suppose we were rather silly teenagers.'

The normal school-leaving age was fourteen. Those who stayed on either went to a high school for further education or to a school for business and trade skills. Anne went to a high school until she was sixteen but then left to become a secretary, working for a company which looked after the property interests of some Junkers, the traditional ruling class in Prussia. 'Aristocratic properties, landed estates, you might say. It did mean I could often get things like eggs.'

She also met, socially, one of Germany's war heroes, Lettow-Vorbeck. I hadn't heard of him, so she got up to check his record in a German reference book. I said, 'Don't bother, it's not important,' but she walked across her spacious drawing room, past her old-master paintings, antique furniture and rare books, to dig out the exact reference. 'Ah, here it is. So. He was a general in the Afrika Korps. I thought that was it.'

I asked what German people of the time thought of the British – were they the dreaded, nasty enemy? 'I don't remember thinking that. Actually I don't remember thinking much about Britain. It seemed a long way away, right across the North Sea. What we all worried about was the Russians.'

Her mother did her bit for the war effort, handing over her jewellery to the authorities. 'There was a big publicity campaign to encourage you. If you handed in a certain amount, you got a diploma which said, "I gave gold for iron." I admired my mother for doing this, but I often wondered later if her jewellery really did go to serve the war, or if someone took it . . .'

She hasn't retained her mother's diploma, alas, but she does have some First World War memorabilia. She went off to look in a desk and came back with army photographs, medals, programmes – all belonging to the man she was to marry, Stephen Westman.

He served in the German Third Foot Artillery Regiment, number 14, during the First World War as an army doctor. She showed me a programme for an Officers' Mess dinner held on 27 January 1918, for the Kaiser's birthday. By this time, the German army was suffering enormous losses, yet in her husband's mess that evening they had roast beef and something called Swedish artichoke, with salad, followed by a pudding, all of it with musical accompaniment. The programme, printed in purple on cheap shiny paper that had made the ink run, gives details of the menu and the music. It included works by Verdi, Rossini and Bizet. It doesn't say who played, but presumably it was the regimental band. Her husband's name is handwritten in ink on the front of the programme – Assistant Field Doctor Westman.

He went on to win the Iron Cross, First Class, and other medals, all of which she still has. He survived the war, returned to Berlin and resumed his old job as a lecturer in the postgraduate medical school.

Anne didn't meet her husband-to-be until the war was over. She first saw him when she happened to attend a public lecture he was giving at the Humboldt Institute. When she met him later, socially, she told him she'd been to his lecture. He soon became a professor and head of the Department of Obstetrics, well-known in German medical circles for his lectures and writings. His first book was published in Germany in 1924 and entitled *Solved and Unsolved Problems of Modern Medicine*. He went on to write three other books, in German, one of which was called *Sport, Womanhood and Physical Training*. As a gynaecologist and obstetrician, he was keen that women should have a proper understanding of their bodies.

It was during the 1920s in Berlin that he and Anne became good friends, but there were several obstacles to their relationship: he was married with three young children, though his marriage was not happy; he was seven years older; he was part Jewish, through his maternal grandmother and, as the Nazis rose to power, this became significant.

Meanwhile, Anne had other boyfriends. 'Two made me definite proposals of marriage, but I said no.' In the end, Stephen divorced and was free to marry her. 'My mother never raised objections. She couldn't have done anything about it anyway. My father was, of course, long dead.'

Before they could get married, Stephen discovered through a friend who was the Police Commissioner in Berlin that he was on Hitler's hit list. When the Nazis took control, he decided to leave Germany.

Tom Westman, born 1928, and Stephen's son by his first marriage, says that the reason his father fled was not his Jewish background but his medical activities. 'He gave public lectures about pregnancy, what women should and should not do to prevent it, and the Nazis thought this obscene. He was really a German Marie Stopes, going round talking about birth control. He upset the Catholics as well as the Nazis. He wanted women to know the facts about themselves, not some old wives' tales. That's what really made him a marked man.'

Stephen fled to Edinburgh, leaving behind his three young children in the care of their mother, though they later joined him in Edinburgh. He knew that Edinburgh University was noted for medicine, but found that his German qualifications were not recognised. He had to start from scratch to qualify as a British doctor and eventually achieved an MB and an FRCS.

'In 1933, I went to Edinburgh and we got married in a register office,' says Anne. 'We lived in a house in Minto Street. I could speak English already. Stephen and I had both learned it at school, along with French and Latin.'

They eventually moved to London where Stephen took premises in Harley Street. Then came the Second World War. Stephen found himself again attending to war wounded, this time on the British side, not as an army doctor but as a civilian doctor, working in the British Emergency Hospitals.

After the war his practice thrived: he became one of London's leading gynaecologists and published medical papers and books – written in English now. Harley Street houses are big, and most doctors usually rent only a few rooms, but Stephen bought the whole of 137 Harley Street, plus the adjoining property behind it, 31 Devonshire Mews West. Tom was sent to Epsom College and the two daughters went to boarding school at Haywards Heath.

They lived a glamorous life, Anne and Stephen, with expensive holidays, buying paintings and antiques. For a while, they had a handsome house in St John's Wood, 29 Carlton Hill, then later moved out to the country, to Chorleywood in Hertfordshire. They attended balls and parties at the German Embassy and Anne became a director of a fine-art publishing company.

Stephen took part in a BBC TV series called *The Great War*, first shown in 1964 and repeated since, giving his memories of the First World War. Not many Germans, after all, had memories of both wars, from different sides. He even had his photograph in the *Radio Times*. Such fame, I said. Anne went off to find a copy.

He died in 1964, not long after the programme was first broadcast. 'He had had minor heart attacks since 1961. Then he had a massive coronary.' His last book, published posthumously, was called *Surgeon with the Kaiser's Army*. That week, Anne had had a request from an Anglo-American TV company, wanting to use some of the material from the book in a new documentary series about the First World War.

In 1977, she decided to leave Chorleywood and moved back into London, taking the apartment in St John's Wood. She never thought of returning to Germany, even though she was now widowed, with her stepchildren grown-up and married. 'I didn't want to uproot myself any further. I've always liked living in Britain.'

Do you feel British? I asked. She answered with a Latin proverb. '"*Ubi bene, ibi patria.*" Where I prosper, that is my country.'

Judging by her possessions, she has sufficient means to provide a comfortable life. I noticed a Brueghel among her paintings, as well as works by Paulus Brill and Ventura Bona-Peeters. She always got her clothes from Norman Hartnell, her favourite dress designer. But, of course, once you get to ninety-seven, money is not enough for a comfortable life. Physical and mental health are what matter, and Anne clearly has both in abundance.

I could see on her desk a neat pile of letters, accounts and documents. She says she attends personally to her affairs, though, of course, she employs lawyers and accountants. She has no help in her apartment, except a cleaner who comes twice a week. She doesn't need to cook because she always eats out at lunch, then sticks to fresh fruit in the evening.

'I go out because I can't sit here all day, can I, doing nothing.' She says it's always a very simple lunch, for which she pays between twenty-five and fifty pounds. She doesn't take cash but uses her Barclaycard, and keeps all the bills, which she files neatly. She usually has fish, such as Dover sole, followed by a light pudding, perhaps crème caramel. No wine, just orange juice.

Anne today

Tom, her stepson, told me that she loves being fussed over by West End head waiters, but she said she wasn't aware of this. 'I don't talk to the head waiters. I try not to keep them back as, of course, they are very busy.'

She does have a couple of gentlemen callers. ('Gallant old codgers' was Tom's phrase.) They occasionally take her out, but naturally, by now, most of her old friends and admirers have long since died. 'I do have one old friend, still living in Berlin, who visits me when he comes to London.' She paused, then gave a half-sigh. 'He hasn't been recently. He is quite a bit younger than me.'

Does he know your age?

'Of course not. He thinks I am much younger than I am. If he were to ask me, I wouldn't tell him. I would reply by saying what Lohengrin said to Elsa when she asked him where he had come from. "Thou must not ask that."'

She has her hair done every two weeks, in the hair salon of a local hotel, and takes great care of her clothes. 'I think there is nothing worse than an old woman who neglects herself. *Ja*, I suppose there is a bit of vanity in me, but why not?

'I did have a couple of proposals after Stephen died, both from doctors, but I refused. I didn't want to get married again.

'The most important thing in my life is to keep my independence. I still have that. Totally. I don't rely or depend on anyone.'

Two years ago she had a fall and broke her hip. 'It was the femur, actually. I had a hip replacement, and now I can walk again perfectly well. I can walk a mile if I want to. These days I usually take a stick, just in case.' She does wear two hearing-aids, but so small and discreet, and her hair is so carefully arranged that I hadn't noticed until she revealed them.

Tom lives on the Isle of Skye, where he and his wife run a pottery studio. 'Westman's Pottery, it's called. That would amuse and amaze Stephen, if he were alive today. He always hoped Tom would be a doctor, but he spent most of his working life as a policeman, ending up at the Police College in Hendon.'

Tom has two children and two grandchildren. One of Anne's step-daughters, also called Anne, lives in California and is married to a doctor. She has two children and seven grandchildren. The other, Elizabeth, lives in Berkshire and for a while was a local councillor and a JP. She is now widowed with four children and ten grandchildren.

'I don't see a great deal of the girls or their families, but I see quite a bit of Tom. As I told you, I like to be independent. I am never bored. I listen to classical music. I read the *Telegraph* every day and watch a bit of television. *Mastermind* used to be my favourite programme.

'All I really miss is foreign travel. I realise those days have gone. I used to love travelling. We went everywhere – Italy, Germany, oh, the holidays we had. Baden-Baden, Capri, Rome, Florence, always in the nicest hotels. We went to America many times, usually on the *Queen Mary*. We did a twelve-day trip on the *Windsor Castle* once to Cape Town. That was so very nice.

'Now, alas, I am more or less pinned down here. Since my fall, I am worried about going too far away. So, that's my only real complaint. No, I don't regret anything. There's nothing I didn't do I wanted to do, or places I never saw. I have had a very nice life. The British people have been very nice to me.

'During the war, we had no problems. Nobody was horrible to us for being German. I can remember nothing nasty being said to us. Internment? No, I can't remember that ever being mentioned.

'I don't think the world as a whole has become a better place. Could anyone say that? I can't think of any areas in which we have progressed – apart from medicine – but a lot in which we have deteriorated. Morality, for example, how people dress, how they behave towards each other. I mean, look at these unmarried mothers. In my day, a girl with an illegitimate baby carried a stigma through life. Now they don't care. They even boast about it . . .

'No, I didn't miss not having children of my own. I did bring up three from when they were fairly small. I had enough to do with them. I never wanted any of my own.'

Despite saying her social life was very quiet these days, I noticed one invitation on her mantelpiece from the German Embassy. And having said she couldn't travel anywhere any more, it came out that she had already booked her Christmas holidays – at the Grand Hotel, Eastbourne.

How did she explain being so active at her age?

'I try to keep up an interest in many things and to enjoy life. I've never smoked and never drank much. Being independent, I think that's the most vital thing to be. I never think about tomorrow, or the fact that the curtain will soon be coming down. That sort of thought is, how do you say? – unpalatable. So I never think about it. As long as the going is good, which it still is, I will continue to enjoy life.'

I then asked Tom for his explanation of her long life. 'I am reminded of the story of the person who was asked that and said it was because he failed to buy a ticket for the *Titanic*. Anne is like that. She has always been very lucky in life. I don't remember her ever having an illness. She eats very little – and all of it healthy.'

Two weeks later she rang me up and invited me to have lunch with her. 'Claridge's or the Savoy?' she asked. 'You choose, darling.'

I chose the Savoy. She said she would do the booking. When I turned up, I found she'd got a very good table facing the river. I sat at it on my own for some time as she arrived late, apologising profusely. She hadn't been able to get a cab. It was a wet and miserable November day and London seemed to have come to a standstill, but she was all smiles and charm, looking stunning in a black suit trimmed with fur, a black lace blouse, large floppy black hat and a black, lacquered cane. I could sense people looking at her, not just because she was about the only woman in the entire dining room but because she looked like she must be Somebody.

We decided to stick to the set lunch and we both started with smoked salmon. I had lamb as my main course while she asked for *pâté de foie gras*. It wasn't on the set menu. The waiter was slightly huffy, saying he'd have to ask the chef. Anne made faces at me when he'd gone. I had a glass of white wine. She had fresh orange juice – and made the waiter pour it into a stem glass as she didn't like the straight glass he'd brought it in. It was a packed dining room, with people constantly being turned away and the staff all in a flurry.

'This is what I like best,' she said, looking round. 'I do like to watch people. What would be the point of cooking a meal at home, just to eat it on my own?'

She asked how my book was getting on – a question no other 1900-er had asked – and I told her one problem was that I was finding roughly twice as many women as men who were born in 1900. She got out her fountain pen from her neat black handbag, and drew me an X chromosome and a Y chromosome, pointing out in passing how a Y is really an X, with a leg missing.

'Women are X, you see. That's why they live longer.' I took her word for it. Well, she is the widow of an eminent doctor.

Over lunch, I asked what happened to her mother and sister, whom she had presumably left behind in Germany, when she'd got married in Edinburgh in 1933. I'd been so interested in her husband's career I'd forgotten to ask.

'We kept in touch until the war began. I tried to ring my sister several times but found I couldn't get through. I wrote letters, but they didn't get through either. Eventually one envelope came back marked "Deceased". It turned out both my sister and mother had been killed by British bombs.'

The set two-course lunch was twenty-five pounds each, according to the menu, but I noticed the bill somehow came to eighty-eight pounds; which she paid. I thanked her, saying it was my treat next time. I would take her to the Groucho Club. She might find it amusing. When I explained it was in Soho, she didn't appear so keen. She much prefers West End hotels.

Outside, it was still pouring. There was some minor drama at the front of the Savoy, which had the porters rushing all over the place. A black cab had broken down in the Strand, right at the entrance to the hotel, preventing vehicles getting in or out. I went out into the Strand. The traffic was stationary, with no sign of a cab, so I picked my way through it and across to the Strand Palace Hotel. I waited for a cab arriving, then nabbed it. I came back triumphant, telling Anne I'd got her a cab. She wasn't at all concerned, standing serenely in a shop doorway, looking cool and elegant. 'I never mind waiting,' she said. 'The older you get, the quicker the years go by . . .'

13

FLORENCE PARSONS

Blitz fire-fighter and suet pudding-eater

Florence Parsons and husband Leslie, Ramsgate, c. 1955

Florence Parsons was born on 1 January 1900, a birthday so enviably neat, so subtly significant, so supremely easy to remember that it's a shame birthdays can't be assumed by deed poll the way names can. What fun to have gone through life writing 1–1–00 on boring official forms. Florence herself thinks her birthday is amusing. She laughed when she told me, as if it were new to her, but then she laughs a great deal, even at her age. Florence Parsons is another happy person, though her life and background were not nearly as fortunate as Anne Westman's.

She was born Florence Hall and when she arrived, at the first light of the new century, her family was living at 3 Chase Road, Southgate, in North London. Her father used to be the driver of a horse-drawn bus, which went every day from Southgate to the City of London. When Florence was born, he was working in private service for a local factory-owner, driving him around in his trap. Florence was only three when her father died, aged thirty-two. She can't quite remember him, but she can still see the horse he drove.

Her parents had eight children, four of whom died in infancy. Florence was the youngest of the four remaining and had two sisters and a brother. As a young widow, her mother was left with very little money and had a great struggle to bring them up. She went out ironing or took in washing to make ends meet. Florence can't remember bare feet, but her shoes were often made out of old pairs cut up, then bits nailed on or stuck together.

They lived mainly on suet puddings, which their mother boiled in a cloth tied up with string. 'One day, when she had to go out all day, doing someone's washing and ironing, she left me and my sister Daisy to buy some apples for the suet pudding. When she got home late, she said, "Where's the apples?" And we'd forgotten to get them. She picked up the suet dough and threw it at the wall! We all had to scrabble around and scrape it off. Then she tied it up in a rag and cooked it, putting a dob of jam inside instead of apples. Oh, we had to eat it. We were starving. We'd been looking forward to that suet pudding all that day, waiting for mum to come home.'

Florence laughed and laughed at this story – as did her daughter Betty, though Betty had presumably heard it umpteen times. Was that typical of your mother, to throw things around?

'Oh, no. She'd just had a hard day. She was exhausted, probably had a bad headache, which she often had. We were little terrors as girls. I remember one Christmas, my mum fell asleep after our Christmas lunch with her mouth open – and me and Daisy threw nuts in it! Oh, we got it for that. Daisy was a caution. She'd often go out and come back dressed as an old woman, in granny clothes, knocking at our front door, and putting on a creaky voice. We always knew it was her, of course.'

Florence went to Chase Road Infants' and then a girls' school in Waterfall Lane until she was fourteen. 'It was very strict. On the day I left, the headmistress said to us, "This is the worst day of your life, girls." I thought, no, it ain't, this is the best day of my life. I couldn't wait to leave school.'

She got a job at ten shillings a week as a nursemaid, looking after two children, but didn't like it. She started looking in the newspapers for other jobs and saw one advertised at Kemp's biscuit factory in York Way, near King's Cross. 'I said to my friend, "Let's both go." She said, "It's factory work, I don't want no factory work." I said, "No, we'll try for the office" – and we did, getting jobs as clerks doing invoices.

'It was while I was working there, when I was about sixteen, I first met my husband, Leslie. He was an apprentice fitter in a factory nearby. Me and the other girls used to walk around in our lunch-hour and talk to some boys. That's how we met him and his mates. My friend got a boy but she didn't carry on with him, so it ended up with just me and him, walking around at lunch-time. In fact, we spent most of our courting time walking. He lived in Tufnell Park, which was about ten miles away, so we were always walking. We couldn't afford the pictures or even the buses. We'd just walk and walk till we found a park and then sit on a seat together. Then we'd walk back.'

Leslie was a year younger than Florence, too young to serve in the First World War, but one of her cousins went off. 'He liked to show off in his posh uniform. He joined the Middlesex Regiment. Their best uniform was red and very splendid and he thought he was one hell of a feller. I think his uncle had got him into it. He was already in the army. You got the King's shilling, if you got someone else to join. Anyway, he never came back, this cousin. Missing presumed dead. I did ask his friend, who joined with him, and he said he was blown to pieces.

'I remember the Zeppelins over our house. We could see them clearly from the windows. Mum used to tell us to stand against the wall in the hall when they started dropping bombs. A fat lot of good that would have done us!

'One of them Zeppelins got shot down not far away, at Cuffley. It seemed just up the road from us, but was probably a mile or so away. We saw it on fire, men falling out of it, and we all ran to see what would happen. There were men in the street shouting and swearing, "Die, you bastards." Not very nice language, was it? I think there were nine Germans in the Zeppelin, and they all died. I did see it on the ground, yes, I saw it, still in flames, or what was left of it.'

'Mother has always had a morbid fascination for accidents,' said her daughter Betty. 'That, and a good funeral.'

After a few years at the biscuit factory, Florence secured a better job in a small printing works, Shaw's, in Fetter Lane. 'Again I saw it advertised.

Oh, I was always on the look-out for better-paid jobs. This was twenty-five shillings a week and they wanted typing. My mum said, "You can't do no typing," and I said, "Why not?" Anyway I applied and got the job. I never got the sack, so I must have done it OK, in my fashion. It was simple typing, really, only a few lines at a time. My job was to address letters and envelopes for invoices.'

Florence and Leslie spent eight years courting before they got married because they had so little money. Leslie had been paid off when he finished his apprenticeship, and was out of work for some time until in 1919 he joined the Royal Engineers as a regular soldier. It was the only way he could secure an income. 'He served in Ireland, fighting with the Irish, keeping them down, I suppose. I dunno, I didn't ask. In Donegal. Is that in Ireland? And then he was in Germany.'

They got married on 3 October 1924, at Islington Register Office. They couldn't afford a proper wedding, or any photographs, or a honeymoon, but Leslie had been given married quarters at Aldershot where he was stationed. Florence became pregnant almost immediately, and their first child, Joan, was born in 1925. Soon after, they moved back to London and lived in rooms in Leslie's mother's house, in Warrenders Road, Tufnell Park. Betty, their second daughter, was born in 1926, at the Royal Northern Hospital in Holloway Road. Then came Alan, in 1928. 'I remember the nurse saying, "You've got a son, Mrs Parsons, to go with your two girls." I said, "Oh, who says I want a son? Boys are just trouble, if you ask me."'

Leslie left the army in 1931 and got a job with a factory near King's Cross, as a fitter and later as a lorry-driver. During the Second World War, he was allocated war work at the De Havilland aircraft factory at Witney, Oxfordshire, where he lived during the week, coming home most weekends. Florence became a fire-fighter. 'Not that I was much good at it, but you had to do something, sign on for some war work. A list came round and you were given things you could do. My husband was all right, he was out of the bombing at Witney, wasn't he? Leaving me in the danger zone in London, trying to fight fires.

'We were given a bit of training, told we had to break windows and get into bombed-out houses and carry people out over our shoulder. I thought, you've got some hopes, there, chum. When the sirens went we all had to rush like billy-oh to this tent place, then we'd go round where the bombs had landed and put out incendiary fires. That was the idea. I don't think I ever put any fires out.

'One weekend, when my husband was home, the siren went so I rushed out leaving him in bed. Ten minutes later, I was back – because I'd forgotten to put my teeth in. He says to me, "Florrie, what you need your teeth for, gel? The Jerries are dropping bombs, not pork pies . . ."'

Florence and Betty laughed so much at this that they had to put their hands over their mouths.

She had had all her teeth taken out just before the war, in her late thirties, which was common practice at the time among people with dental problems and little money. 'Not that I had no dental trouble, mind you. It was me legs. That's all I'd been complaining about, pains in me legs. Then, blow me, he says, "The best thing is have your teeth out" – so I ends up with none of me teeth. But the pains did stop, oh, yes. He was right. Pyorrhoea. I think that's what it's called.'

Betty, then aged about fifteen, remembers many nights spent in their Anderson shelter at the height of the London blitz. 'Then sometimes we wouldn't go down. My sister and I would decide to stay in our beds, which was on the top floor – very silly, I know. Even if we did spend the night in the shelter, which was at the bottom of the garden, we'd creep into the house, looking for something to eat. When the London docks were being attacked, that was the most dramatic. The whole sky would be red. A lot of people, when the sirens went, ran to the Tube at Tufnell Park, and spent the night there. Mum and I didn't. I think that was for people who were really scared. It was horrible down there. We refused to go. In the morning, after the all-clear, we'd go round the streets and pick up any bits of shrapnel as souvenirs.'

'Oh, there was a great spirit during the war,' said Florence. 'Neighbours really did help each other.'

Betty was the only one of her three children to pass the 11-plus and she went to Camden School for Girls, which proved expensive, not in fees but in getting the right summer and winter uniform. 'She had to have a shantung dress in summer, I remember that,' said Florence. 'And her own hockey-stick. Gawd, that was expensive, yet she hardly ever used it. It was always raining on her hockey days.'

'It was a very strict school,' said Betty. 'No eating sweets in the street, that sort of thing. Always wear your hat.'

Traditionally, Camden School had a strong middle-class intellectual base, attracting socialists from the Hampstead area, so I asked Betty if there were any girls from well-known families?

'Only Blossom Brown.' Excuse me? 'She was the daughter of Teddy Brown. Oh, he was very well-known as a xylophonist. He toured all the music halls. His daughter Blossom was in my class.'

Betty went on to work as a secretary in a solicitor's office, married a chartered surveyor, had three children and lived in Sevenoaks in Kent. Her two sons got scholarships to the local public school and went on to university, one to Cambridge, the other to Reading. Florence's other daughter Joan married, had four children and still lives in North London. Alan worked at the offices of the *Daily Mail* and is now retired. Altogether, Florence's three children produced nine grand-children, and she now has nineteen great-grandchildren.

Leslie retired aged sixty-five. One of the things he and Florence did in his retirement was to go to the opera, an interest he had acquired while serving with the army in Germany. He rarely had the money to indulge himself, but sometimes he and Florence would get cheap seats in the gods.

'I didn't really like it, all that screeching, and people dying all over the place, too bloomin' sad for me. But I went with him now and again, just to please him. I'd lean over and watch all the fine ladies arrive in their posh dresses and I'd say, "Oh dear, I think the Duchess of Pimlico has arrived." After Leslie died, I never went again. I prefer Jim Reeves.' She also gave up voting Labour. 'I only did it to please him. When he'd gone, I changed to Tory. I just thought they was better. That's all. I liked Mrs Thatcher.'

Leslie died in 1979, after a heart attack, and Betty's husband Eric died the following year. Florence lived alone in a rented flat in North London, on a Peabody estate, until a couple of years ago. She managed very well, doing her own cooking and shopping, until she started to fall. 'I kept on getting these social services people coming to see me. I didn't want them fussing around, did I? Treating me as if I was barmy.'

'They were only trying to help you, Mother,' said Betty.

'They'd ask me the date, who the Prime Minister was, who the Queen was, as if I was batty.'

'She could have stayed in her flat,' said Betty. 'But Joan and I explained that because of her falls, she'd have to have someone doing her shopping, her cooking – even lighting her own gas cooker as she could be a danger to herself. So she eventually agreed to come here.'

Florence now lives with Betty in Sevenoaks, a small detached house, rather in need of some modernisation, but in a quiet road.

'I didn't want to move,' said Florence. 'I still can't understand why I can't go out and get on buses like I used to.'

'She won't accept she falls. The other day, she'd gone out into the garden. I looked out and she was sitting on the grass. Oh, I thought, that's nice, till I realised she'd fallen and couldn't get up.'

'I can walk,' said Florence, 'if someone holds me arm, but I don't like that. So, you see, I don't go out much now. And I don't like it, not being independent, but I have to lump it. I keep saying I'm going back to my flat, but I know I'm not. What can you do? That's how life goes.'

All the same, she seemed in reasonable shape for ninety-seven: her hearing was still good and her sight only a bit blurred. How did she explain living so long? 'Plenty of suet pudding! No, I mean it. I've always eaten well, and still do eat well. I know suet pudding is supposed to be all wrong for you, but it didn't do me no harm.

'I never drank, except a glass of ruby wine at Christmas. I did smoke – but only other people's cigarettes. When people asked me if I smoked, I said, "Yes, and I'll have one of yours!" So I only ever smoked free ones. I gave that up about twenty years ago.'

Florence today

It then emerged that her older sister Daisy was still alive, aged 103, and in a home, while her mother had lived until she was ninety. So despite her father's early death, there are some long-living genes in Florence's family. Would she like to make 103?

'Hope not,' she said. 'I don't want to end up trouble, being a burden to Betty, do I? With her having to look after me.'

She's been lucky in her health, apart from having her teeth out. Between the births of her babies and some heart trouble at eighty-nine, she had not been to a hospital for over sixty years.

She has been in an aeroplane once and that was at the age of eighty-six when she went abroad for the first time, flying with Betty to Switzerland for the wedding of Richard, one of Betty's sons.

'She kept on looking out of the window,' said Betty, 'staring at the blue sky, saying, "It's not moving, it's not moving." I said, "We'd still be on the ground, Mother, if we weren't moving."'

'Oh, I did like it,' said Florence. 'It was lovely.'

Wouldn't you like to have travelled more in your life?

'Not really. I haven't missed it. Because I knew I never could go abroad, it didn't come into my mind, so I never fancied it. Ballooning, I wouldn't mind a go at ballooning. That looks good fun.'

'Oh, she's not frightened of anything,' said Betty. 'Given the chance, she would step into a balloon now. I wouldn't dare to.'

Life, on the whole, still gives her a laugh, despite her lack of independence. When she switches on the television, she usually finds something to amuse her. No, not comedy programmes. Politicians, usually.

'That Kenneth Clarke, he does make me smile. He's one alone, isn't he? He just don't care, does he, with his tie hanging out, his shoes all scuffed up. I have to laugh the minute I see him. And the Queen Mother, she cheers me up. She was using two sticks the other day, which is more than me, so I'm beating her, ain't I?

'Yes, I've enjoyed it, on the whole. I'd have it over again. Why not? The only thing is, if I came back again, I'd like more money next time. But that's about all . . .'

14

ALBERT CHARLTON

Miner and Newcastle United's oldest supporter

Albert Charlton (centre), at his wedding in 1927

Albert Charlton jumped up the moment I entered the front room of his neat, bright bungalow in Morpeth, Northumberland. He gave a big toothy smile, insisted on shaking hands, then showed me to a comfortable seat. His daughter Gwen wheeled in a trolley with tea and cakes, then handed me a copy of the *Newcastle Journal*, which said that her father, at ninety-six, was Newcastle United's oldest season-ticket holder. The next oldest, according to the paper, is a mere youngster of ninety-one. I could see that he was pretty fit, after all his bounding up, but I know it also takes good lungs and knees to climb up to any seat in the stands these days. 'Aye, but it's no bother,' he said. His seat is in the East Stand, quite a few steps up, but he gets there unaided. Most impressive, considering the hard physical life he's led.

A name like Albert Charlton suggests his family has been around here for some time. But was he related to the famous footballing Charltons? 'No, don't think so. I did know Mrs Charlton, Bobby and Jack's mam, when we lived in Beatrice Street, Ashington. And I have met Jack. Aye, he's a nice chap. But no, we're not related. Except far back, maybes. In the old days all the Charltons were sheep-stealers . . .'

Thomas Albert Charlton was born on 3 June 1900, in the pit village of Ryton-on-Tyne, near Wylam, where George Stephenson, father of railways, was born. He was the youngest of seven, three boys and four girls, and their father was a miner who later became an insurance sales-man. He was spoiled, being the youngest, but that didn't stop one of his brothers trying to do him a bit of damage. 'I was aged about two or three when my brother Joe – Joseph Llewellyn was his full name – asked me to put me hand on a tree trunk. Like this, he said, flat out. So I did. Joe then picked up an axe and tried to chop off me fingers . . .' Big laugh, broad smile, as Albert held up his hand to let me see. Right enough, I could see one finger missing. 'No, not that one. I lost that finger later. This finger here. Look, a bit of the side is still missing. That's the one Joe tried to chop off.'

Albert attended the colliery school, Emma Vale it was called, named after the colliery, and left at fourteen to become an apprentice caddy at Ryton golf course. Sounds a desirable job, healthy and open air, for a miner's son.

'Oh, it was, and the professional was a very nice feller, Mr Ferney. But I'd only been there a few months when in August 1914 the war broke out. Then I had to go into the pit. I remember standing on the pit heap at Emma Vale Colliery watching the Germans shell Hartlepool.'

You say you had to go down the pit. Who forced you? Your father, the village, the government?

Albert stopped in his flow. 'I really divvent know. That's all I can remember, being told to go down the pit. I never asked questions.' Perhaps it was considered war work. Or perhaps the golf course staff had gone off to the war so you had to get another job. Albert looked perplexed. I wished I hadn't asked. One of the things about talking to 96-year-olds, even those as spry as Albert, is not to cross-examine too much. It doesn't just slow them down, it stops them in their tracks, derails them from their memories.

Albert's first job, down the pit, was coupling tubs together. He explained how it worked, how the tubs ran along underground to the coal seams. I asked how much he got, thinking it was an easy question.

Most people can remember their first wage, and are proud to tell you, even if they can't remember later increases.

'I don't know. Me father drew all me pay.'

Being the youngest son, Albert watched as his older brothers went off to war. The eldest was William John, known as Jack, who joined the army and found himself in the Enniskillen Guards. 'They sent him first to Ireland to fight against that feller, what's his name? Didn't really sound Irish. De Valera, that's the one. Then he was sent to France in the Machine Gun Corps. He was killed in France. His wife gave birth to a son while Jack was in France. So he never saw his own son.

'Joe was in the navy. He was a stoker in the *Dreadnought*, the one that split in two and sank, but Joe survived.'

Meanwhile, Albert was down the pit. He graduated to working at the coal face and was called a putter and then a hewer, which meant putting up pit props and then hewing away at the coal seams. In putting up the pit props he suffered his first injury. A pile of logs collapsed and he broke a leg. In a later accident a large chock, which was wedging up the roof, gave way and brought down some enormous stones. They fell straight on to Albert's hand. This was the accident that claimed his finger. 'I was looking the other way, waiting for my marrer [mate] to hand me another chock to put in its place, when it all fell down.'

He showed me his missing finger again, pointing out that there was still a little bit of bone left in place. 'When they operated, they should have taken it right back to the knuckle, but it was the compensation, see. You got paid per joint. If they had taken the whole finger away, right up to that knuckle, I would have got three hundred pound. As it was, I only got a hundred.'

Throughout his mining life, Albert seemed to be constantly involved in accidents. 'Oh, aye. I had a season ticket to the pit infirmary, just as today I have a season ticket to St James's. That's my joke.' Could any of the accidents possibly have been clumsiness? He didn't think so. Just bad luck.

In the General Strike of 1926, all the miners in his pit, as elsewhere, were locked out for six weeks and received no wages. Albert believed the strike was justified. 'We did have some traitors at Emma pit, oh aye, we knew who they were. They'd go straight from the pit to the Buffalo, that was the village social club. You'd see them telling the bosses what had happened at the union meeting.' Why did they do this? 'For a free pint. Some people will do anything for a free pint. Oh, we knew who they were, like, but it was a disgrace. It meant the bosses knew everything that was gannan on.'

When the strike started, Albert and three of his mates, who all worked in the same set, had made an agreement between themselves that if one of them didn't get his job back after the strike was over, none of them would return. Albert and two of his mates were offered their jobs back, but one was not. So Albert and one of them decided to leave. They went to Ashington pit, some twenty-seven miles away, where they both eventually got a job.

By this time Albert was seriously courting a local girl from Greenside near Ryton called Ruth Keenan, and seeing her was a bit awkward once he moved to the new job. They'd met at the same Bible class at Crawcrook Primitive Methodist Church, had courted for seven years and then been engaged for three. Not untypical of the times, to have a long engagement, but Albert says they had the extra problem of his mother. She was an invalid, suffering from asthma, and he was the one who stayed at home till she died.

As the recession began, Albert was often working only part-time, never officially laid off or unemployed, but often without work, and pay, for two or three days a week. The sign for a non-working day was the colliery buzzer blowing loudly in the evening, indicating the pit would be closed next day.

One Wednesday evening just after Albert had moved to Ashington and was living in digs, it blew very loudly. He decided to make the most of the Thursday off, so he put on his best clothes and cycled to Ryton to see Ruth. He stayed the night there and was preparing to spend Friday with her too, when Ruth's mother asked if he was sure his pit was closed on Friday as well as Thursday. He had to admit he'd only guessed that it might be and Ruth's mother told him he'd better go back first thing on Friday morning, just in case.

'As I was getting into Ashington, I met my marrer Bill. He said, "It's working today, man, hurry yourself up." I was in me good suit, of course. I didn't have time to go and change into my old clothes or I'd miss the shift. There was no uniform in the pit, apart from a helmet. You just wore your oldest clothes.

'Bill had two shirts on, a sort of top shirt and undershirt. We often wore them, if the seam was a long way in. You'd get cold and damp walking to it, then take off one shirt when you started working. So I took off my good suit and put on one of Bill's shirts. But that wasn't enough, was it? Then Bill had an idea. He took off his trousers and gave me his underpants. So I went to work that day in his old shirt and his underpants! What a sight I must have looked. But I did the whole shift, and I got paid. I had no bait, of course, but I managed to get a tin bottle of water from someone at the top of the pit.'

This is obviously one of Albert's favourite memories. He could even put a date to it, working out that it must have been 1927. He told it all with relish and a lot of hand gestures. It was a story his daughter Gwen must have heard quite a few times, but she smiled all the way through.

She said she could clearly remember her father going off to work at the pit, leaving at the same time, repeating the same litany. 'He'd always say, "Bait, bottle, candle-box, tabs, midgie," then check all his pockets. Bait meant his sandwiches. His bottle of water was to drink, as mining is very thirsty work. Candle-box held his candles. Midgie was short for midget, meaning a small lamp, which miners stuck on their helmet. Tabs were, of course, cigarettes . . .'

Gwen paused. It had suddenly struck her as a strange thing for her father to have said as he has never smoked. Albert also looked puzzled for a moment, then smiled. 'I must have picked those words up from other miners. From me dad, probably. It was what all miners said in them days, going off to the pit.'

Albert married Ruth on 20 August 1927, at Crawcrook Primitive Methodist Church in Ryton, but he nearly didn't make it. The day before the wedding he was injured in the pit once again. It turned out not too serious, though when he went to pick up Ruth from work on the cash desk at Bainbridge's, the department store, he arrived with his head all bandaged. 'I'm not surprised,' was Ruth's first comment.

It wasn't a white wedding, as they couldn't afford it: they had only twenty pounds in savings between them. She wore beige, as far as Albert recalls. Any honeymoon, or did the money not stretch that far?

'Ooh, we had a grand honeymoon. One week at Robin Hood Farm, Bassenthwaite, over in the Lake District.'

Albert got up to find his wedding photograph and also a snap from the honeymoon. In the wedding photo, his brother Joe is best man. He was the one who could well have been an axe murderer. In the photo he does look rather grim and fierce.

After the wedding, Ruth went back to her parents' house and lived there for several months, while Albert went back to his work, and his digs, in Ashington. They eventually found somewhere to live together and moved into a flat in Beatrice Street, Ashington. Gwen, their only child, was born in 1929. 'One was quite plenty,' says Albert.

They saved hard, and when Gwen was about three they bought a terrace house in Ashington for £350. Ruth's parents also moved in with them and stayed till they died. 'It took twenty years to pay the house off. I'd forgotten about it, really, till one day the Blyth Building Society sent us papers to say we owned our own house.'

In 1937, when Gwen was seven, they went to London for the Coronation, along with Ruth's father. Albert was off sick at the time, recovering from another injury, so they thought they'd take advantage of it, though he still had to get permission from the colliery to leave Ashington and visit London.

'Ruth's brother was an accountant in London. Oh, he had a very good job, it was in a Jewish firm, with offices in Piccadilly. We slept in his office, all of us, overnight, and next day we had a grand view of the Coronation procession. We all hung out of the windows and saw the King and Queen in their open carriage.

'I'll tell you one funny thing about that trip to London. We were walking down Whitehall, me and the wife, and approaching was this man and I said to my wife, "Eeh, that looks the spitting image of Mr Dando." Mr Dando was the minister of the church we'd gone to when we lived in Ryton and he married us. He came across to us and said, "I *am* Mr Dando!"'

Gwen became a nurse and midwife and worked for some years in Australia. She eventually returned to the north-east of England and became a health visitor.

In 1964, Albert retired from the pit after fifty years as a miner. He had been thinking of staying on another year, until he was sixty-five, but a chance conversation with his area manager made him change his mind. 'He was called Isaac and I knew him well because he was in our church. He was giving me a lift home from church one day and I happened to say I could now retire with a pension, so I'd been told. I asked Isaac what he thought and he said, "Take it. If it was me, I'd jump at the chance." He was a younger man than me, and a manager, so it made me think, What's stopping me? So when I got home, I opened the front door and says to the wife, "I'm retiring." She jumped up and down and shouted, "Hallelujah!"'

Albert's passion for Newcastle United began when he was fourteen. His father wasn't a fan, though an uncle was, so he usually went with other young miners from his village, often walking all the way to Newcastle, a distance of some eight miles. 'When we reached the Scotswood bridge, then we'd get a tram to the ground.'

He has been to Wembley for three Cup Finals, but not very recently, as Newcastle's Cup performances have not been as good as they once were. 'I remember the Man City final when an ex-Sunderland feller scored a goal against us. Now what was his name? And, of course, I remember the final where Jackie Milburn scored with a header. That was unusual for him.'

His favourite players have been Hughie Gallacher and Jackie Milburn. 'There was also a centre-forward called White, and a full-back called Mitchell, I liked them. But, really, I liked them all. Oh, they've all been good players.'

His wife, he says, never objected to him going to football. She would travel in from Ashington with him and go shopping in the afternoon. They would meet up afterwards and go to a show in the evening. Albert never drank or smoked, so he wasn't one of those supporters who crowded the pubs before and after a match. Nor has he ever worn a scarf – though he has several Newcastle scarves, given to him as presents. 'When I first started going at fourteen, an uncle said, "Never show your favours. If you wear a scarf, you just draw attention to yourself." So I never have. And I've always kept out of any trouble.'

'My wife did once say she'd like to go to a match. So this Saturday she came with me, but the queues were absolutely enormous. It so happened they were giving out Cup Final vouchers. If you got the right one, you went into the draw to get a Cup Final ticket. Anyway, I didn't get one – but she did. She said she didn't want to go to another match, because of all the queuing. So I took her ticket. That was lucky, wasn't it?'

Until the age of eighty, Albert always stood in the Leazes End, swaying and being jostled by the crowds, but he was eventually persuaded to get a season ticket and therefore have a seat. He has renewed this ticket every season: seat 0052, Row B, in the East Stand. In the 1996–97 season it cost him £389. A bargain, as season tickets go. His season ticket is very desirable, and there is a long waiting list at Newcastle. He never misses a home game, even at ninety-six. These days, he is driven to the ground by two friends, both younger chaps, he says. One is only seventy-six.

'I was in a local shop not long ago with my father,' said Gwen. 'I was paying for whatever I was buying, and I heard him telling the assistant that his new season ticket had just arrived. There he was, showing it to this woman in the shop. She asked him how old he was and was amazed he was ninety-five. She then told her son, who turned out to be a reporter on the *Journal* – so that's how it first came out. Later on, with another man, aged ninety-one, he was taken to St James's Park and they took lovely photographs of them.'

Albert likes the standard of football today but doesn't think the modern footballer could kick the old leather balls. 'They're just like balloons today.' He thinks standing areas should have been kept, with cheap admission, to let ordinary young men see the game. 'That Judge Taylor needs hammering, making them have all these expensive all-

Newcastle United's oldest supporter at St James's Park

seater places. How can a young chap afford to go? If you go to a match today, then take your wife out to the pictures or a show in the evening, as I used to do, you'd need about a hundred pounds. Ridiculous. Aye, that Sir John Hall has done a good job, two good jobs, the Metro Centre and Newcastle United, but now, well, he wants to rule everything, if you ask me.'

Albert's wife Ruth died in 1986, aged eighty-three, after a stroke. He has lived ever since with Gwen in her bungalow in Morpeth. Gwen is unmarried and now retired. She doesn't feel she's in the classic situation – only daughter, obliged to look after elderly parents, ends up trapped: 'Not at all. Don't forget I did leave home at eighteen to work in Australia and other places and was away for many years. I have seen the world, and seen life. So, no, I don't mind looking after my father.

'We get on very well. He's so cheerful and very popular. Everyone loves him. Until a few years ago, he was Father Christmas every year at T. & G. Allan's in Morpeth. He only gave up because they moved the lavatory from the floor he worked on. Old men do need to be near the lavatory. For many years he also helped out at the local primary school, setting up the tables for school dinners. He's been over thirty years retired, but during that time he's always been active.

'He's still in various luncheon clubs, such as Age Concern. He goes to church every week, oh, he goes quite a few places, apart from his football. He's never bored. I took him the other day to the Metro Centre. He does love watching people. For the first time ever, I got him to sit in a wheelchair. He wasn't keen at first, but he enjoyed having a good look round and I didn't have to worry about him.'

'Aye, she bosses me around and nags me these days,' says Albert. 'Getting her own back, I suppose, for when I bossed her around as a little girl.'

When Gwen is away on holiday he goes into a Methodist Home for the Aged. 'She puts me in kennels,' said Albert. He himself doesn't travel much further now than Newcastle, but he went to Australia when he was eighty-eight, and to Canada to see relations. He is the last surviving of his seven brothers and sisters. 'My sister Louie died at ninety-nine, but she died happy. She thought she was a hundred.' Albert hopes to make a hundred. 'I'll have a big party for all my nephews and nieces and friends.'

He was going to vote Labour at the coming election. 'In the old days, all the miners voted Liberal, as my father did, but I've always been Labour. But it depends on the character of the candidate. One year I didn't vote at all because this chap's character wasn't too good. No, I'm not going to say his name, but I remember him, oh, aye. I quite like Tony Blair, he seems decent, but he gets my back up at times.'

How?

Albert thought for a while and decided it was Blair's voice. Too posh? He grunted, but refused to add anything further. Gwen said her father's political hero in recent years had been Lord Tonypandy, the former Speaker of the House of Commons. 'Oh, aye, he had a lovely voice.' He was also a Methodist, which helped. Among his most hated people has been Arthur Scargill, whom he thinks did untold damage to the miners.

He still reads the *Journal* every day, without using specs, and always has a book on the go, though that's now a large-print book. Beside his chair was a mystery adventure by Gwen Moffat. He loves football on TV, sometimes too much so, according to Gwen. 'I've had to get a new carpet because of him. He'd worn a hole in it. Look, just there, in front of him. In fact, it's happening again. He will bang his feet on the carpet when he gets excited. He also tries to lean forward, thinking he'll see more, that he can get round the side of the TV screen and see if the goal really went in . . .' Albert laughed at this, but agreed it was true.

Since he gave up work, he has had some of the healthiest and most active years of his life. 'Aye, that was a funny thing. Since I retired I've never felt better. I used to get terrible bronchitis at the end of my time down the pit, with all the cold and damp. It went to my chest, you see. Once I finished, it all cleared up.'

His only problem was discovering at the age of eighty that he had diabetes. He copes with that well, still eating sweets but rationing them. 'When I go out, I'll eat anything, whether it's spaghetti Bolognese, Indian or Chinese.

'I think the real secret is talking to people. That's what keeps you alive. Oh, and another thing. I've always bathed my chest with cold water all my life, winter and summer. I just dab my chest with a cold facecloth, first thing in the morning. And my eyes. Oh, and I always keep my eyes open when bathing them. My uncle taught me that. I think it's helped my hearing as well.'

Albert today

He does wear a hearing-aid in one ear and has no hearing in the other – a result of his mining years, caused by dripping water. He says the hearing-aid is always falling out, which annoys him. 'I've got a lot of hair in this ear, you see. It grows there, not on my head, and from time to time it makes the hearing-aid pop out.'

His working life has been physically hard, but he thinks it was hard in other ways too. 'We often had to fight hard, argue hard, just to get our wages. We used to be paid in sets at one time, a group of, say, twelve miners would be paid a certain sum by the management for shifting a certain amount of coal, then we'd be left to divide it up. Well, you can imagine the arguments and problems, with fellers having done different shifts, different jobs. That all stopped when they gave us individual cheques. Much better.

'But, on the whole, I'd say I've enjoyed life. It's been hard at times, but I've usually found something to laugh at.'

'The other day,' said Gwen, 'we got a call from Newcastle United. Someone asked for Albert Charlton, but I answered it. It was about this bond they were trying to sell, five hundred pounds a time. I asked what the advantages were and they said, "Oh, it guarantees you'll get your season ticket for the next ten years, till 2006." I said, "My father happens to be ninety-six. I don't think that'll be a very big advantage." The voice at the other end went silent, then he hung up . . .'

Albert had a good laugh at that.

15

WEST HAM UNITED

The club badge

The history of football in the twentieth century shows enormous changes, most of them reflecting the equally enormous social, economic, national, racial, cultural and commercial changes of the century. Looking back to 1900, the year West Ham was born, screwing up the eyes and gazing through the bottom of a glass darkly, with or without a meat pie by the side, we can see the same eleven players, kicking a ball in much the same way, with much the same objective, but everything that surrounds them and their lives has been transformed.

Newcastle United, which become professional in 1889, was going strong in 1900, so Albert Charlton was following a long line of fans when he started to support them. So were many other northern clubs, still household names today.

No one knows where and when football began. The Chinese were supposed to be playing some sort of ball game in 300 BC. Roman soldiers were at it a few centuries later. In Britain, there are written references throughout the Middle Ages. In 1314 Edward II attempted to ban it, considering it violent and dangerous. Mary Queen of Scots, while held in Carlisle Castle in 1568, watched a game of football being played in the castle grounds. Possibly the first captive audience?

Shakespeare mentions it in *A Comedy of Errors*. 'Am I so round with you as you with me / That like a football you do spurn me thus?'

The public schools and the universities took up football in the early nineteenth century, seeing it as a healthy activity for muscular Christians. In 1848, some chaps at Cambridge University refined the rules of the game as it was then played, probably fairly violently, by the working classes.

The Football Association was founded in England in 1863 for the express purpose of codifying the rules, and the world's first international, between England and Scotland, took place in 1872. In 1885, professionalism was legalised and in 1888, the Football League was formed with twelve clubs: Accrington, Aston Villa, Blackburn Rovers, Bolton Wanderers, Burnley, Derby County, Everton, Notts County, Preston North, Stoke, West Bromwich Albion and Wolverhampton Wanderers. All were from the North or Midlands.

Football was well established in Britain by the end of the century, and had been exported by British sailors, soldiers and engineers to Denmark, Austria and Brazil, leading to the foundation in 1904 of a world body for football: FIFA. England declined to join. Typical, some might say. The English felt somehow superior, above all that. It was their game, which they had invented, and they certainly didn't want to play it with a lot of foreigners. Fortunately, the rules of football, as created in Britain, were adopted by the rest of the world. 'Goal' and 'penalty' went into almost every language, just to make it easier for England to know what was going on, if they ever joined, but still they wouldn't. They knew best. They felt they played the best.

In 1893 the Cup Final was held at the Crystal Palace, so it was acknowledged that London should be at the heart of English football, though there was no London team in the final that year – Aston Villa beat West Bromwich Albion before a crowd of 42,560 – or for several years to come. Tottenham Hotspur, Fulham, Brentford and Millwall had all become professional in the 1880s, followed by Arsenal in 1891, but West Ham was still not in existence. (Chelsea and Crystal Palace came even later, in 1905.)

West Ham began as the works team of Thames Ironworks, a shipyard on the bank of the Thames, down-river from London, which specialised in building iron ships. Arnold Hills, the owner, had been educated at

Harrow and Oxford, and had played football for England against Scotland in 1879. He was very keen on the health of his workers, and in 1895 he built a sports complex that cost £20,000, with a cycle track and a football pitch. That first season, on their new pitch, the Thames Ironworks team managed to play some evening matches under floodlight – by stringing electric lightbulbs from poles and dipping the ball in whitewash to make it more visible. It was noted that when the Ironworks were about to shoot, the lights seemed somehow to dim, making it much harder for the opposing goalkeeper.

In 1898, they were promoted to the Southern League, but a bit of fiddling had been going on, unbeknown to Mr Hills, and they were fined twenty-five pounds by the FA. Their crime had been to hire an agent to tempt away players from the Football League. Interesting to realise that money, agents and inducements have been with us so long.

Once Ironworks were in the Southern League, they ceased to be a purely works team. They were employing semi-professionals and soon looking for a much better ground. Arnold Hills realised that he could no longer finance them from his own pocket. On 5 July 1900 a new company was formed called West Ham Football Club, named after the local borough, with a capital of £2,000, to be raised by selling 4,000 ten-shilling shares. The team's colours, from its beginnings as Thames Ironworks, had been claret and blue, the house colours of the shipyard. The crossed hammers on the club's badge also came from the shipyard, representing riveting hammers and not from the name West Ham, which is what many modern fans wrongly imagine. In the early decades of the century, supporters still shouted, 'Come on, you irons.'

In 1904 they moved to the Boleyn Ground, Upton Park, where the railway connections were better. The name Boleyn came from a local castle where Anne Boleyn's family is supposed to have lived. Until 1902, they had virtually been run by the Hills, but that year they acquired an excellent manager, Syd King. They were still in the Southern League, but always managed a good FA Cup run. In 1905 they lost to Woolwich Arsenal, and in 1907 they reached the third round, drawn at home against the mighty Newcastle United. Newcastle offered them £1,000 in cash to play the match at St James's Park, but West Ham refused. They drew 0–0 at home – but lost the replay. In 1913, still in the Southern League, they lost at home to Aston Villa in the second round. Their gate receipts were £2,000, a huge sum for the time.

Professional players in the Football League earned on average about three pounds a week, which was better than the average working man but not all that much – a situation that continued for the next fifty years. That is one of the mysteries to me of pre-war and post-war football in Britain: clubs attracted huge audiences, took in enormous amounts in cash, yet always paid their players so little. Where did all the money go?

A lot went in underhand payments, or tempting players away from other clubs, though of course the official transfer fees were all above board, and soon began to rise. In 1913, Blackburn Rovers paid £2,000 for West Ham's star player, Danny Shea.

Their next star player was Syd Puddefoot, who had been signed as a professional by King when he was only a schoolboy of sixteen. In 1913, they beat Chesterfield in the first round of the cup, 8–1, with Puddefoot scoring five goals. In the next round, they beat Crystal Palace. Then they played Liverpool at Anfield, where they drew 1–1 before a crowd of 45,000, despite being a Southern League team. Puddefoot scored the vital goal. In the replay they got thumped 5–0.

During the First World War, most players, like young men everywhere, joined up. The normal League fixtures were suspended, to reduce travelling, but there was a Khaki Cup Final in 1915, between Chelsea and Sheffield United. In London, there was a Combination League, formed from Southern League and Football League clubs, which West Ham joined. This provided matches for troops on leave from the trenches. Football was even played in the trenches, as we know from that famous incident when British and German troops played football together on Christmas Eve, then went back to killing each other.

After the war, West Ham managed at last to get itself into the Football League, joining the second division. They were in such a hurry to sign that they broke Southern League rules and were fined £500. In 1921, they finished fourth in the second division, but it was their exploits in the FA Cup which always seemed to bring them most glory. In 1923 they beat Derby in the semi-final at Derby, before a crowd of 50,709.

For many reasons the FA Cup Final of 1923 made history, not just for West Ham fans but for most people in England. It was played for the first time ever at Wembley, in a magnificent new concrete stadium, built at a cost of £750,000 as the focal point of the 1924–25 British Empire Exhibition. In the match programme, Wembley was described as 'the Greatest Arena in the world, the largest, the most comfortable, the best equipped . . . In area, it equals the Biblical City of Jericho.' Quite a boast. It was also the so-called White Horse Cup Final. Wembley had been built to accommodate 127,000, but about twice as many turned up. Many managed somehow to get in, which meant that there were around 200,000 in the ground at one time. In trying to save themselves from being crushed or suffocated, people spilled on to the pitch, where there was soon chaos until PC Storey, on his white horse Belle, restored some order, saving hundreds from being trampled to death. The scenes were captured on film – more history. Then, as now, there had been a lot of jostling beforehand for the right to film the event. Pathé News didn't win it but they sneaked in a cameraman disguised as a West Ham supporter. He was carrying a large cardboard hammer, under which he held his camera.

It was a North versus South battle, which always gives extra spice to any football match. West Ham's opponents were Bolton Wanderers, one of the oldest clubs in the country, formed in 1874. The North, along with the Midlands, had dominated football since the beginning: in the forty-seven Cup Finals since 1872, only Clapham Rovers in 1880 and Spurs in 1901 and 1921 had been victorious. In the League, the first division had never been won by a London or Southern club. (Arsenal was the first to do so but not until 1931.)

The King was present, and all the newspapers devoted pages to photographs and descriptions, as well as to the match report. In the East End most houses were covered in West Ham's colours. That West Ham were, of course, still in the second division added an extra degree of excitement.

Alas for West Ham, Bolton beat them 2–0, and were given a grand reception at the House of Commons by Lloyd George. West Ham made do with a civic reception when they arrived back in Canning Town on a special train decked in their colours.

People remembered the day for decades afterwards, almost like the

The 1923 Cup Final team

death of John F. Kennedy, and whole books were devoted to what was considered an extraordinary event. The gate receipts were £27,776. Each club was given £6,365 and the players were more modestly rewarded. Their basic pay at the time was still only eight pounds a week.

In 1924 West Ham were promoted to the first division and finished thirteenth, miles behind the champions, Huddersfield Town, managed by Herbert Chapman, who won the title three times in a row. (In 1930 Arsenal finally won it, having pinched Herbert Chapman.) West Ham didn't have much success in the first division, though they produced the occasional star, like goal-keeper Ted Hufton, who played six times for England, and Vic Watson, who scored six goals against Leeds in 1929 in a game West Ham won 8–2.

In 1931, their long-serving manager Syd King, who had done so much to bring them from a works team to the first division, committed suicide. The next season they finished bottom of the first division and returned to the second. Meanwhile Arsenal went on to be the dominant club of the 1930s, not just in London but in England, while West Ham were reduced to also-rans, their fans having to content themselves by singing 'I'm Forever Blowing Bubbles'.

Why this song was adopted by West Ham fans – it is still sung by them today – is a bit complicated, but the origins of many football chants are shrouded in mystery. It was not meant to be symbolic, though throughout its history West Ham has usually been better at creating froth and bubbles than solid achievement. In fact it was first sung because a young West Ham player called Murray had a head of curly hair that looked like a mass of bubbles, and reminded the crowd of the painting by Millais used in advertisements for Pear's soap. The song itself was written by an American, James Brockman, and didn't reach England until 1926, thus confounding the legend that West Ham fans sang it at the 1923 Cup Final.

Charlie Paynter took over as manager in 1932 and lasted nearly as long as Syd King, until 1950. One of his star captures was Archie Macauley, whom he bought in 1938 from Glasgow Rangers for the then colossal fee of £6,000. Later he moved to Arsenal and represented Great Britain against the Rest of Europe at Hampden Park in 1947.

West Ham's last second division match before the Second World War was at Upton Park on 3 September 1939, the day on which war was declared. Many of the 8,000 spectators present feared an air attack from Germany during the match: mobilisation and evacuation had started two days earlier. Once again, normal League matches were suspended, with football played on a regional basis until 1944.

There was, however, a war Cup Final in 1940. It was held at Wembley where West Ham met Blackburn Rovers, another long-established northern club, founded in 1875, who had won the Cup five times in the 1880s and 1890s. Alfred Wainwright, later famous for his guide-books to the Lakeland fells, was a co-founder and chairman of the Blackburn Rovers Supporters Club. He came down by coach for the final – and saw West Ham win 1–0 before a crowd of 42,399, the club's first real triumph. Even though there was a war on.

During the war, West Ham's ground, so near the London docks, suffered bomb damage. The office staff were moved elsewhere, and many records were destroyed, but the ground itself never closed. Up in Manchester, United, under their new manager Matt Busby, vacated their ground because of bomb damage and had to share with their arch-rivals, Manchester City, at Maine Road. After the war, League programmes resumed and enormous crowds turned out at all matches throughout the country.

In 1950 Ted Fenton took over as manager of West Ham, and in 1958 the club returned to the first division after a break of twenty-six years. Also in that year, Bobby Moore, aged only seventeen, made his first-team début, replacing the club captain, Malcolm Allison, who was recovering from a spell in a TB sanatorium. In the following season Moore made only three appearances, and had to wait for a regular place even though the team was not doing well. In 1960 Ted Fenton was sacked and replaced by Ron Greenwood.

The arrival of Ron Greenwood began the best spell in West Ham's history. He nurtured and trained local boys carefully, giving them what was considered the best football education, and West Ham became known as the Academy of Football.

His three star players were all home-grown: Moore, Martin Peters and Geoff Hurst. Hurst, son of an Oldham professional, had been born in the north, but brought up locally in Essex. Greenwood's other major star, Johnny Byrne, was bought from Crystal Palace for a West Ham record fee of £65,000 in 1962. In 1964, West Ham beat Manchester United in the Cup semi-final and Preston in the final, 3–2. That year Bobby Moore was named Footballer of the Year. At last West Ham supporters had something real to celebrate and there was a victory parade several miles long through the heart of London's East End. In 1965, the team went on to win the European Cup Winners' Cup – only the second British club to take a European trophy. (Spurs had won it two years earlier.)

West Ham was therefore at its strongest and most talented when in 1966 the World Cup at last came to England. England had finally agreed to join FIFA in 1946, forty-two years after it was formed. The World Cup had first been played in 1930 but England had refused to join in until 1950 when – oh, the humiliation – they were beaten 1–0 by the USA of all countries, which had never appeared interested in soccer. Then in 1953 came a further embarrassment when England were beaten 6–3 at Wembley by Hungary, their first defeat on home soil by a foreign team.

I was there on 30 July 1966 when England played Germany in the World Cup Final at Wembley. And I still have my ticket – seat 37, row 36 in block K. The cost was five pounds for one of the best seats. Today it would be at least £150. And I still have my memories, which will probably never fade, especially as it looks unlikely that England will get to another World Cup Final in my lifetime. I have boasted endlessly, despite my children's yawns, that I was present at two of the defining moments of the 1960s: at Wembley that day, along with 90,000 others, and also in the studio at Abbey Road when the Beatles recorded *Sgt Pepper*.

It was also a great day for West Ham. They provided the captain, Moore, and the two goal-scorers, Hurst and Peters, who helped to defeat Germany 4–2. We didn't know then that it was a peak for both England and West Ham.

In the 1970s, West Ham still had a fairly decent team, with the emergence of Trevor Brooking, who made his début in 1967 aged eighteen, and Billy Bonds. Under John Lyall, who replaced Greenwood in 1975, they won the FA Cup, beating Fulham, of the second division, in the final. Next season they got to the final of the European Cup Winners' Cup again, but were beaten by Anderlecht, 4–2. In 1978, they were relegated to the second division. Despite this, they won the Cup Final in 1980 against Arsenal. In 1981 they returned again to the first division.

West Ham have always been known for their lack of consistency: periods of flair, elegance and success, followed by barren times ending in relegation. Sometimes they have played as if they were the Academy of Football, giving lessons in style and tactics. At others they have appeared more like Thames Ironworks, full of cloggers and artisans. They are not alone in this: most teams are not consistent, even the best. But where West Ham have been unusual is in consistency of managers: during their first ninety years they have had only five. And until the 1990s, they were consistently a local team, drawing their support and most of their players from their immediate catchment area. Arsenal, Spurs and Chelsea have always been cosmopolitan, glamorous, big-city clubs, attracting support and stars from all over the country. By comparison, West Ham have been provincial, small-time, loved and supported locally, but with no national following. Very often, as in the 1964 Cup Final, they have put out a team that was not just totally English but heavily local, with most members coming from East London or Essex.

This changed dramatically in the 1990s when West Ham suddenly became the most 'foreign' team in London, if not Britain, a polyglot mixture of races, nations and languages. It is true that in the past there had been the occasional foreign player, such as Clyde Best from Bermuda in 1970, one of the first black players in Britain, and in 1983 there was the Belgian Van der Elst, but these were exceptions.

The change reflected what had happened elsewhere in British football. There was a sudden and enormous increase in income, especially for the big clubs, mainly through television. Between 1997 and the year 2001, the various TV channels will pay a total of £998 million for the right to broadcast matches. It is no longer a purely working-class sport. Football is seen now as a fashionable activity.

When I went to visit West Ham I expected to see some of these changes reflected in the atmosphere and environment. I hadn't been to their ground since the 1970s when I was doing a match report for the *Sunday Times*. Ron Greenwood was then the manager, and after the match, he invited the press into his own office. That wouldn't happen today. There is either a special press room, or statements are made by a spokesman, often in a corridor or car park. That day, Jimmy Hill was there and he sat in Greenwood's chair, pontificating, while Greenwood dispensed whisky to the other hacks.

The ground is on the same site at Upton Park which they have occupied since 1904, but as at most football grounds in Britain, big and small, in the 1990s there have been major structural changes: stands have been rebuilt in line with the Taylor Report, published after the Hillsborough disaster of 1989 when ninety-six spectators were killed. One object was to produce all-seater stadiums, getting rid of the traditional open terraces where supporters had stood, jammed together, for over a hundred years.

The brave new concrete stands, all over the country, have signified the end of football as a rather homely, amateur-run, locally based enterprise. The Big Stands now show that football is Big Business, that it has become a major industry, turning over billions of pounds, with salaries, transfer fees and admission prices that no one could have believed possible back in 1900. Or back in the 1970s, come to that.

In 1972, my season ticket for Spurs cost £17. In 1997, it was £600. A thirty-fold increase over twenty-five years. Until the abolition of the maximum wage in 1961, no player could earn more than £20 a week. In 1972, the average regular first-team player was earning £20,000 a year. By 1997, this had risen to £250,000 a year – a twelve-fold increase over twenty-five years, but the real stars, especially foreign imports, now earn up to £1 million a year, and often the same again from endorsements and marketing – about a hundred times the earnings of a superstar footballer in 1972.

Clubs have been floated on the stock exchange, with Manchester United, the wealthiest British club, being valued at £623 million when it was sold to Rupert Murdoch in September 1998. The club had a turnover in 1997 of £88 million. Today, most top clubs make more from TV and marketing than from supporters at the turnstiles who turn up to watch the matches.

The area around Upton Park is predominantly Asian, full of Asian fashion and food shops. I went into Ken's Caff, next door to the ground, and had a cup of tea, price 30p, but decided against their 'famous Bubble Breakfast'. No, not another reference to 'Blowing Bubbles' but meaning bubble and squeak – potatoes and cabbage – which they offer with eggs and bacon, all day long, for only £1.50. On the walls were West Ham posters, older ones featuring the ever elegant Bobby Moore, and present-day ones showing Julian Dicks, with his shaven head and a suitably ferocious demeanour. On sale was a West Ham fanzine called *Mission*, which I bought and read with my tea.

Fanzines are another feature of the modern game, which would amaze, and probably revolt, any 1900s fan. The language is rather direct, not to say obscene. They are another sign of the popularity of football. It takes enthusiasm and time, plus money and access to cheap printing, to produce such publications, which often sell only a few hundred. In this issue, the main object seemed to be to mock the manager, Harry Redknapp. 'Redknapp conceded his next signing will be coming from a country not noted for its flair players – England.' Another article was even more direct. 'Who do you fear seeing on the telly – Redknapp or Jimmy Knapp? Both talk bollocks, but only one is pissing us off.'

I was given a tour of the Upton Park ground by one of West Ham's sales executives, Wally Morris. No, he doesn't sell players, he sells advertising space and corporate hospitality. For sums ranging up to £300 per person, you can have a four-course meal with wine in a hospitality suite, visit the dressing rooms, have your photo taken with a player, then watch the match. All clubs do this, these days, even in the lower divisions. Or try to.

We toured the Bobby Moore Stand, opened in 1993, where I admired the luxury suites and dining rooms with tables ready for corporate entertaining, wine-glasses, claret and blue paper napkins in place. There are two ultra-modern stands, and two ancient ones which are due to come down. The present capacity is 26,014, but when the new stands are completed it will be 36,000.

It struck me, as it always does in a football ground on non-match days, how underused these massive sites are: they cost millions, yet they only come to life once a fortnight, however much clubs try to be a focal point for the community. Even the players and coaches don't use them, except on match days. West Ham train at Chadwell Heath, where they have three pitches and the manager has his office.

I looked across the empty stadium, at the darkened giant TV screens and the advertising hoardings, announcing their messages to no one. Just twenty-five years ago superior clubs, like Spurs and Arsenal, refused to have adverts in the ground or in their programmes, considering them vulgar and commercial. I noted an advert for Jiffy Condoms. What would people have made of that in 1900?

Wally took me into the dressing rooms, which are in the old West Stand, built in 1925 – and it looks it. Basic wooden park benches and two plunge baths, which were positively Victorian, of the sort used by Thames Ironworks. But, of course, it was a thrill to stand in the very room where Bobby Moore, Martin Peters and Geoff Hurst used to get changed. 'When I take people round,' said Wally, 'I always tell them how Bobby Moore was so immaculate that when he took his clothes off he folded his handkerchief in four.'

I then went to see the club's managing director, Peter Storrie. Most clubs have a similar paid official now, the business boss, who runs the club from day to day and makes all the financial decisions. West Ham, though not one of the top premier clubs, none the less has an annual turnover of £15 million, a third from gate receipts, a third from TV and a third from marketing. There is a staff of fifty-four full-time and twenty-two part-timers, plus a playing staff of thirty-one professionals and eighteen youths.

Mr Storrie came into the business of football relatively late, although he was born 500 yards from the club and has been a supporter from the age of four when he was first taken to a match by his father. His career until 1990 was mainly in furniture, and he was managing director of a Scandinavian firm. Then he became a director of West Ham, acquiring 2,000 shares at a cost of some £60,000, and in 1991 its managing director. The club's major shareholder in 1997 was the chairman Terry Brown, a local property developer, who tended to keep a low profile, especially at a time when there were take-over rumours.

Unlike some chief executives of the big clubs, Mr Storrie always makes himself available to the fans and the media. 'At the beginning of every season, we give a lunch here for the press, to get to know them. I like to think I never say, "No comment," when asked a question but, of course, if some reporter makes things up, you think twice before talking to them again.'

He replies to around a hundred letters a week from fans and fanzines. I told him I had read *Mission* and he made a face. 'Yes, I will talk to them. We have three main fanzines, and several which come and go, but *Mission* is the hardest to please. We could win the League *and* the Cup – and they'd still be attacking us.'

That day, it was towards the end of the 1996–97 season, with West Ham near the bottom of the Premiership. He estimated relegation would result in an instant 50 per cent drop in TV income and a 30 per cent drop in gate and commercial money, though the latter might slowly rise, given a successful team. To avoid such a possibility, they had recently been on another spending spree, paying £5 million for John Hartson from Arsenal, a club record, and £2.3 million for Paul Kitson from Newcastle. The previous year they'd spent £10 million, mostly on foreign players. They had had to borrow some of the money, thus lumbering themselves with massive interest payments in the years to come.

'Finance is my major worry, every day, but I suppose that's like all businesses. But just five years ago football wasn't like other businesses. Then along came Mr Murdoch and Sky TV. More money came in, and transfer fees and salaries started booming. The manager selects the players to buy and sell, but I control the transfer fees and wages. Five years ago, a player on £1,000 a week might come in to demand a rise and he'd ask for £1,100. I'm not going to tell you the wages today, but let's say if it was still £1,000, then the player would be asking for between £2,000 and £3,000.'

He agreed that my estimate of Premiership wages was about right –
£250,000 for an established player, half a million to £1 million for a
superstar. According to West Ham's accounts, their highest-paid player
was earning around £600,000 – a surprisingly large sum, considering
they don't have any current international superstars or even England
players.

'That is what you have to pay. There is just so much competition for
the best players. A centre-forward, on average, will cost 50 per cent
more than any other player because they are in such demand. After that
comes a central defender, who will probably cost 30 per cent above the
others.'

Like most managers and club officials, he is not very pleased about
the rise of the agents, though admits they have helped players' finances.
'Some are good, some bad, but they are slowly controlling the game.
Oh, yes, players are all on contracts, but if an agent gets them a better
deal you can find they lose form or start getting injured, so you might
as well let them go.

'It will be worse in 1998–99 when any player over twenty-four will
be a free agent inside their own country. At the moment, they are only
free to move between countries. It will mean that when their contract
expires you can't charge a transfer fee. Their old club gets nothing. But
to sign a new player, who might have been worth £3 million under the
old system, you will still have to shell out £3 million, which will all go

West Ham United today

to the player himself, and of course his agent. The rich clubs will survive, but the poor will get even poorer.'

In their attempt to survive, West Ham went for foreign players,
which involved Peter Storrie in many foreign negotiations. On the field
they haven't all quite worked out, as the fanzines will tell you.

'They've all spoken good English, except perhaps Futre of Portugal, so
communication has been easy. Food has not been a problem either.
Most British players have pasta the night before a match, these days. The
only little difficulties have arisen when players have come from some of
the very big European clubs, like Milan. What they have there is something called a house manager, whose job it is to look after each player's
domestic life. For example, the club will pay direct their gas bills, electricity, phone calls, everything, so the player need only ever bother
about his football. We don't do anything like that in England. It can be
a shock to some of them, and their wives, having to pay their bills.

'I had a call the other day from a well-known furniture store who had
one of our new signings there, saying that all his bills would be sent
direct to West Ham. That was what happened at his previous club. 'Not
likely,' I said. Another time, we had to arrange for one of our staff to
take a player's wife to a supermarket and explain how it worked. She'd
never had to go to one before. Silly things, really, but we have to sort
them out.'

In the old days, players earned little, and were not much interested in
investments. 'Harry Redknapp was telling me the other day about when
he was a young player. One day, the club arranged for a financial expert
to come and talk to the first team about pensions. They all moaned
because they wanted to go off and play snooker. When the expert had
finished, no one waited to ask him questions except two players. Today,
every first-team member would be dead keen to listen to financial
advice – at least, those who didn't already have their own personal
advisers.'

So far, West Ham hasn't had much luck in attracting the local immigrant community, either as spectators or players. 'There are no Asian
players in the Football League. I don't know why this is, unless it's
because they prefer cricket, or their parents want them to stick at school
and become doctors. But it will happen. We have two Asian YTS boys
who look very promising.'

He is worried about the financial future of football and wonders what will happen if a couple of clubs who have gone public collapse, with their share-value decreasing.

'I don't see a European league in the near future, but perhaps a British League or Cup, with the two big Glasgow clubs joining in. There might then be two premier leagues, a first and a second, with the rest being divided into a northern and southern league with some of their players being semi-professional. The way things are going, the gap in football is going to get wider and wider every season.'

As for football itself, he had no doubts about that. It will go on for ever.

16

LEONARD COOPER

Great days at Radley; not so good at Oxford

Leonard Cooper at Oxford, in his Radley First XI blazer

I caught the train to Norwich with Leo Cooper, the publisher, husband of the author Jilly Cooper, to see his father. I have known Leo and Jilly for almost thirty years, but I knew nothing about Leo's father, or what his profession had been.

I knew that Leo was a sports lover, and gathered his father was as well. I also knew that Leo was something of a *bon viveur*, and wondered if his father had been. On the train, we travelled first-class, as Leo said it was the only way to get a decent breakfast. He promised a good lunch when we got there, because his sister, with whom his father lives, is a jolly good cook. Then we'd catch an afternoon train home, and be able to have a jolly good tea. Sounded good.

His father was always called Leonard, he explained, while he himself was Leo. First-born sons were always christened the same, but they alternated Leonard with Leo. It went back, oh, generations, to the family steel firm in Leeds, Leonard Cooper Ltd. Still in business, in fact.

Leonard has some shares, but the family had long since ceased to be involved.

We were picked up at Norwich station by Rosemary, Leo's sister, in a large Jaguar, the latest and most expensive but badly in need of a wash. Leo teased her about it, saying it was a bit vulgar. She said, yes, it wasn't her image at all. It really belonged to her millionaire son-in-law but they'd been given it on permanent loan.

Their house, in a village about ten miles from Norwich, was stunning. I could see rolling lawns, a walled garden, outhouses, and a river at the bottom of the garden with a boat tied up. Leo said it was Elizabethan. 'Rubbish,' said Rosemary. 'It's only 1690.'

Inside it was equally attractive with nice furniture, paintings, ornaments and a big log fire in the drawing room. Rosemary, addressed as RM by Leo, offered coffee. Leo said he'd have a whisky and water. Seemed a bit early, as it was only eleven in the morning. Leo is large and rather florid, but at sixty-two he does glow with good health. (And since that day he has given up drink.)

I expected his father Leonard, even at ninety-six, to be equally large but he turned out to be quite thin and angular with a small, Clement Attlee moustache. He was wearing a smart suit, striped three-piece, and appeared fit and dapper. He came into the room on his own, but with the help of a zimmer frame.

He shook hands with Leo, called him Old Boy, laughed a lot, asked about Jilly, then settled himself in a seat by the fire.

He was born on 5 December 1900, between two sisters, Lettice and Barbara, at Bramhall in Cheshire. 'That was purely because my father at the time was running the Manchester office of Leonard Cooper. We later moved to Wetherby. A shame I was born there. Much prefer Yorkshire.

'The family firm was based in Leeds and had been going about a hundred years when I was born. We'd originally been farmers at Ulpha in the Lake District, in the Duddon Valley. My sister Lettice was christened Lettice Ulpha Cooper. There's a church bell in Ulpha with the name Leonard Cooper on it.'

His first memory concerns the coronation of Edward VII in 1901. 'Obviously I can't remember it, it's just what I was told. I was apparently pushed in my pram to some coronation party in Wetherby and I stole a lemon bun, then I was sick.

'We moved around a lot when I was young. My father had a passion for larger and larger houses – if the firm was doing well. Then we'd move to smaller places, when things were not as good. The biggest house we had was Roundhay Grange, near Leeds. I'm told it's now a working-men's club. We had four inside staff, plus a chauffeur and two others outside. Those were the palmy days, before the First World War came along.'

His first school was a dame school in Wetherby, then he was sent away to a prep school in Brighton.

'I never understood that,' interrupted Leo. 'Sending you all that way.'

'It was because of a promise my father made,' said Leonard. 'He had a friend at Oxford who wanted to open a prep school. My father said if he ever did, he'd send a son there.'

While he was at prep school, he remembers seeing Graham White land his little plane on the front at Brighton. 'He was married to Pauline Chase, you know, the actress.' While up in London one day, lunching with his father at the Oxford and Cambridge Club, he saw a Zeppelin flying over London.

'You told me you saw it shot down,' said Leo.

'Did I, old boy?' said his father. 'I think you're making that up.'

'That's what you used to tell me,' said Leo. 'The one that was shot down over Cuffley. You said they were trying to bomb the House of Commons but they could never find it and ended up bombing places like the Humber estuary.'

'Did I, old boy? News to me.'

Leo looked a bit aggrieved. He is something of a military expert, being a publisher who specialises in military subjects.

'I do remember the war breaking out,' continued Leonard. 'We were living in St Albans at the time. I think my father must have been running the London office. I went into the streets of St Albans, which was a garrison town, with Lettice and we kept on coming across troops cooking their breakfast by the side of the road.'

The discipline at his Brighton prep school was very fierce. 'Savage, even. The head once gave me fourteen strokes on the bottom with a rope end. I had helped another boy to cheat in an exam, by letting him copy from me. It didn't do him any good as it was all wrong anyway. The boy himself got fifteen strokes.'

Leonard went on to Radley at thirteen, like his father before him, and young Leo after him. 'And Felix,' added Leo, referring to his son.

'Oh, I loved Radley,' said Leonard.

'So did I,' said Leo. 'I thought it was magic. But Felix never liked it . . .'

'What I remember most from all my school days is cricket,' said Leonard. 'In 1912, I saw Ranjitsinhji make a duck at Hove. I saw my first Test match at Headingley in 1910. I was passionate about cricket. It was my ambition in life to be a cricketer. I can still remember the 1910 Yorkshire Eleven . . .'

He went on to recite the names, one by one, but I didn't get them all down. '. . . Hurst, Rhodes, Denton, Wilkinson, Rothery, Newstead, Lord Hawk, Hunter. They have a nice rhythm, don't you think? That's why I've never forgotten them.

'The most marvellous memory I have is when I was in Radley's First Eleven. I wasn't really much good . . .'

'Oh, you were,' said Leo. 'Better than me. You played for the Eleven for two years.'

'Anyway, the best moment was in my last year. We were playing against Bradfield. Their captain did an enormous hit to the boundary. I was fielding by Dormitory Dump, a clump of elm trees, now gone. At first I misjudged the ball and went too far forward, then I ran back – and I caught it! What a moment that was. The sub-warden – that's what we called the deputy head – was standing on the boundary. He put his stick under his arm and he started clapping me. He had never liked me. Oh, it was marvellous. It's my single happiest moment. A wonderful memory. I always think about it when I'm feeling miserable.'

The happiest moment in your whole life? He nodded and smiled, savouring it.

'Oh, I can understand that,' said Leo. 'I once made a century in a school match.'

Leonard then went up to Oxford, which was more than Leo did. 'Oh, I was useless at school,' said Leo. 'Hopeless.'

'Were you, dear boy? Oh, yes, I remember you asking who is this feller George Eliot.'

'And translating Bognor Regis as the King of Bognor. I brought home one school report which was so awful you burned it in the fire. Do you remember that?'

Leonard nodded, but it was Leonard I wanted to hear about. In 1919, he went up to Oxford, to the same college, Corpus Christi, as his own father, and had the same room and same scout.

'He was called Walter, an old man with grey hair. When I arrived, I asked him if he remembered my father. He said, yes, he remembered the smell. My father apparently used to keep a Roquefort cheese in his cupboard. Strange that, remembering the cheese but not his sporting triumphs. My father got a Blue for soccer, the first Oxford soccer Blue to have come from Radley. He was a goalkeeper, by the way.'

Leonard played for his college cricket team, where he once scored 93 not out. Another wondrous day.

'I went to Parson's Pleasure in the morning and had a swim. Naked, of course, as it was Parson's Pleasure. Then I went hacking in Port Meadow, on a pony. In the afternoon, I scored 93 against Merton. In the evening, well, perhaps I'd better not remember that. But I did enjoy myself. A wonderful day . . .'

Alas, his studies were not quite as wonderful. He went up to read classics, but changed to history. 'I wasn't very good at classics. Turned out I wasn't very good at history either.'

The war had just ended, so Oxford was full of men who had served in the war, along with boys straight from school, such as himself. 'There was a great divide, and we were awfully jealous of them.'

He didn't meet any girls. Wasn't interested in them, anyway. 'Girls bored me. I never went out with a girl until I got married.'

He doesn't remember any wild parties, or living it up in dining clubs. Weren't there any dining clubs, full of public schoolboys like yourself? 'Oh, yes, but I was never invited to join the dining clubs.' Why not? 'Because I wasn't very popular.' I waited, hoping he might explain. 'People didn't like me. So I wasn't elected to anything.'

Leonard said all this calmly, matter-of-fact, as a statement, not looking for sympathy. Leo sat quietly, saying nothing.

He didn't get a degree, which was a terrible blow. 'I ploughed my final exam. It was all my fault.'

He had thought that he might be a parson, having long since given up the fantasy of being a cricketer, but without a degree, there wasn't much he could do. His father was very upset, and told him he would have to join the family firm, which he did and looked after a subsidiary that ran quarries in Ribblesdale. He quite enjoyed that, living in the countryside. He joined the Territorial Army and went on annual camps with the King's Own Yorkshire Light Infantry. He met the Queen Mother, then the Duchess of York, who was Colonel-in-Chief.

In those days, he wore a monocle, mainly because his father did, and he had always admired his father. He also grew a moustache. 'I sold my first one for thirty bob. My mother never liked it, and offered me money if I would shave it off. I did, then a few months later I grew another one. Since then I've always had a moustache.'

During the General Strike of 1926, he worked on the railway, helping to keep it going. Didn't local workers in Leeds consider him a scab? 'That term was never used. It was all good fun, really. I oiled points on the Leeds–Holbeck line. And we got paid. We also got food tokens which said, "Two Fish Teas". At Holbeck, there was a pub where they would accept the fish-tea tokens and give you beer instead.'

His sister Lettice, meanwhile, had also been to Oxford, to Lady Margaret Hall, and had had a novel published. 'I was proud of her, and a bit envious, so when I was going off for a few weeks to Edinburgh, on business to do with the quarries, I said to her at the station that while I was away I'd write a novel as well. She immediately went off to a stationer's and came back with an exercise book and said, "Here, write it in this." It had really been a boast. Anyway, I did it. It took me some time to finish, then Lettice introduced me to her agent, Miss Huntsman, and her publisher, Hodder & Stoughton. It came out in 1921 – on the same day as Lettice's second novel. I remember getting on a train at Waterloo to go and watch the boat race at Barnes, and I saw both our books being displayed on the station bookstall. That was rather thrilling.'

The book was a historical novel called *The Iron Cage*. His advance was a hundred pounds. That was all he made, as it didn't sell very well, but Hodder took his second novel, *The Little Island*, about Napoleon on St Helena, somewhere Leonard had never visited. His third novel was turned down. 'Some reader's report said that Dick, the chief character, was too shadowy a figure. Well, Dick wasn't the chief character anyway. Hodder-Williams wrote nicely to say they were turning it down. I changed my agent, because Miss Huntsman was charming, but not much good, and went to A. D. Peters. I later left them as well and went to A. M. Heath. I suppose they are still my agents, if I have any now . . .'

His third novel was eventually published, and then he turned to non-fiction, and wrote biographies of Radical Jack, the Earl of Durham, and Surtees, the author of the Jorrocks books. But he never made enough money to give up his job at Leonard Cooper Ltd and become a full-time writer like his sister. Especially when he started thinking that it was about time he got married.

'My father and mother thought I'd never get married. They were always trying to fix me up with suitable girls, inviting them for dinner, or to stay the weekend, that sort of thing. "Nubile bits," that's Jilly's phrase for them. Funnily enough, one of them was Jilly's mother, Elaine Whincup. Oh, a very pretty girl. She went to school with my younger sister, Barbara.'

The woman he did marry, Stella Jupp, had also been at the same school – Queen Margaret's, Scarborough – with Barbara. She was one of those invited by his parents to stay in their house during the holidays. She had been born in Hong Kong where her father was a wealthy businessman. They married on 18 June 1932. 'Waterloo Day,' said Leonard.

It was a big wedding, at Chislehurst parish church in Kent. They had their honeymoon at Carbis Bay in Cornwall, then moved into a rented house back in Yorkshire, at Malham. They later moved to Long Preston, which became the family home.

They had three children. Leo was born in 1934, Rosemary in 1938 and finally Johnny in 1946. That was a big gap. 'Was it? I suppose it was. Can't remember the reason. The war, probably.'

'I know exactly where my father was the day war broke out,' said Leo, 'because my mother told me. He was in the Wenhaven Café in Settle.'

His father looked a bit taken aback, wondering what was coming.

'When the news of the outbreak of war came through, he pretended to be Hitler. He put on a little moustache with his finger and did goose-stepping round the restaurant, and then he went outside and up the street. He'd probably had a few drinks. I always thought this was a

Marriage to Stella, 1932

funny story, as everyone already hated Hitler. But my mother never thought so.'

'I have no memory of that,' said Leonard. 'I think you are exaggerating.'

'No, Mother told me. The story was all round Settle.'

Leonard went into the army at once, having already been in the TA, with the rank of major. After six months or so, he had to leave, for health reasons. For the rest of the war, he was busy in the local Home Guard, still as a major.

'It was just like *Dad's Army*,' said Leo, 'only funnier. I remember it well, even though I was only seven or eight. Our car was once dressed up in a sheet and I was told it was to be a German tank, which they would then attack.'

'You were a pretty useless German tank,' said Leonard. 'That I do remember.'

'Another time, his men were supposed to be making an attack on a crashed German aeroplane. He was to wait for them at an agreed position, in his major's uniform. They eventually all arrived – in the back of a furniture van. And all of them singing! He was absolutely furious. He had every bugger get off the van, go back up the road, then come back, marching in order.'

Leonard agreed that that story was true. They both laughed heartily at the memory.

After the war, Leonard expected to go back into the family business, but his father had agreed an amalgamation with another firm. They emerged as the controlling partner, and they didn't want Leonard. 'They pushed me out. They hated me, that was the reason. I didn't like them. Some London wide-boys, that was what I thought of them. So that was the second disaster in my life. I'd lost my military job – and then I lost my civilian job.

'I had to look around for another job, to support my family. I couldn't survive on my books. They'd come to an end during the way anyway. All I could get was a job as an insurance salesman. I joined Canada Life Assurance, based in Leeds. I was out in the country most of the time, so that wasn't so bad. But I hated it. All the time I hated it. I was very pleased to retire at the age of sixty-five.'

'Didn't they give you a watch when you retired?' asked Leo. 'And you said you were going to burn it in the fire?'

Leonard rolled up his sleeve to reveal that he was still wearing the watch. He'd never destroyed it, after all.

He did write a few more books after the war and had some modest success with a biography of the Duke of Wellington, which was also published in the USA. It made him a thousand pounds, the most he earned from any book.

Leo and Rosemary remember their father sitting typing in the kitchen in the evening when they were young, after his insurance work. 'My wife hated the noise of the typewriter,' said Leonard. 'She said I had to type in the kitchen. She also didn't like me smoking my pipe. I had to do that in the garden shed. She never read any of my books. They didn't do well because they weren't very good. That's all there is to it.'

Leo came to his defence. His father had done jolly well to get published. Some of his books were pretty good, such as *Many Roads to Moscow*. Then there was one called *Wanted at His Office*. At one time, he was going to do a joint biography with Lettice, each doing half, but it was never finished. Then Rosemary weighed in: her father was a man who was jolly useful round the house, cooking the evening meal. That surprised me, considering his class and generation.

'I had to do the cooking,' explained Leonard. 'My wife didn't know a thing about it. She'd been brought up with masses of servants. When we first married, and the business was going well, we had a couple of staff in the house, so she never had to cook. During the war, they went off to do war work, so I started doing a bit. After the war, when I lost my job, and started in insurance, we had no money for staff so I had to cook.'

'What was nice about him cooking,' said Rosemary, 'was that he always sang when he was doing it. In fact, he sang all the time, very loudly. Wagner was a great favourite. I remember being on a bus with him during the war and he was singing Wagner, in German, at the top of his voice. I was so embarrassed, imagining people would think he was a spy.'

He was always keen on music. From his early married life, he played the organ and ran the choir in his local church.

'I remember some of the rows he had with the vicars,' said Leo. 'Those rows went on for years, with every vicar in turn, arguing about things like which hymns. My father thought they were all ill-educated, that was the real reason, and knew nothing. He could be very outspoken and rather sharp. What about that row you had with Mr Milner?'

'Remind me,' said Leonard, flatly, but quite interested to hear stories about himself he had forgotten.

'He was a very pompous man in the village who wore plus-fours. My father hated him, but Mr Milner often gave him a lift from the railway station. He made Father sit in the back while he put his bowler on the passenger seat and said, "Now don't sit on my hat, Leonard." Every day he said the same thing. Then one day my father got fed up. While he was getting out of the car, he deliberately shoved his hand through Mr Milner's bowler hat. He was never given a lift again.'

Leonard gave a slight smile, but neither denied nor confirmed this story. I said it seemed surprising that Leo and his brother and sister all went to boarding schools, when their father was clearly poorly paid, and didn't even own a car. Leonard couldn't remember. Leo and Rosemary said, yes, money had been tight at home, but they always presumed a family trust had paid for their education.

Leonard's wife, Stella, died in 1979 of cancer. He lived on his own for a while, then came to Norfolk to share a house with Lettice. Neither of his sisters ever married. Lettice died at ninety-seven. Barbara, who was an amateur singer, became secretary to John Lehman. During the war, Lettice gave up writing for war work, and was secretary to the Minister of Food, Lord Woolton, famous for encouraging the population to eat pies made out of scraps.

'It was thought that as a novelist she could help Lord Woolton with his recipes,' said Leonard. 'As they were fiction as well.'

When Lettice died, Leonard moved in with Rosemary and her family. Her husband, David, is a doctor, senior partner in a local GP practice. They have three children. Justin went to Cambridge and for five years was a master at Eton, then gave it up to go into the City, hoping to make some money.

Leonard has two rooms to himself and tries to be as independent as possible, but recently had a fall. Two nurses now come in to help during the day, or take him out for car rides. I complimented him on his appearance, saying he didn't look ninety-six.

'My father had a good complexion. I remember having lunch with him once in Settle and someone came up to him and said how well he looked. "Drink, sir, just drink," he replied.

'I've no idea how I've got to ninety-six. And that's the truth. There must be some good genes somewhere. My mother got to ninety, as well as my sister. My mother was one of fifteen children, and several got to ninety. Apart from that I've no idea. It really is a mystery.'

Did you smoke and drink? 'I smoked a pipe from the age of eighteen until just two years ago. I had a fall, and after I came out of hospital, I just seemed to have lost the taste for my pipe.'

And what about drinking? There was a long pause.

'I don't know if you need to know this,' said Leonard, slowly. 'Oh, well, I suppose you do. I was an alcoholic. I overdid it when I was young. A doctor finally warned me, saying I had to stop or else.'

This was thirty-nine years ago. He hasn't had a drop since. Quite an achievement, I said. When similar things happen to film stars, or pop stars, they go around boasting about it, making their past even worse than it was to show how well they have done to recover.

'No, I've been a damn fool. There's no need to say I did well to recover, old boy. I know I made a mess of everything in life. I didn't suc-ceed in anything – in the army or in business.'

But you had a long marriage, three children who have turned out well, lots of grandchildren. You've had three different sorts of careers, counting the books. That's quite a lot to do in life.

'No, it's not. I didn't do well at any of them. I never succeeded.'

So what would you have liked to have done, apart from being a famous cricketer?

'A musician. I should really have studied music. I would have loved to have been a professional musician. Or, best of all, a conductor. But I did get a lot of pleasure from playing the organ.'

And playing cricket. So would you have your life over again?

'Not likely.'

Because it was hard?

'Oh, it was easy rather than hard. I've been very lucky in not having to do hard jobs. But I've been unsuccessful. That's been the problem.'

'Well, I haven't done well either in life,' said Leo. 'I wasn't clever enough for university. I haven't been good at anything, really.'

'You were good at rugger, old boy,' said his father. 'I can see you now in a match, picking up this feller, bodily, and throwing him into touch. That was pretty remarkable.'

'You obviously didn't see me the time I was sent off for being drunk during a match,' said Leo, laughing. 'We were on a tour of France at the time. And I was the captain as well.' More laughter.

I asked about politics, if he had ever been interested, but Leonard shook his head.

'I thought you were left-wing,' said Leo. 'That's what you told me when I was young.'

'That's because I said I hated Churchill. Which was true. Never liked the chap. But it was mainly because my father-in-law loved him so much. I just said it to annoy. In every election, I did vote Tory. No, I think I once voted Liberal because I liked the chap. Lettice, now she really was left-wing.'

He thought the arrival of women priests was a pretty good thing, but on the whole that the world is a pretty awful place today. 'Going to hell, that's what. Manners have got worse, but that may be just my prejudice. And morals, they've gone to hell as well. My father was the best man I ever knew. Quixotically honest.'

Then we all went in for lunch, made by Rosemary, which was

delicious – pheasant, bred on their estate, which Leonard ate heartily. Leo and I did the wine proud. Leonard drank orange juice.

On the way home, on the train, Leo said his father had told stories he had never heard before. And had also been very honest. The years when he drank were terrible, especially for his mother. 'I don't know how she stood it. They probably thought I'd turn out a drunk as well. But my father did survive it, which is remarkable – thirty-nine years without a drink. I don't know how he did it.'

I said I was more struck, disturbed even, by the way he said he had failed in life, made a mess of everything. An unusual thing to say, for a gentleman of his background, and at his age, though in a way, rather brave. Was it typical, or had I just got him on a bad day, feeling depressed?

'I have heard him say that before. He does have a strong self-deprecating side to him. I think part of the problem was his father. He adored him, but I don't think his father thought much of him, thinking he was a bit of a wimp.

'He didn't tell you one of the dramas in his writing life. He once got sued for a line in one of his books. "Give me a really good sherry, not Amontillado," he had someone say. It turned out that that was then a brand name. They brought an action and he had to pay a thousand

Leonard today

pounds. It set him back for a good many years. That's the story my mother told me anyway.

'On the other hand, he has done a lot in his life, when you think about it. I'm rather proud of him. And I do think some of his books are really rather good. He published seventeen in all. I've got copies of them all at home. Somewhere. I hope one day one or two might be reprinted.'

17

PEARL NEWMAN

Still a star in her Salford nursing home

Pearl Newman in the 1920s

Pearl Newman met me at Reception, looking resplendent in a sparkling white blouse and some very nice pearls, but it was her complexion that struck me most: beautifully and delicately made-up, with hardly a wrinkle, scarcely a crease. Could she possibly be ninety-six? She had sent me a typewritten letter promising she had 'lived quite an exceptional life'. When I rang to make an arrangement it sounded even better. She said I would be 'flabbergasted' by what she had to tell me.

'Two hours? That's all you are coming for? You'll need to come and live with me for the next twenty-five years to get anywhere near my life story . . .'

Her progress through the luxury nursing home where she lives in Salford was quite stately, at times peremptory, barely acknowledging people who said hello to her, although her speed was somewhat limited by a zimmer frame on wheels, which she uses not for reasons of ill health, certainly not, she has always had perfect health. It is purely a temporary measure. 'It wasn't my fault at all. It was one of the lifts. It threw me out and I've damaged my hip.'

She made her way slowly along a corridor to a lift on the far side of the building, as she now refuses to use the offending one. I realised we were being followed by a woman of about eighty, rather well dressed, hair coiffured, but she did have a faintly abstracted air.

'Take no notice of her,' hissed Pearl, taking my arm. 'She follows me everywhere.'

'Where are you going, Pearl?' asked the woman, plaintively, as we got into the lift.

'With this young man.'

'Where to?'

'We're running away.'

'How long will you be away, Pearl?'

'Two weeks.'

'Can I come with you, Pearl?'

'No, you cannot.'

We got to the first floor, along another corridor, and finally into Pearl's room. It was a mass of cards and bouquets, presents on her recent birthday. Around the room were rows of glossy photographs in glitzy frames, mostly of one person. 'My brother Philip. He was one of the most famous violinists in the world. Look, this is him with Trevor Howard. And that's my father. He'll go down in history, oh, he really will. You've landed lucky. You've never met anyone in your life like me, have you? Now look at that photo over there – not that one, in the folder . . . No, don't open it that way – oh, no! What are you doing? Give it here, I'll open it. Now fetch that to me. Not that, over there . . .'

Such energy, such power at ninety-six. I wanted to smile, sit down and admire, but found myself sent whizzing round the room, to fetch things, take them back, put them straight, while all the time she talked non-stop, telling stories, going off at tangents, opening packets of cuttings, explaining photographs. One of them showed her in a wedding dress, on her own, which seemed strange, so when there was a pause, I asked when it had been taken.

'When I was twenty-three. I'm a widow, you know. Look at these cuttings. Over here. I said, look. Four photographers – four, are you listening? – covered my ninety-sixth birthday, the *Jewish Chronicle*, the

Jewish Advertiser, the *Salford Advertiser*, the *Manchester Evening News*. Oh, they all came to photograph me on my birthday. Well, I do look amazing, don't I? My brother, he was so famous, so famous. I've lots of copies, so yes, have one. No, don't take that cutting, take this one. They said I had no relations in the whole world. Wasn't that cruel? What will my relations think? So that's why there's a bit missing. I cut that paragraph out. Here, you can have this one instead . . .'

On that first visit to Pearl, I hardly got a word in. It was highly entertaining, but she mostly talked about her brother Philip, even though I explained it was her life story I wanted. When I had to leave to catch a train, she tried to stop me, saying stay for dinner, stay the night, but I promised to come back in a fortnight.

She was just as lively on my second visit, but this time I made it clear I wanted her memories of her own life, not her brother's, famous though I am sure he was.

'You don't believe me? He doesn't believe me,' she said, making a mock grimace as if to an audience, though there was no one else in the room. She then insisted on getting out a photograph of her brother, which showed him standing in front of a street in Portugal called 'Calle Philip Newman'.

'See, they named a street after him. Is that not famous? Is that not famous, Mr Davies? You tell me.'

I agreed that he had obviously been famous, no question, but let's come to him later. After her story.

Pearl was born on 14 August 1900 in Cheetham Hill, Manchester, where her father, Harris Newman, was cantor of the Great Synagogue in Cheetham Hill Road. He had been born and brought up in Russia and always spoke English with an accent. Her mother, Augusta, had come originally from Cracow, but her accent was perfect, according to Pearl.

'So perfect that people used to stop her in the street to hear her speaking. Oh, yes, they did. She was a small woman, very beautiful, very good family, very good, very well-off. Her brother was Barnet L. Hollander, you'll have heard of him. He wrote a book later in life, so of course you must know about him. It was a book about art. He wrote it after he retired. He was a lawyer, very famous, an international lawyer, with offices in New York, 44 Wall Street – see, I still remember his address. You wouldn't believe I was ninety-six, would you? And in London his offices were at Paper Buildings, in the City.'

Your father, the cantor, what else did he do?

'Nothing, that was it. A cantor leads the singing, as you know. These days, anyone can do it, but in those days, that was his job, full-time working in the synagogue, taking services, everything. He was a reverend, you would say, a very clever man as well as a great singer – look, here he is in his robes. We had the finest people in his congregation, the finest in Manchester. My mother used to say he should have gone to London, but he liked it here. We had Nathan Laski, the Ashkenazis, the Adlers, oh, everyone . . .'

Pearl had an older brother, Montague, and her beloved younger brother Philip, born 12 May 1904. They were all musical, like their father. The boys played the violin and Pearl the piano.

'I don't remember a time when I couldn't play the piano. One of my earliest memories is going to the Free Trade Hall when I must have been about eight to hear Kreisler. We went behind the stage afterwards to meet him, me and my family, and he put his hand on my shoulder and said, "Pearl, your little brother is going to be a great violinist." For weeks, afterwards, I said to people, "Don't put your hand on my shoulder, that's where Kreisler touched me."'

Pearl went to a Jewish infants' school, then to Heath Street Secondary High School. 'I was excellent at everything except geography. After school, I had my piano lessons. If there was ever half an hour to spare, my father would say go and practise, and I did. I also went to elocution lessons. Since I came in here, my accent hasn't been as good as it was. You should hear some of the girls who work here. "Coom 'ere. You wot?"'

Pearl gave a very good imitation, then offered to sing me a song, 'The Roses Are Shining In Picardy'. 'I know all the verses, even now. I have sung in cabaret, just for charity, of course, and the classics, oh, yes.'

She left school at fourteen and stayed at home. 'I didn't go out to work. A reverend's daughter, going out to work? I stayed at home and helped my mother, learned to cook, practised my piano, did elocution lessons and German lessons. We had maids when I was young, but my mother said I had to learn to cook in case I married someone who couldn't afford to have staff.'

Typical of the times, I said. The daughter kept at home till Mr Right came along. So that's what happened till you were twenty-three and got married?

'What, dear?' she said, affecting for once not to have perfect hearing, which she clearly has. I said that was what she'd said on my first visit.

'Oh, that's what I tell them in here. The thing about Jewish people, they are so nosy, they want to know everything. So I've always said I was twenty-three when I got married. I do look twenty-three in the photograph, don't I? They believe it. I've always had very wonderful skin. People always said, "Oh, what wonderful skin . . ."'

So what did happen?

'Oh, I had lots of people. One very rich man asked my mother if he could take me off to South Africa, but I refused.

'Then one day a *chachunzen* arrived to see my father. That's a Jewish match-maker, sort of matrimonial agent. He wanted to know about any eligible Jewish girls in the area, in my father's synagogue. In those days, people often had arranged marriages. The parents would agree it all, and the settlements, and the children would go along with it.

'Anyway, this match-maker was acting on behalf of a Glasgow family, looking for someone said to be the richest boy in Glasgow. When he went back and reported, it turned out this boy fancied me most! He was very plain, I thought, but his family, they had two very big shops in the middle of Glasgow. They sold umbrellas and leather goods. My father took me to Glasgow to see him and his family. He said to my father he didn't want any money from him as dowry, he just wanted to get married and have a home.

'I quite liked him, even though he was plain, so we got engaged. I bought him some nice clothes as he didn't spend much on himself, in fact he wore a billy-pot on his head, which looked as if he'd had it since his bar mitzvah at thirteen. No, not a skull cap, nothing to do with that. It was an old hat he wore, which I called a billy-pot because to me it looked like a billy-pot. You know, a billy-pot, to drink out of. Okay then, a billy-can. But his family had a gorgeous house and their shops were lovely.

'We found somewhere to live in Glasgow and I started furnishing it. I went to London, to Galeries Lafayette, and chose curtains. I ordered furniture, bought sheets and blankets. Everything was ready. We'd even booked our honeymoon in Germany. Then, six weeks before the wedding, with everything arranged, he said he wasn't going through with it. It was all off. It was terrible. I was so shocked. Yes, he was plain, and people used to say to me, "What are you doing with such a plain man?" but I wanted to get married and I would have made a very good wife. Oh, it was terrible . . .'

What was the reason? Had he found someone else?

'No, no. All he said was that I was extravagant. Me, extravagant! I would not have cost him a penny. I knew all the presents we were going to get. Isaac Wolfson's father, you've heard of him, he was going to give me a grand piano. My Uncle Barnet, he'd promised me an allowance.

'I was so distraught, I had to get away. So I went to Blackpool and booked into a Jewish boarding house, Freeman and Bowman, or Bowman and Freeman, I don't remember. Jewish people, well, they can be cruel. Some of them found out what had happened to me. Well, my father, he was so famous, everyone in Manchester knew about the wedding. Two people stopped me outside the boarding house one day, asking me what happened, what happened, and I didn't want to tell them, so what did I do? I fainted. Right there, in the street. I woke up in hospital. A very nice doctor said it was terrible, people not leaving me alone when my engagement was broken. I wrote to the doctor later, he was so nice . . .'

Pearl returned home, to life with her parents, helping her mother, playing the piano, but her rich uncle did give her a small allowance, so she had a bit of money of her own.

By this time her younger brother Philip had gone to the Manchester School of Music and become a violinist. 'He met Geraldo in London and was offered a job at Lyons Corner House. "Not for me," said Philip. Instead he went off to Brussels where he studied at the Conservatoire and became a professor.

'Once he was established, I went with my parents to visit him. We'd go every year, on the boat to Ostend. I once saw the Dolly Sisters. They were going to gamble at the casino. I remember they wore bracelets right up to here.

'It was then decided I should try to get into the Conservatoire. I always had a beautiful voice, though I say it myself. I went across for the audition, ready to sing "One Fine Day" from *Madam Butterfly*. I was then told the director didn't like Puccini. I said, "Hard luck, 'One Fine Day' is my perfect piece, I'm going to sing it." I did, and half-way through the director clicked his fingers. He held up his hand and said, "Passed." So I was in.

'My brother got me a little flat in the Avenue Geeborn. There were twelve girls in my class and one of them, Olga Calmeyn, went on to be very famous. Have you heard of her?

'I'm not saying I would have got a first prize. I'm sure I would have got a second. But it was not to be. After about three months, my brother came to me one day and said, "Here's the ticket for the boat. You've got to go home, mother is very ill."'

So that was the end, she says, of her musical career. She had to stay with her mother instead, though for many years she did the occasional charity concert, both classical and cabaret. She showed me a photograph taken at a charity occasion at the River Room, New York. On the back, it was stamped 'River Room, New York', so I could see it was genuine.

But she continued to visit Brussels most years to see her brother. 'Now I am going to tell you something amazing. He became a friend of the Queen.'

Our Queen, now the Queen Mother?

'No, Queen Elizabeth of the Belgians. She loved music and went to hear Philip one night giving a concert. He was playing Beethoven's violin concerto and she thought he was so wonderful she wanted him to be her teacher. So for about thirty years, he was her teacher.

'Let me tell you about the Command Performance. No, please. This is the last story about Philip, but you will love it.

'He sent me a telegram this year to come, as it was going to be a special occasion. And it was. The lovely clothes and jewellery, oh, you wouldn't believe it. Such gorgeous people, such finery, and all so cultured. The orchestra was marvellous, as good as the Hallé – no, better than the Hallé. The leader was Van Zundant and, of course, Philip was the soloist. Afterwards we were all presented to the Queen in the Royal Box. I was with Philip, as his partner. Oh, it was gorgeous.

'Then we went in carriages to the British Embassy for a reception. As Philip got into his carriage, he leaned down to kiss this little old woman who was standing on the pavement. "Who is she?" I said. "She is the old woman who brings me my fish to my door," said Philip.

'At the reception, I was with Van Zundant and Philip was with Van Zundant's wife. Oh, it was wonderful. We had fresh strawberries, flown in from, well, wherever fresh strawberries get flown in from. Oh, it was gorgeous.

'Then do you know what? Philip leaned over and gave me a kiss and whispered in my ear, "Not so bad for a little boy from Cheetham Hill."'

Montague, her older brother, also played the violin, but he doesn't seem to have figured much in her life, or in her memories. 'That's because he went off to America. Mother begged him to come home, but he wouldn't. Then when she heard he was riding a motorbike, she begged him to give it up, to make a vow that he would. He made the vow but didn't keep it. He later got injured in an accident and became a cripple. But he still gave concerts in his wheelchair. He was even on the radio.'

In 1939, just before the outbreak of war, another man came into Pearl's life, a much older man, though she wouldn't say how much older. Her father, by now retired, thought he seemed a suitable enough person. 'Though he was from a very different background from our family.'

You mean not Jewish? Pearl laughed aloud at this. 'Of course he was Jewish. You think a reverend's daughter would not marry a Jew? I mean

Pearl today

he wasn't cultured or musical. He was in antiques, buying and selling. But he had a nice sister. She had a shop in Oxford Road called Madame Amelia, a gown shop, full of lovely things. When we got engaged, she took me to London, to the Bond Street model shops, to pick my wedding dress. In brocade, you've seen it, you've seen the photo, people said it was the nicest wedding dress they'd ever seen.

'We got married on the twentieth of June 1939, in my father's synagogue, of course. It was full, queues outside, with a policeman on a horse to keep back the people. Inside, the synagogue was done in pink and white peonies. There were three choirs.

'We had our honeymoon in Bournemouth, in a Jewish hotel. I forget the name, because I don't want to think about it. It was all a mistake . . .'

How long did it take you to realise it was a mistake?

'Ten minutes. The moment we got to the hotel he was so nasty with the staff, so aggressive and horrible.

'But we came back and moved into this wonderful flat in Whalley Range, beautiful flat, beautiful block. They didn't usually take Jewish people, but I had got it through my father. I paid for all the furniture. I even bought him a car, with my money.'

Where did you get the money from, with your father a retired cantor and you had never worked?

'You trying to catch me out? I told you already about the allowance from my Uncle Barnet. That wasn't much, but on my wedding I got a lot more. When my father got to seventy, there was a presentation at the synagogue for him, a *chazan* it's called. He decided not to keep it for himself but to put it away for me, his only daughter, for when I got married. Someone in the synagogue said, "Don't put it in the bank, invest it in this cap manufacturer." He was also in the synagogue, this cap manufacturer, and he said the shares would soon be worth a lot, which they were. When I got married, I got all the money. That's how I paid for his car, and everything else. What a mistake.

'He was a gambler. I never knew that before. When I found out, he promised not to gamble any more, but he went through my money. All my rings, bracelets. And he was so jealous. When we walked out, he said men were looking at me. He had no need to be jealous of me, because I was so very ugly . . .' She paused. 'There, I'm making you smile.'

After about a year, Pearl decided she'd had enough. She asked him to leave the flat, but he wouldn't go.

'I went to see my lawyer, David Lever, you know father of all those famous Lever lawyers. Some of the people in the block had complained because of my husband's shouting, shouting at me, so David Lever had to settle all that.'

Did he ever hit you? 'Oh, no, just shouted, and was jealous. I put his divan under the window and said, "Sleep there." I refused to cook for him, or do anything. In the end we got divorced. It lasted two years, I suppose. The grounds were incompatibility.'

What was his name? 'I don't want to tell you. I changed my name back to Newman afterwards. It made it easier when I went to visit Philip in Spain. We could go to places, book in easier, instead of people thinking, What is Mr Newman doing with a Mrs X?'

What was he doing in Spain? 'Ah,' said Pearl, seeing a chance to get back to Philip, 'when the war started, and the Germans were about to invade Belgium, the Queen helped Philip to escape. She provided a car and a chauffeur and they drove across Europe. He lay on the floor of the car when people shot bullets at them. He got to the Iberian peninsula – is that what you say? He lived in Spain and then Portugal. He met Casals, oh, they were great friends, and he started this festival in the town of Pollensa. That's where they named the street after him, Calle Philip Newman.'

Philip died on 23 November 1966. He never married. 'He was too busy to marry. Oh, I do miss him. Every day I miss him so.' Her other brother is also long since dead. He didn't marry either. So she has, indeed, no close relatives left in the world. She nursed her mother at home until she died. Her father died in a home, aged ninety. 'A Jewish nursing home, Dr Schlossburg's.'

Pearl gave up her Whalley Range flat when the neighbourhood deteriorated. 'Oh, it did. It became so dangerous. I then moved to Salford, to a very lovely flat. Then in 1992 I came here. Another mistake. I must have had a brain storm. They are so jealous of me here, because I look so marvellous. I was fit and well, I had no need to come here at all.' So what happened?

'My very good friend Dolly Sheer, oh, she was so pretty, and so rich, she had a car and a chauffeur. I used to play the piano for her. Anyway

she moved in here, taking the best suite, and she kept on at me to move
in as well. I was still fit and well, but she said, "Come and be with me."
So I finally agreed. I must have been mad. Nobody can do as much
harm to yourself in life than yourself. She died three weeks after I'd
moved in. So that was it. I'm stuck here. Pick up my telephone, ring
down and say you are staying for lunch, as my guest, go on.'

I said I really had to get back, but it had been fascinating talking to
her. Would she say it had been an easy or hard life?

'Oh, easy. It's never been hard at all. Oh, the wonderful weddings I
have been to . . .'

Yet a shame about her own wedding. She presumably had no children?

'I don't miss not having children. That doesn't worry me. How could
I have had any anyway? I put his divan under the window. If someone
had said to me, "You will have twenty Philips," then, well, that way I
would have had a baby.

'But it's also been a sad life. I've made many sacrifices. There have
been many heartbreaks. When I lost Philip I was in despair for six
weeks. I wanted to die, but I came round.

'I think what you can say about me is that I've been brave. Very
brave. But please don't go. Stay, or at least say you'll come again. I've so
enjoyed talking to you . . .'

18

FREUD AND
THE INTERPRETATION OF DREAMS

Sigmund Freud in 1909

Many books were published in 1900, most of them forgotten now, like most books, most years. Among novelists, about the only ones still known to the general public are Conrad, who published *Lord Jim* in 1900, and H. G. Wells, whose *Love and Mr Lewisham* appeared. Beatrix Potter was writing *Peter Rabbit* that year, her first book, but it didn't appear until the following year, mainly because nobody wanted it; she had to publish it herself. In the USA, Theodore Dreiser's *Sister Carrie* was published by Doubleday, until Doubleday's wife said it was too sordid, so Doubleday withdrew it and Dreiser had a nervous breakdown.

In non-fiction, there was a book that, among other things, considered breakdowns of various sorts, and has gone on to be seen as the book that has probably been more influential than any other published in any other year during this century. This was Sigmund Freud's *The Interpretation of Dreams*, his most important work, the one that helped to introduce his basic theories.

Freud had finished the book in 1899 but publication was dated 1900. He was worn out and exhausted with the struggle to complete it, that was one reason. He felt it was not going to be well received, as he himself at the time was not being well received. But it also looks as if he delayed the official publication day to coincide with the new century. Freud was never knowingly unaware of his own genius, and was convinced that the book would be seen as important. All the same, how smart, how apt, what foresight, what confidence, to present the book at the birth of the twentieth century. Looking back, we can see that, in so many ways, our century has been greatly influenced by Dr Freud. Whether or not we approve of or agree with psychoanalysis, it has entered our lives, how we talk to each other, how we think about ourselves.

Freud was forty-three when the book was first published, quite old for a genius, quite old for a seminal work. He had been born on 6 May 1856 in Freiberg, a small town of some five thousand people in Moravia, later Czechoslovakia, but at the time part of the vast Austro-Hungarian empire. His father Jacob, a wool merchant, had been married before, and had a grown-up family, when he married Amalie Nathanson, twenty years his junior. Sigmund was her first-born, followed by another boy, Julius, who died young, then five girls and finally another boy, ten years younger than Sigmund. When Sigmund was three, his family moved to Vienna and that became his home town from then on.

He learned English and French at school, taught himself Italian and Spanish at home, wrote a diary in Greek and was reading Shakespeare for pleasure by the age of ten. His mother gave him every encouragement, making sure he had the best oil lamp for his studies while the rest of the family crouched by candlelight. She removed the piano belonging to his sister Anna in case her practising might disturb him. When he was about eight, he urinated in his parents' bedroom, which did not please his father, who said, 'That boy will never amount to anything.'

He was top of his class every year and when he had graduated from high school aged nineteen, in 1875, his father rewarded him with a trip to England to stay with a half-brother in Manchester. He liked England, was impressed by its history, especially Oliver Cromwell, and that the Prime Minister, Benjamin Disraeli, was Jewish-born.

In Vienna, Freud entered the medical school and, on graduation, did some research into physiology, cutting up things like fish to analyse their nervous systems. He might have continued as a research scientist, on a very low salary, but for two events. First, his father lost his money in a wool venture and Sigmund felt, as the oldest child, he should find a proper job; second, he had a girlfriend. It had been love at first sight when he met a young Jewish girl called Martha Bernays and in 1882 they got engaged. That same year he set up as a doctor in Vienna, on his own, taking on patients.

He was experimenting for medical purposes with cocaine, which he found exhilarating as it helped his migraine. One of the people to whom he recommended it later died, and he seems then to have given it up, but during his experiments he came to the original conclusion that it would be useful as an anaesthetic in eye operations. He didn't get round to writing up his discovery because he went off on a long trip to Hamburg to see his Martha. By the time he returned, another Viennese doctor had already published the same theory.

'It was the fault of my fiancée that I was not famous at an earlier age,' so he wrote later. Sounds rather ungallant, but it's more likely he was being ironical. In the flesh, he was seen by some strangers as terribly serious and detached, giving away little about himself, but he could write amusingly and graphically.

In 1885, he was awarded a grant to go to Paris for several months to study under Jean Martin Charcot, Europe's leading neurologist. Charcot specialised in the use of hypnosis for mental and nervous problems in women – or hysteria, as it was normally called. Nineteenth-century fiction, and real life, was filled with women having fainting fits, the vapours, trouble with their nerves, all of which came under the general heading of hysteria.

Mental disorders were known about and classified in 1900, but the ways of treating them, if they were treated at all, were mainly physical. There were various forms of water treatment, such as hydrotherapy, which basically meant having buckets of cold water flung over you.

With hypnosis, Charcot suggested to women that they were cured, the hysteria had gone. Freud was impressed by this, and when he returned to Vienna, he started treating his women patients in a similar way.

Freud and Martha got married on 13 September 1886, and not long afterwards they moved to 19 Berggasse, the address in Vienna that also became his consulting rooms. They had six children, three girls and three boys, including Martin (named after Charcot) and Oliver (after Oliver Cromwell). Last came Anna. His medical practice was doing well and they employed a cook, housemaid, nurse and governess for the children.

He was now specialising in neurology, using hypnosis. So was a close colleague and friend, some fifteen years older, Dr Josef Breuer, who was apparently the first to use the word 'cathartic' in describing such treatment. There did appear to be some sort of catharsis taking place, a cleansing of the mind, when the method worked. Together, they wrote a book called *Studies in Hysteria*. In it, Freud described four of his cases. Breuer wrote about one of his patients, to whom he referred as Anna O. She went on to fall in love with Breuer and imagined herself pregnant by him, which didn't do much to help her hysteria. It was around this time that Freud himself decided hypnosis wasn't such a good treatment: it didn't explain or get to the real roots of the problems, and often had the reverse effect.

Breuer refused to delve any deeper into Anna O.'s problems, though he could sense the sexual content. He didn't want to know or investigate what might be there. Freud, a bolder spirit, considered that a true scientist had a duty to delve and research further, whatever the consequences. So he carried on, but instead of hypnosis, he used the 'concentration technique'. This meant laying people on his couch, putting his hand to particular spots on their heads, and getting them to talk about their problems.

He moved on to a new way of achieving this in which he, as the doctor, was no longer the dominant and leading partner. Instead, the patient took over, thus reversing the traditional doctor–patient relationship. He would say some words and the patient, still lying on the couch with Freud out of sight, would say the first words and thoughts that came into her head. (It was usually a woman patient.) Freud called this new treatment Free Association. By recording and analysing his patient's free associations and thoughts, Freud came to a dramatic conclusion: sex was at the bottom of everything. Well, almost everything.

Then he wondered why human beings kept these thoughts secret and named this 'repression'. Hiding these dark, nasty thoughts resulted in a 'conversion' taking place, by which the original events or traumas manifested themselves, almost as an act of revenge, in physical symptoms – hysteria.

He also discovered what he called 'transference'. This meant the patient could transfer his or her feelings, which could be love or hate, from the original cause to the doctor who was doing the treatment. In 1896, he gave this new treatment a new name: psychoanalysis.

Psychoanalysis seemed to help his patients, if only because they were talking about their problems. Freud listened to them without comment or criticism, accepting anything they might tell him.

However, some people in Vienna were horrified: word went round that Freud was weird, that he was sick himself, that he was being excited by all this sex talk. His practice suffered – especially when he put forward another theory as a result of his psychoanalytical work with his patients: that at the base of all hysteria was seduction by parents. Well, this led to even further shocks and horrors, which culminated in the Department of Neurology at Vienna University refusing to let him enter the building.

Freud had a large family and assorted relations to support, and he needed patients and recommendations from the medical world: he had a problem. In the past, other doctors and scientists in other places had realised that there might be a sexual undertone to some forms of hysteria, but the society in which they lived and worked had made their ideas unacceptable. The nineteenth century was a particularly repressive period, in which people's sexual thoughts and sexual behaviour were never discussed. None the less, Freud carried on, determined in his arrogance to see it through, to prove his point.

In 1896 his father died, aged eighty-one. Freud had respected and admired his father, considered they had got on well, but after his death, he began to examine his own reactions. This led to what became his own self-analysis. And the main form of his own treatment was to examine his dreams.

For the next three years, he studied all his dreams, forced himself to dream, night and day, even sleeping on a harder bed when he found it made him remember more dreams. In trying to work out what they meant, he came to several conclusions. He discovered he had not loved his father, as he had thought, but was jealous of him because his father had loved Sigmund's mother. He realised he had been pleased by the death of his brother Julius, because he had seen Julius as a rival for his mother's love. He called this mother-love the Oedipus complex. Freud had always been a student of Greek and the classics and he often adopted classical terms for his new theories.

He also came to the conclusion that there was indeed such a thing as infantile sexuality. He later grouped it into types: oral, anal and genital. Along with the theory of repression, the study of the unconscious and the interpretation of dreams, these formed the original elements of psychoanalysis.

He started to write a book about his dreams, and was shocked by the discoveries he made about his real self. It revealed that he was vain and egotistical, wanting to do down his enemies. He worked out a system to describe different dreams, the different stages of dream work as he called it, and how to look for symbolic meanings in dreams. A penis might appear as a stick, a sword, a snake. The female genitalia were a cave, a bottle, a bag, a shoe, anything that was hollow or enclosed. Emperors and kings were parents. Vermin were brothers and sisters. Water equalled birth. Journeys meant death. Riding or sliding or any other rhythmic exercise meant sex. In the book, he didn't actually say that all dreams were sexual, though his detractors said he did, but he was convinced that sex was their primary source.

Only 600 copies of the book were printed and in the first two years only 228 were sold. His royalties amounted to little more than a hundred pounds. He was very disappointed by the lack of reviews or recognition. No one, he moaned in a letter to a friend, had detected the importance in it that he himself thought was 'the only discovery I have made which will survive'. Later in 1900 he gave a lecture on dreams at the university in Vienna. Only three people turned up.

Being the first analyst, he naturally had his own analysis of what the problem was. The world at large, just like the individual human being, was experiencing a form of repression. The world was refusing to admit what he had revealed.

In 1902, for his medical work in general, he was given the title of professor, which was conferred upon him by the Emperor Franz Josef in

DIE

TRAUMDEUTUNG

VON

DR SIGM. FREUD.

«FLECTERE SI NEQUEO SUPEROS, ACHERONTA MOVEBO.»

LEIPZIG UND WIEN.
FRANZ DEUTICKE.
1900.

Title page of Freud's book

person, even though Freud was a Jew in a city where Jews were already stigmatised and where Hitler was soon to arrive. This enabled him to start building up a decent clientele. He worked from eight until one, seeing five patients, each for fifty-five minutes. Then he had lunch and walked for two hours round Vienna. From three o'clock until nine, he saw more patients, most of whom were middle-class, well-off women, and wrote up his notes.

Having a decent income meant he could travel and Freud often went to Italy, which he loved, and made another visit in 1908 to England. He also had money to spend on his two personal luxuries – antiquaries and cigars. The cigars were a strange, not to say Freudian, indulgence. He didn't drink, or hanker after any of the new toys or machines of his time, such as a Mercedes car – or even a bicycle, which he thought undignified. He refused a typewriter, preferring to write all his books with pen and ink. Cigars were his passion and he smoked twenty a day. Perhaps that's why he saw his patients in fifty-five-minute sessions, so that he had time between them for a quick smoke.

Most weekends, and much of his spare time, were spent in writing. Even when translated into English, his work shows a surprising fluency and wit – well, surprising for a scientist. In 1901 he published *The Psychopathology of Everyday Life*, based on a series of lectures he had given, which became his best-selling book so far. In it, he explained how we can all make little mistakes in talking or writing, using the wrong words, which actually give away what we really mean – the Freudian slip, as they became known.

In 1905 two books appeared that he had written simultaneously, the manuscripts worked on side by side at his desk. One was *Wit and its Relation to the Unconscious*, which showed how jokes appeal to our repressed and/or our sexual side, allowing us to laugh in private at rude or childish things we might suppress in polite company. The other was *Three Essays on the Theory of Sexuality*, in which he enlarged on his theory of infantile sexuality. It also made clear that he considered sex was meant for pleasure, not simply for reproduction – which upset almost every civic dignitory and churchman (and most people born in 1900).

However, Freud was attracting followers, in Austria and elsewhere. Inspired by his work, the world's first Psycho-Analytical Society had been formed in Vienna. All the members were Jewish, and included Alfred Adler, and in 1906 they gave Freud a special medallion on his fiftieth birthday.

In 1908 the first international psycho-analytical congress was held in Salzburg. A. A. Brill came from New York, and Ernest Jones from London. He was a Welshman from Swansea, educated at University College, Cardiff, and then University College Hospital, London. He had been greatly influenced by reading *The Interpretation of Dreams* and in 1906 had started using psychoanalysis on his own patients. Out of the first international congress came Freud's first journal.

In 1909 Freud, along with Jung, visited America for the first time. He was invited to lecture at Clark University in Worcester, Massachusetts, all expenses paid, plus a fee of $700. On the boat from Hamburg he was surprised, but delighted, to find his cabin steward reading *The Psychopathology of Everyday Life*. The lectures were a great success, but a professor in Toronto said that Freud's theories were disgusting, an incitement to free love and savagery.

Freud began to realise that his theories could be applied not just to his patients and their problems but to people in history and the world at large, so he turned his attention to religion, anthropology, myth, painting and literature. In 1910 he wrote a biography of Leonardo da Vinci, using the basic facts about him that had been known for centuries, though mainly ignored, such as his dreams, and came up with some interesting theories: Leonardo's obsession with flying, for example, was clearly sexual, Freud said. The Mona Lisa's smile was his mother's smile: he remembered her sensuousness from when he had been a baby. The book, which sold well, was the world's first psychoanalytical biography. There have been many since. It made a pleasant change from the hagiographies of the nineteenth century.

By 1911, Freud found himself increasingly at odds with Adler, one of his earliest pupils. Adler made use of the term 'complex', as in obsessional complex or inferiority complex. One of their differences centred on an explanation for the behaviour of Kaiser Wilhelm II, known for his arrogance and boasting. Compensating for something or other, we might say today, but while Adler put it down to his withered arm, Freud said, oh, no, it was due to the loss in childhood of his mother's love, though, of course, the withdrawal of her love might have been caused by the withered arm.

Adler had begun to believe anyway that Freud was over-emphasising the sexual element in his theories. He eventually broke with him and went to America. (Alder died in 1937 in Aberdeen; he suffered a heart attack while walking down a street.)

In Britain, Ernest Jones remained a supporter of Freudian methods and worked hard to have them accepted in medical circles. In 1911, Freud was made a fellow of the Society of Psychical Research. 'The first sign of interest from dear old England,' Jones wrote. At the British Medical Association's conference that year, a paper was read that included for the first time a case history of psychoanalysis. When the British Psycho-Analytical Society was founded in 1919, Jones was made its president.

At the outbreak of the First World War, Freud's three sons all went into the German army. Martin, the eldest, became a dashing cavalry officer. When the full horror quickly became apparent, Freud was in the depth of despair, worrying about his sons and about the future of humanity. He continued to write to Jones in London, through intermediaries in Switzerland, about the bad conditions, his poverty and lack of patients.

He was also worried that the psychoanalytical movement, which in just ten years since the foundation of the first society had attracted followers in almost every major country, including India and Japan, would collapse because of the war. But many doctors were, in fact, employing Freudian methods to treat war victims. Freud's three sons all survived the war, but in January 1920, his second daughter Sophie, aged twenty-six, died as a result of the flu epidemic which had been sweeping through Europe.

Perhaps because of the horrors of the First World War, and the mental problems of the shell-shocked victims struggling to recover, Freud modified his theory of dreams. He admitted that not all dreams were wish fulfilment but could be recurring traumas. He also propounded a death-instinct theory. All living organisms are conscious of moving forward to death, though they hope to arrive there in their own time, not through illness or accident. At the same time he developed the pleasure principle, that part of each person was interested only in reckless enjoyment. This grew into another book, *The Ego and Id*, published in 1923. The *id*, he said, was the unconscious part devoted to pleasurable and impulsive behaviour. The *ego* was the conscious self, striving to be good and moral, according to the standards of the times. These new theories, he said, showed that psychoanalysis did not, after all, ignore the moral and spiritual side of human nature.

He himself was convinced that he would die relatively young, in his fifties, and then he decided he would die in February 1918, between the ages of sixty-one and sixty-two. He became obsessed by these numbers, seeing them everywhere, from hotel rooms to house numbers. He once booked into a room numbered thirty-one and immediately saw that as significant because it was half of sixty-two. His first telephone number in 1900 was 4362, and he noted that forty-three was the age he then was, while sixty-two was the age at which he would die. Clever, logical people are, of course, as likely to be influenced by supposed signs and symbols as the rest of us. What he was really afraid of, he said, was that he would die before his mother, leaving her to grieve for a son, which was not how things should be.

In 1923, he had an operation for cancer of the jaw, the first of thirty-three operations over the next sixteen years during which bits were chopped out of his mouth and tongue. Eventually he had to wear a prosthesis, which affected his speech but he tried hard not to let it stop him smoking. When he was desperate he asked for a cigar to be shoved into his mouth, even though he was well aware that smoking was making his problems worse. So much for self-knowledge.

By the 1920s he had become a household name, at least in the so-called civilised world. He was still being attacked by opponents as evil, with harmful and malevolent sexual theories and practices, but generally he had been accepted as someone who had made humanity look at itself in a new light. In 1924, the main prize at the Welsh Eisteddfod was given for a poem about psychoanalysis – not the sort of event at which you expect to meet the avant garde.

That same year, the *Chicago Tribune* offered Freud $25,000 if he would come and analyse two famous murderers, Leopold and Loeb. William Randolph Hearst's rival newspaper group offered more, plus a luxury liner to take him to America if his health was too poor. Sam Goldwyn tried to get him into films, willing to pay him $100,000 as a script adviser, starting with *Antony and Cleopatra*. All of these offers were turned down, dismissed as nonsense, along with other more academic awards and honours. Distinguished visitors to Freud in Vienna included H. G. Wells and Thornton Wilder. 'When I am attacked,' Freud said, 'I can defend myself, but when I am praised, I am helpless.' He was admired by Jews around the world as one of the great Jews of the century, along with Einstein, even though he was not religious. 'The Jews have celebrated me like a national hero, although my service to the Jewish cause is confined to the single point that I have never denied my Jewishness.'

When Freudians claimed more for Freud's theories and methods than even he himself would claim, he was careful to make it clear that 'no analysis was ever concluded, or finally successful'. He saw analysis as fundamentally an unsatisfactory occupation, one of three areas in which you could never be wholly right – the other two were bringing up children and governing nations. He also observed that he didn't think the success of psychoanalysis 'can ever compete with the success of Lourdes'.

In 1933, when Hitler came to power in Germany, Freud's writings were publicly burned in Berlin. At first, it didn't seem to worry him unduly: he'd been attacked often enough already. And while he was horrified by Hitler's growing persecution of Jews in Germany, making

Jewish doctors scrub the streets with toothbrushes and other humiliations, he believed for a long time that such things would never happen
in democratic Austria. Friends around the world urged him to leave
Austria, but although he had always moaned that he disliked Vienna, he
ignored their warnings.

On the afternoon of 12 March 1938, he heard some unusual noises
out in his quiet street. He sent out his maid Paula to buy a newspaper.
The headline announced that the Nazis had arrived in Austria.
Suddenly Nazi tanks were rolling through the centre of Vienna,
swastikas were daubed on buildings, Jews were attacked and ridiculed in
the streets. Three days later they arrived at Freud's house. His wife let
them in, as if it were a social visit, telling them to put their rifles in the
umbrella stand. Ernest Jones was visiting at the time and recalled later
that Freud, despite being 'gaunt and frail', shouted at them, his dark
eyes blazing. They left fairly hurriedly, confiscating the Freuds' passports
and 6,000 schillings. At the same time, the offices of the psychoanalytical publishing company, which had produced all Freud's books and
papers, were ransacked.

On 22 March the Nazis arrived again at Freud's house and took
away Anna, his daughter. She returned within twenty-four hours, yet
it had become obvious to the Freuds that it was not their possessions
but their lives that were in danger. After some behind-the-scenes
negotiations, involving two friends in Paris – Princess Bonaparte and
the American ambassador to France, who had been a patient of
Freud – a deal was done, some money paid, and Freud, his wife,
daughter Anna and maid Paula were allowed to leave Vienna. All
their money was taken from them, but Freud was allowed to keep his
personal library and collection of antique figures. The rest of his children were already safely out of Vienna, three in London, but he left
behind his four elderly sisters, all in their seventies. Along with his
brother, Freud had previously set up a fund to support them in their
declining years.

At the age of eighty-two, and in poor health, he left the city that had
been his home for almost seventy-nine years. On 8 June 1938, he
arrived at Dover after a night train and boat trip from Paris. He had a
dream in the night in which he was William the Conqueror, landing at
Pevensey in 1066, about to conquer England. Wish fulfilment, or what?

Customs formalities were waived, and the British government allowed him diplomatic privileges.

The Freuds took rented accommodation in North London, at 39 Elsworthy Road, where they lived for three months. Then they moved into a house in Hampstead, at 20 Maresfield Gardens. Paula arranged Freud's desk and couch, books and antiques, as they had been for all those decades in Vienna. The Royal Society made him a fellow and the *Lancet* praised him, saying that since Darwin no one had aroused more controversy. Letters arrived from all over the world addressed simply to Dr Freud, London. Questions were asked in the House of Commons, trying to hurry through his British citizenship, but it was felt that he should be a resident for five years, like everyone else.

Salvador Dalí came to see him, saying that reading *The Interpretation of Dreams* had been one of the chief experiences of his life. Freud considered surrealists were 'complete fools', even though they had made him one of their heroes. He much preferred classical art. He took a few patients, saw one or two a day, and continued writing and revising. *The Interpretation of Dreams* had been republished several times with new introductions adding his latest thinking.

His health grew worse and he had another operation for the cancer in his jaw, plus some radium treatment, but he continued to enjoy his house and garden and his dog. He said he liked the British people, felt welcomed and at ease, but at times he was homesick for Vienna and the life he had once led.

Freud died on 23 September 1939, aged eighty-three. He had heard the first air-raid sirens, but he never knew what happened to his sisters in Vienna. Just a few months later, all four went into concentration camps. Three were burned to death, the other died of starvation.

Freud was cremated at Golders Green, and Ernest Jones gave an address at his funeral. He later produced the authoritative book on the life and work of Freud, which appeared in three volumes in the 1950s. W. H. Auden wrote a poem in memory of Sigmund Freud, in which he said that Freud was no longer a person but a 'whole climate of opinion, under whom we conduct our differing lives'.

That was true then and is still true today. Writers who can be said to have been influenced by Freud include Proust, Joyce, Kafka, Thomas Mann, William Faulkner, Eugene O'Neill, Graham Greene. Lawyers, sociologists and criminologists are equally influenced by Freud. Ordinary people, in their ordinary lives, go around the planet using Freudian phrases and references, such as repression, denial, defence mechanism, Oedipus complex, death wish, pleasure principle, libido, neurosis, without realising where they have come from. As for the analysts, more of them are around today, of all persuasions, than ever before. Even if many don't accept all Freud's theories, particularly some of those about women, they agree that he started the whole process of the examination of our inner selves. He was the first to make us aware of the unconscious.

The British Psycho-Analytical Society today has 430 members, mostly based in London. Many are medically trained, as Freud was, and have gone through many years of analysis themselves, as well as training in analysis. Judging by the number of institutes turning them out and the number of adverts from those offering their services, there must be around a hundred thousand other analysts, assorted counsellors and therapists, many with little professional training. All of them are trying to relieve our problems and fears, stresses and anxieties, by using psychological means, not medication or physical treatment. Just as Freud first tried to do. Does it work? Well, millions think so, though solid scientific proof is hard to find.

Today dreams are still studied by psychoanalysts, especially when monitoring psychic change during treatment, and *The Interpretation of Dreams* is still in print in most languages.

After Freud's death, his family continued to live in Maresfield Gardens. His youngest daughter Anna, the only one to follow him into psychoanalysis, had her consulting room in the house. His wife Martha died in 1951 aged ninety-two. Anna died in 1982 aged eighty-seven. In 1986, the house opened to the public as the Freud Museum.

It is a typical 1920s Hampstead house, red-brick, double-fronted, three storeys, trying hard to be imposing. Freud's son, Ernst, father of Lucien and Clement Freud, found it for him. He was already living in London, working as an architect, but his father appears to have paid for it. Although he was not able to bring any money with him, royalties were coming in, plus payments of around four guineas a time from patients, so he managed to get a mortgage from Barclays Bank.

The director of the Freud Museum is Erica Davies, who is Welsh, like

Ernest Jones, Freud's friend and biographer. There is a staff of five, including a research director, Michael Molnar, English-born but of Austro-Hungarian parents. They receive around 14,000 visitors a year, most from abroad. At one time, they were mainly American, but after Freud was attacked in the American press, which said that psycho-analysis was a mere cult and its theories undemonstrable, the numbers of Americans decreased. However, Latin American and Japanese visitors have increased, so keeping up the total numbers.

'It's a shame we don't have more British visitors,' said Erica. 'The general image of him in Britain is of a cold person. We don't get finan-cial help from the government or any other body in Britain, which we could do with. If this house was in New York or Paris or São Paulo, we would get enormous funding because there would be such pride in having the home of one of the great makers of the twentieth century. He actually chose to come to England, when he could easily have gone to America or elsewhere. He was an Anglophile, but the official attitude to him here is indifference. I find him personally rather cuddly, but I admit we are a bit low on the Bambi factor . . .'

Freud cuddly? I wouldn't put it quite as strongly as that, but anyone who reads his books will find he can write amusingly. Hard to give examples as out of context few things sound funny, but he made a bad-taste joke after the Nazi thugs had ransacked his house and gone off with the 6,000 schillings – about three hundred pounds: 'That's more than I get for one visit.'

The house itself, and the furniture and furnishings, are warm and friendly, not what one might expect from a cold, clinical analyst. Everything, of course, came from Vienna and is still arranged as Freud had it. There is a thirty-minute home movie of his life in Vienna from 1930, and also from his year in Hampstead. He hated having his photo taken, but he didn't seem to be aware that wealthy visitors, such as Princess Marie Bonaparte, were sometimes capturing him on a moving film camera. It's a silent film, but with a voice-over commentary made later by Anna Freud. One of the highlights is his golden wedding anniversary in 1936 when friends and relatives arrived in a garden to give him presents while he sat in a deck-chair. In the film, when talking to close friends, he gestures a lot with his hands as he makes a point. When silent, you can see his mouth still moving. I thought at first he

The Freud Museum in Hampstead

was chewing gum, till I realised he was trying to make his prosthesis more comfortable. In one of the last shots, he is in the garden in Hampstead, looking for goldfish in the pond to show to his grandchildren. Even at the end, he has the inevitable cigar.

Perhaps the most surprising part of the whole house is his consulting room. It is absolutely crammed with Greek, Egyptian and other antiquarian ornaments and objects. On his desk alone I counted forty different pieces. There was also a little brush, about the size of a toothbrush, which I presume he used to dust his treasures.

The centrepiece is his couch where his patients lay down. Freud sat unseen in a tub-shaped seat to the side. He said he didn't want to be stared at, but perhaps it was to allow his face, and his mind, a rest from time to time. His seat didn't look very comfortable, not for eight hours of listening to people talking.

He never made notes during consultations, but later in the evening, so he said, which I find hard to understand. How could he remember the exact details of eight different patients? When I interview more than three people in a day, I can easily confuse them in my mind, but at least I have my notes. Freud was often criticised for fudging and fiddling his case histories, taking liberties, putting disparate elements together to make his point.

The couch itself, the famous couch, which came with him from

Vienna, is covered in a multi-coloured Persian rug. On it were lots of pretty embroidered cushions. Behind it, on the wall, hangs another attractive rug. I had expected something leather and brutal, with no colour or anything to distract the eyes. In reality the room feels more like a Turkish brothel. Not that I know what a Turkish brothel looks like. Only in my unconscious dreams.

19

Dr David Davies

Welsh wizard of ruby and medicine

David Davies (front row, fourth from right), aged 11

Dr Davies, like Ernest Jones, comes from Wales, graduated from the same university, then trained at a London medical school. Unlike Jones, he didn't devote his life to the new and wonderful world of psychoanalysis. Dr Davies became a traditional GP, relying on basic common sense and a great deal of experience rather than Freudian theories to build up his own medical practice and minister to the good people of Preston.

For over sixty-six years, patients in his practice have been relying on Dr Davies for their aches and pains. No, he himself did not carry on his doctoring for quite that long. What he did was found a Davies Doctoring Dynasty. At one time three members of his family worked in the same practice and between them totted up 109 years of doctoring.

David John Davies, known to his patients as Dr DJ to distinguish him from the other two, still lives in the same house in Liverpool Road,

Penwortham, Preston, where he had his practice. His present bedroom is his old surgery. He lives alone, but the other two Dr Ds live next door to keep an eye on him. They both have English, public-school accents, while he retains the lilting Welsh tones of his boyhood.

He was born on 19 March 1900 in Llanelli, and at home they spoke only Welsh. His father, a foreman in the local tinplate works, owned his own house, which had a big garden surrounded by fields. He was a pillar of the local Calvinist Methodist Chapel where he was a deacon. David's earliest memory is of going to chapel, with his two older sisters and an older brother, and listening to the singing.

At school he was a star, good at everything from all sports to all learning. School reports show a long list of prizes and awards. At eleven, he won a scholarship from the local board school to Llanelli Grammar School. There he became head boy, captain of rugby and captain of cricket. 'And there were some good 'uns in my year,' he said, unmodestly. 'One of them went on to be a vice-chancellor. I was the captain of every darn thing, despite being one of the smallest boys.'

I could see from his school photos that he was small compared with most of the others. His height, at his tallest, was five feet seven. Now he is about five feet five, having shrunk with age, but you can still see the build of a wiry but muscular scrum-half.

His daughter Dilys had got out the school reports and photographs. She also handed me his full CV, bang up to date, beautifully presented, which surprised me. I mean, persons of ninety-six don't usually need a CV. Where are they going? Their next situation probably won't need an interview.

He wears an Eton collar in his first photo at Llanelli Grammar, along with a serge jacket, knickerbockers, black boots and long thick socks, which must have been warm in winter but hot in summer. When he was at school his ambition was to play rugby for Wales, while his parents and the school wanted him to go on to university and be an academic star. At seventeen, the school put him in for a Drapers' Company Open Scholarship to University College, Cardiff, which he won. 'But the war was still on when I got to eighteen, so I was called up instead.'

Called up in 1918, towards the end of the war? Could that be correct?

'Well, I'd been in the OTC at school, so if you joined that it was automatic. It felt like being called up. And I was pleased to go.'

He would have liked to have been sent abroad, and seen foreign service, but he found himself in the RNVR and posted to Crystal Palace, in South London. It was his cleverness on paper, especially in the sciences, that presumably had impressed them. 'They made me an instructor. I had to teach electricity and magnetism, about which I knew nothing at all. Still don't. I can't even change a plug.'

He served for only a year, by which time the war was over, and achieved the rank of O. Tel., or Ordinary Telegrapher, at least he thinks that's what it stood for. He has a photograph of himself in his naval uniform, looking about thirteen, not eighteen, a cabin boy perhaps in a Noël Coward musical. Where was the photograph taken? He could remember exactly, as many people can, even looking back eighty years, recalling what they were wearing, the colours and texture still lodged in their brain, and often what was happening in their life that day. A pity old photos don't come with a commentary, that it has to be applied later, as with that old film of Freud.

'I was in Regent Street, London. I'd come up with a pal to London to sing in a Welsh choir, a naval choir, in Hertfordshire. We happened to pass this photographic place in Regent Street and we both decided to have our photographs taken.'

David aged 18

At nineteen, he finally went up to university in Cardiff, where he was captain of cricket and also managed to get his BSc. By this time he had decided to be a doctor. 'My parents had always wanted me to,' he said, giving a mock shrug. 'I was doomed, you see.' He won a scholarship to the Middlesex Hospital and after his second-year exams was awarded the Broderip Prize. All the way through his education he won scholarships, which meant his parents never had any fees to pay.

'Middlesex was the best teaching hospital. Oh, certainly. There was Samson Handley, who was an outstanding surgeon, and Lord Webb Johnson who went on to be one of the architects of the health service.'

He graduated MRCP and LRCS, to add to his BSc. He also has an MB and is an FRCS from Edinburgh. Dilys explained that his qualifications are many because, over the years, he qualified three times in different disciplines and places – the University of Wales, London University and then professional bodies.

When he had finally qualified as a doctor at the Middlesex, he went out and bought his first car. 'It was a Riley,' said Dilys. 'He just went out into this showroom in the West End of London and bought it. He couldn't drive, of course. The salesman showed him how to turn the engine on, how to change gears, then Father got into it and drove all the way home to Wales.

'The next day, he took his relations out for a spin in the countryside, to show off his new car. They came to a gated road, where you had to get out and open gates. One of his old uncles kindly got out to open the last gate – and Father forgot him! Drove off and went back home, leaving him behind. Well, that's the family story . . .'

Her father smiled and nodded. 'Now I think about it, it was a Kleino car. Not a Riley. I bought a Riley later on.'

He carried on working at the Middlesex as a doctor, and was promised a permanent job but he got fed up waiting. 'They wanted to keep me, but they said it would be six to eight months before a certain position came up, so I decided to look around for another opening. I went to the library, got out the *BMJ* and applied for several jobs.

'It was a Saturday when I heard from two of them. They both sent telegrams. I know it was a Saturday because I was playing rugby for Middlesex Hospital against London Welsh. The two places being offered were in Preston and in Poole. I'd never heard of either. No idea where they were. One of the players in the dressing room suggested going to Euston and asking for directions. Then one friend said he'd heard of Preston, and knew vaguely where it was. So that's how I decided to come to Preston, let me see, seventy years ago. It was all by chance.'

'I wish you'd gone to Poole,' muttered Dilys.

In 1926 he went for an interview at Preston Royal Infirmary and was offered a position as a house surgeon, on a six-month contract. 'I was most impressed by them. There were three superb surgeons, and a very good gynaecologist. I arrived to take up the position on a Sunday, as a total stranger, and on the Tuesday I had two invitations to put up on my mantelpiece in my digs. One was to the hospital ball the coming Friday and the other was to play rugby for Preston Grasshoppers on the Saturday. I'd never even heard of the Grasshoppers. Wasn't that strange? Two invites in such a short time.'

So how did it happen?

'Well, I only discovered much later. Turned out there was a dentist at Preston Hospital who had two sons at Tommy's — St Thomas's, in London. They knew I played rugby so they had told their father that a boy called Davies was coming up to be the new houseman.'

After his six months, he was appointed assistant surgeon. 'There were no registrars in those days. What you had were surgeons and assistant surgeons who were part-time consultants. You worked half the time as a consultant in the hospital and the other half you worked as a GP. As a consultant, I saw people in the hospital two mornings a week, and then I did operations on a Thursday. The rest of the week I was in Pole Street at old Lake's, doing my GP work in Dr Lake's partnership.'

Pole Street is in the centre of Preston, where Dr Lake had his practice. 'I was told there had been a surgery on the same site for about a hundred and fifty years, back to the times when surgeons were barbers. In fact, that was why it was called Pole Street. When I joined Dr Lake in 1926, he still had a pole outside his surgery. At the front door, there was a mouthpiece into which you could talk and be heard inside, though not very well. This was long before the days of telephones, of course. The idea was that if you had a real emergency in the middle of the night, you could reach Dr Lake in his bedroom. What it mostly meant was that you woke up his wife . . .'

Dr Davies got married in 1929 to Gladys Johnson. According to Dilys, her mother was a well-brought-up girl, on the rebound from a long engagement which had been broken because the boy in question was under his mother's thumb. Dr Davies feigned surprise when such intimate family details were revealed, as if they were all new to him.

'I think Mother was his first girlfriend,' continued Dilys. 'Father didn't go in for that sort of thing. He wasn't a ladies' man. He lived for rugby when he wasn't working.'

'I see,' said her father, rolling his eyes.

'In fact, Mother told me their first meeting had been arranged. When her engagement finished, some friends of hers, a dentist and his wife, decided she must meet somebody new as quickly as possible. So they organised a dinner party to which Father was invited. They actually met on the doorstep going in.'

'Did we?' enquired her father.

The marriage took place on 12 August 1929, just a year after they'd met. Not a white wedding, said Dilys, her mother wore a peach dress, which they still have. In fact, it was worn recently by one of the grand-daughters. But it was a large family occasion none the less. In the photograph I noticed Dr Davies wore spats. 'Oh, they were very fashionable.' He smiled, looking at the photo of himself. The honeymoon was in Llangollen where an eisteddfod was taking place.

In 1932, Dr Davies decided to set up his own GP practice and built the property in which he still lives. It's a rather grand, double-fronted building, which was his home and his surgery, with a dispensary at the front, facing the street. Where had the money come from?

'Money?' he asked.

To build such a place. You were only thirty-two. Did you take out a mortgage?

'I really can't remember,' he said.

'Oh, doctors were very well off in those days,' said Dilys. 'In 1935, I can remember clearly that we had two living-in maids here, Cathy and Mary, a nanny to walk the children and a gardener, Mr Walmsley. Do you remember him, Father?'

Dilys's other pre-war memories include her mother's driving. 'She was a demon driver. She had her own car and would go to places like

Marshall and Snelgrove in Southport, taking her sister Nan to squeeze the horn. She always maintained she couldn't drive and squeeze the horn at the same time. She also couldn't reverse. I went with her once, to Marshall and Snelgrove, and we drove three times round the block to find a space she could drive into without backing.'

Dilys was born in 1930 and her sister Enid in 1935. Just two girls? 'Oh, that was enough,' says Dr Davies.

'You forget that Mother did have at least one miscarriage that I know about,' said Dilys. 'Of course, he would have liked a son. In his fantasy, he had a son who went to Charterhouse, Cambridge, Middlesex Hospital, and played rugby for Wales. That's what Father really would have liked.'

In reality, he still did pretty well. Dilys was a boarder at Liverpool College for Girls. She said she was the naughty, bolshie one, while her sister was good. 'I was once asked if I'd like a baby brother and I said yes, to stuff him up the chimney.'

All the same, Dilys went on to study medicine at the Middlesex Hospital, as her father had. It was there she met another Davies, the man she later married, Tudor.

'I fell pregnant before I had qualified, which was a really stupid thing to do. My excuse is that we hadn't got to that part of the curriculum . . .

'I wanted to have a career and never to have to do anything domestic, like slicing loaves of bread. I've never been good at that.'

She had the baby, Gareth, then finished her medical training and her house jobs at Preston Royal Infirmary. For a few years, she and her husband worked as doctors elsewhere in Lancashire, then came back to Preston to join her father in his practice, which is how the three Davieses came about. She was always Dr Dilys while her husband was Dr Tudor.

She has now retired as a GP, but has another career as a gardening expert. She is chairman of the Hardy Plants Society, a national organisation with twelve thousand members. Her speciality is onions – the ornamental sort, not the ones you fry – or alliums as they are correctly known. She has toured the USA giving lectures on them, and published a book, the first on ornamental onions since 1875. She gave me the full title and I said I'd look for it in the library.

Enid went on to be a businesswoman and lives in Vancouver, Canada. She is married to a doctor and has four children. 'I speak to her every Sunday on the phone,' said Dr Davies. Dilys has two children, both lawyers. Dr Davies Senior has six grandchildren and four great-grandchildren, the oldest of whom is at Shrewsbury and is jolly good at cricket, he said.

He, his daughter and son-in-law have seen tremendous changes in general medicine over the last seventy years, notably the arrival of antibiotics, vaccinations and the Pill, but the major upheaval in Dr Davies's professional life came with the National Health Service in 1948.

'I had to decide whether to be a surgeon or a GP. As I told you, I was doing each of them, and had done so for many years. The hospital secretary wrote to me, saying I had to choose. I could have become a full-time surgeon at the hospital, but then I thought of all the things I was involved in – medical officer to Lancashire fire brigade, and the police, Ribble Motors and others. I didn't want to give them up, as I enjoyed it. So I decided to stay as a GP. As a hospital surgeon you had to retire at sixty-five, whereas a GP could go on much longer.'

'I think there was also the strain of operations,' said Dilys. 'I remember something being wrong with his nose, because of the atmosphere in the operating theatre. It was incredibly hot in there. Operating is really a young man's game.'

What about the political implications of the National Health Service? Were you in favour?

'Certainly,' said Dr Davies firmly. 'It was the best thing that ever happened to this country. From then on, I could decide on treatment for purely medical needs. Before then I had always to choose treatment dependent on the finances of people, on what they could afford.'

Did most GPs think like you?

'I think so, except for a few, the ones who perhaps had recently bought into their practices. That was the system at the time – as a young doctor you very often had to buy into an existing practice. They didn't get any compensation when their practices were nationalised, which in effect was what happened. That didn't concern me because we hadn't bought this practice. It was our own family practice.'

Not long after he first opened, one sister joined him from Wales, having qualified as a pharmacist, to look after his dispensary. She then married a junior doctor, whom Dr Davies had taken into his practice. 'So my partner became my brother-in-law.' Later, his other sister, who was also a pharmacist, joined the practice. At one time, there was a total of eight working doctors in his immediate family. But not all called Davies.

Dr Davies retired from his own practice in 1971, leaving his daughter and son-in-law to continue. His wife Gladys died in 1986, by which time she had Parkinson's disease.

'My parents had the happiest marriage of any couple I have known,' said Dilys. 'They revolved around each other. Even when they were apart for a short time they always wrote. My mother went to Canada every year to see Enid and her children. My father couldn't always go, because of various activities, but they wrote to each other every day they were apart.'

Dr Davies's numerous activities included the Masons, where he was an Assistant Provincial Grand Master, but rugby was his major pleasure. He became captain of the Grasshoppers in 1925–26 and played with them for many years. Dilys dug out some team photos but he was a bit upset not to find the one in which he was captain. Then they remembered: it hangs in the club-house. He never played for Lancashire, but he managed a county trial. 'That year the trial was held down at Waterloo. I got through it all right and was picked to play against Vale of Lune, but I was operating the day of the match so I couldn't make it. I was never picked again.'

He maintains his wife did not feel neglected during his years of rugby and masonry, plus all his many positions as medical officer. He made sure he went out with her one night a week.

'In the old days, it was always a Thursday evening, after my operating day. We always went to the pictures, to the Palladium in Preston, even right through the war. We watched whatever was on – westerns, gangsters, comedies. I loved them all. I always sat in the back row, in the same place, so the usherette knew where I was in case I was wanted in an emergency at the hospital.'

He himself has always had good health. Until he was ninety, the worst that ever happened was tonsillitis in 1934. Then, at ninety, his eyes began to weaken and he started to use a stick for walking, in case he fell. A cataract operation corrected his sight. 'At the age of ninety, he threw away his walking stick,' said Dilys. 'Then he bought himself a new evening suit.'

He lives on his own, makes his own breakfast, then later his help arrives to tidy his house and prepare his lunch. In the evening, Dilys pops in from the main part of the house with his evening meal. He has his TV set specially tuned to S4C, the Welsh ITV station, so that he can enjoy the language of his fathers. On Sunday he listens on the radio to the Welsh religious programme, but just for the singing: it takes him back to his boyhood in the chapel. 'I listen to the hymns in bed, then fall asleep at eleven o'clock.'

Despite his strict Calvinist Methodist upbringing he doesn't go to church or chapel these days. Did that mean he no longer believed in God? 'Oh, I suppose I do believe in God. Who at ninety-six would say otherwise?'

He has never been much interested in politics. He usually voted Tory, said Dilys, while holding socialist views. 'I think, as GPs, my father and I always felt we should not be known for any strong political views because we worked for the whole community.'

'I was once asked,' said her father, leaning forward in his chair, 'if I would stand as the Liberal candidate in the General Election. I nearly

Dr David Davies today

fell through the floor. I asked the lady who had come to see me why she had thought of me. "Because you're Welsh," she said. "We like you and you're a good talker." I just laughed at the very idea.'

I asked Dr Davies Senior if he had any explanations for reaching such a great age. 'No idea. You tell me.' Dilys put it down to his natural optimism, thinking the best of everyone and never getting worried or depressed. 'His is a soul which has not been bothered with philosophical problems. I can't remember him ever railing against anything or anyone in his life.'

'I have, of course, been very lucky as far as health goes,' said her father. 'I've batted very well in life, don't you think? I haven't smoked for the last forty years, and hardly drank, except for a glass of wine at official functions. Perhaps a whisky, if pressed. I suppose it was my Welsh teetotal background which kept me away from drink.'

He has no regrets, no places he would like to have seen, nothing he would like to have done. 'I've seen Europe and North America. Quite enough. It's never come into my head to shoot off to Africa. On the whole, people have been so damn kind to me.'

Would he go through it all again?

'Yes, I could give life another go. I'd enjoy starting again, as long as there were not too many fools or nasty people in my path. I'm not sure about being a GP next time round. The bureaucracy has gone mad. And you have people complaining all the time now. I don't think I would have liked that. But life generally, yes, I've enjoyed it all.'

In the car, taking me to the station, Dilys said her father was a joy to look after, no problems, no moans. 'Except he still thinks I'm fifteen. One of the things which make him easy is that, for ninety-six, he is not cranky in any way. That does happen.

'As a child, I thought he was very strict, and rebelled against him when he said I couldn't read comics on a Sunday. That was just his own Calvinist upbringing. He wasn't strict at all.'

I said I was grateful she had printed out his full CV, so useful, so helpful. It meant I didn't have to ask boring things like dates and sequence of events, which always slow down conversations and interrupt thought processes. But why had she done it?

'It's for his obituary,' she said. 'He's been a fellow of the *BMJ* for many years, so I know they'll want a proper obituary when he goes. So will other medical and local publications. When I decided I'd better get everything down in order for all the obituaries, I thought the best person on him is himself. So he helped me compile it. He was most amused . . .'

20

MONTY HEDGES

Ex-brickie; ex-two World Wars

Monty Hedges, aged about 6

Montague Hedges would not like it all over again. On the face of it, he has been one of the lucky ones in life, one of the few who saw active service in both world wars and survived. At ninety-six, he has all his wits about him, appears as bright as a button, his memory remarkable, exact dates tripping readily off his tongue, but when it came to summing it all up, his first reaction was to say it was depressing. Not just the world in general but how he had ended up.

He was born in London, on 9 November 1900, given the rather posh-sounding name of Montague but never known as such in his own family. He was always Taggy, which was how his five sisters and his two brothers referred to him.

'I was born at one o'clock in the morning,' he added, giving me all the facts. 'At 13 Manor Road, South Norwood.' This is a suburb of London where his father was a jobbing builder, sometimes doing well, sometimes not so well.

'My first memory was when I was three. Does that count as an early memory? We were living in Wembley and I was in the back bedroom when I stood too near the fire in my nightdress and I caught fire. My sister who was eight rushed to put it out and burned her hands saving me.'

He has no real memory of school – there were just so many of them, and so many houses in which he lived when he was young. 'We moved from Wembley to Beaconsfield, High Wycombe, Isleworth, Guildford, Kilburn, Wimbledon, oh, all over, wherever my father could find work.

'I wasn't much good at school, but it was only when I was eight they realised I was unable to see the blackboard. They decided I needed specs. My eyes were dodgy, see. I've worn specs ever since. Not that they do me much good now. I finally left school at fourteen, thank Gawd. I joined my father, of course. It's all I wanted to do. From him I learned to be a bricklayer and a carpenter, and a good brickie and carpenter, excuse me for boasting. Yes, there were apprenticeships in those days, but I just worked with my father, picked it up from him.'

He was in Guildford the day the First World War broke out, but can't remember any feeling of excitement because it was bad for the building trade. Most building work came to a halt as the men went into the services. 'I tried to join up when I was sixteen, and went to a recruiting office in Kilburn. I said I was seventeen and a half. The recruiting sergeant looked at me and said, "Go home and get your birth certificate, sonny."

'My dad then got a job in Scotland, at Ayr, where they were building an aerodrome. He was doing the reinforced concrete for the foundations and I went with him. That's when I first became interested in aeroplanes. When the Ayr hangar was finished, we then moved to this loch near Dunoon where they were building a hangar for the flying-boats. I worked on that with my dad – but when we'd finished it, the flying-boats turned out to be bigger than the hangars. We had to pull them down again. You'd have thought they'd have worked that out beforehand.

'It was while pulling down the hangar I had a nasty accident, caused by a German prisoner-of-war. It wasn't his fault, mind, just an accident. He was pulling down a beam and it crashed into the ladder I was standing on and I fell to the ground. I was in hospital for three weeks.

'Early in 1918, around March, when I was still just seventeen and a bit, I went to Glasgow and volunteered again, this time for the Royal Flying Corps. And I got in. I wanted to be a pilot, as I loved planes, but at my medical test they could see I wore specs. They said I couldn't be a pilot, not wearing specs. So I became an aircraftsman. I went to Halton Camp in Wendover in Buckinghamshire for my square-bashing. I passed out at Weybridge and then I went to Biggin Hill. When they'd asked me what trade I had I'd said I was a carpenter, so they made me a rigger. I looked after the rigging on the planes. Planes were just like kites, really, with wooden frames and bits of canvas, all held together with wires.

'I had to check the struts and the control wires before they set off. I did go up now and again, when a pilot took me for a spin. They were all two-seater planes – Avros and Bristol fighters. If the Bristol fighter went up with just one person, we had to fill it up with ballast. Oh, any old rubbish we could find just to balance the plane. No, I wasn't scared when I went up. The pilot would turn to me and say, "Everything all right?" I'd shout back, "If it's good enough for you, it's good enough for me."

'A lot of them didn't come back when they went on bombing missions, but I remember thinking they were lucky, really, compared with the army. I mean, they went off in their little planes, and they'd drop their little bombs over the side by hand, or try to shoot German planes through the open window with their pistols, then they'd come back and get a good night's sleep in their nice quarters with good food in the Mess. Now, the lads fighting in the trenches, they were stuck there, weren't they? They had no decent bed to go to. I had two brothers-in-law fighting out in France. One of them got killed.'

Some time in 1918, after several months in the Royal Flying Corps, he was told he was now in the RAF. 'No, I didn't ask any questions. You did what you were told. We'd been in khaki, with a sort of fold-over jacket, but when we became the RAF we went into blue uniform. I got ten shillings a week when I first joined the Royal Flying Corps. By the time I left the RAF, still as an aircraftsman, I was getting a pound a week.

'I was demobbed in 1919. I was given a demob suit, sort of brownish, with a bit of grey in it, and a hat, well, a flat cap. I went back to Wembley and joined my dad in the building trade.'

Monty in 1920

He didn't work on the Wembley Exhibition of 1924–25, but when it finished, and most of the exhibition halls were pulled down, he remembers his dad managing to buy a load of timber at a very reasonable price.

There were many lean times, when Monty was out of work and forced to look for employment elsewhere, or in different fields. In 1920 he spent three months working in the bakehouse of a shop in Oxford Street. 'It was called Buzzard's. A patisserie, very high-class, very posh.'

On the counter, at the front, was a young girl called Marie Louise Phillips, who turned out to live not far from him in Wembley. They started courting and she became his first real girlfriend. 'Well, I had a cousin I was fond of, but that didn't come to anything.'

One day, on the way to work, he saw that a new photographic shop had opened in Oxford Street, offering three snaps for ten shillings, so he went in and had his photograph taken. He gave one to Marie and one to his mother. (Could it have been the same shop where Dr Davies had his photograph taken? Monty was adamant it had been in Oxford Street and not Regent Street. No doubt there were many.)

Monty and Marie married on 6 October 1923, at St John's Church in Wembley. Quite a lavish wedding, for a working man, with the bride in white and six bridesmaids – four adult girls and two younger ones – all clutching chrysanthemums. They even had a honeymoon, two weeks in Southampton. 'Not a hotel. We stayed at the home of one of Marie's relations.'

Then they moved into their own house, built by his father. 'He was the builder, but I had to pay for it. It should have cost £1,250, because it was a good house, detached. Oh, yes. I can remember the address – 36 District Road, Sudbury, Middlesex. All I had to pay was £840. I didn't have a penny, but I got an £840 mortgage from the Cheltenham & Gloucester.'

It was in that house that their first four children were born, all girls – Marie in 1925, Pam in 1930, Patricia in 1932 and Brenda in 1933.

He eventually gave up working with his father, but was never employed in the normal sense, preferring to be a freelance bricklayer or carpenter. 'I did piecework, getting a certain price for a set job. It meant if it went well, I got a pound more than an ordinary brickie.' It also meant he was often out of work.

In 1935, twelve years into his mortgage, he ran out of money and started accumulating debts. 'I had a sequence of bad luck. They were pestering and pestering me for the money, and it got so bad I decided to hop it. I just did a bunk. I took my wife and children and we hopped it to Harrow Weald where I rented a small flat. It was a bad turning, really. I was told later that if only I'd been able to find twenty-five pounds, they would have let me stay, and then, whatever happened, they would have been forced to pay me something if they'd taken the house off me.'

Were there, er, other reasons for getting behind with the money, such as gambling or drink?

'No,' said Monty. 'I've never gambled. I often had a few drinks and a game of dominoes, after a hard day at work, just to relax, but that wasn't the reason.'

Later I asked Brenda, his youngest daughter, if there was more to the story than he'd told me. 'I don't think so,' she said. 'Daddy has gone through life saying that if only he'd had that twenty-five pounds things would have been so much different. I believe him.'

Things were still bad when the Second World War broke out, by which time they had a fifth and final child, Doug, born in 1935.

'The winter of 1939 to 1940 was terrible. The war had stopped most house building, then the bad winter made any sort of building work impossible. The only way I could think of to get a regular income was to join up. I didn't want to leave home and my young family, but I knew they would be guaranteed money for the rent and for food if I was in the army. So I joined the Royal Engineers. I was thirty-nine at the time. No, I don't know what the age limit was, or whether they perhaps waived it. But anyway, the Engineers took me.'

So, once again, he was into uniform, and once again he had to go through square-bashing, even though he had done all that in the last war. 'I did my training at Dover then we went across to France. Near Deauville. We were set to work to build fences round the gun emplacements, in case the Jerries came and tried to get at the guns. They were pretty useless fences. Any Jerry could have knocked them down with his jack-boot.

'The Germans were soon advancing, invading Denmark, Holland and Belgium. I remember saying to our lieutenant, Mr Chapman, that we'd better be doing something soon or the Germans would be through the Maginot Line, just as they were in the First World War.'

Towards the end of May 1940 the Germans had entered France and were working their way down the coast to Boulogne. On 27 May the British began the evacuation from Dunkirk. Over the next week, 299 British warships and 420 other vessels, many of them makeshift and fragile, managed to rescue 335,490 Allied officers and men from the beaches of Dunkirk.

'We didn't make it. While most of the lads were being chased into the boats, we got lost. We just got cut off, isolated inland. There was still some French resistance, and we were supposed to help them, but they soon fell. When that happened, we were stuck. No communications line, no grub, no nothing.

'For two weeks we did nothing but march, march, march. No idea where we were going. We just had hardtack to keep us alive, sort of dry biscuits. Then we found a few abandoned lorries, left by the British, which had some bully beef on board and some MacConachie. That was a tinned stew.

'We didn't do any fighting. We spent most of the time either marching or hiding. Can you blame us? We slept in the open or in tents, if we happened to find any lying around.

'On 17 June 1940, we got to St Malo and we were taken aboard the troopship *Britannic*. There was about eight hundred of us got away on it. I can remember clearly going on board, absolutely exhausted, but it's funny, I can't remember getting off. The moment I got on board, I spotted this mattress and I just fell on it and went straight to sleep. I was so flaked out. I wasn't so young, don't forget. I was just about to turn forty.

'Some time afterwards, an officer woke me up and said, "You can't sleep there, corporal, we've got some wounded." So I got up, and then fell back to sleep again on the deck. That's probably why I can't remember us landing. It was at Southampton, I know that, but I have no memory of arriving. I can remember getting the train to Bournemouth, and when we got there we were given bread and marmalade, but I can't remember Southampton. Funny, that . . .'

Brenda, then aged seven, remembers her father coming home from France. She hardly recognised him as he'd been away so long.

After a spell of home leave, he reported back to barracks. 'I had to see the MO, of course. As you'll know, after you'd been on leave you always had to have a medical inspection. As I was getting my clothes on afterwards, he says to me, "Corporal, you're having trouble doing up your buttons. What's the problem?" He then examined me and found I had Reynaud's disease. It's to do with the capillaries in the cold weather. They're meant to open but they don't, not if you've got Reynaud's disease. Your fingers go mauve then blue, then white and you can't use them 'cos they go numb.

'I'd known I had the problem, but I'd always been able to manage in the summer or warm weather, whenever I was on rifle practice, machine-gun practice or whatever. It was just in cold weather I had any real trouble. That was when it was dodgy.

'I went before a full medical board and they went into it all, lots of examinations and that. I was then discharged from the army. They said they didn't want to do it but they were pushing me out. At the board, I was asked if I'd had it before I joined the army, if I'd had it in civilian life. I said yes. That was a silly mistake. If I'd said no, I would have got an army pension on medical grounds, but I never did. I got no pension, not a sausage, for serving in either war.

'Oh, yes, I knew I'd got it. So it would have been a lie. My father had

it. He could never use his hands in cold weather. Brenda and Doug have
it as well. It doesn't affect me now, stuck in here. It's never cold in here,
is it?'

In October 1941, having done nearly two years in the army, Monty
tried to find a job. Which was why he had joined up in the first place –
and nearly lost his life, or at least his freedom, in the process.

In the army, as a corporal, he had been on twenty-eight shillings a
week – little more than he'd had as an RAF aircraftsman in the First
World War. In those decades between the wars, there had been little or
no inflation; if anything, the pound had been worth more in 1920
than in 1940.

The war had one minor good effect, though: when Monty returned
to civilian life, there was more work around, thanks to the London
Blitz. 'I got a job building shelters. No, not the ones you had in your
house or garden but the public ones, built of concrete, which were put
up in the streets or open spaces.

'We had an Anderson shelter in our own house, the steel sort, under
the table. We got a lot of doodle-bugs in our area. There was a gasworks
behind our house, which the Germans were trying to get. One night,
during the bombing, my wife and the kids got under the table, but I
went on sitting in a chair, reading the paper, when damn me, all the
windows were blown in. I was lifted up in the air, right out of my
chair. They were good windows as well, with leaded lights.'

Monty finished his working years as a foreman for Wembley
Borough Council, retiring in 1964. By then his children had grown up
and he and his wife bought a flat in Lewisham for his retirement. His
wife died in 1980, aged eighty, after suffering from cancer of the bowel.
'Our wedding anniversary was on 6 October and she died the next
day, 7 October.'

As ever, Monty was exact when it came to dates, ticking them off in
his mind, noting anniversaries of every sort. 'Next 15 February I'll have
been in this place four years. Worse luck . . .'

For eight years after his wife's death, he lived alone, and managed
well, he said, caring for himself. Then his eyes began to fade and his legs
grew weaker. His son Doug had moved to Australia, to work for a tool-
making firm, but all his four daughters continued to live in London or
the south of England. Naturally they worried about him living alone,

with his poor sight, fearing he would fall and hurt himself. For a few years he moved round between them, living with each in turn. Four years ago, he moved into a nursing home in Hertfordshire, where he now lives, in order to get professional care. Brenda, his youngest daughter, with whom he had lived for the previous couple of years, is not far away and comes to see him almost every day.

Apart from his weak eyes, and stiff legs, he seemed in reasonable physical condition for ninety-six. There was no doubt that he was as sharp mentally as he had ever been. His own father and mother lived to eighty-three and eighty-seven, but Monty has long since outlived his four sisters and two brothers. How did he explain living so long?

'Dunno.' He sighed. 'Haven't a clue.' He didn't seem the slightest bit interested in the topic. Of everyone else I spoke to who had been born in 1900 most had had their pet theories, only too pleased to pass them on. But not Monty.

So I asked if he had advice for other people hoping to live to a ripe old age. 'Nope,' he said, giving another sigh, indicating this was a very boring line of questioning. 'No ideas.'

I then asked if he would say it had been a hard life. He immediately brightened up.

'Oh, very, very hard life, but hard work never hurt anyone. Hard work is good for you.'

How about regrets? 'Can't think of any. I never had much money but that's the way it went.'

How about travel? 'Perhaps I regret not going to South Africa. My father's brother asked me to, after the last war, but I didn't. So that was it.' Monty's uncle had emigrated to South Africa earlier on and become a successful architect, so he would have had several family connections there, if he had gone.

He has never been abroad, apart from war service in France, and has never been on a plane, apart from quick flips round the aerodrome in his First World War years. But no, he wouldn't say he missed not having travelled or having been on a foreign holiday. He never owned a car either, though now and again he drove the builder's van illegally.

'I did sit the test once and failed. I got tricked, if you ask me. The tester said at the bottom of this street turn right, and when we got there, it was a dual carriageway, so I tried to turn into it because he'd said go right, but of course I couldn't. So he failed me. I was cheated, if you ask me. So I never sat the test again.'

He said he had never been interested much in politics, but always voted Tory. 'I remember feeling sorry for Churchill in 1945. I voted for him, and was very surprised when he didn't get in.' He never joined a trade union: he was against unions on principle.

Looking at the world in general, he can see no improvements in his lifetime, apart from television. 'There's been no other advances. Everything's gone from bad to worse. There's too many people today. Too many cars. When I was young, the place was empty. I can remember going on my motorbike in 1923 from Wembley to Rickmansworth, which is about fifteen miles, and never seeing a car, not one car. Look at the population. We've got fifty million here today. There were only thirty million when I was young. When I was seven, I'd never seen a coloured person, a black person. If you did, you'd point him out. Now everyone's black, aren't they?

'And everywhere you go it's rape and murders and knifings. The papers are full of it, all the time. Terrible.'

His favourite newspaper has been the *News of the World*, not that he can read it, these days. He has a TV in his room and tries to watch it, but says it's a bit of a blur. He dresses and shaves himself, but doesn't go to the dining room for meals as he finds he walks into walls, unless there's a good hand-rail. Anyway, his knees have now become so weak that any walking is an effort.

'If only I could see a bit better, but I look through a glass darkly.' He paused, as if knowing that was a strange phrase for him to use. 'When I try to walk, I usually go arse over tit . . .'

He stopped and put his hand over his mouth in mock apology. It was the first time I'd noticed a smile. While he was totally lucid, with perfect hearing, understood everything and never faltered for a date or a memory, he had looked faintly miserable all the time. I'd presumed at first it was mainly due to the pain in his knees.

Brenda, who had been sitting with me, said she was going outside to have a smoke. As soon as she'd gone, Monty got up from his bed, with some effort. He had been lying on it during our conversation, fully clothed. He said he wanted to have a word with Terry.

Terry is his budgerigar, his companion for the last three years. The bird belongs to the home and used to live in the sitting room, but no one seemed interested in it. 'The women couldn't be bothered so I took it over. I gave it the name Terry just because I used to have a budgie of my own called Terry.'

Monty asked where Brenda had gone and I said just outside, for a smoke. Monty himself had smoked a pipe most of his life, and loved it dearly, but gave it up after his wife died. He felt it had begun to make him feel dizzy.

'You're sure she's outside?' asked Monty, getting back on his bed. I reassured him that she was.

'I never thought I'd end up here,' he said, leaning towards me. 'I never did. If I could see properly and my legs were up to it I wouldn't be here, not another minute. I just never thought it would happen.

'It's no life this, you know. I'll be glad when I've had enough. I'll be glad when it's over . . .

'I'm *compos mentis*, but I'm stuck here with all these women. I'm the only man here, you know. I'm stuck with eighteen women – and some are disturbed. They walk into my room in the middle of the night in their nightdress. It's not funny. I know they can't help it, poor old souls, but I didn't want to come here. Oh, I never thought it would come to this. I've got no pleasures left . . .'

Brenda came back at this point, and gave her father a cuddle. She checked that his legs were not hurting him, and asked if he'd like a little drink, a spot of his usual: his mouth must be tired with all the talking. He grunted a reply and she poured him a whisky, which he sipped slowly.

'Hasn't he got lovely hands?' she said. 'Daddy, you've got lovely thin hands, haven't you? People always remarked on that. Lovely hands, for a builder.'

Monty continued to sip his whisky. He has one every morning, usually about eleven o'clock, his daily treat. In his working days he would sink a few pints every evening, either beer or Guinness. He would like to have a whisky in the evening as well as the morning, as his nightcap, but he says the home won't allow it because he has medicines to take at night.

Brenda had brought a pile of photographs for me to look through.

There was one of Monty from the First World War, wearing a Royal Flying Corps cap, but very worn, flaky and very small, too delicate to remove from its frame. It had been worn as a miniature, hung on a necklace that his wife had carried round her neck.

'That was my happiest time,' said Monty. 'After I got married. Those were the happy years. It all ended for me, really, after she died. Now I've lost so much. I've completely and utterly lost my independence. So that's it, then. That wraps it up, you might say . . .'

I twittered on about the home, which had nice gardens and the staff seemed pleasant, though I hadn't seen many of the other residents. Monty groaned. He'd had enough of me, so I thanked him for all his time and effort and memories.

I was grateful to see him. I'd arranged to talk to him three months earlier, but he had cancelled, saying he couldn't be bothered with talking about his life. He couldn't be bothered with anything, really.

Outside, I told Brenda what he'd said when she'd left the room. 'I thought he would,' she said. 'That's why I left. I knew he wanted a good moan. There's been a lot of moans since he went into this home, but what else could we do? Once his eyesight went, and he started to fall, he needed proper care.

'But that wasn't the only reason he was falling. Until recently, he was getting through two bottles of Scotch a week. Which, of course, didn't

Monty today

please the nurses here, not when he started falling down in the home. That's really why he's just allowed a glass a day in the morning.'

I said it seemed a harmless enough pleasure, as long as he wasn't harming others, considering his age and what he has been through. In his position, I'd be moaning much worse, and probably not be as honest, looking back on my life.

'Yes, he has had a hard life, but he's been a good father and a good husband.'

21

HAMBURGERS

The famous golden arches

Hamburgers are a twentieth-century creation, born in 1900, so most students of hamburger history agree, though we in Britain had to stagger on without them till many decades later. But we had already experienced that other defining ingredient of modern life, Coca-Cola. That first arrived in London in 1900 from the USA, where it had already existed for fourteen years. We can't therefore say soft drinks were of this century, but fast food certainly has been.

There was no fast food as such in 1900, apart from stalls in the street selling chestnuts, fruit and sweetmeats, or any pre-packaged food in the home. Mass production of food in advance began with the First World War, when catering on a large scale was first attempted. Cafeteria-style eating, where you queued up at a counter, was also a wartime innovation.

In ordinary people's homes, a lot of potatoes and a lot of bread were eaten, the latter sometimes with jam, and a lot of beer drunk. Beer was the only luxury food, or luxury of any sort, for ordinary working people. Sometimes it was taken to excess, hence the rise of the teetotal movement and the proliferation of those illustrations, all too typical, of underfed children, hanging around the door of the pub, waiting for their father to come out with what was left, if anything, of his wages.

The better-off had meat and poultry and lots of vegetables – at least, those native to our shores and in the appropriate season. They could indulge themselves with fancier fare at restaurants and hotels, sitting down to be served by uniformed staff.

I have in front of me *The Times* for 4 December 1900, which I bought as a present for my father-in-law – that was the day of his birth – but, of course, I really bought it for myself. On the front page, the Royal Palace Hotel, Kensington, was offering lunch that day for three shillings and dinner for five shillings, which also included music by the Blue Hungarian Band who played daily. Electric light throughout was another attraction, which most posh London hotels boasted, and also electric lifts.

No mention anywhere in the prints of the day of hamburgers. We are, of course, talking hamburgers as we know them today. Should the talk get round to hamburger meat, then that's another story. Who knows when that began? There was some form of minced or chopped-up beef long before there was recorded history.

One form of that chopped-up meat began to be called a 'hamburger steak' early in the nineteenth century in the USA, introduced by German seamen who had come originally from Hamburg. The word itself is said to have been first used on a menu in a restaurant called Delmonico's in New York in 1836. Frankfurter sausages were named in much the same way – a sausage produced by people in or from Frankfurt. Likewise, a certain sauce favoured by people from Bologna became Bolognese sauce.

At this stage, the hamburger steak referred simply to the meat. Hard to believe that for centuries no one had thought of doing anything else with it. Equally hard to believe no one had thought of a sandwich – until it was 'invented' in 1762. That's the official birth of the sandwich, the year when the 4th Earl of Sandwich, during a hard day and night at the gambling table, decided he was far too busy to get up and eat proper food, and kept himself going by eating meat shoved between two bits of bread. Everything else he did in his life, such as being First Lord of the Admiralty during the American Revolution, or serving as postmaster general, has been forgotten. He has gone down in history because the sandwich was named after him.

The first known person said to have put a piece of hot hamburger steak between two bits of bread was a certain Louis Lassen of New Haven, Connecticut, some time in 1900. No day or month is recorded but it happened at his three-seater, roadside café called Louis Lunch. His name didn't pass into the language, unlike Lord Sandwich's, partly because presumably there were other people, in other cafés, in other towns, doing much the same, and because the meat itself already had a name. In that same year, 1900, the word hamburger, still meaning the steak, appeared in a dictionary for the first time, a new French–German–English dictionary of food compiled by a Mr Blüher.

What established the hamburger, meaning hamburger steak in a bun, was the 1904 World Exposition in St Louis, where the Olympic Games, the first in the USA, were also being held. Scores of vendors, mostly of German extraction, did a roaring trade by cooking hamburgers, shoving them in buns and selling them to people who wanted to wander round, watching the excitements, eating as they went. It was from that year that the word hamburger came to mean not just the meat but the meat in a bun.

There was never, of course, any connection with ham. The hamburger, like the Hamburger steak, contained beef, not pork. Later on, the word was shortened further, though etymologists are still arguing about exactly when, and the rather ugly little word burger emerged and sneaked into most known languages.

For the next fifteen years or so, hamburgers were eaten widely across America, but they were considered standing-up food, on-the-move food, cooked and sold at wayside barbecues and stalls.

It was not until 1921 that the first of a chain of proper hamburger restaurants was opened, where you sat down at counters, ordered and ate your hamburger. The restaurants were created by W. E. Ingram in Kansas and he called them, rather grandly, White Castle, giving a hint of elegance to a very cheap and modest meal. Each hamburger cost only five cents, but they were only about a third of the size of the modern hamburger. Customers were encouraged to buy them by the bag. Within a few years, he had eleven White Castle restaurants, by which time they were being copied by similar-sounding small chains, such as Royal Castle and White Tower.

The first literary reference to a hamburger was made by the American writer Thomas Wolfe in his novel *You Can't Go Home Again*, published in 1947, but set in 1929. His description of a group of truck drivers sitting in a transport café, eating hamburgers, has hardly dated, and hardly been bettered: 'They poured great gobs and gluts of thick tomato ketchup on their sizzling hamburgers, then tore with blackened fingers at the slabs of pungent bread and ate with jungle lust, thrusting at their plates and cups with quick and savage gulpings.'

The small chains of hamburger restaurants that sprang up across America in the 1920s varied slightly from state to state. In California, they favoured open-air, drive-in hamburger places. It wasn't simply because of the weather, local affluence played a part, with so many people, especially teenagers, having access to their own car.

One of these was created in San Bernardino, California, by two brothers, Maurice and Richard McDonald. They had moved to California from New England around 1926 and got jobs as scene-shifters and truck-drivers in the movie business. They saved enough money to buy their own little cinema, which they opened in 1932. It didn't do very well. Then they noticed that a hot-dog salesman, working from a stall nearby, was making more money than they were, so in 1937 they decided to try opening an eating place instead. It was a simple, drive-in restaurant, doing barbecued food, such as hot dogs.

After the war, though they seemed to be working as hard and there were always queues in their car park, business was not as profitable. They analysed the reasons, then closed down, and reopened in 1948 with a newly designed restaurant. It was still a drive-in but with a streamlined service, like one of Mr Ford's car assembly plants. It produced only hamburgers, french fries and soft drinks. It was a big success, and became well-known locally.

Their name would never have been known outside San Bernardino but for a soda-fountain salesman in Chicago called Ray Kroc. Which brings us to one of America's all-time legends. Every American knows about Kroc, the man behind McDonald's. There are even those who believe there never was a McDonald. That it was just a neat name Kroc picked at random. McDonald's themselves do little to suggest they had any history pre-Kroc.

In 1954, Ray Kroc was fifty-two, suffering from diabetes and arthritis and missing a gall bladder. He'd had a varied career as a pianist in a brothel, a salesman of paper cups, and was currently selling Multi-mixers, a new machine that mixed five milk shakes at a time, a good idea, but not one that most restaurants needed unless they had a lot of customers. He was surprised therefore when a drive-in hamburger joint in California, of which he had never heard, ordered eight of his Multimixers. He decided to go down to see their operation, hoping to sell them even more of his machines.

He was amazed by the queues, impressed by the efficiency, liked the taste of their hamburgers, loved their french fries. He met the McDonald brothers and suggested they should open more places on the same lines, hoping, of course, that they would therefore need more Multimixers. They said that one was enough, thank you. They had their retirement homes all planned, didn't want to expand, were happy as they were. In that case, said Ray Kroc, perhaps they might let other people copy their format. Such as, well, himself.

After some discussion, they agreed he could have the right to franchise their idea throughout the whole of the USA – apart from those the brothers had already sold: they had licensed their idea to ten other drive-ins, mainly in California. This did not perturb Ray Kroc, who went ahead with the deal. He agreed that the brothers would receive 0.5 per cent of the turnover from any future McDonald's, which he would pay them out of the 1.9 per cent he would personally take from every franchise.

He went back to Chicago and borrowed the money to start the first restaurant, following the principles and the architecture the brothers had established. This proved a bit difficult. An open air drive-in built for the heat of California could not readily translate to the freezing winters of Chicago, yet he had agreed with the brothers not to deviate from their master plan, unless he had signed permission from them to do so, sent by registered letter. However, whenever he made any changes, they spoke on the phone, but nothing was ever written. From the beginning, he was technically in breach of the agreement.

In California they had stored goods outside, in the fresh air, but that was impossible in Chicago, so he built a storage basement. Then he found that although he was using the same potatoes, same oils, same methods, the french fries were nothing like as nice. It turned out that storing the spuds outside in California, in baskets made of chicken wire, dried them. Spuds are mostly water so the effect had been to create a dry spud, perfect for frying. To get the same taste in Chicago, Kroc had to use hot-air blowers, belting out in his basement.

He opened his first version of a McDonald's in Des Plaines, a suburb of Chicago, on 15 April 1955. It was a big success, but then he discovered that the McDonald brothers had, in fact, sold a franchise to someone else in Chicago. He had presumed he had exclusive rights everywhere outside California. He was forced to buy the other restaurant for $25,000, all of which he borrowed.

The McDonald brothers had taken little interest in the ten franchises they had sold for a thousand dollars each before Kroc came along. They kept no control, made no checks, allowed each operation to go its own way, with different menus, different prices. They took no royalty income either, so it didn't matter to them what happened. Neither had children, they had made their pile and were quite happy with what they had done in San Bernardino. By 1955 their own little restaurant had a turnover of $350,000, all from 15-cent hamburgers, which gave them a profit of $100,000. Their kitchen was open for all to see, and they didn't seem to mind if people copied their methods and style for nothing.

Long before Kroc had appeared on the scene they had even created the Golden Arches symbol over their restaurant. In many senses, then, Kroc was not an innovator. But, as with many creations in human history, from steam engines to cars and aeroplanes, the person who makes new ideas work, perfects them and makes them available to all, is just as much a genius as whoever had the idea in the first place. Kroc is certainly considered as such in the USA, the Henry Ford of hamburgers. Neither man invented what he is best known for, but each made the invention they took up part of the American way of life.

Kroc didn't even invent franchising – that's yet another American creation. Its origins go back to the early nineteenth century when the Singer Sewing Machine Company sold franchises to local operators, letting them run their own Singer stores. A similar system was taken up by the early motor-car manufacturers in the 1900s, but this, again, was a manufacturer's franchise, a dealership, like Singer, selling a product.

It wasn't until the 1920s that franchises moved into food services. It began with identical little roadside stalls selling the same root beer, or the same make of ice cream; then in the 1930s, franchised restaurants appeared, the best-known being the Howard Johnson roadside chain in 1935.

From the long years he had spent in selling paper cups and soda fountains to restaurants and chains all over the States, Kroc knew about the franchise business, all the problems, all the tricks. Many franchises went bust because they were a con, no more than pyramid selling, with franchise holders buying the rights to a large area, such as a state, then making their money by selling on local franchises. Their income was purely from selling franchises, not from producing any product. They didn't care about that.

From the beginning, Kroc took total control and worked on a long-term plan; he was not out to make a fast buck. He realised that if customers were happy, the local franchisees made money and were happy. In turn, he made money. And he was happy.

Another trick used by many franchisers was to make money on the actual goods and services they supplied: they forced individual restaurants to buy everything from them, often at higher prices and inferior quality. Kroc made sure that his highly controlled mass purchasing was not to make money for himself but to help his franchisees, in the knowledge they could not get burgers or buns cheaper or better than his.

In the first year, eight McDonald's restaurants were opened in Chicago. Kroc laid down exactly the system, prices, décor and furnishings. He banned juke-boxes, pay-phones and vending-machines, all of which provided an easy income for most American restaurants, but Kroc believed they encouraged loitering and unproductive traffic, which he didn't want in his restaurants. Neither did he want the undesirable connections associated with vending-machines, which were often supplied by criminal gangs. Kroc trained his managers personally, instilling in them his mantra of Q, S, C and V – Quality, Service, Cleanliness and Value.

By 1957 there were twenty-five restaurants, but Kroc himself had still not made any money. He was still living on his salary from the Multimixer business, though he soon gave that up. By 1959 there were a hundred McDonald's, all still in the Chicago area.

He hired a full-time property agent to look for new sites, but this led to a financial crisis when the agent turned out to be a crook and ran up huge debts, which had to be settled by Kroc himself. Now, though, he was finding it easy to borrow from banks and other institutions: they could all see the enormous amount of cash each McDonald's outlet was bringing in.

In 1961 he offered to buy out the McDonald brothers. His relationship with them had deteriorated and they had no interest in what he was doing, so he asked them to name their price. They said $2.7 million would cover everything, including their original restaurant, which they were still running. They reckoned that that would give them a million each, with the rest for tax. Kroc considered it extortionate, but agreed to pay up, borrowing the money from the banks at a high rate. (He ended up paying back £12 million, as the banks had cleverly written into the deal a share of future profits for themselves.)

At the last moment, the McDonalds changed their mind, saying they wanted to keep their restaurant, though Kroc could have everything else, their name, the whole concept, all royalties. Otherwise the deal was off. Kroc was furious, but had to give in. Eventually, he opened one of his McDonald's opposite theirs, and ran them out of business.

For their $2.7 million, the brothers had, of course, given up the 0.5 per cent royalties they held under their original deal with Kroc. If only they had hung on to that for a little while longer they would have made $2.7 million a year. Today, well, their royalty total would be in billions rather than millions.

In 1963, the five hundredth student graduated from the Hamburger University, which Kroc had opened to teach his management staff. In 1966, McDonald's went public. In 1967, the first McDonald's opened outside the USA – in Canada. In 1968, the thousandth restaurant opened – back in Des Plaines. In 1972 the two-thousandth opened, again in Des Plaines. McDonald's love all these facts and figures, which they issue in a glossy booklet after every big event, congratulating themselves and the genius of Kroc.

The three-thousandth restaurant opened in 1974 – in little old London, England. The five-thousandth opened in 1975 in Japan. The six-thousandth opened in 1980 in Germany. In 1990 they opened in Moscow. Today, there are over eighteen thousand McDonald's worldwide, in eighty-nine different countries. And still counting.

Kroc died in 1984, aged eighty-two, by which time he had indulged his boyhood interest in sport by buying a national baseball team and a hockey team. He'd set up Ronald McDonald children's homes around the world, created the Kroc Foundation, received honorary degrees from all the best US universities and written his life story. He married three times, but had no children. (Maurice McDonald died in 1971 and Dick McDonald in 1998.)

In the USA today, McDonald's is still the leader in its field, but has been facing serious competition from its rival Burger King, which also opened in 1954. McDonald's had an embarrassing failure in the USA with the launch of a superior, so-called adult burger, the Arch Deluxe, which they withdrew. It was never tried in the UK. Here McDonald's still reigns supreme, at least commercially, and is under little threat from its rivals.

It is now almost forgotten that Britain had hamburgers long before McDonald's opened here in 1974. They were first heard of during the Second World War, with the arrival of thousands of American troops – over here, over-sexed and over-filled with fast foods. American troops were the vanguard of the American way of life, our first glimpse in the flesh, as opposed to films, of people with crew-cuts who chewed gum, ate hamburgers, drank Coke and seemed terribly glamorous.

The Wimpy Bar was unveiled in Britain at the Ideal Home Exhibition of 1954, our first chain of hamburger restaurants, still going, but fairly modestly, now owned by a management buy-out. Wendy's is another hamburger chain, which disappeared for a while, but has now reopened. In the UK, Burger King is owned by Grand Metropolitan. It is very successful, and the nearest rival to McDonald's, with 417 restaurants. But McDonald's, with 750 restaurants in 1997, is the brand leader, the acknowledged heavy in the hamburger hierarchy, both here and around the planet.

The British headquarters of McDonald's is in East Finchley, North London, housed in a rather austere brick-built office block, functional rather than flash, which looks more East European than American. In the entrance hall, along with various framed awards, such as the Queen Mother's Birthday Award for Tidy Britain, there is a plaque commemorating the opening ceremony in 1989 by the local Tory MP, who also happened to be the Prime Minister of the day, Margaret Thatcher.

In an office I noticed a framed motto on the wall exhorting the virtues of being a mature human, signed by the President of McDonald's in the US, though it read more like Patience Strong. This wasn't typical of the company in this country, I was told. They were really very British. For example, they call their management training school a management training school, not a university, as they do in the States. It's part of their headquarters and I went round it later and was most impressed. It is well worth the title of a university department, judging by the lavish audio-visual lecture rooms. It has a full-time staff of twenty and trains several hundred managers every year, almost all of them graduates.

When McDonald's first arrived in the UK, the first priority was to find and create their own suppliers, starting as Kroc did with potatoes. They wanted Russet Burbank, a variety not known in the UK, so they had to be imported and grown. They needed bakers to provide buns to their precise specifications. Most of the original suppliers have become multi-million-pound companies. None is owned by McDonald's and none has a contract. It is all done on a handshake, just as Mr Kroc insisted.

The UK McDonald's differs from the American model in that the UK restaurants are mostly owned and operated by the company. Only 23 per cent are franchised, compared with over 80 per cent in the US. This is to do with their British history, and also because the notion of franchising was not as common in the UK as in America.

In Britain, all McDonald's sites are owned by the company, even

Ray Kroc of McDonald's

those that have been franchised. That explains why you don't see many McDonald's on motorways, at least not so far. The company always insists on having total control over the way a restaurant operates. Other burger restaurants can be seen in motorway service stations, but whatever the name, they are usually run by the service stations, which McDonald's won't allow.

A McDonald's in the UK might appear to be an exact clone of a McDonald's in New York or Moscow, offering the same burger at the same sort of price in the same sort of environment, all of which McDonald's believe is vital to their world-wide appeal, but a discerning eye can spot certain regional differences. In France, a stronger pepper sauce is added to the burgers. Britain created its own veggie burger, which it took five years to perfect.

McDonald's UK says it was purely to offer a choice, not to replace the Big Mac. If there are four or five people coming to eat in a McDonald's, the chances are, these days, that one will be a vegetarian. They thought it sensible to offer a vegetarian alternative, otherwise all five might decide to eat elsewhere.

In Britain, they have done trials with pizzas, as a minor item on the menu, but after two years they were dropped. They also offered mixed salads and most recently a pre-packed pasta salad.

Unlike America, Britain is still in the throes of expansion. In the USA, they have been going twenty years longer and there is one McDonald's for every 20,000 of the population. In the UK it is still only one to 80,000. So the march of the mighty McDonald's army goes on, still with fields to conquer.

Despite what some people might think, there has not been a lot of opposition. The best-known campaign against the arrival of a McDonald's was in Hampstead, London. The local preservation society felt a McDonald's would ruin the look of the High Street and battled against it for about ten years. McDonald's won and the Hampstead McDonald's is well established. In fact, it looks relatively discreet, compared with some more recent High Street arrivals. It also has the cleanest lavatories in Hampstead.

There is one less well-known battle they didn't win, and that was on their own doorstep in East Finchley. The High Road outside their headquarters is of little historical or architectural interest and looks just the sort of place you'd expect to find a McDonald's – but there isn't one. McDonald's put forward a proposal but it was refused planning permission. They withdrew without appealing, and opened another restaurant half a mile up the road.

There is a McDonald's restaurant on the headquarters site, but purely for the staff. At first glance, it looks a typical McDonald's, in design and staff uniform, but the menu is wider: it offers a salad bar and a choice of main course. That day, watching the staff having their own lunch, I noted half were eating burgers and the other half spaghetti Bolognese. A burger every day of the week wouldn't, of course, be good for you, as even they agree.

Elsewhere in Britain the plan is to open up to a hundred new McDonald's every year, well into the millennium. If you'd like to manage one, or even own a franchise, you should apply now. There will be lots of opportunities – but the conditions are pretty strict.

There are two sorts of McDonald's franchises. The traditional one costs over £250,000, depending on size and location. For that money, you are buying the business for twenty years, with fixtures and fittings, but not the building. That always belongs to McDonald's. You also pay a percentage of your turnover to McDonald's. They think of this not as a royalty but as a contribution towards the McDonald's marketing and publicity budget, from which, of course, you will gain.

The second franchise is for only three years. For this you pay nothing but have to show that you have £40,000 available to cover your running costs, wages and supplies in the first few months before the cash rolls in. This scheme is meant to encourage suitable employees to have a go. If they do it successfully, their three-year lease can be converted to a full twenty-year franchise.

Some franchise holders are employees who have worked their way up and been on the management courses, then helped by McDonald's to become franchise owners. Another rule makes it easier for McDonald's staff to succeed: all franchise holders must be hands-on active participants. They don't want investors, absentee owners or companies. They won't tell you how much you might make, which is something all would-be franchisees want to know. After being trained, you will be offered a restaurant and then you'll hear about the budget plan of the store in question.

McDonald's is not obliged to publish its figures as it is a private company, but the average turnover for the average store is around £1.5 million (in-house, they talk about 'stores', not restaurants). If you estimate a 10 per cent profit on such a turnover, and take off the royalty fee, a franchise owner must therefore make around £100,000 a year.

In Britain, they don't consider Burger King a real worry, or any of the other smaller hamburger chains, but they acknowledge the competition from Britain's thousands of fish-and-chip shops, which, of course, provide an older version of fast food, and the rise and rise of pub food, which offers a serious alternative for quick snackers.

The two most serious threats to McDonald's business have come from other sources. The first was the BSE crisis of 1996, when British cattle were found to be carrying the disease and which led to widespread banning and general fear of British beef. It was a catastrophe for British farmers, the Tory government and the meat industry. Overnight, McDonald's UK business fell by 50 per cent. They instantly withdrew British beef, then issued reassuring messages. Their suppliers had to import all their beef, which wasn't a major problem as 50 per cent was already coming from abroad. Business eventually returned to the normal rate, but it took over a year before McDonald's felt confidence was strong enough to reintroduce British beef.

The other and possibly even more damaging event has been the so-called 'McLibel' case, which ate right into the heart of McDonald's and what they think they stand for. It began back in 1984 when leaflets started appearing alleging, among other things, that McDonald's hamburgers were bad for your health, that the company was a bad employer and that it damaged the environment. McDonald's took steps to stop the leaflets before it all ended up in court. The trial lasted three years – 314 days actually in court – and was the longest in British history, and produced a book, acres of newsprint and hours of television.

During the course of the trial, McDonald's had made few public statements, and were not going to say much now. The trial had made it hard for anyone trying to get even harmless information about McDonald's, such as myself, wanting only their history. When I first tried to contact them, it was as if they were under siege, and I found it hard even to get the names of their executives.

The biggest mystery about the whole affair was why they bothered to take to court two unknown, unemployed people who managed their own defence, without lawyers, and became national heroes, glamorous figures, representing the Little People against McDonald's, the Big International Bullies.

McDonald's didn't see it in those terms. They say McDonald's is a family, with lots of family members. Many of the staff are shareholders through stock option schemes. Staff were saying their children were coming home from school having been told by their teachers that McDonald's cut down rainforests. Was it true? Could their company possibly do such a thing? If so, could they trust them any more? They decided they had to act to stop such untruths being repeated and repeated, though they were reluctant to let it reach the court.

The judge's verdict was given in June 1997. It took him over two hours to read out a 45-page summary of his 800-page conclusions. McDonald's emerged the victors, in that they were awarded £60,000 damages for most, but not all, of the allegations that had been made. They were cleared of cutting down rainforests, creating starvation in the Third World, causing cancer and food poisoning, but found guilty of paying low wages, of cruelty to some animals and of exploiting children in their advertising campaigns.

McDonald's claimed they were broadly satisfied, and promised to look into the areas in which they were criticised. It was estimated that their legal costs would reach £10 million – a huge amount, but minuscule compared with their worldwide turnover of $32 billion.

It remains to be seen what long-term damage the case has done to their image in Britain. Not a lot, probably, in terms of business and commercial success. Whatever some people might think of their burgers, McDonald's is here for a bit longer. In 1998, they had 760 outlets in Britain, which were visited by 10 million people every week. McDonald's create 5,000 new jobs every year and by 2000 they will have 1,000 outlets.

Of all the births in 1900, few would seem to have a rosier future than the Big Mac. Unless, of course, in the twenty-first century the whole world goes over to veggie burgers . . .

22

MARY ELLIS

A real star of the silver screen and West End

Mary Ellis in Harper's Bazaar, *1925*

Mary Ellis lives in Eaton Square, about the most attractive, most famous residential square in London, which is only as it should be, as Mary Ellis is one of our most famous, attractive stage stars. She might not be a household name with today's theatregoers, as it is over thirty years since she last appeared on a West End stage, but anyone who knows about the theatre will know her name. She will be for ever associated with several of the century's best loved theatrical experiences, such as *Rose-Marie*, which was written for her, and Ivor Novello's *Glamorous Night* and *The Dancing Years*.

Outside her house is a blue plaque to Vivien Leigh, who lived at the same address, in the apartment next door to Miss Ellis, until her death in 1967. Terence Rattigan was another theatrical legend who at one time lived in Eaton Square. Today her best-known theatrical neighbour is Andrew Lloyd Webber. He is one of the few who has the whole house.

Miss Ellis's West Indian housekeeper and companion, Lyris, who lives with her, let me in. She has been with Miss Ellis for forty years and originally came from Grenada. She escorted me into Miss Ellis's drawing room, past rows of books, paintings and memorabilia. I noticed a Chagall poster, signed to Miss Ellis, and a Magritte over the fireplace.

Later Lyris reappeared with China tea, biscuits, hot scones and jam on a trolley. It was wheeled in, just as they used to do on the West End stage, all those years ago, when Ivor and Noël and Binkie were but boys, long before kitchen sink. Kitchen sink, of course, has been and gone. Many of those pre-war plays and musicals, in which Miss Ellis starred, have seen their time come round again. Some are now considered classics. Just like Miss Ellis.

She was wearing an elegant two-piece fawn suit, sitting bird-like on the edge of her chair, watching me beadily, taking in everything I said and did, putting me firmly in my place if I asked what she considered was too personal a question, reprimanding me when I did anything silly, such as putting a cup on the floor. She was quick to smile and utterly charming, as one might expect from a successful actress, but also very sharp.

She was my second 'famous' person born in 1900, in the sense that, like Dame Elizabeth Hill, she is in *Who's Who* and greatly distinguished in her profession, but what was really unusual about her was her self-awareness. Many people of ninety-seven, however well-educated, however successful they may have been in their working life, seem to lose the capacity, or perhaps just the desire, to stand back and look at themselves objectively. Leonard Cooper did it, and Monty Hedges. Perhaps too truthfully. Most of us, of course, never manage it.

Mary Ellis is American, a rather more refined export than either hamburgers or Coke, but you would be hard pressed to tell it from her accent, which is clipped, upper-class period English, as befits a lady living in Eaton Square. She was born in New York on 15 June 1900. Her father, Herman Elsas, had come from Alsace (then in Germany) to the USA as a young man, starting work as an office boy in a paper-mill in Texas. He rose to become President of Consolidated Paper Mills. His wife, Caroline Reinhardt, had also come from Germany. They had two daughters; Lucille was ten years older than Mary. Mary was born at

West 98th Street, near the Hudson river, in a red-brick house where she was looked after by her own nanny, Alice.

'My first memory is of when I was about the age of two. I am sitting under a piano, watching the pedals move while my mother played. But most of my other early memories are usually with Alice. When I was about five, Alice took me to the theatre for the first time. It was some kind of indoor circus at the New York Hippodrome. We were in a box at the side of the stage. Someone on stage shouted, "What time is it?" and the main clown, Marcelline, took out a huge watch and said, "Three o'clock", whereupon I said, in a very loud voice, "Time for my cocoa, Allie." Everyone heard me. I can remember the startled but amused look of Marcelline, who stopped and ran across the stage to give me a wave. That could be the first spark which fired me to want an audience.'

Mary went to Leetes School for Girls in New York. She thought at one time about going to university, until she fell in love with classical music. 'I was first taken to the opera when I was ten, to see *Madam Butterfly*, and I developed a schoolgirl crush on Geraldine Farrar. From then on, I went every Thursday, usually with my mother, either to the opera or a concert.

'I saw Pavlova dance – and then next day I saw her in the street in New York. She was going into a department store, so I followed her. She was dressed very strangely, like an old aunt, with lots of chiffon veiling and a floppy hat. I also saw Sarah Bernhardt on her last tour. She must have had her wooden leg already because she sat cross-legged for all her scenes.'

At the age of fifteen, Mary left school to study music and singing full-time, hoping to become a professional singer and join the New York Met. 'My first singing teacher in New York was Frieda Ashford, a Belgian woman, married to an Englishman. When I had to sing softly she would say, "Put the teacup over that note." If I had to sing loudly, she'd say, "Sing across Brooklyn Bridge."'

She put on a slight American accent, to tell that story, so I asked if in those days, as a New York teenager, she had a New York accent. 'Never. I always spoke standard English. You forget my parents were both German, and didn't speak American English. In many ways, we were still European. Every summer, we sailed to Europe and spent several

months in London, Switzerland, Austria, Italy and Germany. I spent my
fifth birthday in London. I can't remember the hotel or the house we
were staying in, but I can remember waking up and finding a golden
heart placed on a red plush chair beside my bed. It was a birthday present from my father. I wore it on a chain round my neck for years and
years – till it was stolen by robbers.'

It was when she was around twelve, spending the summer in Zürich,
that she fell in love for the first time. The boy was from Manchester,
Rupert Sternberg, a few years older; he was spending his summer in
Europe. His parents, too, had originally come from Germany. 'I met
him every summer from then on, even when he went up to Clare
College, Cambridge, to study medicine. When I was back in New York,
he wrote me enormous letters. Oh, there is nothing as wonderful as first
love. I have never had that same quality of love in my life, ever again.

'He smoked a pipe, a Meerschaum, and I got great comfort out of
holding it when it was hot. He always smiled at this – perhaps already
aware of such Freudian manifestations. When he first asked to kiss me,
I said I would have to ask my mother. "You must decide that for yourself," my mother replied. So I went back and said he could kiss me on
the cheek. He laughed and tied my two long braids under my chin and
made me promise I would never cut them off.

'I can remember everything about him, but it was never fulfilled.
Ever afterwards I thought, Why didn't I do that, why didn't I say that?
He joined up when the war began, and was killed on the Somme in
1916. When I heard, I at once cut off my braids.'

In 1918, Mary at last got an audition with the New York Metropolitan Opera and was taken on as a junior singer, on a four-year
contract at $150 a week. It meant she sang the juvenile – young girls' –
roles, rather than simply being in the chorus, so from the beginning she
had fairly important parts. On joining the Met, she was persuaded to
change her surname from Elsas to Ellis.

Her début was on 14 December 1918 in a world première of three
Puccini mini-operas. She also sang with Chaliapin and Caruso. 'When
Chaliapin "died" in my arms, his voice vibrated through my whole
body like a church bell.'

Caruso almost literally died in her arms. This was in *L'Elisir d'Amore*
at the Met. 'Just before the final scene, he asked me to wipe his face of

sweat. Then, during our last duet, I noticed a trickle of blood in the corner of his mouth. I think he sang only one more performance before he died. He was a darling man, great fun, yet somehow absurd. He wasn't attractive, like, say, Domingo. He was just a jolly little fat peasant of a man. But what a voice. None of his records do it justice. It was like honey and wine . . .'

She was never aware as a young girl, she said, about all the affairs going on behind the scenes, despite being occasionally pinched on the bottom by elderly Italian baritones or invited to candlelit suppers with musical directors. She remained pure and intact until swept off her feet by an American air force pilot, Louis Bernheimer. 'It was crazy. Till then, I'd been thinking only of my career, then I fell into his arms. He was a war hero and it was like the Second World War, but not so sophisticated. People did crazy things, just because of the war.'

They married in 1919 and had their honeymoon in Paris, where it turned out he had had a mistress since his war years. 'I remember her name, Marie Delorme, and even her address, the rue Moscou. He had a photo of her and I tried my best to look like her. He was obviously still obsessed, so I said he should go and visit her. So off he went. He said if he wasn't back in six hours, well, we could take it from there. I sat on a bench on the Champs-Elysées all afternoon, then eventually headed back to our hotel, the Hôtel Byron. He was already there – in great distress, weeping and wailing. It turned out Marie Delorme had died, some months earlier. He was inconsolable. He also had piles. I had to apply some ointment every few hours, which didn't help our honeymoon. That was it, really. We went back to New York, but he never recovered.

'After a year of watching my misery, my father whisked me off, like a young rabbit, to some state in the west and got me a divorce. It was a very bad experience. I can't tell you the half of it. Some years later, I heard he was in some scandal in California and killed himself.'

When her contract at the Met was about to end, she was approached by a famous stage director of the time called David Belasco who persuaded her that, as it would be years before she was a leading opera star, she should turn from classical opera to classical theatre. He said he would give her a part in his next Shakespeare production, but first she should do six months in stock – at a repertory company – learning the

Programme for Rose-Marie

basics. She appeared in her first New York dramatic role as Nerissa in *The Merchant of Venice* at the Lyceum in 1922.

Two years later, while in another stage play, she was seen by the producer Arthur Hammerstein, father of Oscar. He thought she would be perfect for light opera as she could act as well as sing. He asked her to meet him, along with his son Oscar, then a young lyricist, and the composer Rudolf Friml. 'At that meeting, *Rose-Marie* was born.' She played the title role of a French-Canadian girl in love with Jim, a fur trapper, wrongly accused of murder. It opened on 2 September 1924, and overnight almost the whole of New York was singing 'The Indian Love Call'. Mary Ellis was the toast of the town, invited to parties with George Gershwin, Fred Astaire, Harpo Marx and Yasha Heifitz. 'I had a bad cold once and George Gershwin came to see me. To amuse me, he played bits from "Rhapsody in Blue" which he was composing.'

She says she didn't do the big starry things, preferring to remain as private and anonymous as possible. 'I didn't think of myself as in "show-biz". I was a classical singer who happened to be in a light opera. I sang it very seriously, like an opera singer, as if I was doing Puccini. I suppose that was part of the show's attraction. My salary was good, about five hundred dollars a week, but no, I had no feeling of fame. I was just doing a job I loved. There was a London production, at Drury Lane in 1925. I could have gone with it, but I refused. After a year, singing the same stuff, I'd had enough.'

To many people's amazement, she went back to the classical theatre, appearing in an off-Broadway arts theatre production of the Jewish folklore classic, *The Dybbuk*. By this time, she had married for a second time, to Edwin Knopf, an actor and brother of the famous publisher. She met him through her sister Lucille who had married another well-known New York publisher, Horace Liveright. When he first proposed, she turned him down. He then went off to Germany, had a shooting accident and lost part of his arm. 'When he returned to New York, I felt somehow responsible. I thought I might help him overcome his disability – so when he proposed again, I married him. It didn't work. I behaved badly and have always felt sorry and ashamed. He later married a lovely young woman, a friend of mine, so it turned out happily – for him, at least.'

The next serious relationship in her life was with Basil Sydney, the well-known English actor, whom she met in New York when he was playing in a modern-dress *Hamlet*. At the time he was still married to someone else. They acted together in Laurence Irving's version of Dostoevsky's *Crime and Punishment*, and soon started living together.

When talking films arrived, Fox offered them both screen tests. Mary passed hers and was offered a contract, but Basil failed so Mary turned hers down and they both took parts instead in New York in *The Taming of the Shrew*.

'My mother was always unhappy about us living together, which we'd done for about three years. One day she started crying, saying, "What can I tell my friends?" as if I'd done something terrible naughty. At the end of *Shrew*, we had a weekend away in Connecticut. We knocked at a minister's door and got married.'

In 1930, they both came to London, Basil's home town, where his parents were still living. Mary made her West End début in a play called *Knave and Queen* at the Ambassadors, alongside the young Robert Donat. She then appeared in Eugene O'Neill's *Strange Interlude*, which was then considered very avant-garde. A young English actress called Peggy Ashcroft was one of the people who wrote her a fan letter.

While in her next West End play, a comedy drama about the upper classes called *Double Harness*, she was approached by C. B. Cochrane, the great English impresario. He knew about her success in *Rose-Marie*, all those years ago, and said it was about time she returned to singing.

He persuaded her to appear in *Music in the Air*, a play with music by Jerome Kern and Oscar Hammerstein at His Majesty's.

'The morning after it opened, Mr Cochrane asked me to come to the front entrance, not the stage door, when I arrived for the evening performance. I almost fainted. Every poster, and all the signs up in lights, announced MARY ELLIS IN MUSIC IN THE AIR.'

She and Basil had taken a small mews house off Berkeley Square, but with her new status they moved to a larger house near Regent's Park, with a cook and housekeeper. He was doing equally well in a play called *Dinner at Eight*. When that finished, in 1934, he was offered a play in New York.

'I remember leaning out of the window, early in the morning, waving goodbye to him. He never came back. The next thing I heard, he was living in a hotel with a young actress he'd met in *Dinner at Eight*.' Ah, these show-business people. That was the end of her marriage number three.

Her career, however, went from success to success. After a matinée for *Music in the Air* a young man, who had been watching her from a box, sent up a card bearing the name Ivor Novello. 'I did vaguely know his name, but all I knew was that he'd written "Keep The Home Fires Burning".' She agreed to meet him, and they discussed possible ideas, but at the same time she was invited to Hollywood. She'd done one film in England, at Teddington studios, *Bella Donna*, with Cecil Hardwicke, but Hollywood was offering a great deal more money.

In 1935 she went off to do her first Hollywood film, travelling with her dresser, Maudie, as her companion. She met most of the film stars of the time, like Gloria Swanson, Bette Davis, Charles Boyer, and starred in three Paramount films – *All the King's Horses*, *Paris Love Song* and *Fatal Lady*.

On the boat home, she had to learn the script for the musical Novello had written for her return – *Glamorous Night*. It opened at Drury Lane in 1935, during the Silver Jubilee celebrations for George V and Queen Mary. 'Ivor and I hung out of the windows of his Aldwych flat to catch sight of the royal coaches. At the weekend, we went to his country home, Redroofs. I remember his mother, Madame Clara Novello-Davies, standing up every time the National Anthem was on the radio. Which it was, about every ten minutes.'

Mary with Carl Brisson in All the King's Horses

In 1936, she made her TV début. This was during the early weeks of the world's first regular TV broadcasts, made by the BBC from Alexandra Palace in North London. 'Our faces had to be painted pale ochre, so we all looked ghastly, like Frankenstein's monsters. I sang a Noël Coward song, but I can't remember which. People had to go and stand outside radio shops to see what TV was all about, as only a couple of thousand people had sets.'

In 1938, she was in Edinburgh, for the provincial run of a new West End play called *Innocent Party* playing opposite Cecil Parker, when a young stage-door johnny sent in his card, saying he was a devoted fan of her singing and her acting, had been for years. That same evening she heard from New York that her father had died, aged seventy-four. She refused to see the young man.

But he persevered, kept on pestering, so she checked out his name, Jock Muir Stewart Roberts. 'A clergyman I knew in Edinburgh told me he came from a very good family.' Eventually she agreed to meet him. He lived on the Scottish border, son of a wealthy wool manufacturer, drove a Jaguar and was a keen pilot, skier, fisherman and climber. After a hectic six-month courtship, he became husband number four.

Despite his privileged background, he was very left-wing and idealistic. He was keen to see her continue her career, which Mary would have been willing to give up. In 1939 came the second of the shows written for her by Ivor Novello, *The Dancing Years*. That opened on

2 March 1939, and was yet another success. She was still appearing in it when the Second World War broke out. 'People had been saying, "It won't happen, it won't happen," but that day we heard the air-raid siren. There was only a very small audience that night in Drury Lane and Ivor came on stage to tell people to move nearer the front. We managed to get through that performance, then the theatre went dark. Every London theatre was closed.'

During the war, she shut up her London house and her housekeeper went into a munitions factory. She handed over her country home for use by evacuees. Jock, her husband, enlisted, hoping to be an RAF pilot, but was commissioned instead into RAF Intelligence.

Mary was asked to tour with ENSA, in shows for the troops, but chose instead to take a relatively humble job as a welfare officer in emergency hospitals, working in various parts of Britain. Looking back, it may have been the influence of her idealistic husband, encouraging her to do something worthwhile. They didn't often see each other during the war, and when they did meet, she didn't care to ask about his work.

After three years' war work, she returned to the West End theatre in 1943, appearing in a Novello drama about Joan of Arc. She and Jock took a flat near Marylebone High Street where they spent many nights in public shelters or up on their roof, clearing away smouldering bomb debris.

'One of the most inspiring London theatrical events during the war was towards the end of 1943. Cochrane took over the Albert Hall for a show in aid of Toc H called *Seventy Years of Song*. The place was filled with army, navy and air force people. Most of the stars from the West End did their bit. I sang the "The Indian Love Call" from *Rose-Marie*. Then we all sang First and Second World War songs. It finished, after three hours, with a thousand people singing "Jerusalem". It lifted everyone into a blissful limbo. For one evening, we all forgot the war.'

Her post-war successes included Rattigan's *The Browning Version*, Noël Coward's *After the Ball* and O'Neill's *Mourning Becomes Electra*, directed by the young Peter Hall.

Jock died in 1950 from a freak accident: he fell to his death in the Scottish borders while testing out some nylon rope in preparation for climbing in the Alps. She never married again and threw herself into work for the next twenty years. This included further West End plays, a season at the Royal Shakespeare Company, plus radio and TV dramas. Her last West End play was *Look Homeward, Angel* with Peter McEnery at the Phoenix Theatre in 1962. Her last stage performance was in Shaw's *Mrs Warren's Profession* at the Yvonne Arnaud Theatre, Guildford in 1970.

Today she doesn't go out much and gets around her flat with the aid of a frame – she had a couple of falls – but she still entertains and keeps in touch by phone and letters with many of her old friends. She published her autobiography, *Those Dancing Years*, in 1982, handy for those who might want more details of her many hundreds of roles.

'Yes, it has been a packed life. You see I did have three careers – in opera, straight theatre and musicals. In fact, I've done most things on stage, except pantomimes and circuses. I'd perform now, if anyone asked me to be an old lady in a TV play.

'No, I have no regrets about my careers, though I often wonder what might have happened if I'd stayed at the Met, and continued as an opera singer. But I'll never know.'

How about four marriages – surely some regrets there?

'I don't think four love affairs is very much,' she replied smartly, 'not for someone of my great age. I suppose I regret I didn't just live with them, which I would have done today. I did make several terrible mistakes, but in those days, you had to get married to live with someone. That's what one did.'

So it would have been better to have been born later, and taken advantage of today's greater sexual freedoms?

'I disagree. I think it's very sloppy, though I know everyone does today. I think it's animalistic. You can't ever get to really know someone when it's simply a case of careless rapture. Anything real and important in life takes time, takes analysis. Otherwise it's just sloppy. You should be prepared to take the responsibility for making promises to another human being. A promise is a sacrifice or it is nothing. I believe in marriage. You should want to be with someone, as part of their life. So no, I don't prefer today.'

She had no children. When I tried to question her further, asking if she had perhaps prevented it happening, I was told I was being too personal. 'It just didn't happen. I was far too busy with my career. I put that first, till it was too late. I never missed having children but I suppose it is a regret now, that I never did. On the other hand, if I'd had any, they might all have died in the Second World War.

'I think every age has wonderful things about it. I never think about trying to be younger than I am – and never have done.'

Never? 'Well, as an actress, there was a time when newspapers put my age a couple of years younger than I was, which for a while I never corrected, but I never actually lied.

'Now at ninety-six I'd say I am enjoying life as much as I did at sixteen. At sixteen, you have a lot of worries, a lot of fears. I don't have any now. I don't think "old" because I accept the fact that every stage in life has a cause for celebration. You should accept that, balance the good and the bad, the yes and the no, as you go along.

'One of the pluses for me now is that I have become much more interested in other people. They fascinate me. When I was younger, let's say up to sixty, I had little interest in other people, only in myself and my career. I now take pleasure in meeting new people, hearing about them and their lives.'

She could give no quick explanation for reaching her age. Her elder sister survived until she was ninety. Her mother died at seventy-eight.

'I suppose I have not had excesses in life, apart from those I'm not going to tell you about. I mean, I have never smoked and hardly drank – just one glass at social occasions. Holding a champagne glass was enough for me. I suppose I come from a fairly abstemious family. I've never much been interested in eating.

'My health has always been good, apart from a hip operation, and two nasty falls, but I don't want to think about them. I have been very fortunate. I sold my house in France, but I don't miss it. I couldn't travel that far now. Friends keep me in touch with what's happening. I read the *Telegraph* every day and watch a bit of television. I keep an open mind. I like to think I do nothing tightly.'

She finds it hard to believe the huge salaries film and stage stars are paid today. 'When they can neither sing nor act better than we could,' she added, tightly. When she herself was making good money, she acted sensibly. 'My father always told me never to pay a monthly rent which was more than two weeks' salary.' Her paintings and antiques were bought for modest amounts, many years ago. 'I got the Magritte in

1918 for fifteen pounds. The Chagall was a present from him. I had lunch with him once. He wore a plaid shawl, a Panama hat and he ate everything that was put in front of him – melon, ham, lobster, ice-cream.'

She didn't spend a lot on herself. 'I only wore make-up when I was working – masses of cold cream plastered on. You had to, in those days, as the lights were so strong. I think putting it on, then taking it off, was like giving yourself a face massage. In my private life I never wore make-up, except lipstick. I have never in my life washed my face with soap. I always use plain water. That was something my mother taught me.

'My first love was probably my greatest love. The one who died in the First World War. If he came into this room now, I would still recognise and love him. But I was happy with Basil for those six years or so. He was lovely and intelligent and clever and he did spoil me – till he ran off with someone else.

'Ivor Novello was such a dear and good friend, and so very talented. It was tragic he died in his fifties. I wasn't quite as close to Coward. He couldn't actually write music, I mean write it down, the way Ivor could. He got Elsie April to write it out for him. We had words when I was in one of his shows, *After the Ball*, which was his musical version of *Lady Windermere's Fan*. I thought him rather vindictive. He had persuaded me to play in it but there were several cast changes before we began. The two people I ended up playing beside were both very tall – and I am very small, though I usually looked taller on stage. This time it was very obvious. One critic wrote, "Why did Miss Ellis make her entrance on her knees?" It made me feel like a female Toulouse-Lautrec. Coward wasn't very supportive. But we remained friends and I later visited him in Switzerland.

'Of course bad reviews are hurtful. You always remember the bad ones more than the good ones. On the whole, I had good reviews.'

A lot of her closest theatrical friends were homosexual, not that she realised in her early years, but she always got on well with them. 'I found them very comforting as friends. I suppose my unhappy experiences with the total male made such relationships a relief . . .'

The peak of her professional fame was in *Rose-Marie*, followed by *The Dancing Years*, but she thinks her greatest professional satisfaction came with *The Dybbuk*. 'It's about a girl's lover who dies and his spirit enters her body. The vocal challenges are great, but I was happy with how I did it. *Rose-Marie* was more exciting, I suppose, as it was written with me in mind.

'As a person, I was happiest when I was with Basil in New York, when we were doing *Taming of the Shrew*. But each period has had a peak. I was lucky, but I also made things happen. I didn't just sit and wait. I was willing to try new things, and go hell for leather to achieve them.

'I can think of many things to celebrate which have happened in my lifetime, such as man getting to the Moon. That was wonderful. But I also think that life, more or less, is much the same as it always has been. If you read all the histories and sagas about people who have lived on this Earth, you'll realise that if you were to be planted down at almost any period, you would understand basically what was happening to them, what they were doing and worrying about. People don't change. Only the music changes. There is the same beauty and the same sort of ugliness in every age. There's always comedy and tragedy, only they appear in different costumes.

'I suppose today people's expectations of life are a bit different from the past. And I suppose there is a loss of tenderness and kindness to one another. Those are two changes I can see. But as for morals, I don't think people have really changed. Not even sexual morals. We are all much the same, behaving basically in the same way. We all have to make

Mary today

the same sorts of mistakes, as we grow up and go through life. Just as I did. A person who doesn't make mistakes has missed all the lessons in life. I can think of many mistakes I made, but I now think of them with something approaching tenderness. I seldom think, Yes, I was right there.

'The older one gets, the more one gives thanks for simple things, like waking up to a new day. I don't fear death. I look upon it as another adventure. I imagine myself saying, "Hello, excuse me, can I come in?" and someone saying, "How do you do?"

'And if I am in pain at the time, then I'll be glad of death. Death means no pain. But I don't want it, because I don't want to leave this marvellous and terrible life. Yes, it is both marvellous and terrible, being alive. I want it to go on as long as possible. Let's hope I do live until I'm a hundred . . .'

23

CISSIE REID

Mayoress of Stretford

Cissie Reid (second left), Mayoress of Stretford, 1957

Cissie Reid, sitting in the little two-up and two-down terrace house in Stretford, Manchester, where she has lived since 1933, started with a confession. I had been told she was born on 20 October 1900. That's the day she celebrates her birthday, and what she has always told her friends and family, including two of her relations, niece Edna and husband Bill, who were sitting with her, as we all had tea and Dundee. But when I came to check her date of birth, and she saw me writing down 20 October, she said she'd better tell the truth. She always did, on things like official forms . . . but, well, er, since 1920 she has been living a slight fib.

Oh, no, I thought. I had a self-imposed rule of sticking strictly to people born in 1900. No other year would do, which had meant turning down several people born in 1899. All that tea and Dundee cake. Cissie sitting there in her best frock. I can't just stand up and leave if she wasn't born in 1900.

It all began, explained Cissie, when she met the man she was to marry, Ted Reid. It turned out his birthday was 20 October. Cissie, quick as a flash, said wasn't that funny, her birthday was also 20 October.

'You see, I've always wanted things to be nice in life,' said Cissie, smiling sweetly. Her niece and husband stared at each other, somewhat mystified by this fairly pointless bit of deception. Her real birthday, said Cissie, was 21 October 1900. 'Only one day different, so it wasn't really much of a lie, was it? My husband never, never knew, but it did make things nice and neat.' Phew. So she is still a 1900-er.

She was born Elizabeth Herrity, one of ten children – six girls and four boys – but always known by her sisters as Sis, hence Cissie. Her father was an Irish labourer who volunteered for the First World War, got badly injured in the trenches and was sent home as a cripple. One brother, Alec, followed his father into the army and joined the Cheshire Regiment.

'That's his photo on the wall,' said Cissie, standing up to point it out to me. All her walls were covered with family photographs, many of them professional as Cissie and her husband had something of a ceremonial life. Alec's photo was framed with the crest of the Cheshire Regiment, and adorned with some medals. I admired the arrangement but noticed that Alec was not in uniform. Why not?

'He wasn't in the army long enough to have his photograph taken, because he never came home on leave. He joined at eighteen and a half and was killed at Ypres before he'd reached nineteen. He took the King's shilling, I suppose. He and a pal went to Eccles and joined up. I think you got more, another shilling, if you got a pal to join up as well. I expect my father joined for the same reason, to get the King's shilling.

'I remember the day Alec went off. We went to Patricroft station to see him go, me and my father. The last words my father shouted at him, as the train drew out, were "Keep your head down, son."'

Cissie went to a convent school, St Patrick's, in Livesey Street, where she was taught by nuns. 'These nuns never went out, never went anywhere, so they never knew anything about evil or bad things.' Her education finished at twelve when her mother took her away from school to help at home with the younger children. At sixteen, things were a bit easier, so she started work at a rubber factory. 'My job was blowing up rubber balls. I wasn't very good at it.' But she stuck at it for the next seven years, till Ted Reid came into her life.

They met at a Labour Party social at Patricroft Bridge. He was a locomotive fireman on the works railway of the Manchester Ship Canal. 'He lived in the next street to us, but I didn't know him till then. He said he'd seen me often, watching me from the top of a bus. At the Labour social, he asked if he could take me home. I said, "Well, it won't be far, because my mum will be waiting for me at the end of our street."

'I was a good dancer, thanks to the rubber works.'

You mean it was an extra, provided by the management? Sounds very enlightened.

'Oh, gosh, no,' laughed Cissie. 'Nothing like that. It was just that I worked with a girl who went to town dances, and she knew all the latest steps. There was also a boy at work who had a mouth organ, so in our lunch breaks we used to dance. My friend taught me the latest things. It meant when I went to dances I always got picked up right away.'

Cissie and Ted got married on 29 December 1923, the Saturday between Christmas and New Year. Ted was on shift work over Christmas but was able to get that day off. They didn't have a honeymoon till six months later, in the following summer, during Lancashire's annual fair week, and went to the fashionable honeymoon place for young Lancashire couples, the Isle of Man.

Cissie stopped work immediately on her marriage, not because she really wanted to, as a job in the rubber works was a job after all, but because that was what married women in the 1920s and 1930s did. Earlier, during the First World War, it had been possible to continue to work, but when the men returned, things had gone back to normal. The rationale was that men were the breadwinners, so if a married woman continued to work, she was depriving a man of a job.

'We lived first of all in Eccles with an old lady who had a shop. She was fifty-three, so I'm saying she was an old lady, she seemed so at the time to me. She'd been in service and had a baby and then lost it, so she was living alone above the shop and had a spare room.'

A year later they managed to get a house of their own in Chorlton, putting up ten pounds as key money and agreeing a rent of 16s. 6d. a week. The timing was good because Cissie had her first baby, Joyce, in 1925.

'You aimed to have a baby twelve months after you married. That was why you got married, to have a baby, but of course you really needed a house to have a baby, so that was what all the hurry was about.'

In 1930, she was pregnant again, hoping for a boy. 'It was the same time as the Queen Mother was pregnant – Duchess of York as was. She's exactly the same age as me, of course. She'd had a baby girl first, like me, so naturally I'd been following everything that happened to her. Everyone was expecting her to have a boy. Oh, gosh, they were, it was in all the papers. Bonfires were being prepared in Scotland to celebrate the birth of a boy. He would one day be King, not Princess Elizabeth.

'I remember saying to the nurse looking after me, "If it's not a little boy, will I have to go through all this again?"'

In the event, she had a boy, Howard, while the Duchess of York had another daughter. Was there by chance the slightest feeling of being one up?

'Oh, gosh, no. I felt sorry for her. I remember one of the papers of the time said, "It's a bouncing daughter." That was a nice way to put it, wasn't it?'

Despite having met at a Labour Party dance, neither Cissie nor Ted had so far been very interested in politics. They had gone to the dance for purely social reasons.

'It was when Dad – that's what I always called Ted and he called me Mum – was ill one time. He was off work and getting bored and was looking for things to occupy himself, so we bought him a piano. He'd been awarded certificates for piano-playing when he was sixteen or seventeen. It was the only thing we ever bought on the HP. It cost fifty pounds for the piano, plus twenty-seven shillings for the stool, and we had to pay back three shillings a week for years. He thought he might give piano lessons from home, but he never did.

'He never liked being at home with a crying baby. On the first night Joyce woke up crying, he said, "I didn't think it would be like this." He wanted to be out, doing things, helping people, meeting people. He thought that made people more useful, more interesting.

'I remember one thing Dad always used to say. "People wrapped up in themselves make a very small parcel."

'So that's really how it all started, how he came to be a union man.

One day at work the person who had been their railway union man announced he was giving it up. Someone said to Dad he should do it. I can't honestly remember him being active till then. It was just someone thinking he was up to it, he was the man, so he took it on.'

Ted progressed from being a union man to becoming a councillor, representing the Talbot North ward on Stretford Council for almost thirty years. He first took his seat in 1945, and served until 1972. He even attempted to become a Labour MP, standing for Davyhulme.

'He didn't win, but he did reduce the Tory's majority. Sir Samuel Storie, the sitting Tory MP, was nice enough and we became friends. He used to send us a Christmas card from the House of Commons.'

Did she regret he didn't become an MP?

'Gosh, no. He would never have been at home at all if he'd become an MP. He was out all the time as it was. He was a man who couldn't stop still. Perhaps he relied on me too much to look after him, run the house and family, wash and starch his overalls for work. Yes, I starched them. People used to say, "Who does your overalls?" he'd say, "Mum does them."

'He didn't try again to be an MP. It wasn't any lack of determination. He stood six times to be a councillor, before he got elected. He just realised it was too late to be an MP.'

The highlight of Ted's political career was 1957–58 when he became mayor of Stretford, with Cissie as his mayoress. Nephew Bill was sent upstairs to get the album of that year. He returned with the wrong one and was sent back. Again he brought down the wrong album, and was told off by Cissie, by which time he was puffing. The stairs to Cissie's bedroom, where she still sleeps, are incredibly steep. At last he found the right photographs for the year in question. They were in a monster suitcase, which he had to drag down the stairs, puffing even more.

Ted, as mayor, got the year off work with full pay. He and Cissie attended hundreds of engagements, each of them carefully recorded photographically. 'We had our own photographer, you see, who followed us everywhere.'

The year in question happened to be the year of the Munich air disaster. On 6 February 1958, eight members of the Manchester United football team, the so-called Busby Babes, were killed. Old Trafford, the home of Manchester United, is in Stretford, so Ted and Cissie, as the mayor and mayoress, were present at many of the funerals and other events connected with the disaster. 'At the end of the season, United got to Wembley, and we were invited to the match as the club's guests.'

Ted died in 1976. For most of their married life, they had rented their house, but four years before he died they had managed to buy it, as sitting tenants, for six hundred pounds. 'It was nice to know I wouldn't be put out in the street. Still does feel nice.'

By the time of his death, both children had long since left home. Joyce had failed the 11-plus to go to grammar school, which her parents had hoped she would pass, and left school in 1939, aged fourteen. 'I wanted her to do more with her life than I did, so we paid for her to go to a Rapid Course in Manchester.' She became a typist and got a job in the typing pool at the Manchester Ship Canal Company, where her father worked.

'She was very attractive, though I say it myself as her mother. She played the piano and got awards for her soprano singing. She had lots of boyfriends. I always encouraged her to bring them to the house. Well, that way you know what they're up to. During the war, she was once writing to six boys in all.' Local boys, mostly away at the war, but along came one boy who was fighting his war in Manchester. 'We didn't know what was going on at first, till she came home and said she was going to become a Catholic.

'I remember saying to Dad, 'She'll probably tell us next we're not married.'' Although I was brought up a Catholic, Dad wasn't, so I'd given up the Church and never gone.'

It turned out Joyce was going out with a Catholic boy – serving in the US Air Force. And they wanted to get married.

'I was against it. She was only twenty, too young, I thought. I refused to sign the forms. Under twenty-one, you had to have your forms signed by your parents, in those days. Dad wasn't really bothered. He left all family things like that to me. In the end I gave in and they got married in 1945. She went off with her husband to Ohio. I think she was the first GI bride in Ohio.

'Oh, I had nothing against him. He was a fine fellow. I just thought our Joyce was too young.'

In 1947, two years after Joyce had got married, and already had one baby, Cissie went out to see them. They didn't have enough money for

Cissie today

Ted to go as well, and anyway he was working. 'Gosh, that was exciting. I went on the Cunard line. Out on the *Mauritania*, which cost forty-eight pounds. Then back on the *Queen Mary* for fifty-six pounds.'

'Can you get us some tickets at that price, Cissie?' said Bill, now recovered from humping the suitcase.

'His family were lovely, really looked after me, gave me presents, and I had a great time. They even gave me a string of pearls. They couldn't have been nicer. But while I was there I noticed little things. Well, just little things, but very soon they were breaking my heart, even when I was smiling and having a good time. I can't really describe them. There was one time Joyce asked me to look after little Denny, her baby. That was OK, but it turned out she wanted to go out and look for a job. That's Denny on the wall. He became a PFC and is now aged fifty. PFC? That's Private First Class. He served in Vietnam.

'I couldn't understand why Joyce didn't seem to have any money and wanted a job, yet the family appeared to be doing so well. While I was there, her husband had taken over the family shop after his father had died. It was doing very well. I remember the excitement when it got a liquor licence, which was hard to get. You remember all the Prohibition years?'

Because of the shop's success, Cissie came home from her 1947 trip hoping all was well with Joyce's life, despite what Cissie says were her inner fears.

'I didn't see her again till 1966 when we both flew out to see them. During all those twenty years, she managed to keep it from me what was happening. She wouldn't talk about it. It was only later I learned that she'd sold her rings. It was the liquor licence that did it. Her husband was an alcoholic. When it all came out eventually, Joyce never said anything awful about him. She just used to say, "It's a disease, Mother."'

In the end Joyce got divorced, by which time she'd had four children. Her first husband is long since dead. She remarried and had another three children, which means Cissie now has seven American grandchildren.

'Joyce carried on working all these years, very good job as a legal secretary, they thought very highly of her, but she retired last year at the age of seventy.'

Cissie's son Howard has also been married and divorced and married again. He has two children and lives in Shropshire. He recently retired after working in hotel management. One up, in a way, to the Queen Mother, of whose children only one went through a divorce.

'I missed having none of my grandchildren growing up near me. It would be nice to have children around me today, to run messages or post letters.'

Cissie kept very active after her husband died, involved in many local organisations and activities. She has only recently given up running a luncheon club for old people. She did this well into her eighties, despite being twenty years older than many of those she was helping. 'It's like Dad always said, "Being wanted". That's what keeps you active.'

She cooks, cleans her house on her own, has good sight and hearing, has not yet suffered any falling, hardly ever stops talking and clearly enjoys life, despite having little money.

'Dad never got a pension from the Ship Canal. Yes, after all those long years. He was too old, you see, when a graduated pension began, and we didn't have any money to pay into it. He did used to say to me, "When I go, love, you won't have anything." But I do get income support and a home help comes two hours a week to do my shopping. I gave up doing my own shopping last year. I do miss it, gassing to all the neighbours in the street and in the shops.

'I remember when I moved into this street in 1933, there was an old woman across the road called Mrs Britton. All the neighbours told me not to walk down her side, or I'd never get past her door. That's what happened to me, I suppose. I'm the old woman in the street who loves talking.

'I've got a knocker, the only one left in the street. They all have front-door bells now. Children love a knocker. I used to get a lot of little kids knocking at the door and running away, as kids do. It never interfered with my life, not really, though their parents told them off. It didn't bother me.

'I went out one day to see who it was and this little boy was there, banging on my knocker. "How old are you?" he said to me. He'd obviously been told not to bother me because I was a very old woman.' Cissie stood up to illustrate, with appropriate gestures, how she'd told the little boy she was twenty-one, putting her finger in her mouth and fluttering her eyelashes like Shirley Temple. 'The little boy then turned to his little friend and said, in a loud whisper, "She doesn't know how old she is." So it rebounded on me. He didn't realise I was being funny.'

It was only three weeks earlier that Cissie finally gave up going out in the street on her own. 'I just went to the pillar box, that was all. I knew I was being a bit silly, and that I might fall, but I'd gone all the same. Howard, my son, has said that to me all my life. "You just can't wait, can you?"

'On the way back, I suddenly didn't feel at all safe, so I said to myself, "If I get home this time, I won't do it again." So that's it.

'I've been told not to do my own cleaning, but I still do. I wait till it's dark, then I get my little step-ladder out, climb up and clean my windows. If I do it in the dark, no one knows I'm being silly.'

She gets most lonely at weekends, if she has no visitors, when her street goes quiet and there's not much happening. During the week, she finds it easier to keep busy. All the same, she knows she has done well to be in her own home, looking after herself, at ninety-six.

'Oh, I've had a good life. I've been lucky. We didn't have much money but we had good friends. I think that's why I've lived so long – being thankful and content.

'Dad and I always trusted each other. I always knew where he was and what he was doing when he went off to Labour Party conferences.'

She kept up her Labour Party work and support after her husband died, although she had never been a serious political animal. 'I did it really for Dad's sake. To my simple mind, I don't like either party to get a big majority. It makes them big-headed. I want Tony Blair to get in, of course, but not to get too powerful.'

24

THE LABOUR PARTY

The birth of the Labour Party

A rather important meeting took place in London in 1900. It didn't seem exceptionally important at the time, as there was a war on so most people had other things to think about. However, when they look back triumphantly a hundred years later, as they doubtless will, that meeting at the Memorial Hall, Farringdon Street, on Tuesday, 27 February 1900, will be seen as the meeting at which it really began. Out of it emerged what we now call the British Labour Party.

The meeting was called by the Parliamentary Committee of the Trades Union Congress. Its purpose, so the posters announced, was 'Labour Representation', to 'establish a distinct Labour Group in Parliament'. In other words, a proper party, with its own whips and policy. The roots and causes, strands and influences go back decades, if not centuries, but political historians are agreed: this was the meeting that mattered.

The union movement had grown considerably over the century,

despite periods when its activities had been banned. It currently had over half a million members, but felt it needed its own representatives in Parliament. At the time MPs were not paid, so it was almost impossible for a working man to be elected, unless he was sponsored in some way.

The railway unions were particularly keen to have some sort of representation in Parliament. All new railway lines had to be approved by Parliament, where they were backed and supported by the relevant Tory landowners and railway companies. The workers had no say in the matter.

The miners, on the other hand, were not so keen on forming a Labour Party. Their union had struck deals with the Liberal Party in several coal-mining areas where the Liberals had put up candidates approved by the miners, and were unofficially known as Lib-Labs. The miners had been quite happy with this arrangement.

However, the unions generally considered the Liberal Party, despite the radical leanings of some of its members, no more supportive of the aspirations of the new working classes than the Conservatives, so they had called the meeting.

The Memorial Hall, now gone, was just round the corner from Fleet Street where in 1900 the presses of the *Daily Mail* and other mighty organs were pounding out the latest dramas in the Boer War. Ladysmith had been under siege since January but on 28 February, the day after the Labour meeting, it was finally relieved, which was one of the many reasons why the meeting didn't make many column inches. It didn't make any in the *Daily Express* – but that wasn't born until two months later.

There were 129 delegates at the meeting, all of whom were men, and most of whom came from the unions. There were representatives of some of the country's biggest, the railway workers, and some of the smallest, such as the Vellum Bookbinders' Union, the Match Makers' Union and the Waiters' Union. The latter had only 200 members, so it had done well to send a representative.

The meeting was also attended by delegates of three socialist groups. First there were members of the Fabian Society, clever, middle-class intellectuals, such as Sidney and Beatrice Webb and George Bernard Shaw. The second group, the Social Democratic Federation, was also fairly middle-class but more extreme, not to say exotic.

The Independent Labour Party (ILP), the third of the socialist groups, had been set up in Bradford in 1893. Despite its name, it was not a properly organised party, more a socialist society, but Keir Hardie was a member. Earlier he had failed to be adopted as a parliamentary candidate by the Liberals but in 1892 had been elected as the ILP Member for West Ham South, the first socialist to be elected to the House of Commons. He was born in Lanarkshire in 1856, never went to school, started work at seven then was a coal-miner from the age of ten until he was twenty, before he became a trade-union official and later a journalist. When he lost his seat in 1895 the ILP had begun to fade.

At the Memorial Hall meeting, the Socialist Democratic Federation tried to get it formally agreed that the new Labour Representation Committee (LRC) should accept the concept of the class war. After some discussion, it did not. (The SDF representatives soon left the committee.)

Another motion was put forward that only members of the working class should represent the new party in Parliament. John Burns, the ILP MP for Battersea, stood up to oppose it. 'I am tired of working-class boots, working-class brains, working-class houses and working-class margarine,' he said. He argued that Labour should not be prisoners of class prejudice and the motion was defeated. All classes were allowed to join, which was fortunate for Tony Blair and the Labour Party as we know it today.

The meeting elected as its first secretary young Ramsay MacDonald, a member of the ILP. Like Keir Hardie, he was a Scotsman, and also illegitimate. He had been born in Lossiemouth in 1866 and brought up by his mother and grandmother. His intelligence was spotted by a local dominie and, unlike Hardie, he acquired some education: he attended school till he was twelve, then became a pupil-teacher. He, too, later became a journalist. Hardie was considered a rough visionary while MacDonald, ten years younger, was seen as more sophisticated and accomplished; he had travelled, taught himself science and married well, to Margaret Gladstone, a doctor's daughter and niece of Lord Kelvin. He was a handsome, romantic figure with an attractive speaking voice.

The first General Election in which the new LRC took part occurred

just six months after its foundation, in October 1900, the so-called
Khaki election. The Tories, under Lord Salisbury, played the patriotic
card and were re-elected with a large majority – 401 MPs against 268
for the opposition. There was even a Tory majority in Scotland for the
first time in many years.

In the following two years, membership more than doubled to
861,000, mainly due to the Taff Vale judgement. Some Welsh railway
workers, who had gone on strike in 1900, were successfully sued by the
railway owners for damages. In 1901 the House of Lords upheld the
judgement, and £23,000 had to be paid by the workers. This seemed
like a mortal blow at the time, but in fact it saved the Labour Party. It
made unions such as the miners, the textile workers and others who had
not supported the original meeting realise it was vital to have parliamentary representation.

At the LRC's annual meeting in 1903, held in Newcastle, subscrip-
tions were increased to provide a fund from which in future MPs would
be paid. In return for their wage, MPs would have to 'strictly abstain
from identifying themselves with or promoting the interests of any sections of the Liberal or Conservative parties'. Hints of discipline to
come. This did not stop Ramsay MacDonald from arranging a secret
deal with the Liberals whereby they would not put up candidates in certain places where the Labour candidates were strongest. Hints of deals
to come.

In the 1906 General Election, the LRC put up fifty candidates and
got twenty-nine MPs, which included Keir Hardie again, Ramsay
MacDonald and Philip Snowden. All twenty-nine came from working-
class backgrounds, many from the north, particularly Lancashire and
Scotland, most were union officials and nearly all were Methodists or
Congregationalists.

The Conservatives, under Balfour, were soundly beaten and the
Liberals, under Campbell-Bannerman, took power. Balfour mocked
the triumphant Liberals by sneering that they were a 'mere cork' on the
socialist tide. Bernard Shaw thought it was the other way round, that
the LRC had ridden along like a cork in the Liberal tide.

Once the new Parliament assembled, the LRC assumed the name the
Labour Party and formalised itself by appointing whips and officers.
Keir Hardie was elected leader of the party (though the formal title for

some years was chairman) and Ramsay MacDonald continued as party secretary.

By the January 1910 election, there were signs that Labour's initial impetus had faded somewhat, although they now had forty MPs. The Liberals, spurred on by Lloyd George, were embarking on a series of radical social reforms while socialists in the Labour Party were beginning to argue among themselves. Hardie, who tended to be a lone wolf, was suspicious of Arthur Henderson, who had taken over as leader in 1908, thinking him timid and reactionary. In 1910, he admitted that, 'The Labour Party has almost ceased to count.'

In 1911, the Liberal government introduced state payments for MPs, in return for which the Labour Party agreed to support Lloyd George's Insurance Bill. In 1913, a Trade Union Act allowed unions to raise contributions from their members for political purposes. Both these changes helped the Labour Party, but the First World War stopped any real growth. The Labour Party had been against armaments, and in August 1914, Hardie and Henderson took part in a Trafalgar Square demonstration to oppose the war, which didn't make them very popular: the nation's young men were soon rushing like lemmings to join up. Once the war began, most Labour MPs felt they had to support it. Arthur Henderson, who again took over as leader in 1914, joined the war coalition government with a seat in the Cabinet.

In 1918, the Fabian and socialist wings of the Labour Party managed to have some important additions made to the party's constitution. Sidney Webb drafted Clause Four of the party's ultimate objectives, which explicitly committed it to common ownership of the means of production. The party also aimed to introduce a minimum wage. The two policies were to run and run.

The December 1918 General Election was virtually a vote for or against Lloyd George as the architect of victory. The Labour Party put up a massive number of candidates – 361 compared to 78 in 1910 – but won only fifty-seven seats. Their anti-war history had worked against them. Some of their best and ablest members, such as MacDonald, Henderson and Snowden, lost their seats. A Scottish miner called Willie Anderson was elected leader, and dismissed by Beatrice Webb as 'respectable but dull-witted'.

In the 1922 election, Labour put up 414 candidates of whom 142 were elected. This was the party's breakthrough, not in gaining power but in achieving real influence. The Liberals were routed, and Labour emerged in second place, becoming the official opposition, which gave them additional status and importance. Their leaders had now to be seen and treated as a prospective government.

Ramsay MacDonald was elected once more as leader, and therefore Leader of His Majesty's Opposition – but he was worried. He wrote in a letter to an American friend that he was the first person ever in such a position without a private income and without proper support. 'Whereas my predecessors inherited secretaries and a going machine, I inherited nothing and am having to make everything.'

One of the significant aspects of the party's astonishing success was that, for the first time, their MPs came from a much broader spectrum of society. While the leaders, like MacDonald, were still working-class in origin, some new MPs were middle-class: Clement Attlee, aged thirty-nine, was the son of a well-known lawyer and had been educated at Haileybury and Oxford. He had qualified as a barrister, then taken up lecturing. He lived in the East End of London, where he became mayor of Stepney, and entered the House of Commons as the Member for Limehouse.

One of the newcomers at the next election in 1923 was Susan Lawrence, MP for East Ham North, who became Labour's first woman MP. (The Tories had the first woman in the House, Nancy Astor, in 1919.) Miss Lawrence had earlier been a Conservative, and wore a monocle. On turning Labour, she sported an Eton crop. In *Who's Who* she gave her age, which at the time women did not do, and listed her hobbies as 'parties, Tolstoy, rowdy meetings, mountaineering and reading Government Blue books'. She was always irritated when she was referred to as a woman MP, and would ask why people didn't speak of Churchill as a man MP.

The 1923 election had been called suddenly, on the issue of tariff reform, and Labour won 191 seats. The Tories no longer had an overall majority and the Liberals decided to support Labour. On 23 January 1924, Stanley Baldwin, the Conservative Prime Minister, resigned and the King called upon Ramsay MacDonald to form a government. After twenty-four years, the Labour Party was at last in power.

MacDonald was now fifty-seven, a widower since the tragic early death of his wife. His daughter become his hostess at 10 Downing Street. Since becoming its first secretary in 1900 he had proved himself a good leader: he had kept the party afloat and its rival factions relatively happy, as well as surviving ups and downs in his own career. He was now an experienced, knowledgeable politician. He had some blind spots, on economics, for example, but then, as we well know, going to university or even studying under Maynard Keynes doesn't make you right on economics.

He had confidence enough in his own position in the party to appoint the first ever woman minister, Margaret Bondfield, who had left school at fourteen to work as a shop assistant. She became Minister of Labour and entered the Cabinet in 1929. MacDonald perhaps showed too much confidence in his own diplomatic abilities by appointing himself Foreign Secretary, which upset those colleagues who had fancied the job.

One of his decisions was to give unconditional recognition to the new Soviet government. This handed the Conservatives a chance to accuse Labour of being leftie, not to say Communist. It also worried his Liberal supporters and, after only nine months in office, it contributed to his downfall. The government was defeated by the Conservatives and Liberals in a vote, and MacDonald called a General Election. Alas for him, the Tories romped home with 413 seats to Labour's 151, although Labour's total vote went up by a million to 5.5 million. The Liberals only got forty seats, which meant that this time the Tories had a comfortable majority and were able to survive the full five years, including the General Strike of May 1926.

However, Labour bounced back in 1929, thanks to a worsening economic situation for which the Tories were blamed. Labour got 287 seats, their largest number so far, and for the first time they had 'won' the election, in that they were the biggest party, though without a clear majority. MacDonald came back into power as Prime Minister, but with Arthur Henderson as Foreign Secretary. One of the junior ministers was Oswald Mosley, who put forward a plan to relieve the economic situation by imposing state control on all foreign imports. The Cabinet turned it down. Mosley resigned and was replaced by Clement Attlee.

By 1930, unemployment had reached two million. Labour's handling of the economy was no better than the Tories' and MacDonald seemed more interested in foreign than home affairs. Mosley went off in a huff, put on a black shirt and started his own party, leaving Labour to fight among themselves or snipe at MacDonald and Philip Snowden, the Chancellor, for the economic problems. MacDonald wanted sacrifices made, which he said was for the good of the nation, but the trade unions opposed him.

On 23 August 1931, MacDonald decided he'd had enough. He persuaded all his Cabinet to resign, then went to the King with his own resignation. Two hours later, to the astonishment of his Labour colleagues, he had returned as Prime Minister to form a coalition government with the Liberals and Tories.

No discussions, apparently, had taken place with his Labour Cabinet. He had acted almost alone, out of pique or fury, despair or madness, depending on which political historian you prefer. For nine years, he had been the Labour Party's strongest leader, had twice been Prime Minister, if just for short periods, but now he was isolated and virtually ostracised. The parliamentary party, meeting at Transport House (which had become the party's headquarters, as well as that of the unions) voted for Arthur Henderson to replace him as leader.

MacDonald struggled on as Prime Minister with his coalition Cabinet for a few more weeks, keeping neither his Liberal nor Tory

Ramsay MacDonald

associates happy, but hoping to sit tight until the Labour Party saw the sense in his actions. That didn't work either. Then came the bitterest blow: the National Executive expelled him from the Labour Party.

He was forced to call a General Election in October 1931 which, naturally enough, ended in humiliation for Labour. MacDonald and Snowden, who were seen as the villains, stood as members of their own little National Labour group. MacDonald was elected again and remained as Prime Minister of a coalition – but only forty-six Labour MPs were returned, compared with 287 at the previous election. Oh, what a tragedy, what a farce. The Labour Party, almost at one stroke, had been as good as wiped out. Or had it wiped itself out?

The new leader of the Labour Party, who took it into the 1935 election, was Clement Attlee, who had been appointed temporary leader a few months earlier after the resignation of George Lansbury. The party recovered a lot of ground, and gained 154 seats. MacDonald, standing again as National Labour, lost his seat to Emmanuel Shinwell and retired. He died in 1937, aged seventy, at sea, while on a voyage to South America.

Attlee wasn't really expected to remain as leader: he lacked charisma. He was small, weedy, more a civil servant than a rabble-rouser. 'A natural adjutant, but not a general,' as the *New Statesman* described him. But at the next leadership election, fierce rivalry between his two opponents, Herbert Morrison and Arthur Greenwood, allowed him to win through on the second vote.

Quietly and diligently, Attlee worked to restore the status of the party, and as the 1930s progressed, he was helped by a resurgence in romantic and intellectual socialism, as seen in the Spanish Civil War, when young men went off to support the republican side, and the success of the Left Wing Book Club founded by Victor Gollancz. Attlee proved stronger than he appeared, especially when he opposed Chamberlain on appeasement and came out against any further concessions to the advance of Hitler. This endeared him to Churchill who rang him to say, 'Your declaration does honour to the British nation.'

In effect, Attlee became deputy Prime Minister to Churchill. During the war, he tended to look after domestic issues, with little fuss or publicity, a quiet man with a quiet personality, while Churchill ran the war itself, brilliantly, flamboyantly and ultimately victoriously, proving a perfect wartime leader.

Naturally, when the 1945 General Election was called, Churchill expected a grateful nation to do their duty. Instead, Labour stormed in with 393 MPs – an astonishing figure that gave the party a clear majority of 146. For the first time in their short and rather bumpy history they were in total control, dependent on no favours, no deals with others.

How had they done it? Even with hindsight political success is often as difficult to explain as political failure. The MacDonald coalition shambles was down to a combination of his personality, trade-union pressure and the economic climate. The 1945 landslide Labour victory is usually attributed to two elements: the electorate were fed up with the Tories, had not forgotten their pre-war record, and were excited by Labour's promises.

Political parties are in the business of making promises. We expect it of them, even when we scoff and sneer and remain suspicious. Perhaps the most striking aspect of the 1945–50 Labour government was that it kept its promises: it brought in a vast programme of nationalisation, which included coal, transport, electricity and steel, and introduced the National Health Service. At the same time, India, Burma and Ceylon were given independence. During this government, Labour did not lose one by-election, another remarkable record.

There was a slight backlash in the 1950 election, thanks to the austerity measures imposed by Stafford Cripps, the Chancellor, but Labour were re-elected, if only just, with an overall majority of five. Then the leaders started to fall out with each other, as they often do in tight times. Hugh Gaitskell, aged forty-four, took over from Cripps as Chancellor. In his 1951 budget he introduced charges for dentures and spectacles, which seemed to make a nonsense of a free National Health Service, according to the young Harold Wilson, President of the Board of Trade, and Aneurin Bevan, Minister of Labour, both of whom resigned.

Attlee called a General Election in 1951, hoping for a more workable majority, and though Labour polled almost 14 million votes, their biggest share so far, the Tories were back in power with a majority of seventeen and Churchill as Prime Minister. They increased this in the

1955 election, after which Attlee resigned as Labour leader. He was replaced by Gaitskell, another public-school, Oxbridge product.

The Tories won again in 1959, their third consecutive victory. Gaitskell decided that Clause Four was at the root of the trouble, but failed to get it ditched. A more serious, deeper division was caused by the Campaign for Nuclear Disarmament, supported by many Labour Party members and others in the country, and Gaitskell found himself at odds with his left wing.

In 1963, Gaitskell died suddenly, aged fifty-six, and Harold Wilson took his place as leader: another clever – nay, brilliant – Oxford scholar and don, but this time from a working-class background. His boasts about his barefooted childhood were exaggerated but his Yorkshire accent was intact and his knowledge of football immaculate. (I went to interview him once and he insisted on reciting Huddersfield Town's team from 1930.) After thirteen years in opposition Labour won the 1964 election. Wilson became Prime Minister at forty-eight, the youngest since Rosebery in 1894. His majority was tiny, only four, but he was a trained economist – the first to lead Labour – and a smart tactician. He managed to appear popular and modern, by showing interest in the Beatles, football and technology, unlike the aristocratic Tory leader, Sir Alec Douglas-Home. He carefully chose the time of the next election, in March 1966 (before, not after England's World Cup win), and Labour emerged with a majority of 96. It was the party's second time in government with real power; over half its MPs were graduates and there were twice as many teachers as miners.

But the trade unions, with their block votes, were still an immensely strong influence. Wilson found it harder than Attlee to retain their support and loyalty – he usually achieved it by giving in to them, treating them with deference, beer and sandwiches at Downing Street. The economic situation worsened, strikes increased, terrorists became active in Northern Ireland and the Tories returned to power in 1970 with a majority of thirty.

Edward Heath, the new Tory leader, did little better than his Labour predecessor, with even more strikes and a three-day (working) week which culminated in the miners' strike of 1974. The public had had enough of both main parties and there was a brief upturn in Liberal fortunes but Labour won the 1974 election with another minuscule majority. The nation held its breath for a few moments, while Heath tried to strike a coalition deal with the Liberal MPs, all fourteen of them, but it came to nothing, and for the next two years, Mr Wilson did another balancing act.

Then, in March 1976, he did something that no Labour leader – in fact, no Prime Minister this century – has done: he resigned, for no obvious reason, five days after his sixtieth birthday while apparently at the height of his political powers. He'd led Labour to three General Election victories and had been Prime Minister for eight years, during which time homosexuality had been legalised, capital punishment abolished and the Open University founded.

James Callaghan took over as Prime Minister, but managed only three years in office before the Tories stormed back in 1979 with Margaret Thatcher as their leader, the first woman Prime Minister in British history. She reigned supreme throughout the 1980s, a period upon which most Labour voters prefer not to dwell.

In the meantime, Labour leaders suffered endless humiliations. Michael Foot, a throwback to the intellectual, high-minded and badly dressed Fabians, sneaked in as leader almost by default, but lasted only two years. Neil Kinnock took over and began to modernise the party. It seemed, according to most pollsters, that he might even have triumphed in the 1992 election, but the power of the Tory tabloid press, his supporters claimed, robbed him of victory. John Smith succeeded him but died in May 1994.

Tony Blair, the next leader, like Attlee and Gaitskell, was public-school and Oxford educated. He was born in Edinburgh, but considered Durham his home town. He was brought up in a Tory household and joined the Labour Party relatively late in life. As leader, he set about real reform, and started with Clause Four.

In 1995 I spent a day with Tony Blair when he was touring the country during his anti-Clause Four campaign. I went with him from London to Glasgow, then on to Leeds. I noticed how in speeches to the Labour faithful he referred constantly to New Labour, and made clear his contempt for the Labour old guard, which for too many years had wasted its energies on outdated arguments and ideologies. I also noticed that after each speech women asked for his autograph.

I came back to London by train with Alastair Campbell, his press adviser, while Blair went on to Sedgefield to spend the weekend in his constituency and watch Newcastle United. On the train, I asked Campbell what Blair was really like. 'He's the same in public as he is in private, as you saw today. He doesn't have one message for the party insiders and one for the rest. He's in touch, compared with some old-time Labour people in the '80s who lived on another planet.'

All the same, there seemed something buttoned up, almost unemotional, about him. Then Campbell told a rather revealing story about something that had happened at the previous Labour Conference in Blackpool when the change to Clause Four had been first proposed. There had been weeks of discussions, talk of splits and attacks, but Blair's speech received an ovation. 'Afterwards, I was high on adrenaline, and so was John Prescott. All of us were buzzing, but when Tony came off the platform, all he said was, "Right, what's next?"'

Sounded like lack of emotion to me. 'No, it doesn't. It shows he has a focused mind. He had got worked up and worried beforehand, but once it was over he was ready to move on.'

Tony Blair became Labour leader with no Labour Party roots, carrying no political baggage, which was obviously an asset. What I hadn't realised until that day was how radical he was, how coldly determined to transform politics, just as Margaret Thatcher had. If, of course, he ever became Prime Minister.

As the 1997 General Election approached, Blair had emerged as a charismatic Labour leader and had convinced the country that the party really was New Labour now. It was ahead in the polls – but would the polls be wrong, just like last time?

The month before the election I went to visit the Labour Party's headquarters, now in a rather ugly glass and concrete block on London's Millbank, very handy for the Houses of Parliament and just along the street from the Tate Gallery. It is almost next door to MI5, housed in an equally soulless edifice. These buildings might be blank and anonymous on the outside, but inside . . . what plots, schemes and emotions were seething and fizzling away.

When it all began in 1900, Labour had only one official in Ramsay MacDonald, its unpaid secretary. In 1997, I counted 250 paid officials,

200 in that building alone, but that was just before an election. In normal times, they get by with 150.

The security was intense, not just because of the normal 1990s worries about terrorists, but also the realisation that political opponents or media spies might be trying to infiltrate, hoping to pick up a few secrets.

As I waited, I began to notice that almost all the ants were young, in their twenties and thirties. There were equal numbers of men and women. There was no standard dress: some were in sparkling white shirts and suits, like the *Express* hacks (the most sparkling of all being Peter Mandelson, whom I spotted gliding among the desks like a lounge-suit lizard), but just as many were wearing jeans or casual clothes. Most surprising of all was that many were doing something not everyone in open-plan offices does today: they were talking to each other. Gossip, office love affairs, football or what happened last night on the telly?

Certainly not, said David Hill, the Labour Party's chief spokesman, when he led me through the rows of desks. They're all working while they're talking. Well, he added, there might be some gossiping as today's Labour people know how to party, but the units were structured so that people *could* talk to each other, to keep in touch with what other units were doing.

Units? Structure? It turned out the floor had been arranged into four main task forces, in their own areas with their own leaders but connected to each other. One was called the Attack Unit – until recently, it had been the Rapid Rebuttal Unit, but its name had been changed to make it sound, well, less negative and defensive. As only its staff know what they call themselves, it didn't seem a very important change but, of course, this is to misunderstand the nature of modern politics.

The Attack Unit's purpose was to attack the Tories, either full-frontal attacking or full-frontal defending and denying, whether the attack had come first or not. To aid them in this work they had installed a very expensive piece of computer equipment called Excalibur, which had cost some £300,000. Into this, they were feeding all Tory pronouncements, on every subject, by almost every Tory, so that by keying in a vital word, they could bring out in seconds all relevant references and show the Tories contradicting themselves or lying or both.

Then there was the Information Briefing Unit. Among other things, it passed on whatever the Attack Unit had come up with. There was also the Media and Monitoring Unit and the Key Seats Unit. It was vital, said Mr Hill, for all of them to know what the other was doing, its aims and progress. Yes, Peter Mandelson, MP for Hartlepool, was in overall charge, having been made the party's General Election campaign co-ordinator and, indeed, as the grandson of Herbert Morrison he has Old Labour in his blood.

Some of New Labour's modern methods have come from the USA, such as the interlinking task forces. 'But we have helped them as well. We helped the Democrats in 1992, telling them what the Republicans might do and say because, at that time, the Republicans were copying the Tories.'

Both Labour and the Conservatives were using much the same methods in the election of 1997, arming themselves as if for battle, talking about war rooms, but Labour, which since 1900 had tended to be the more amateur, raggle-taggle political machine, for once seemed more efficient, cleverer and with more manpower. Round the corner in Smith Square, at the Tory Party headquarters, their forces numbered only forty. The Tories had also recently acquired their own Excalibur, but that didn't frighten David Hill: 'They'll have teething troubles, just as we did. It's only as good as the material put in and the capacity of the people to use it. It did help us with the Scott Report. The Tory government wouldn't let us see it in advance, but the minute we got it, we downloaded all 1,800 pages into Excalibur. When Tory spokesmen started quoting selected bits without having read the whole report, we immediately found the context and quoted the bits missed out which, of course, caught their spokesmen on the hop . . .

'There are a few young people who can get over-keen, but there's always an excited buzz. A lot won't be employed here after the election, but they all know it will look good on their CV. I'm about the oldest person working here.'

David Hill was born in Birmingham in 1948, into a strong Labour family. He has retained his Brummy accent, and his allegiance to Aston Villa Football Club, despite his Oxford education. His first two years after graduation were spent with Unigate, where he might have become manager of a dairy if he hadn't left in 1972 to work with a local

Tony Blair

Birmingham MP, Roy Hattersley, rising with him through the Labour hierarchy. He became the party's chief spokesman in 1993. In many ways, in his style and experience, he is Old Labour.

'The process of change began with Neil Kinnock, but it was hard for him as he was seen as someone coming from the left, so it was suspected he didn't believe in the changes. The Tories played up these fears. John Smith made the next leap forward, introducing an element of trust. Tony Blair was what we needed for the final move forward – someone without any political baggage.

'I only hope that when we do get in, after we have completed all our pledges, that we'll start some social changes. Last time we were in, under Callaghan, there was a raft of social measures we never got round to. Nothing very shattering, just things like equality before the law, freedom of the press. If Tony Blair's Cabinet turns out as competent as I know they are, having seen them from inside, then there should be time for some radical social measures. As for me, and all Labour Party officials, my job will start the day after the election – working for re-election in five years' time.'

To the amazement of almost everyone, including the Labour leaders, there was a landslide victory on 1 May 1997, with Labour winning 419 seats and the Tories only 165. The swing to Labour was 10 per cent, the biggest for fifty-two years since the 1945 landslide, when the swing was

12 per cent, but the 1997 landslide resulted in twenty-six more Labour MPs than in 1945. So it was the party's biggest victory ever.

At forty-three Tony Blair came in as the youngest Prime Minister since Lord Liverpool made it at forty-two in 1812. The total number of women MPs more than doubled, from 62 to 119. Almost all were Labour, who had 101 compared with only 39 in the previous Parliament. The first Labour Cabinet of 1997 included five women, plus nineteen female ministers. Many were very young and were immediately christened Blair's Babes by the tabloid press. There were also three openly gay Labour MPs, one in the Cabinet, Chris Smith, which would have been impossible in 1900, and hard to imagine in 1945 or even 1979.

Like the rest of the population, the new Labour MPs were better educated. In the 1923 election, which led to Labour's first government, just 14 per cent of the party's MPs were graduates. In 1945, this had risen to 33 per cent. In 1997, it was 64 per cent. There was a strong Scottish element among its leaders: the Foreign Secretary, Robin Cook, the Chancellor, Gordon Brown, and Blair himself are all Scottish-born, which reflects Labour's historic association with Scotland, although unlike Ramsay MacDonald and Keir Hardie, no one could say that the present Labour leaders are horny-handed sons of toil. In 1997, the place to hear true working-class voices was in the House of Lords, among the Labour life peers, rather than in the House of Commons.

The Tories, meanwhile, had been well and truly vanquished. Not one MP in either Scotland or Wales. Their total of 165 was their lowest since the Liberal landslide of 1906 when they were left with 157. In 1997, they lost seven Cabinet ministers – not quite as bad as 1906, when they lost eight. But the Tories have been a dominant force for two hundred years and have rarely been in the wilderness for long. Since 1866, their worst spell out of office has been eleven years between 1905 and 1916, while until they returned in 1997, Labour had been out of office for eighteen.

But Labour looked certain to end the century not just in power but confident of repeating their success in the twenty-first century. After all, in this one they had pulled off two of the three landslides. Now, as New Labour, they appeared to have pulled off an even better trick in taking over the mantle of Tory economic efficiency and appealing to all sections of the populace. Just forty days after the 1997 election, the *Express*, which had supported the Tories since it had been born in 1900, came out in favour of Tony Blair and Labour. That was a reassuring sign.

Then, in 1998, just a year after the famous victory, David Hill left the Labour Party to work for a commercial PR firm, at reportedly twice the salary. Could that be a more worrying sign?

25

Dr Daly Briscoe

Suffolk GP, writer and lecturer

Daly Briscoe, aged 11

Dr Arnold Daly Briscoe is a Tory, used to be a Tory councillor, but he is not your modern, thrusting, pushy Tory. He is a caring, benevolent Tory of the old school. In a word he is a gentleman, proud and patriotic, smart and well-dressed, kind and considerate. That's one reason why at ninety-seven he is such a popular, well-loved figure. The other reason is that he never moans or groans. At that great age you are allowed to, for the chances are you'll have a few aches and pains, plus complaints about the modern world, but Dr Briscoe combines a stiff upper lip in the face of life's problems with an engaging good humour and cheerfulness, bursting into schoolboy laughter at the slightest amusing remark. Small wonder he has a waiting list of nice neighbours, mostly middle-aged, middle-class, his fans – his groupies, even – ever eager and willing to help him in any way they can. There is a rota, for example, of people who come in to read to him for two or three hours most days. He lives alone, and is very independent, but his vision is poor now. One pops in to help him read and answer his post, or just to have a chat. Dr Briscoe is a legend in his local lifetime, known by all. In a way, they are paying him back for the many he has helped in his professional and personal life.

He has a large house in Woodbridge, Suffolk, an affluent market town of period houses, attractive streets and some twelve thousand souls. He doesn't actually live in the house in autumn and winter but in a flat above his garage. The main part of the house is so cold and he hasn't got central heating, but he has a gardener and a cleaner and he opens it all up when he is entertaining friends or relations, which he often does. He is very keen on entertaining and social activities, especially of an uplifting literary, cultural or historical nature.

The moment I arrived, he offered me a glass of sherry, dry, medium or sweet, and I could see he had three decanters filled in readiness. Then, to my surprise, he said he'd taken the liberty of booking a table at the local inn for lunch, after we had finished our chat. I said I couldn't possibly take up more of his time but he was adamant that I must join him, along with Margaret, one of his neighbours. At his expense, oh, yes.

He is known as Daly to all his friends, never Arnold, but I was wary of addressing him as such on a first meeting. It was clear from remarks he made, ever so politely, that he does not care for the habit of addressing a total stranger by their first name. It gets his goat when petty officials, reading from forms or applications, call out 'Daly' or even worse 'Arnold'. In his day, at school and university, it was surnames only, even between friends, until you had known each other many years.

He was born in Whitefield, north of Manchester, in Lancashire, on 2 July 1900, where his father had a brewery. When he was five, they moved to Hereford, for reasons he didn't understand at the time, but later his mother told him there had been some problems at the family brewery. Rumours of arsenic in local water, the beer perhaps not up to scratch, had begun to worry his father, who decided to sell out, a decision he later regretted. The move itself was a success, for his father became general manager of the Hereford and Tredegar Brewery. They lived in some style and young Daly was sent to Hereford Cathedral School as a day boy.

He had two brothers and two sisters, but one sister died of scarlet fever at five. 'I can still see my father in tears when he spoke of her. There were no antibiotics in those days. Most families lost a child.'

He idolised his oldest brother, born in 1894, who went off to the First World War aged twenty. 'He was gassed at the second battle of Ypres and was invalided home, but he recovered and returned to the Somme. He survived that, then joined the Royal Flying Corps. He flew in biplanes, as an observer, and was shot down. But he survived that as well! Alas, he later contracted pulmonary tuberculosis and died aged forty-six. I think his war service had a lot to do with it.'

At the Cathedral School, in his Eton collar and cap with three yellow rings round it, Daly was considered clever at most subjects, good at games, but a bit small. 'That was rather embarrassing. I was so small and lightweight most of my schooldays and didn't grow till I was over sixteen. It meant I was the cox in the school's first boat for four years. No, I wasn't bullied, but I can't say I enjoyed being so small. My nickname in the school was Goliath!'

Out burst his schoolboy, rather high-pitched laughter and he held his mouth in mock horror. By the age of eighteen, his growth spurt had started and he soon made it to five feet eleven.

'I've always had good health, all my life, but I'll tell you about one nasty accident when I was seven. My father had a horse and trap and we kept a couple of horses in our stable. There was a Jacob's ladder against the stable wall and I had been warned not to climb it – so I did. I fell off and broke the femur in my right leg. There were no X-rays in those days. The local doctor put my leg in wooden splints, from my armpit to my foot, and rigged up a pulley. He weighted it with a can of shot, for me to use as a form of traction. Do you know, it worked so well that when I recovered, my right leg, the broken one, was five-eighths of an inch longer than my left leg. It is to this day. Ha ha ha . . .'

Caning was practised regularly at his school, as it was at all schools of the time, both private and state, but fortunately, just before he arrived, the privilege of senior boys, the monitors, to cane younger boys was taken away. 'The headmaster, of course, still regularly exercised his cane. It was known as a "flissing". It's a nice onomatopoeic name for the sound of a cane.'

The day war broke out, 4 August 1914, he was with the school's officer cadet corps at a camp near Aldershot. 'It was in a place called Mytchett's Farm. There were OTCs from lots of public schools, making up a battalion. We were being drilled by regular army officers under Captain Berners of the Grenadier Guards. His adjutant was Lieutenant the Honourable H. R. L. G. Alexander. You must know that name. He later became Field Marshal Earl Alexander, who directed the retreat from Dunkirk in the Second World War. Oh, he was a fine-looking man. An Irish Guardsman, if I remember rightly. I can still see him galloping all over the place on his horse.

'We were there, drilling away, when the news came through. It was a Sunday. We were told war had broken out and we were being suddenly sent away, before the camp had finished. So we all arrived back home very unexpectedly.

'Oh, yes, what you know is true. Young men everywhere fell over themselves to get into khaki. I was personally very disappointed that I was too young. When I reached eighteen in July 1918, I fully expected to be called up. In fact I waited at home for my call-up papers, but August went by, then September and October. I began to wonder if they had been mislaid.'

The call never came, so in January 1919, he went up to Cambridge and registered as a medical student at St John's College. 'I can't remember when I thought of becoming a doctor. It was probably talking to an uncle who said that medicine was far more worthwhile than brewing. Without sounding too priggish, I think that has been a motivating force in my life, wanting to do something worthwhile.'

In June 1918 he had been entered for the Somerset Exhibition at St John's College, Cambridge, an award limited to Manchester Grammar School, Marlborough Grammar School and his own school. 'We were a fairly small school, with just a hundred and twenty boys, with only the most primitive of science labs, but we regularly sent ten each year to Oxford and Cambridge. I sat the exam in St John's, in the Combination Room. I remember it was full of soldiers who'd been billeted in the College.' He got the award, and ever after felt grateful to Sarah, Duchess of Somerset, who had endowed the money in the seventeenth century.

Daly spent his first year on E Staircase in New Court where he had his own sitting room and a bedroom. 'It's been made into two rooms now as students have much less space. I know – because I went back and had my ninetieth birthday there.'

He also had a college servant to look after him. 'My gyp's name was Bailey. His favourite remark, which he said all the time, was "Don't you know, sir." I suppose the modern version would be "you know". Oh, he was very agreeable. He brought me a jug of hot water every morning and poured it into my washstand so I could shave. He even turned my socks inside out so I could slip into them easily.'

He doesn't remember any social snobbery with chaps from the major public schools feeling superior to people from lesser schools like himself. 'Not at all – at least I never saw it, nor did I suffer from it. St John's was a closeknit community. I didn't know a soul when I went up and felt lost for a couple of days, but by dining in college each evening I soon felt part of the place. You had to dine in at least five nights a week, in your gown, of course, which you wore to all lectures. The head porter would parade up and down between the tables in Hall, putting pins in a board to check you were in for dinner.

'Nobody I knew had lots of money or went around getting drunk and behaving badly at dining clubs. The war had just ended so there wasn't a lot of food and drink around. I think the only time we made merry was at bump suppers – and then I'd say we were merry, not sozzled.'

What about girls? 'Oh, we had nothing to do with them. We lived a monastic life. There were undergraduettes at Girton and Newnham but they were technically not full members of the university, and not allowed to wear gowns, but they could attend lectures. I remember going to an open lecture given by Q – Sir Arthur Quiller-Couch – who had been made professor of literature. His lectures were splendid and very popular. The undergraduettes always sat in the front two rows but Q deliberately looked right over them and would begin each lecture by saying, "Gentlemen." Imagine that happening now! What a fuss there would be. Ha ha ha . . .

'I suppose some girls were entertained in the men's colleges, but they always had to be chaperoned. In the science labs, doing physiology, I did see one or two, but I can't say I ever knew any. I certainly didn't have a girlfriend. I didn't know anyone who had. I had never met any girls, socially, at home or at Cambridge.'

What chaps like Daly did, to get rid of all their energies, was a great deal of hearty rowing. Now that he had shot up to almost six feet, he was soon stroking the college boat. 'In 1919 we managed four bumps, which was a great achievement. I still have my college oar. I'll go and get it, if you like. No? All right, then, later perhaps . . .

'I was awfully lucky because in the summer of 1919 I rowed at Henley. It was called the Royal Peace Regatta. I was fortunate to row for Lady Margaret, the College Boat Club. We reached the semi-final but got beaten by Shrewsbury, alas.'

His hero at the time was Hubert Hartley, who stroked the Cambridge University boat to victory in the Varsity Race three times in a row and went on to be a master at Eton. 'Oh, he was a marvellous chap. I suppose I have always looked up to admirable people. Ranjitsinhji, the cricketer, with his marvellous leg glide, he was another of my heroes. Churchill, of course, he's my all-time hero. Also Sir William . . . now what's his name? The Home Office pathologist, a long time ago, before Spilsbury. I thought he was a marvellous man. Sir William Willcox – that's the name!'

During his time at Cambridge the medical lecturers included Sir Clifford Allbutt. Of course, they were all admirable men. 'Allbutt invented the clinical thermometer. Strange to think that, until then, everyone used a bath thermometer. He was still lecturing well into his eighties. There was no retirement age in those days. He used to ride to Addenbrooke's hospital on a tricycle, with his little goatee beard and his morning coat. All physicians wore morning coats. Usually with a top hat.'

After Cambridge Daly went on to St Thomas's Hospital in London in 1922. 'We spent the first three months in casualty, seeing everything coming in, doing a lot of minor stitching. Then you did six months on a medical ward. After that six months dressing on a surgical ward. My surgeon was Mr Nitch. I helped him in the operating theatre, dressing wounds. Then you had several months in various specialities, eyes, ears, nose and throat, mental diseases. Dr Stoddart was the physician for mental diseases. He looked like Edward VII with his summer beard and grey morning suit and topper and we students jokingly said he had an Edward VII complex. For our mental work, we visited Bedlam in Lambeth – the Bethlehem Royal Hospital, to give its correct name. But known as Bedlam. Hence the phrase. You had to ring outside on a bell on a long pole, then a porter with enormous keys would unlock the gate and let you in, then lock it all up again. The security was intense.'

When he first arrived in London, he lived in Cambridge House, a university settlement in Camberwell, with fifteen or so other students, each in a bedsitter. One day, out of the blue, he got an invitation from a family he'd never heard of called Nicholson who lived in Brockley, near Lewisham.

'What had happened was that my father had been visited in the brewery in Hereford by a Mr Nicholson who sold him malt. My father had mentioned he had a son who'd gone to London as a medical student so Mr Nicholson had immediately said, "We must have him out." So this invitation to supper on Saturday arrived, along with instructions on how to get there, which bus to catch, how I would be met at a certain bus stop. I got off at the correct bus stop and walked right past a young woman who was waiting, though I vaguely glanced at her, thinking she was nice-looking. She then came after me and said, "Mr Briscoe." I'd never thought they might send their elder daughter to meet me. But that was it . . .'

You mean love at first sight? 'Oh, absolutely!'

Doris Winifred Nicholson worked in a bank, one of the earliest female bank workers, thanks to the male shortage during the war. She was also two years older than Daly, but that never worried him.

'Shall I tell you something interesting? My mother was two years older than my father. My son has married a woman two years older. So that's three times in a row we've gone for older women. Extraordinary.'

They married on 15 September 1925 at St Cyprian's, Brockley, a small but white wedding, and they had their honeymoon at Hereford. 'My parents kindly went off on holiday so we could enjoy the family home and also have the maidservant to look after us.'

Later that year they moved to Cornwall where he acquired his first post as a GP, working with a Dr Harman. Their first two children were born there, Dorothy-Anne in 1928 and Susan in 1930. Then Daly decided that the Cornish practice was too remote, too rural, and that he wanted to be nearer London. In 1932 they moved to Woodbridge, where he has remained ever since. Their son John was born there in 1933 and another daughter, Jane, in 1936.

Marriage to Doris, 1925

In 1928, Daly had joined the Territorial Army as a lieutenant in the Royal Army Medical Corps and had been very active from then on. 'I actually joined up on 2 September 1939, the day before war broke out. I was in khaki till 3 September 1945, soon after VJ Day.'

Another example of a professional gentleman of thirty-nine, getting on a bit, yet determined to join the army. I could understand the disappointment of a very young man at missing the supposed fun and adventure of the First World War, but all these years later, by which time they all knew what war was really like, it seems a bit hard to have gone off and left a wife and four young children. Did he have to go?

He stared at me for a while, as if not comprehending my question. 'Of course I had to go. I was a soldier. My wife always accepted that. I remember having a discussion with a major, a friend of mine. He said that the most important thing in life was King and country. That's the number-one priority. After that, in second place, comes business. Third is family. And that's still what I believe. If you think about it, if your country is in danger then that will affect your family. And if your business, whatever it is, goes to pot, your family will suffer. So that's it – King and country first, business next, and then family.'

Most people today, I suggested, would put the order the other way round. He nodded in agreement. 'You're probably right. Shocking, isn't it?'

His wife, he says, was always a wonderful support in everything he did. 'On the big issues we always clicked. We only ever disagreed on minor things.' Such as? 'Oh, too trivial to even think of. Food, perhaps. I've never had much interest in food, which she did.'

Dr Briscoe had a distinguished war, serving as an army doctor, ending as a lieutenant-colonel. Almost straight away he was sent to France and was there during the evacuation of Dunkirk, escaping on HMS *Whitehall*, and was mentioned in dispatches. He kept his own Dunkirk diary, which one day he might publish. In October 1940 he was sent to Iceland and was the medical officer on duty treating survivors from HMS *Hood*, of which there were only three. When the war ended, he was serving in Bangalore.

Afterwards, he returned to the relative peace and quiet of his general practice in Woodbridge. He sent all three of his daughters to Cheltenham Ladies' College while his son John won a scholarship to Winchester. From there he went to his father's old college in Cambridge, then his father's old hospital, St Thomas's. Today, Dr Briscoe junior is an Apothecary to the Queen and the Queen Mother at Windsor Castle, and also medical officer to Eton College. He lives in Eton, where he has his own general practice. So he's done frightfully well. 'Oh, yes, he has, we're very proud of him. When the Royal Family are coming to Windsor for the weekend or whatever, he is always notified in advance so he will be available if needed.' Bit of a bind, though, having to be on hand, mucking up your own social life. 'Not really. He always knows he'll have the long summer free. In the summer they're always at Balmoral.'

None of his daughters went to university: one went to art college, another became a nurse and the third an occupational therapist. They are now all married with children and Daly has thirteen grandchildren, plus sixteen great-grandchildren.

'Susan, the one who went to art college, emigrated to Canada, with a girlfriend. She'd tried to be a dress designer here, but didn't manage it. In Canada, she worked at first as a pastry-cook then finally got into fashion design, doing women's underwear. She designed for Linda's Under Lovelies. That was the firm's name. Can you beat it? Ha ha ha. She's now given up work and is married to a farmer, but they still live in Quebec. I've been to Canada to see her several times. I went this year, in fact. In January I've been invited to join them for a two-month holiday in Mexico. They'll probably go overland by car, through the USA, to Mexico. I'm planning to drive with them, all the way. Certainly. Why not? I enjoy driving.'

His wife Doris died in 1985 after a stroke. She never liked her Christian name and was always known as Doosra, the name by which she is commemorated on a seat on Woodbridge railway station. I said I would look out for it on the way back to town.

'As a girl, she had a friend also called Doris – and they both hated their name, so the other Doris's husband rechristened them. He'd been a tea-planter in India so he called his Doris Didi, which is Urdu for "this one". My Doris got Doosra, meaning "the other one". And that's what she was always called.'

Dr Briscoe has long given up his work as a Tory councillor, which he did for many years, becoming chairman of the local district council. 'It all began after I retired in 1966. I was approached one day by someone who said that as I was very interested in the local community, why not stand as a councillor? I really hadn't thought about it. So I said I'd sleep on it. Next day I said, "Yes, I'll throw my hat in the ring." I was fearfully lucky, and got in straight away. I'd always voted Tory, of course, but never thought of being a councillor.

'I had the great pleasure, as chairman of the Council in 1977, Jubilee year, of meeting Prince Charles who came on a visit. I also met Sir Alec Douglas-Home. No, not here. That happened at Hawarden, Gladstone's old home, where I had gone to use the library. You know Gladstone married an heiress? That's where he got his money from. At the library I was fortunate to meet Sir Alec Douglas-Home. He shook me by the hand and I said, "Sir, I must tell you we share the same birthday." And he said to me, "Ah, but do you know who the third is? King Olaf of Norway." Now, wasn't that interesting?'

I asked what he thought of Tony Blair and New Labour. He thought for a while and said, 'Plausible.' Did he consider voting for him? 'Ah, that would be giving away a secret. You shouldn't ask that. It's a secret ballot, isn't it? I did admire Mrs Thatcher. I thought she did a lot for the country, knocking the unions into shape.'

Since his retirement as a GP, he has also emerged as an author. He has written three books, which have been published locally: one on Sarah,

Duchess of Somerset, his benefactress; one on Thomas Seckford of Woodbridge; and the other on Sir Thomas White, who became Lord Mayor of London in 1553. 'Alas, they didn't do very well. I thought the Duchess might sell well in Cambridge, but St John's only bought one copy for their library! Ha ha ha.'

He has also been, and still is, a noted public lecturer around Suffolk, addressing literary groups, churches, women's institutes and other bodies, raising money for good causes as he always lectures for free. At present he has three set lectures. One is on Edward Fitzgerald, who translated *The Rubáiyát* by Omar Khayyám. Dr Briscoe used to live in the house in Woodbridge where Fitzgerald himself lived, and thus became interested in his life. He also lectures on the Seckford family of Woodbridge, and on medical practice before the National Health Service. Book him now, if you'd like to hear him. He doesn't mind travelling. He laughed and laughed, but agreed that, yes, he was still accepting engagements.

Over lunch, it emerged that he was working on a fourth lecture. Well, he has given his staple three lectures quite often, and most locals have now heard them. The following week he was going to give his new lecture on a totally new topic – Quebec. He has, of course, been there on several occasions to see his daughter, so he has first-hand experience but he had to research its history.

Over lunch, his dear friend and neighbour Margaret, one of those who reads to him, confessed she rather wished he'd stuck to his tried and tested three lectures. As his eyes are not up to any books these days, she has had to read aloud to him all the books about Quebec, make notes for him, then write out his lecture. It has proved a trifle . . . well, exhausting. But she clearly loves her labours. Especially reading to him.

'He's only fallen asleep once since I've been reading to him. It was a biography of Bismarck. Yes, it was pretty heavy. I was quite pleased when he grew tired of it. Oh, we only ever read biographies and history, never fiction.'

'I also have talking books,' said Daly, 'which I can play to myself, but I do so like being read to. It means we can discuss as we go along. I also hear the local gossip from all my readers. But, best of all, I like their company.'

He has a talking watch on his wrist for telling the time and he goes out to do all his own shopping, in the local shops, walking with the aid of a white stick. 'I can see about fifteen yards, but it's all blurry. I find it impossible to read or watch television, but I don't actually walk into bollards. Avoiding cars is quite easy. I can hear them. I'm most in danger with bicycles as I can't see or hear them coming and have jolly nearly been knocked down by one or two.'

He doesn't do much real cooking, sticking to cereal for breakfast and convenience food for his other meals. 'I buy buffet pork pies, iceberg lettuce, Bakewell tart and cup-of-soup powders – the sort of fast food I don't need to prepare or cook. As you get older, you should eat less. The vital thing is exercise. It's totally wrong for the elderly to live in bungalows. That's the wrong advice. You need all the exercise you can get.'

To get up and down to his own apartment above his garage he has to climb fourteen bare wooden steps, all at a very steep angle, almost like getting up into a loft. He says he finds them no problem. He doesn't have to see the steps, he knows them so well.

His eyes started to go when he was eighty, which was when he gave up driving. 'Macular degeneration of the retina, that's all it is. Nothing too serious.' That was the no-nonsense GP speaking. Margaret said his walking was excellent: he was able to go most places locally, up to a three-mile walk.

He still travels alone to London to visit his club, the Army and Navy, and for meetings of a dining club called the Omar Khayyám Club. 'It's limited to fifty-nine members because Fitzgerald published *The Rubáiyát* in 1859.' Locally he is a member of the Woodbridge Probus Club, which he helped to found. 'That's for retired professional and business men. For men of probity, from the Latin word *probus.*'

So how has he managed still to be living a rich and active life at ninety-seven? He put it down firstly to genes. 'My father lived till ninety-nine – in fact he got within three months of a hundred. My elder sister reached ninety-eight. So I'm lucky in that respect. Medicine has also helped me. In 1960 I had a bronchial pneumonia, but M & B tablets cured it. I've been an abstemious eater, and that's also helped. I have always said that if people ate half as much our hospitals would be half as full. There are too many fat people around. Moderation is vital in all things.'

At that moment we were both drinking rather heartily at the village inn, having had a couple of sherries earlier.

'Ha, ha! Er, well, yes, I don't actually stick to that rule with alcohol. I think alcohol is good in old age. I always have a glass of sherry before lunch, pour myself a glass of ale with lunch, then some wine with my evening meal.'

Over lunch that day, he ate scampi and chips – but was a bit upset when his children's size portion, as ordered, proved to be a large one. He managed most of it, and two large glasses of white wine. As he was lunching out.

He smoked as a young man, but not more than ten a day. 'Gave it up in 1940 after I'd joined the army. It was everyone coughing in the morning, that's what put me off. I realised then how bad smoking must be, yet the army at the time was giving out twenty cigarettes a day to every soldier serving overseas. For free. Can you believe it? If you didn't smoke you were allowed a bar of chocolate instead, so I switched to chocolate. No, I didn't eat them. I saved them up. So when I came home on leave I had all these bars of chocolate for my children. They were absolutely delighted. Ha ha ha . . .

'Yes, I'd say I have had a very lucky life. Very fortunate. Very fulfilled. People say you shouldn't boast about your luck, so I suppose I shouldn't do so – but I have been lucky!'

Daly today

Any regrets, things not done, places not visited? 'I've been to most countries I wanted to see – Australia, New Zealand, America. Mexico will be a first.'

There are some things he regrets about the modern world, such as the lack of courtesy in public places, but mostly he sees huge improvements. 'In medicine the changes have been phenomenal. I wonder all the time at the marvellous health of today's children. When I started as a doctor, children were always taking ill and dying – of diphtheria, scarlet fever, measles, polio, TB. They've all gone, or can be controlled.

'I spent so much of my early working days feeling swollen glands in necks because people had drunk infected milk. That doesn't happen any more. Running ears, that happened all the time, but the sulphonamides have eliminated them. Pneumonia – that used to take away the strongest and the fittest. There was nothing you could do for them, except a poultice on the chest and good nursing. It was marvellous when M & B 693 came in. This was in 1936. I remember I was treating a very strong, very well-built farm labourer who didn't appear to have any chance of survival – but I gave him the new M & B tablets, and in forty-eight hours he was on the mend. It was astonishing.

'The National Health Service has been a wonderful thing. The first few years there were teething troubles. They took over every doctor at once, you see, every man jack, and also every hospital, even the little old-fashioned voluntary ones, so the quality was uneven. It was a large amount to digest and the administrative side had to grow and grow. We waited a long time to renew hospitals. There was no money because of the war. I remember first visiting Canada after the war and seeing all their wonderful new hospitals. We had none.

'The first ten years after the war, those were my hardest years. I was in my surgery at eight-thirty each morning and did a fourteen-hour day. People knew they could call you in the night, all for free, if they were at all worried about little Jimmy. My patients on the whole tried to do it in the evening, not the middle of the night, which was thoughtful, but it meant I was called out almost every evening. I was never home till ten.

'But I would do it all again. I'd live the same life. Why not? Good gracious me, I've enjoyed it all. And I still do. I don't think about being ninety-seven. With my eyes, I can't look in the mirror any more and see the lines. I do often wonder how old I look.

'Yes, of course I hope to make a hundred, but I honestly don't think about it. You may never see tomorrow. Come on, another glass of wine. Why not, what? Ha ha ha . . .'

26

AMY WILKINSON

Spinster and heavy-duty worker

Amy Wilkinson, c. 1903

Miss Amy Wilkinson is a single woman, one of millions in the twentieth century who never married, never had children. Today, many women have deliberately chosen to remain single, though that doesn't necessarily mean that they don't or won't have children. For someone born in 1900, though, society made marriage the norm, then played a rather nasty trick in taking away several million men in two world wars. Did it matter? Does it matter? And do you miss what you have never known?

Amy lives alone on the sixth floor of a large and rather brutal twenty-three-storey council block in Stretford, Manchester, one of those concrete and glass towers put up with almost religious fervour in the 1960s, many of which then came down again in the 1990s as architects and town planners confessed that they had sinned and now regretted their wicked ways.

Amy's building, though, is not noticeably vandalised, so that was something. And there was a modern intercom at the front entrance that stopped intruders from walking straight in. I pressed the button for her flat number, could hear it working, but there was no response. I tried again. Nothing. Was it not working? Was it me? Or was it Amy's hearing? A middle-aged couple arrived and opened the door with a key so I followed them in and stood beside them in front of a lift. I told them I was going to visit Miss Wilkinson. Wrong lift, they said. This lift only goes to odd numbers. You want the even-numbers' lift over there. Shows how much I know about high-rise blocks.

Amy came to the door of her flat pushing a lightweight, collapsible three-wheel trolley, a nippy version of a zimmer frame. She bought it herself, she said. She also has a lightweight wheelchair, which she takes down in the lift and uses when she goes out. She is a big, strong-looking woman for her age. Most people lose weight and height as they get older until they almost disappear, but Amy still looked large and fit enough to cope with the modern world, apart from a nasty touch of arthritis in her knees. She was wearing a cardigan over a floral flock. There was a no-nonsense, take-me-as-I-am air about her as she beckoned me to a chair.

She was born on 29 November 1900 in Pendleton, Manchester. Her father had been a miner originally, but her mother wouldn't marry him, said Amy, until he gave it up so he went into a dyeworks and rose to become foreman. She had a sister, four years older, and a brother, two years older. Both died many years ago. Her mother died aged forty-five and her father at sixty-seven.

Her first home, where she was born, was in Sedan Street, two up and two down, but it had a flush toilet. Then they moved to a house in Strawberry Hill, which had been converted from a house once lived in by Lord Lissadel. She thinks that was his name. Some lord anyway.

'I went to London Street School and, oh, yes, I enjoyed it. We all wore clogs, knitted black stockings and a saddle pinny. This was a pinny which flowed free at the sides. Under it we'd wear a jersey with long sleeves. If you passed an exam at thirteen, you could leave school right away, which my sister had done. I passed, but for some reason, they added some months on for me and I didn't leave till I was fourteen. So I was still at school when the war broke out. We thought it would be all over in a month.

'My first job, when I left school, was at the old *Evening Chronicle* offices in Withy Grove. I had to put a picture of Kitchener into every paper. It was some sort of special offer. There were me and lots of other girls in this little room and we were given a packet of a thousand Kitchener pictures and told to place one carefully in every paper. Well, me and some of the girls used to put two or three in the one paper . . .' She lowered her voice with this guilty secret, as if eighty-three years later someone might burst into her flat and shop her.

Then she was put on to football forecasts, opening envelopes that had been sent in to the paper. Her particular job was to check that all the envelopes were empty. Not a physically hard job, but deadly boring, though she had a good laugh with the other girls. Her wage was fourteen shillings a week, but she left after six months. 'I couldn't stand the smell of glue.' From the newspaper? 'No, I don't know what it was from. They just put us into this little room which was next to a place where they were gluing. Never discovered what they were gluing.'

Then she went into a cotton mill, working on a loom. 'We had to knit this thing like a long stocking, made out of a sort of thick string. Do you know what it was? The lining for hosepipes. They needed them for the war.'

She stayed there for four years, then moved to a wire factory, working on a machine, and then in 1923 she joined Glover's, cable makers in Trafford Park, where she worked for the next thirty-eight years.

'You haven't heard of it? Oh, it was a very famous firm. We made the world's biggest cable, seventy-two miles long, which was laid from Vancouver Island across the sea to the mainland. When we were making these big cables in the factory, they went for miles and miles round the inside of the works, in huge coils, then as they got bigger, they went outside, round the buildings, across the ship canal, oh, everywhere.'

Were they for telegraphic purposes or electricity or what?

'Oh, all of that. They didn't tell us the details, of course, or take us to see them, but by chance I did see once one being laid in the sea. I happened to be visiting my sister in Hastings and they were doing it, just off-shore. Yes, that was interesting.

'My job was what they called tinning. I had to put a copper wire through acid and water to make it look silver.'

Sounds a tough job for a woman. 'Oh, it was hot, like, but we wore clogs and overalls and a cap. Once I didn't have my cap on properly and the whole of my hair, on this side, turned green. It must have been the fumes, you see.

'The machine I was working on cost two and a quarter million pounds. Can you believe that? They made a little film once, of the cables being made, and I was in the film. No, I've never seen it. I've nothing at all. No photographs of my working years, nothing, really, nothing at all . . .'

Most people I had been to see had dug out for me various albums, boxes, files, or folders, assorted memorabilia of their lives, at school, on holiday, the army, their courting days or wedding day. Amy has none of these. She has never had a camera, and the few family snaps she had she left behind in her last house.

'All I've got is this,' she said, getting up and going to a little table. I hadn't noticed that she'd laid out a stiff white-backed booklet, which had been published to commemorate the centenary of Glover's, 1868–1968, the firm to which she had devoted her working life. Her whole life, really.

I admired the silver lettering on the front and let her open it to take me through the pages. It seemed to be full of small print and large photographs of, well, cables. No sign of any workers, though there was a photo of about twenty serious men in suits and moustaches, arms folded. 'Them's the bosses. Hold on, I'll show you my name in a minute.'

Inside the booklet she had folded a printed list of names. She went down them carefully, bending over, peering closely. I said, 'There's a Wilkinson,' being helpful. 'No, no, that's not me. That's another Wilkinson.' At last she found the right one – A. Wilkinson. Not even her full Christian name, just the initial. It was a list of the company's pensioners, printed later, which she had kept with the centenary book, but it was proof of her existence, that she had been and worked there, given them thirty-eight years of hard labour.

'Yes, it was hard, but I enjoyed it. Oh, I really did. After I'd been there twenty-five years, we got amalgamated with another firm. The new bosses came to me one day and said I'd been doing a man's job, I couldn't do it any more. I wasn't very pleased, I can tell you.

'I was then taken off the tinning, away from the acid baths and the copper, and put on to plastic. This was working on machines where you had to cover wires with plastic. It was just coming in and they couldn't get the colours right at first. We had a good laugh at that. The colours would come out like mottled soap. You know mottled soap? No colour at all.

'But I didn't like it. In fact, I couldn't do it very well. I preferred tinning. You had to get the plastic the exact thickness and I never seemed to get it right. So I went to Mr Westwood and I said, "I don't like this job, Mr Westwood." He said, "Stick it for another month, and then you can take your pick."

'So I stuck it for a month and they moved me to cutting cloth. We worked on this machine, a man and myself, which cut the cloth, really thick stuff. They used it for wrapping up the wire and cable.'

For a while, during her early Glover years, she was on a machine where she needed to use pliers to bend wires. 'I was strong enough to do it, but they didn't like the way I was doing it. They said I had to use them this way, not that way. In the end, I threw the pliers down on the factory floor and said, "Sod you and the bloody job an' all." That's the only time, honestly, I ever swore. Anyway, I came back and they had to let me do it my way.'

Most of the time she was on piecework, her wages linked to productivity, so much money for a certain number.

'Over that number, you got a bonus. Usually the targets were so high few people ever got any bonus. Anyway, one week, towards the end of my time there, I worked out my bonus was nine and three, but when the wage packet came, I hadn't got anything. They said I'd worked it out wrong. They told me I was illiterate. Well, I wasn't taking that. I went up to the offices and made them do it all again – and I was right. The boss made this woman, who'd said I was illiterate, come down to the factory floor and apologise to me, on my bench, to my face.

'I then got a smashing job for the last four months I was there. When they realised I could do figures, they gave me some book work to do. Then I retired, aged sixty-two.

'The best week's wages, with bonus, I ever had was near the end. I got seven pounds and tuppence. I didn't spend the tuppence. I kept it. As a – well, as a sign, I s'pose, I dunno. Well, I just kept it, just for luck.'

She stopped, as if wondering about the symbolism that had made her keep the tuppence.

Don't you regret, or even feel resentful, that you hadn't an easier, better job all those years earlier, when you were clearly capable of it?

'I didn't have the education, so how could I have had a better job?' She said this flatly, without anger, stating a truth I should have understood. 'Anyway, I was very strong . . . The week I left, there was some sort of mix-up. I was just finishing work and someone in the office said I was being made redundant. I knew it wasn't true, but I was hurrying home to go to a funeral, so I hadn't time to argue. But next day I went in and sorted it all out. I was retiring, not being chucked out. I wanted that made clear.

'For my leaving present, I got a leather wallet with a pound for each year I'd worked, so that was thirty-eight pounds. I got a pension of four pounds, four and sevenpence a month. It's now sixty pounds a month. So I didn't do so badly, did I?'

Meanwhile, during all those decades of hard work, her private and domestic life went on, such as it was, because she was still living at home with her parents. After her mother died her father remarried, and when he died Amy was left to care for her stepmother. She was also looking after her sister, who had cancer.

'I nursed my stepmother for her last six years when she was bedridden. We only had one tap, in our old rented house, so I used to do everything for her, wash her hair, everything. Sometimes, when I'm sitting here thinking, I think how did I do it? Up early every morning for work, wash myself, wash my stepmother and get her dressed, make her bed, come home at lunch-time and give her a meal, then come home at eight in the evening and do the housework. How did I manage all that? Eee . . .'

Her stepmother died in 1967. 'I'd washed her hair in front of the fire, and got her up the stairs, pushing from behind to make sure she didn't fall down. I can see her now, stopping at the top of the stairs and saying to me, "You've been good to me, Amy. Better than any daughter would have been." That was on the Thursday night. By the next Thursday morning, she was dead.'

In 1968 Amy moved to her present flat, one of the first tenants when the block opened. Despite her arthritis, she still leads an active life, going out three times a week, to St Matthew's Church, to a day centre and to a handicapped club. 'I can get myself downstairs OK, then someone comes to pick me up and drives me to the club.'

She has one relation left, her sister's son Harold, who lives not far away in Davyhulme, and there is also a neighbour who helps. They get her shopping for her, but she does her own cooking. 'They usually get stuff from Marks, ready prepared, which I just have to heat.' She also has a home help for two hours a week.

That day she was feeling a bit weak, and hoped it wasn't the return of a mystery illness that had hit her in 1993. 'I suddenly got these terrible pains in my chest. I was taken into the Withington but they said I was too old at ninety-three to be operated on, the operation was too serious for my age. They didn't expect me to live. I just lay there for three weeks and I lost three stone. But then I recovered. I don't know what it was. They said it was a bubble in my bowel, whatever that means.

'I can't explain why I've got to this age. I don't know if there is a secret. Plain living, I suppose. I never smoked – well, when I was young, I might have a cigarette in the pictures, but if I got through one packet of ten in a twelve-month, that was a lot for me. I used to like whisky and dry ginger, and a sherry with my Sunday dinner, but do you know, I've lost the taste for either of them. It's just gone.

'I've always tried to eat well. In the first war there was no rationing, so you just had to peg out what you could get. I used to queue up for hours on Saturdays at the Maypole. In the Second World War, we had rationing, of course. You got one egg to last you two weeks. When the war ended, they were shoving eggs at you. What I want to know is, where did all the eggs go during the war, then?'

She has always voted Tory, as her father did, though she never discussed politics with him. 'In the General Election of 1922, I went around in an open carriage, standing at the back in a Tory blue dress. I also put some blue ribbon in my hair. Oh, we went all round the place. I said to my dad afterwards, "But you still don't know how I voted." He said to me, "If you've voted Labour, I'll break your neck."

'I did once, just once, vote Labour. That was for Mr Kinnock. I was disgusted with the Tories at the time. Can't remember why. But I liked Mrs Thatcher. Still do. She had brains. Still has.

'I've never been abroad. We looked upon the Isle of Man as being

Amy today

abroad. That was an adventure. But I have been in aeroplane. When I was eighty-three, in 1983, my nephew Harold said was I doing anything on a certain day because he and his wife, Rene, wanted to give me a treat. I said no, I was doing nothing that day, so they said they'd come and pick me up. I put on my best frock because I thought we were going to have a drink at the Last Drop. That's a pub. But then I see we're driving along the motorway, heading for the airport, and I thought, Oh, my God.

'Seemingly, Harold had seen in the *Evening News* that you could have a short flight for fifteen pounds. So this was my treat. What he hadn't realised was it was part of an air show. So we get in this little plane, and I'm looking round for here, you know, this block, Stretford House, to see if I can see it from the air but, blow me, in two minutes we're over Blackpool Tower! I can look down and see it. We went right out to sea and back again.

'Then the pilot starts flapping his wings and doing tricks. He came down twice really low and was only four feet off the ground. Honestly. Only four feet. He was in this air show, you see, doing his tricks. Well, afterwards I staggered out thinking, If I can stand this, I can stand anything in life. The pilot came round and shook my hand. It was in the paper. "Woman of 83 Has Her First Flight at an Air Show." Oh, that was a day.'

Looking back, she could think of nothing she'd missed, no places she'd like to have seen. 'Apart from the Niagara Falls. I always had a fancy to see that. Dunno why.'

Did she think it had been a happy life?

'Oh, I'd say a hard life. I can remember walking home crying, I was that tired. This was when I was looking after my sister, who was dying. There's been a lot of tragedy. Losing my mother, my brother, my sister. Then two world wars. Before the first war you could leave your door unlocked all the time. My father never locked up his racing pigeons, you know . . .'

What about never marrying? Was that a regret?

'That's the way it was. With two wars there were few men around. But I did have one good offer. It was when I was nineteen and he was thirty-three. I was frightened to death of my father, that he'd find out I was going out with someone aged thirty-three. My father got very fierce after my mother died.

'He was a tester at work. I liked him fine enough. He used to wait for me at the end of the street with a taxi and take me to the Princess Theatre, to see musicals. Oh, I loved them. On my birthday, he sent me flowers and a blue blouse. I don't know how he found out my birthday, but I asked him where he'd got the blouse. He said his sister had bought it for him.

'Anyway, he got offered a job in India, to work in a factory there. He wanted me to come with him. I wasn't against India and that, but I said, no, I couldn't. It was fear of my father, that was the problem, really. And the fact that he was thirty-three.

'I must have told him this, about his age, and he said to me one day, "You know, when you get to thirty-three, you won't think thirty-three is old at all." Girls at work used to say to me, "He's a real decent man, you're a fool to say no." I was just nineteen, you see. You were very young in those days at nineteen.

'Well, in the end he went off to India to his new job. Many, many years later, I was walking down Market Street and I saw him coming towards me. Well, my knees went like water. I didn't say anything. And he didn't see me. Sam, that was his name. Sam . . .

'Well, that's the way life worked out. You just have to accept it, don't you? No use regretting things . . .'

27

NANCY LAMBERT

Leather-cutter and sender of royal verses

Nancy Lambert

Nancy Lambert lives alone in a very smart, very expensive block of luxury apartments in Gosforth, one of Newcastle's most desirable suburbs. There's a gatehouse for security, sculpted gardens and a sauna for residents. She has two rooms, kitchen and bathroom complete with gold-plated taps, gold-plated shower and deep pile carpets throughout. Her apartment is on the first floor, but she manages the lift and the corridor quite easily, being very spry, very independent. What could be nicer, smarter, more convenient?

Well, she does wish there were more people nearer her age in the block. No, not folks of ninety-six, just some younger persons, around sixty, say. She happens to be surrounded by young, affluent, upwardly mobile couples who are out all day. Above her, for example, Les Ferdinand, the England and then Newcastle United striker, was living. 'Oh, he's very nice,' said Nancy. 'He's got a very cultured voice.'

The presence of Mr Ferdinand indicates the affluence of her fellow residents. Not many people these days earn footballers' salaries. As an indication of her mental agility, the moment I sat down she produced a poem she had written especially for me, in excellent handwriting.

> A gentleman is coming to see me today
> I really don't know what he'll have to say
> I think it's because of my age, don't you see
> I wonder if he'd like a cup of tea . . .

It went on for another thirteen lines. Then she produced her own thirty-page life story, which she has been writing in a notebook, off and on, since she was eighty-seven. So far, she's only got herself up to the age of sixteen. She's been too busy to finish it.

Nancy was born in Newcastle on 1 August 1900, the sixth child of a family of eight, six girls and two boys. 'We were called Ethel, David, Isabelle, Jane Elizabeth, Elizabeth, me, Mitchel and Jessie. I was christened Annie, but always called Nancy. I was supposed to be christened Ann Elizabeth, which is what my mother told my father, but I think he'd had a few drinks on the way to register my birth. All he put down was "Annie". My mother was also called Annie. They realised I would be called Little Annie and she would be Big Annie, so I became Nancy.'

Her surname was Sced. Most unusual, I said. Yes, they traced it back to a grandfather from Edinburgh who walked down to Newcastle, looking for work. Before that, it was probably Danish.

Nancy's first memory is of soldiers coming home from the Boer War. A good memory, considering the Boer War finished in 1902, but she was positive it was that war. They lived in Stanhope Street, beside Leazes Park, not far from Fenham barracks, and there were always lots of soldiers around.

'On Sunday mornings the military band used to pass the bottom of Stanhope Street on their way to St Andrew's Church and we'd all rush to see them. I loved the music. The drummer wore a leopardskin and we thought he looked really grand. All the soldiers were smart in their bearskin hats.'

Another early memory is of sitting beside the fire while her mother was bathing her baby brother Mitchel in a tin bath. 'I can see his blanket warming in readiness, his wooden cradle waiting to receive him. But then suddenly, he started having a fit, a spasm. My mother was so worried she rushed out with him to get a neighbour to help.'

Her father James was a sign-writer and decorator, supposedly from a better class of family than her mother, said Nancy. 'His father, when we were little children, used to travel on a tram car down Stanhope Street. When he got near our house, he'd ask the driver to stop and he'd throw out a penny for us children, waiting for the tram to appear.'

So your mother did well? 'Ee, I don't think so. His family thought my mother was too good for their son.'

James, apparently, liked a drink and having a good time. He did monologues, played the piano, the concertina and a tin whistle shaped like a boat, and went around the local pubs and clubs on Saturday nights being plied with free drinks by customers. This did not go down too well with his long-suffering wife, who had to look after eight children with not much money.

'I remember one Saturday night when my father came home a bit tipsy and my mother was very annoyed. "Right, I'll pack me bags and go off to London," he replied. "Go on, then," she said, taking him at his word and packing his bags for him. He must have asked me and my sister Lizzie to come with him to the boat, because we both put on our best dresses and walked with him to the quayside. He gave me and Lizzie a penny, then he got on the boat.

'I think this happened a few times, him going off to London. He was always a very smart man, well dressed. His friends used to call him the "London Masher" when he came back from London. Oh, that was the word at the time. It means a smasher, a sort of toff, a dandy, I suppose. On that occasion he brought my sister Jessie a lovely doll. We were very jealous. He also brought a rubber baby doll, which was called the Lloyd George Thirty Bob Baby. I'm not sure why it was called that. Something to do with Lloyd George giving thirty bob to mothers?'

Nancy went to Snow Street School, as did all her sisters and brothers. 'All us six sisters had our photographs taken once, in steps-and-stairs style, in ascending order. When I took it to school to show the teacher, he and another teacher liked it so much they wanted one, so my mother got one made for them.'

At home they played games in the street, skipping, spinning tops, marbles, chucks. Inside, on wet days, they played with something they called a prick book. This consisted of cutting out pretty pictures from newspapers and putting them between the pages of a hardback book. Then you'd "sell" them to your friends for one pin each. The collected pins were given to their mother. In Nancy's memory, she was permanently sewing, making dresses for all six girls.

'Another thing we did was fix a line of string on a wall and hang it with dolls' clothes. Then we'd sing to all the people going past. "Bring your rags and bones here, next door is very dear, bring your rags and bones here." When we'd collected any rags we took them to the rag store and got a copper or two.

'At Easter, we were dressed in white dresses and coloured sashes and we all went with our parents to the Town Moor. In June we were taken to the Hoppings.

'All us sisters had curly hair, except for one, and my mother really slaved over it, washing it and twisting it into ringlets. We had to sit on the steel fender in front of the fire till it dried. We all had good complexions. One day a neighbour asked my mother what make of soap she used and she said carbolic, white Windsor or blue mottled. The first of us to get our hair washed got the cleanest water. We had no bathroom or scullery. All water had to be carried up- and downstairs. We had a wash basin in a bedroom for face washings.

Reference from Nancy's school, 1914

'Every spring, Mother would make up a tonic of scalded lemons, sugar, cream of tartar and Epsom salts, which we each had to take. It wasn't too bad, unless there was too much Epsom salts in it. Other times, we younger ones had to take spoonfuls of gregory or liquorice mixed with milk. We hated that. To make us swallow it, Mother nipped our noses and we were usually in tears. She also gave us a mixture of sulphur and treacle. I suppose the main object was to clean our systems. Anyway, I don't remember the doctor being called out for any of us.'

While she was still at school, she and her sister Betty, being monitors and thought responsible, were chosen to sell programmes at concerts in Newcastle. 'This was for Harrison's concerts, in the old Town Hall in the Bigg Market. It was a great privilege to be chosen because they had the very best artists. I heard Caruso, Madame Melba, Rachmaninov, Madam Clara Butt, oh, many others. Paderewsky as well. We were in white dresses and the ushers were in evening suits with red satin cummerbunds. Oh, it was a wonderful sight. We got a few pennies commission on how many programmes we sold. Next day at school we had to relate to the masters and the class what we'd seen and heard.'

While she was still at school, in 1910, all the children went to St James's Park football ground to celebrate the coronation of King George V and Queen Mary. 'Every school had a team who did marches, drills, swinging clubs, that sort of thing. The boys wore a coloured cap, to tell you which school they came from. It looked really wonderful. My sister was in the club-swinging team for our school. We had a sergeant from the military barracks who had taught us club swinging, so we were very good. The ground, and all the stands, were packed. Each child was given either a mug, a plate or a tin box of chocolates with pictures of the King and Queen on them. They're collectors' items now, you know.'

Nancy left school a few weeks before her fourteenth birthday. 'On the way home I saw a notice in a fruit shop window when I was coming down Stanhope Street saying "Errand Girl Wanted". So I went in and got it. I got two shillings a week and a cabbage at the end of each day to take home. My mother didn't like me doing it. "I'm not having you humping heavy bags of potatoes," she said. So I left after three weeks.

'I then became a nursemaid to Mrs Robson, of Robson's furniture – oh, they were a very well-known family. I looked after her little girl, taking her for walks on the moor. I got three shillings a week for that. I remember exactly the day war broke out because the father, Captain Robson, was in the army. It meant he was going off to war, and I lost my job. Mrs Robson wanted me to live in, you see, while he was away, but I didn't want to leave home, so they got someone who would live in.

'Next I worked at Mr Lane's, High-class Ladies' Tailoring. That was only one shilling a week, but I was learning tailoring. After seven months, he said he was giving me a raise, but said not to open it till I got home. I always gave my wage packet to my mother. She opened it and said, "The greedy blighter, he might have made it two and six." He'd only put it up to two shillings, you see. Not that we said anything to him, of course.'

Nancy's father went into a munitions factory during the First World War and one brother, David, was called up. Some time during the war, around 1917 or 1918 she thinks, an epidemic of flu hit the whole of Newcastle. Her older sister Bella died, aged twenty-three and her mother was so upset that Nancy left work for a while to look after her.

Her next job was at the Co-op handbag factory in Thornton Street, where she stayed. 'Oh, you didn't leave the Co-op if you could help it, because people would think you must have done something wrong. Nobody left the Co-op, unless they were getting married.'

Her job was as a hand-cutter, working with best-quality leather for wallets and handbags, for which she got 8s. 6d. a week, but had to work very hard. 'Miss Cox stood over us with a stop-watch. She was a dragon, but she was quite nice, really. I remember one morning being a bit late for work, which I sometimes was, rushing to punch my card in the clock, then hurrying up five flights of steps to my workbench – only to discover we were on strike. So that was lucky.

'Every time I thought of leaving my mother said I couldn't leave the Co-op. It would be a stain on my character. My wage was needed because my father died suddenly when I was eighteen and a half. He'd been kicked by someone in a pub. He could be a bit argumentative while tipsy, but never rowdy, oh, no. I think his death had something to do with his appendix bursting. Peritonitis, I think.'

Nancy remembers the excitement at the end of the war, and still has a photo of the peace party she attended. 'It was in Diana Street and we had trestle tables filled with all sorts of food and decorations and flags.

There was a grand fancy dress parade. My sister Jessie was dressed as a Boy Scout, look, you can see her hat. I was an Irish colleen.

'And, of course, there was a lot of dancing. All the Sced girls loved dancing. It was in the blood, you see. When I talk about it now, people think it must have been the boys I was interested in, but that wasn't it. I just loved the dancing.'

Her first proper boyfriend was John William Lambert, known as Jack, who was in the same church as Nancy, Westgate Hall Methodist Church. He never cared much for dancing, which partly explains, she says, why their friendship was off and on for so many years.

So you went out with other boys? 'Oh, just as friends. We were very strictly brought up, even though we might have been flighty. No, I never remember any of my friends falling pregnant. Well, they might have done, but I never heard of it. Our mother trusted us. She never said we had to be home by a certain time, but she always stayed up for us. In fact, one night I never came home and stayed at a boy's house . . .'

Nancy laughed, looked coquettish, but didn't need much prompting to go through the whole evening, doing all the voices.

'We'd gone to the Empress ballroom, Whitley Bay. That night they had two dance bands till three a.m. and I was dancing with this boy, Hedley Fenn. He told me he'd heard some fellers saying they were going to trick me and my sister Betty out of missing the train back to Newcastle, so I'd better go and get it now with him. We went to the station with him, to see the last train leaving.

'"If you can trust me," said Hedley Fenn, "I'll take you home to my mother."

'Well, he had such a big house, much bigger than ours. When we got there, his mother and three of his brothers were still up and we all sat around drinking chocolate. Then his eldest brother Tom came home and said, "Oh, my goodness, our Hedley, with two girls."

'Next morning, we got a lovely breakfast, then Mr Fenn, the father, said he'd like a word with us. He gave us a lecture about what our poor mother must have been thinking, not knowing where we were. There were, of course, no phones in those days.'

And what did she think? 'Oh, she had been worried, but not too much. She trusted us, you see. And she presumed we'd stayed the night with friends we had at Cullercoats. I then sat down and did some pen painting for Mrs Fenn. No one understands pen painting today, but you did it on satin with a sort of oil pen. I made Mrs Fenn a table centre on black satin. Me and Betty went on the train to give it to her, as a present for having us. That was the start of a long friendship with the Fenn family.

'But I had lots of boyfriends. Several wanted to marry me, all nice enough lads. Oh, I never met a bad one. Really, I don't remember a nasty lad. Sex never seemed to come into it. Perhaps I was just lucky . . .'

She eventually married Jack Lambert in 1931, after knowing him for fifteen years, and four years of being engaged. He was an engineer at Vickers Armstrong, later becoming a draughtsman. By the time they married, they had saved a bit of money, enough to buy a house divided into two flats. They lived in one and let the other.

So you were upwardly mobile from the beginning, I said, looking round her luxury apartment. 'Oh, absolutely. We were the first in either family to own our own house. We also paid for our own wedding. My mother didn't have to pay a penny. The house was on a mortgage, of course, and it took years to pay it off.'

Their first and only child, Anne, was born in 1940, after nine years of marriage. Quite a gap. Had they been taking precautions?

'Never thought of it. We didn't try to have a baby, or take precautions either. We must have been very innocent. Sex didn't seem very important. But I was thrilled when I was pregnant.

'You are a married man, are you? Right, I'll tell you what happened. I didn't know for five months, till my periods suddenly stopped. I didn't feel so good either, so I went to see the doctor. He said I just might be pregnant. He could send a sample of my urine to Edinburgh, but that would cost money, or he could come to my house on a certain day and examine me. I said he could examine me.

'I waited at home for him with the curtains closed. When the doorbell rang, I thought it was him, Dr Mitchell, so I went down and it was one of my girlfriends. "Why aren't you inviting me in?" she said. I told her I was expecting the doctor. She could come in but she'd have to sit in the other room while he examined me.

'Anyway, I was pregnant. My husband was away at the time, working for his firm. When he came home, I told him I was pregnant. "I don't know how," he said.

'The doctor wanted me to have it in a nursing-home, because of my age, being almost forty, but I didn't want to. I had Anne at home. Natural childbirth. My friend Mrs Jennings was there, Lily Jennings. I've known her all my life, eighty years. We worked together as girls, you see. She died only last year and I do miss her. Anyway, Lily was there for the birth. The doctor said, "Here, hold this leg and pull." She saw it born. Jack stayed in the kitchen. My mother died the year before Anne was born. That's one of the regrets of my life, that she never saw her.'

Anne passed for the grammar school, Rutherford High School, and went to a teacher-training college at Hereford. She inherited her mother's musical ability and spent her working life as a music teacher in a local comprehensive, from which she has recently retired. She and her husband John – they have no children – are both keen on amateur dramatics and opera, and worked for many years to save and revive a Victorian theatre in Newcastle, now called the Tyne Theatre.

'That's how I met Sir Geraint Evans and Placido Domingo,' says Nancy. 'Sir Geraint did the reopening ceremony after the fire in 1986 while Domingo came in 1983 to sing in a special performance of *Tosca*. The connection was that back in 1897 Sarah Bernhardt had starred at the theatre in the original play, *Tosca*, before Puccini turned it into an opera.

'I was in the car with Domingo. I told him I'd heard Caruso singing when I was young. He said to me he'd come back and see me again in the year 2000. I'll be waiting for him.'

Nancy's husband Jack died in 1973, aged seventy-two. They had moved to a bungalow by then, in the West End of Newcastle. Nancy lived there alone for the next twenty years, always busy in lots of local activities.

Every lunch-time, for nearly thirty years, until Nancy was ninety-three, Anne and John came to her house for their lunch, Anne rushing from her school, John from his wholesale meat business.

'I was spoiled rotten,' says John, a large, jovial, bearded gentleman, who looks more like an opera star than a meat trader. 'Nancy made marvellous meals but ate nothing herself.'

Nancy agrees she has never had much of an appetite. 'As a child, I used to hide my food on a window-sill, then drop it in the yard so my mother wouldn't know. I confessed this to her once and she said, "You'll come to want."

'I enjoyed those years making lunches for Anne and John. That's how I was brought up,' she said demurely, 'to serve my family and my husband.'

Anne said later not to be fooled by the servile, compliant side of her mother's nature, which used to be there but has long since gone.

'She was once timid and nervous, scared in a restaurant, for example, to pour out the tea in case people were watching. Dad, in those days, ruled the roost. Now she's very confident and independent. Too much so at times, as I know to my cost.

'No, I don't think it was his death that changed her. It started earlier, when she was in her fifties and I was a teenager, having the usual sort of teenage arguments with my father. I think she picked some of that up from me and started arguing back. She's now so fiercely independent we argue all the time. People say, "Oh it must be nice for you and your mother, having such a good relationship," and I go, "Ho-hummm . . ."'

When I asked Nancy if she had been aware of her newly found independence, she agreed at once, and could even remember the first time she broke out.

'It was the Cup Final of 1953. Newcastle were going to Wembley to play Blackpool. My husband Jack was very keen to go and was trying to get a ticket. My brother knew the mayor and I wrote to him – and eventually we got one ticket. "I'm taking that," said my husband. I said, "Oh, no, you're not. I got it and I want to go. It's my ticket." It was the first time in my life I'd ever opposed my husband. I should have done it earlier. For years I was a Masonic widow. You know what that is? He'd go off to his Masonic lodges, and just leave me behind. Anyway, I stuck to my guns about Wembley. But we eventually got two tickets, so we both went.'

Two years ago she asked Anne and John to sell her house and she moved to the luxury flat, bought on a 999-year lease, to be nearer them and to be safer: there had been several robberies in her area. Ill-health, or fragility, had not come in to it.

'I've only had one operation in my life, and that was back in 1968. I was washing myself at the sink this morning, as I always do, down to my waist, and I thought, There's a bit of dirt on my left breast. I washed it, but it was still there. I thought it was a crease, a wrinkle. Next day it was still there, so I began to wonder about it. Two of my sisters had cancer of the breast – in fact, three of my family have had the same thing, all over the age of sixty. I thought I'd better do something about it.

'I'd not been to the doctor, not for ages and ages, but I didn't feel all that well anyway, so I thought I'd go. He sent me to the RVI to see Mr McEvedy. I saw him on the Monday and he said to come in on Friday, and if necessary, they'd operate. Well, they did. I had a mastectomy. When I came round, and was ready to come out, I told the sister that I'd already booked a holiday. With Lily, not Jack. He didn't like holidays. Wouldn't go anywhere. I asked if I could still go. She was very kind and thought for a bit, checked me and said, yes, count it as recuperation – as long as I come back afterwards for treatment. After the holiday, I went to see the radiology people. They checked me and thought, well, no treatment was necessary. So that was it. Life went on as normal.'

Did you feel no ill-effects? 'Well, I was a bit tired for about a month and used a stick.'

How about Jack and Anne, were they worried?

'They were more nervous than me, I think. Jack was always a bit of a hammy.' Excuse me?

'A scaredy. He'd faint at the sight of a piece of Elastoplast. I had to have check-ups, every three months at first, then six months, then every year. When I got to the tenth year I was thinking, What a waste of time – I meant their time, because they only looked at me for two minutes, so I asked the sister, "How much longer do I have to come?" She checked her notes and said, "We'll call it a day." So that was it.'

How did she explain her long and active life? 'I'm a small eater. I think that's the secret. I've never smoked, except when I was sixteen with Lily. We went into Leazes Park at seven o'clock in the morning of my sixteenth birthday and said, "Let's have a cigarette, now we're both sixteen." We thought we were really wicked. I didn't have another. One was enough.

'I don't drink, just a whisky at Christmas and a sherry if pushed. My mother always used to say, "A whisky for the heart, a brandy for the stomach", but I've never had those sort of problems. I've always been healthy. I've lived a sensible life. You'll be thinking I'm too good to live!'

As lives go, had it been particularly lucky or unlucky, hard or easy? 'Just ordinary. A normal life. We never had too much, and had to do a lot of scraping, but I had a damn good mother. That was a help. And I've been lucky having a very good daughter and a very good son-in-law. Oh, I did have a spot of bother in 1984. Something funny happened in my legs, as if I was walking on lumps of lead. I looked it up in a medical book and it could be Reynaud's disease. Have you heard of it? My legs can still feel like that, but we managed. I think I'm pretty good for my age. Let's say I'm well endowed.'

But looking back at all those years cutting up bits of leather, then being a good obedient little wife, wouldn't she have liked a proper career like her daughter, to have been able to express herself? Didn't she feel cheated?

'Nooh,' she said, surprised at such a question, as if she had never considered it before. 'I had no education, did I?'

Then wouldn't it have been better to have been born, say, fifty years later, after the Butler Education Act, when she would have had a better chance of an education? 'I don't know. I've been quite happy. Feminism is okay, if that's what people want, but it's never interested me.'

On the whole, she thinks the world in her lifetime has changed for the better, except in a few respects. 'There were no gays in my days, nobody was molested. It seems to me the world has gone mad, sex-wise. But, really, I don't think there's any more badness in the world than there ever has been. What badness there is is usually to do with sex or, more likely, money. I'd hate to bring up a child today, in this wicked world.'

She has always voted Labour, despite her upward mobility and her home-owning capitalism. 'Mind you, I admired Mrs Thatcher. I think she's a wonderful woman. But I'm Labour. That's how I was brought up. How about you, Anne?'

Anne had been sitting in a corner during most of this chat, pretending to read a book, but listening to her mother, sometimes smiling, sometimes groaning, but never interrupting.

'I have a memory of a very early election,' continued Nancy, not

Nancy today

waiting to hear her daughter's political views. 'It was Mr Short against Mr Renwick and we all went around the streets shouting, "Vote, vote vote for Mr Short." Or for Mr Renwick. Can't remember when it was now. Or who won. It was a long time ago.

'Would you like to see some more of my poems? You can have this one, specially for you, as I know you've come over from the Lake District today.'

She gave me a beautifully printed, ornate little postcard containing a poem entitled 'Lakeland, by Nancy Lambert'. It was one of her daughter's many ingenious birthday presents. Behind her mother's back, she'd taken some of her poems and had them printed for her to give out to friends.

Every birthday, since Nancy was eighty, Anne has arranged a surprise, ranging from a tour of the Metro Centre to a flight on Concorde. She didn't expect, back in 1980, she'd still have to be dreaming them up today.

'Nancy's problems,' said Anne, when her mother had gone off to find some more poems, 'is that she is marvellous and wonderful when there's something happening, when she's active, going to one of her many church clubs, for bingo, bridge, whist or whatever, or when she's sitting talking to people, such as you – but, oh God, she goes right down and gets depressed when there's nothing happening in her life. Just like me, really . . .'

One of the minor amusements Anne suggested for her ninetieth birthday was that she should send a birthday card to the Queen Mother. After all, they were born within three days of each other. Like everyone else born in 1900, Nancy has followed her progress. She has sent her a card every year since, including a personal message and one of her little poems. She has always got back a nicely typed thank-you letter from a lady-in-waiting. Well, they are well brought-up at Clarence House.

'I've always written poems for people's birthdays or Christmas. They're just silly little verses, but my friends seem to get fun out of them. I hope the Queen Mother does . . .'

28

THE QUEEN MOTHER

The Queen Mother

The Queen Mother is the best-known person born in 1900. She went on to be the most loved and most popular person in Britain this century. An exaggeration, a tease, a ridiculous sweeping generalisation? Or just an example of that old-fashioned, uncritical royal genuflection that was typical of so much of this century and which we'll probably never see again?

If you look back over the decades to 1900, it is hard to think of anyone who has been loved more by the British public. Winston Churchill was greatly loved, but only for a while and then not enough to see him triumph in 1945. Margaret Thatcher, while greatly loved by some, was equally greatly hated, even at the height of her power. The present Queen has never been unloved, but it has to be said she commands admiration and respect rather than adoration. Diana, Princess of Wales, is now an icon, but still has her detractors. As for sports stars and entertainers, explorers and innovators, they have had their moments of glory and hero-worship, but none has stayed constantly in general affection for seventy-five years, which is how long the Queen Mother has been a public figure.

I asked to interview her. Fat chance, but worth a try. I received a polite reply from Sir Alastair Aird, her private secretary, in which he said he had discussed it with the Queen Mother who was 'most interested to hear' about my book and was sure it will 'contain much fascinating information' but, alas, she must stick to her rule of not granting interviews. (He did give me permission to quote the letter, so that was something.)

The Queen Mother has not given an interview since 1923, the year she became engaged, and was ticked off sharply for doing so by George V. She has only twice, as far as we know, given background help to any biographers, to Lady Cynthia Asquith in 1927 and to Dorothy Laird in 1966. But, goodness, the millions of newspaper pages, the hundreds of books, hours of radio and TV that have been devoted to her long life. With more to come, after her death. Will there be revelations, things we didn't know or understand, when an official biography eventually appears? There are certainly a few minor mysteries about her life that need to be explained.

She was born on 4 August 1900, the ninth of ten children, and her

Letter from the Queen Mother's Household

father was Lord Glamis, soon to be the 14th Earl of Strathmore. The aristocracy, just like the working classes, had clearly little knowledge of, interest in or access to birth control. And, like most large families of the time, one was lost in childhood – Violet, who died in 1893, aged eleven, from diphtheria.

Most of my other twenty people born in 1900 also came from large or large-ish families, so Elizabeth was typical of the times. Two came from families of ten children, one from nine and three from eight, making in all an average of five children per family in my random sample. Many also lost a brother or sister in childhood.

Her birth took place in England, not Scotland, despite her ancient Scottish background. That much has been agreed upon. But where in England? Until 1980, all biographies agreed her birthplace was St Paul's, Walden Bury, which is near Hitchin in Hertfordshire, about thirty miles north of London where her father had their southern home. Her father registered her birth at Hitchin over six weeks later, on 21 September 1900, and was fined 7s. 6d. for being late.

On the certificate, he registered her as a local birth and gave his occupation as 'peer's eldest son', the sort of occupation you rarely come across today in the job centres. (He didn't become earl till 1904.) He gave his name as Claude George Bowes Lyon, signing himself Glamis (for Lord Glamis) and his new daughter as Elizabeth Angela Marguerite. Note there was no hyphen in Bowes Lyon. That was an optional extra, sometimes used by the family, sometimes not. For many years Elizabeth often introduced herself as Elizabeth Lyon.

It appears Lord Glamis was not around during the birth or even the first few weeks of his new daughter's life. He was up in Scotland, at Glamis Castle, his main home, where he was busy playing cricket, according to a report in the *Forfar Herald* on 24 August 1900. His wife had actually given birth in London, while staying at her family's home in Grosvenor Gardens, before returning to St Paul's, Walden Bury. There has been a suggestion that the birth was sudden, often the case when you have had lots of babies already, and it took place in a taxi or an ambulance. An even wilder new suggestion, dreamed up in 1997 by an American writer, is that Elizabeth might have been illegitimate, that Lord Glamis was not her father. This all comes about because of the continuing mystery of her exact birthplace. Clarence House has confirmed in recent years that she was born in London, not Hertfordshire, but has given no further details. The Queen Mother looks upon herself as Scottish, with her childhood home Glamis Castle, and doubtless considers a birth in either London or Hertfordshire faintly irrelevant.

Her father, whose family history can be traced back to King Robert the Bruce, had come into a fortune of some £250,000 when he became earl, equal to around £37.5 million today, plus thousands of acres and four handsome homes, so she was brought up in near-royal wealth and affluence. Glamis Castle is, in fact, much older and much nicer than Balmoral. Her father was a country-loving gentleman who grew his moustache so long and silky that he had to part it when he came to kiss his grandchildren. He made his own cocoa for breakfast and ate plum pudding every day for lunch and generally sounded a good egg.

As a child Elizabeth was taught at home by governesses for many years then briefly attended a girls' school in Sloane Street, London, run by the Birtwhistle sisters, where she passed her Junior Oxford Examination. On 4 August 1914, as her fourteenth birthday present, she was taken to the theatre, the London Coliseum, where she saw a variety show. It also happened to be the day war broke out, and the streets to and from the theatre were filled with excited crowds.

Four of her older brothers immediately joined up, like young men everywhere; two of them hurriedly married their sweethearts before going off to fight. One brother, Fergus, who joined the Black Watch, was killed at Loos in 1915. Another brother, Michael, was reported dead, but three months later was found alive in a prisoner-of-war camp.

Glamis Castle was turned into a military hospital during the war and Elizabeth acted as an unofficial orderly, along with one of her sisters, Rose, who had trained as a nurse. During those first few months, so she later told Cynthia Asquith, she was busy 'knitting, knitting, knitting'. She also made shirts for the local battalion, the 5th Black Watch. 'My chief occupation was crumpling up tissue paper until it was so soft it no longer crackled, to put into the linings of sleeping bags.' Doesn't sound exactly like medical assistance, but after the war many survivors reported how she had been endlessly cheerful and kind, helping the sick and wounded of all ranks.

In 1919, she was given a coming-out party in London but doesn't appear to have been officially presented at court, despite her age and aristocratic background. Yet another small mystery, which nobody has explained, not even Dorothy Laird, though she did offer the comment that the Queen Mother has always liked to keep secret, even from her own household, inconsequential personal matters.

She loved dancing and parties, everyone agrees on that, and the society pages described her as one of the beauties of the season. She was small at only five feet two, but perfectly formed. It was at a ball in May 1920 that she met Prince Albert, known as Bertie, the King's second son. They had met as children, at parties, and at one she is said to have palmed off some crystallised cherries on his plate.

Bertie fell madly in love with her, as others had before. On the face of it he was not a brilliant catch, as he had a stammer and bandy legs, which had been put in splints when he was a child to straighten them. He was also shy and moody, quite unlike his elder brother David, the Prince of Wales, who was the golden boy, the fun person, the toast of London society. Eventually, Bertie proposed to Lady Elizabeth – and was turned down. He tried again, and was still rejected.

Most biographers, including the so-called authorised ones, have explained her refusal by suggesting 'she could not face public life'. Elizabeth had always been known for her social gifts, her ability to smile and charm her way in any company, perhaps too sweetly at times, and perhaps her choice of pink frocks and hats was a little too sickly, but there seems little doubt that she was the sort of person well able to face the public. Penelope Mortimer, in a highly unauthorised biography in 1986, but forward another explanation – that at the time there was someone else she fancied. Which would make sense. But who? It could have been a young blade called Captain James Stuart who was then shipped off to Canada, or perhaps even the Prince of Wales himself. There had been newspaper reports that the heir to the throne was about to get engaged 'to the daughter of a well-known Scottish peer', though she had not been named. Looking back, it does seem unlikely. The Prince of Wales, like our present Prince of Wales, always had a fancy for the older, more mature, experienced woman.

Bertie persevered, with the support and good wishes of the Royal Family, who saw Elizabeth as a perfect partner for him. He visited her at Glamis, where she showed him round, and they met elsewhere at social functions. He proposed again, in January 1923, in the wood beside Elizabeth's Hertfordshire home, and this time she accepted. He at once sent a telegram to his parents at Sandringham: 'ALL RIGHT – BERTIE.' Three days later he wrote to his mother, Queen Mary: 'I know I am very lucky to have won her over at last.'

They were married quite soon afterwards, on 26 April 1923, and she became the Duchess of York. She was twenty-two, young by today's standards, but typical of the times. He wore his RAF uniform, as a group captain. Her wedding dress was deep ivory and she wore a veil made from an ancient piece of lace lent by Queen Mary. The ceremony was at Westminster Abbey, conducted by the Archbishop of Canterbury, Cosmo Lang, but the service was not broadcast over the wireless in case, so it was said, people might be listening while wearing hats or, even worse, sitting in public houses.

Their honeymoon was spent in Britain not abroad, like young couples of all classes, at least those who could afford a honeymoon. Most of it was spent in Scotland at Glamis Castle where it was cold and wet and Elizabeth caught whooping cough. Not very romantic. They returned to London and a grace-and-favour house, White Lodge, in Richmond Park.

As a second son, the Duke had few royal duties to perform, but he had several charitable posts and involved himself with boys' camps and factory visits. All his life he had felt in the shadow of his brother David. 'Rather like a human buff slip marked "Passed on to you for action",' he once remarked rather bitterly. But thanks to his wife, he did grow in confidence. She encouraged him to get treatment for his stammer from an Australian speech therapist, and together they managed to cope with it, if not quite overcome it.

Their first child, Elizabeth, was born in 1926, just as the General Strike began, and their second, Margaret Rose, in 1930. They had hoped for a son, all the papers said, and the birth had taken place in Scotland, as the Duchess hoped for a Scottish son, so again the papers said. Then that was it. Could she not manage any more? A pram was kept just in case, which would suggest they did hope for another. Or was he not up to it? How awful to have everyone speculating about such personal affairs but, of course, they did. There again, they were typical of the times in producing a relatively small family. Of my twenty people born in 1900 the average number of children per couple was 1.85, almost exactly the same as the Yorks. Was it decreasing fertility, fashion or birth control?

The Royal Tour of Australia in 1927 established the Yorks as a couple in the public eye. They travelled 30,000 miles, three books were published about their trip and the Duchess charmed everyone she met. They were away for six months, leaving behind their baby daughter, but they saw it as part of their duty as minor royals to put up with such sacrifices.

Not for a moment did anyone expect them to become major royals. George V died in January 1936 and the Prince of Wales automatically became King. When he married someone suitable, as Bertie had, and produced children, the succession would bypass the Yorks. Even when the possibility first leaked out that David, as Edward VIII, might do the unimaginable and abdicate to marry the divorced Mrs Simpson, there was talk that Bertie would not succeed to the throne because of his stammer and his general lack of charisma. It was suggested that his younger brother, the Duke of Kent, who was considered more glamorous and also had a son, might become King instead.

On 10 December 1936, Edward VIII abdicated. Stirring times, never forgotten by anyone alive and listening at the time. Bertie became King and the Archbishop of Canterbury, in a broadcast about the abdication, said the new King had 'a momentary hesitation in his speech' but as the King didn't find it embarrassing neither should we. Very thoughtful, but hard to believe that either Bertie or his wife felt grateful to him for pointing it out.

Elizabeth, as Queen, became the first consort since Tudor times who was truly British. Wherever her exact place of birth, she had definitely been born in Britain, from pure British blood on either side, unlike all those foreign consorts who had gone before – and since. (Prince Philip, after all, is Greek–German.)

Queen Mary had been born in London, but her father was German. She had the advantage as consort of always looking regal, as she was tall and stately, whereas Elizabeth was small, with a tendency to dumpiness, and dressed more like a suburban wife, with her passion for unsubtle pinks and baby blue, though after the Coronation she acquired her own official dress-maker in Norman Hartnell. Unlike Queen Mary, too, she exuded charm and naturalness – and, dare one say it, sex appeal.

Two weeks after the Coronation, Ramsay MacDonald told the new Queen that the King had 'come on magnificently' since his accession. She was naturally pleased, then asked how she herself was doing. 'Oh, you,' said MacDonald, with a flourish of his hands, indicating that everyone knew she was perfect for the job, as if to the manner born.

She and the King devoted themselves to their royal duties, endlessly touring the empire. In May 1939, they made a successful visit to Canada and the USA, which, royal apologists later claimed, helped to encourage pro-British feelings in North America when the war began.

During the war, many members of the aristocracy fled abroad, or sent their families to the country for safety, but the King and Queen refused to leave. The Queen made a point of visiting bomb-damaged cities all over Britain, turning up in her high heels and brightest frocks, though some thought more sombre clothes might have been more suitable. 'They would wear their best dresses if they were coming to see me,' she commented. When eventually Buckingham Palace was hit by a bomb, she was quite glad, in a way, as she could now face the East End of London. Buckingham Palace was actually hit nine times. Windows were blown out, walls were damaged, the garden ruined and they were invaded by a plague of rats.

Inside, they insisted on living like everyone else with ration books, the minimum of heat and only five inches of hot water in a bath, which rather appalled Mrs Roosevelt, who came on a visit in 1942 to see how British women were surviving. During her visit, they ate Lord Woolton's famous pie and when she enquired what was in it, the Queen airily replied, 'Sawdust, probably.' The pie, made mostly of carrots, was served on gold plates by liveried flunkeys and when the King and Queen retreated to the Buckingham Palace shelters, they were able to sit on gilt chairs. Some standards were maintained.

The Queen practised in the gardens with a revolver and a rifle, much to the alarm of visitors when they heard the shots. She insisted that if London and the Palace were invaded, she would personally shoot any enemies. Hitler described her as "The most dangerous woman in London." This could have been propaganda, or even irony. It made a change from a more frequently heard description of her, made many times over the years: "The person you would most like to live in the bungalow next door."

King Haakon of Norway, on a wartime visit, was surprised to find the palace so badly guarded, and pointed out that German parachutists could land in the Mall at any time and easily invade the Palace. The King, rather smugly, said there was a secret system for countering any attack: all he had to do was press a certain button. To demonstrate, he pressed it – and nothing happened. Again he pressed. Still no reply. He rang the guard on duty to ask why he hadn't reacted. The guard said there couldn't have been an attack or he would have been informed. The King and Queen found this funny, but the King of Norway went away worried about their safety.

Where possible they spent weekends at Windsor. On one visit, the Queen went into her bedroom to find a man hiding behind the curtains. He jumped out and grabbed her by the ankles. 'For a moment, my heart stood still,' she is reported to have said. 'Then I realised he meant no harm.' The man poured out all his grievances, how he had lost all his family in the blitz, before he was taken away and found to be an army deserter. 'Poor man, I was so sorry for him.' (A similar thing happened many years later to the present Queen, which could indicate that King Haakon had been right to worry.)

After the war, the royal tours of the colonies began again. In South Africa in 1947 the Queen spoke to a Boer War veteran, who said he was pleased to meet her, but he still couldn't forgive the English. 'I understand perfectly,' she replied. 'We feel much the same in Scotland.'

From 1948 onwards, the King's health began to deteriorate. He suffered pains in his legs and it was thought at one time he might have to have one amputated. His ill-health was kept secret as much as possible, even from Princess Elizabeth who in 1947 had married Prince Philip. The King was eventually diagnosed as having lung cancer. He had been a smoker, as can be seen from many of the early photographs of him with the Queen, but it was normal, not to say smart, to smoke in those days. He died on 6 February 1952. Elizabeth was left a widow, at the age of only fifty-one. As ever, she said her duty was to soldier on. One of the distractions she organised for herself was to buy and renovate a castle in the far north of Scotland, the Castle of Mey, which became her private holiday home.

Apart from her royal duties, she has devoted a lot of time to fishing and horse-racing. At her London home, Clarence House, where she has lived for over forty years, she had a satellite dish installed as early as 1987 so she could watch the racing. She has a collection of paintings, from Matisse to L. S. Lowry, and fine furniture, but Clarence House has never been open to the public, unlike Buckingham Palace, so the general public has never seen her treasures or been able to estimate her personal tastes.

I managed to get myself into the Castle of Mey once, which was even more isolated and windswept than I had expected, and observed some of her paintings. There were a few water-colours by Prince Philip, relegated to the corners, while pride of place was given to some local amateur works of art, made out of sea shells. Very nice, I thought. The week before I was there, a wild-looking Canadian had been picked up by the police while wandering round the castle grounds carrying a black bag. In it was found a paintbrush. He said he had come to paint the castle walls. He had met the Queen Mother in Canada and she'd told him she needed a jolly lot of work done on her castle. That's what happens, of course, when you make polite conversation as charmingly as the Queen Mother. The man was allowed to go free.

Her taste in TV programmes, racing aside, is much the same as everyone else's. A guest was once very late for a dinner party at a country house where she was staying and apologised profusely for getting lost. She accepted the apologies with a smile. 'It was lovely. For once I could watch the whole of *Dad's Army.*'

She has rarely ever had to cancel an official function, which is an indication of her excellent health. Even aged ninety-six, she turned out in the winter cold for Remembrance Day ceremonies and Black Watch engagements, and at ninety-seven was still going to race meetings. Not many of my others born in 1900 were quite so active.

Her worst illness, as far as is known, was in 1966 when she had an operation 'to clear an abdominal blockage', as her surgeons reported at the time. It was thirteen years later that Helen Cathcart declared that it had been a colostomy, which has never been denied. The news was applauded by the Colostomy Welfare Group – who said it had always known – because it would give encouragement to the 20,000 others who have the operation each year. In 1996 Elizabeth had a hip replacement and was seen for a while hobbling on two sticks, but in 1997, Prince Charles said she was fit and well again and had gone back to Scottish country dancing.

The world's media has had obituaries ready since 1980. In 1993, the news swept Australia that she had died: a Sky TV technician had seen an internal notice, thought it was real, and had rung his mum in Brisbane to tell her. The Governor General of Australia had to come on air to announce that the Queen Mother was still very much alive. In 1994, BBC TV had to apologise after her death had been accidentally flashed on Ceefax.

If I had been granted an interview with her, aged ninety-seven, she would certainly have been up to it, judging by all the accounts of her physical and mental condition. I might have had to put up with the racing on in the background, but I would have coped. After all, Dorothy, the ex-Birmingham University student, had the snooker on throughout our two-hour chat.

Most people of the Queen Mother's age find their eyesight fading, but if she can still watch the racing then it can't be too bad. Hearing also causes problems, but you don't really need that to watch horse-races. I've studied photographs, but haven't noticed any signs of a hearing aid, though she probably has one. For most people of her age, two hours of chat is more than enough before they tire or start to repeat themselves. Falling will be her main worry, but Clarence House is doubtless arranged like high-class sheltered housing with nurses and helpers on twenty-four-hour duty.

I have no doubt that her early memories will be much clearer than recent ones. Her first memory in life is probably of Glamis Castle, playing with the dressing-up box perhaps. Those First World War years, looking after the wounded, will be as fresh in her mind as they have always been. I would probably have to cut her short on the early stuff, as I did with many of the others, to get on to her dancing years and early boyfriends. Those days would also be clear, and probably every frock she ever wore, but getting her to admit she turned Bertie down twice might be difficult. The evidence has been published, in books about George VI, but she has probably rationalised it, not wanting to give offence to the memory of her dear husband.

She is now the last survivor of the main participants in the abdication crisis and, with a bit of luck, I might have got her to talk about it. She might even have said it was all lust and sex, selfishness and lack of moral fibre, that was the top and bottom of it, but I can't believe she would blame the Duke of Windsor for Bertie's death, as some royal writers have alleged. The cause was lung cancer, after all. She would probably deny there was any hint of revenge in the treatment of the Windsors from then on, saying it was for the good of the monarchy and the country. Most probably, though, any mention of the Windsors would result in a blank stare, or a pretence of not having heard, which would make clear that they were not to be discussed.

The Second World War years would probably have brought out the best in her. She is said to be a good mimic, and there are probably many funny stories of wartime Buck House with which she has regaled her children and grandchildren. The last forty-five years, since the death of her husband, will yield little. I would try, of course, to bring up one or two of the more dramatic royal disasters – sorry, events – and be told pretty sharpish that such topics are personal.

I would guess she was at her happiest in the 1920s, dancing the nights away, and in the 1930s, as a young mother. Apart from the death of her husband, the unhappiest period was in the 1970s when Princess Margaret's marriage collapsed, ending in divorce from Lord Snowdon in 1978.

She is not alone, of course, in having a divorced child. It happened to several others born in 1900. But where the Royal Family has exceeded the national norm in marital problems is in the next generation. The Princess Royal, the Duke of York and the Prince of Wales all divorced, which left the present Queen with six grandchildren all from broken homes, and the Queen Mother as the matriarch of one of the country's most dysfunctional families. I don't think she would have talked about any of that, unless she'd had a few drinks or was feeling unusually maudlin, when Di and Fergie might have got much of the blame. Grandmas do tend to take the side of their own.

To get on to more cheerful subjects, I would have asked her, as I asked all my subjects, for her own explanation for getting to ninety-seven. She would have pointed to the fact that her father was almost ninety, her mother seventy-eight when they died, so her genes were pretty good. No doubt she would have boasted about moderation in most things, as they all do. She doesn't appear to smoke, though there is an early photograph of her with a pipe stuck in her mouth, but that is said to have been a joke. She's always liked a drink, and probably still has one every evening, which again is not untypical.

She would probably say that being cheerful and optimistic have kept her going, managing to look on the bright side, and I would nod sagely in agreement. There would be few regrets about things she hadn't done, places she hadn't seen, as she has been everywhere. She once talked in her late sixties about regrets to Dorothy Laird: 'The only regret one has as one grows older is that things do not matter so strongly.' True, but most people would see it as a pleasure of age.

I would have asked about people she had met, such as Winston Churchill, and probably not have got very far. People at ninety-seven have unusual gaps in their memories: events and people are erased. She would be more likely to remember details of long-dead corgis and race-horses that didn't win.

On the subject of the modern world she would doubtless say there is too much violence, too much obsession with sex. Everyone else said so. I would point to the medical advances in her lifetime, such as hip replacements, and the joys of radio and TV, and she would charmingly agree, then add that fishing and horses, two of her favourite pleasures, are rather ancient.

I'd hope to hear her reflections on one of the institutions that has changed most in this century: the Royal Family. It must often appear incredible to her. Even looking back at my own lifetime, it is hard to believe what has happened.

As a child, during the war years, one of my treats when visiting my grandmother was being allowed to look through her *Daily Express* picture books about the Royal Family, of course having first washed my hands. I knew all about the little Princesses, their dolls' house, their pet dogs. In the 1950s, I stood up with everyone else when the National Anthem was played in cinemas. All stories in all newspapers about the Royal Family were reverential. Even in the 1960s, no one was allowed to impersonate a member of the Royal Family on the West End stage. The royals were sacred, untouchable, a model for us all.

Now the Royal Family are routinely mocked and parodied. No journalist worth his or her salt would write a piece without getting in some sneer. The present Queen is pitied rather than looked up to. Every member of her family has at some time been derided or ridiculed and the most intimate details of their personal lives revealed, with pictures, or speculated upon.

A BBC TV film in 1969, *Royal Family* by Richard Cawston, is often said to have started this trend by focusing for the first time on the Royal Family in private, at home, instead of in public at a formal occasion. It seems respectful now, compared with what came after, such as *Spitting Image*, but it was the beginning of a new approach.

The Royal Family themselves helped the desanctifying process by appearing in *It's a Royal Knockout* and by making public admissions about personal matters, as the Prince of Wales did in his TV interview with Jonathan Dimbleby, when he talked about his adultery, followed by the Princess of Wales on *Panorama*, who regaled the nation with her suicidal tendencies, affairs and marital problems. What on earth did the Queen Mother make of all that? Turned off, probably, or switched to the horse-racing channel.

In 1997, she was photographed by Lord Snowdon for *Country Life* – which she first appeared in in 1923 on her engagement to Bertie. She was rather mocked for wearing a silly-looking hat with a feather and a bright blue raincoat. At ninety-seven, you are allowed to be a bit eccentric, but back in 1923 she was only being herself, wearing the bright colours she has always gone for. If you look back over the century, she hasn't changed.

Who knows if the Royal Family will survive the next century? Who knows if the Queen Mother, or any of those others born in 1900, will survive this one? But they were there, from the beginning.

EPILOGUE

In 1922 Winston Churchill sighed wearily and observed, 'What a disappointment the twentieth century has been.' In 1933 Trotsky, in exile, considered it had been 'the most disturbed century within living memory'. Views of this century, or of any century, depend on where and when you stand and on what has happened so far in your own lifetime.

During the funeral of Diana, Princess of Wales, in September 1997, the nation was amazed by itself, at its own outpouring of public grief. Her death in a car crash in Paris at the age of thirty-six was sudden and unexpected and gave us what in effect was a royal funeral, though a rather different one from that which began the century, Queen Victoria's in January 1901.

We were all astonished by the reaction to the Princess's death, but perhaps its comprehensiveness was the most interesting aspect, with people from all classes, all ages, native Brits as well as immigrants, people at home and abroad, experiencing similar emotions. The nation appeared united, coming together as it had during the blitz, though the emotions were a bit more open and messier, a triumph in a way for the therapists, the ones who encourage us all to let it show, be touchy and feely, just like the Princess herself.

She was seen as a Person Who Cared in what many felt was an uncaring world, where profits are put before people. Technology and science, greed and money had swept away a sense of community and the value of the individual, which supposedly we once all enjoyed back in 1900 or in some other distant but rosy past.

I don't feel as depressed as many people in this book felt about the way the world is going. I have enjoyed most of the technological advances, such as wireless, TV, computers, jet travel. I am thankful for the enormous advances in medicine. We will all now live longer – even if pessimists say that all this longer life will do is give us more life in which to be ill or to worry about being ill.

It has been a good century for women, with universal suffrage and equal opportunities in the workplace. Now women have a chance to be themselves, to fulfil their potential, which many in this book were not able to do.

This century has also seen the most appalling horrors: machine-guns, gas chambers, atom bombs, biological warfare, ethnic cleansing and other examples of man's inhumanity to man. Such horrors have not, alas, been unique to this century. Only the scale. It has also seen the rise and fall of Communism.

The Internet, we are told, will turn the globe not just into an electronic village, but a machine in one room of one house that we can all use and share. A lot of good it will do us. All media are only as good or as illuminating as their content. The medium itself has no message. It's just another tool, no better than chalk on slate, pen and ink, print on paper. I predict now there will still be books in the year 2099.

I also predict that all predictions will be wrong. They always are, because they are based on what appears to be happening now, taking a straight line forward, saying this is now, so that will be then, but lines in history, like lines in human lives, are rarely straight. They wiggle about, take unexpected bends and bumps, which we can't imagine now as we look darkly forward. The next horror predicted for us is that we will pollute, poison, then destroy the ozone layer and, ultimately, the whole planet. I bet we will be here in 2099. Breathing heavily.

Of the twentieth-century arrivals in this book, no one at this moment doubts that the Labour Party is here to stay, but political parties do have their own lifespan, their own organic growth and death. Birmingham University, or similar, will be here for ever, as it seems impossible to imagine a world without a need for training and education. West Ham United might drop divisions, or even out of sight, but football, here and across the world, is still growing – 172 nations entered the 1998 World Cup. Freud is clearly not forgotten, however much his theories are denounced, nor has psychoanalysis disappeared, but there will be new theories, new ways of explaining ourselves to ourselves.

It doesn't look as though food will disappear, as was predicted earlier in the century, to be replaced by pills, but fast food in the future will probably get faster and less foody, with more fads and fashions that might kill off the mighty hamburger. It's hard to believe that motorcars, as we know them now, will still be here in another century. The mystery is why they have lasted so long, when they have clearly outstayed their welcome. The death of the *Daily Express* is predicted daily but, then, that has been so throughout much of its life.

The lives of the individuals in this book show that you can't predict anything. They have all come through two world wars, plus other passing problems. Become an alcoholic in your early years, fall out of the sky in countless aeroplanes, yet you can still survive to the age of ninety-eight. Smoking won't necessarily get you either, or eating fatty, unhealthy foods all your life.

Moderation in all things is useful, and most observed that the right genes are probably important. An interest in the outside world, in other people and things, rather than being wrapped up in yourself, is also helpful in surviving to a great age. Being cheerful would seem vital, to have an optimistic view of life, yet two or three struck me as clearly miserable and pessimistic and, according to their families, that tendency had always been there. The rule is – there are no rules. Surviving the twentieth century is a matter of luck.

How many of my interviewees will actually make it? That macabre thought struck me frequently. As the book goes to press, seven have died – Richard Joyce, Dame Elizabeth Hill, Leonard Cooper, Dr David Davies, Nancy Lambert, Monty Hedges and Dorothy Ellis. My father-in-law, Arthur Forster, who inspired the book, has also died, aged ninety-six.

Before he went into his nursing home, he had given the family two instructions. 'Straight to the crem,' was the first, meaning no religious ceremony, no fancy funeral, just straight to the crematorium. His other instruction was 'Check the pockets, mind.'

His younger daughter did so before she took his clothes to an Oxfam shop, and found £300, stuffed in various pockets. Under his mattress, she came across another £300. Under the lino and the carpets, there was more money. Altogether, in crisp ten-pound notes, she discovered he had hidden almost £3,000. He had never had any capital or owned his own house, so this was a surprise. Then we found old betting slips, which gave it all away. He'd won in life, in his own way, surviving to a great age and producing a loving, successful family. And he'd also won on the horses.

Loweswater
July 1998

APPENDIX

Useful Books, Chapter Notes

Useful Books

ON THE ELDERLY

DGAA Homelife, *Centenarian Study* (London: DGAA Homelife, 1997). Copies are available for £25 from DGAA, 1 Derry Street, London W8 5HY.

ON THE YEAR 1900

John Montgomery, *1900* (London: Allen & Unwin, 1968).
Rebecca West, *1900* (London: Weidenfeld & Nicolson, 1982).

ON THE CENTURY

Peter Clarke, *Hope and Glory: Britain 1900–1990* (London: Penguin Press, 1997).
Derrik Mercer (ed.), *Chronicle of the 20th Century* (London: Chronicle, 1988).

Chapter Notes

CHAPTER 3: THE *DAILY EXPRESS*

R. Allen, *Voice of Britain: A History of the Daily Express* (London: Patrick Stephens, 1983).

The newspaper's address is: Ludgate House, 245 Blackfriars Road, London SE1 9UX; telephone: 0171 928 8000.

CHAPTER 7: BIRMINGHAM UNIVERSITY

Prof. E. Barker, *Universities in Great Britain* (SCM Press, 1931).

F. Burstall and C. Burton, *A Souvenir History of Mason College and the University of Birmingham* (Birmingham: University of Birmingham Press, 1930).

Maurice Cheesewright, *Mirror to a Mermaid: A History of Birmingham University* (Birmingham: University of Birmingham Press, 1975).

Eric Vincent and Percival Hinton, *The University of Birmingham* (Birmingham: Cornish Bros, 1947).

The university's address is: University of Birmingham, Edgbaston, Birmingham B15 2TT; telephone: 0121 414 3344. Further information on universities in the UK can be obtained from the Committee of Vice-Chancellors, 29 Tavistock Square, London WC1H 9EZ; telephone: 0171 387 9231.

CHAPTER 11: MERCEDES

Erik Johnson, *The Dawn of Motoring* (Milton Keynes: Mercedes UK, 1986).

Brian Laban, *Classic Mercedes-Benz* (London: Salamander, 1994).

Society of Motor Manufacturers and Traders, *The Motor Industry of Britain Centenary Book, 1896–1996* (London, 1996).

The company's address in the UK is: Mercedes-Benz, Tongwell, Milton Keynes, Beds MK15 8BA; telephone: 01908 245000.

CHAPTER 15: WEST HAM UNITED

John Moynihan, *The West Ham Story* (London: Arthur Barker, 1984).

Peter Steele, 'When West Ham Built Battleships: A History of the Thames Iron Works, 1846–1912'.

The club's address is: West Ham United, Boleyn Ground, Green Street, Upton Park, London E13 9AZ; telephone 0181 548 2748.

CHAPTER 18: FREUD AND *THE INTERPRETATION OF DREAMS*

Giovanni Costigan, *Freud: A Short Biography* (London: Hale, 1965).

Sigmund Freud, *The Interpretation of Dreams* (first published 1900; now available as Volume 4 of the Penguin Freud Library).

Jonathan Miller (ed.), *Freud* (London: Weidenfeld & Nicolson, 1995).

Michael Molnar, *The Diary of Sigmund Freud, 1929–39* (London: Hogarth Press, 1992).

Anthony Storr, *Freud* (Oxford, OUP, 1989).

James Strachey (trs.), *Freud: An Autobiographic Study* (London: Hogarth Press, 1946).

The address of the Freud Museum is: 20 Maresfield Gardens, Hampstead, London NW3 5SX; telephone: 0171 435 2002.

CHAPTER 21: HAMBURGERS

Ray Kroc, *Grinding It Out* (New York: St Martin's Press, 1987).

John F. Love, *McDonald's: Behind the Arches* (New York: Bantam Books, 1995).

Roger St Pierre, *McDonald's* (London: Carlton Books, 1994).

McDonald's in the UK are based at: 11–59 High Road, East Finchley, London N2 8AW; telephone: 0181 700 7000.

CHAPTER 24: THE LABOUR PARTY

Henry Pelling, *A Short History of the Labour Party* (London: Macmillan, 1968).

The party's HQ is: Millbank Towers, Millbank, London SW1P 4GT.

CHAPTER 28: THE QUEEN MOTHER

Helen Cathcart, *The Queen Mother Herself* (London: W. H. Allen, 1979).

John Cornforth, *The Queen Mother at Clarence House* (London: Michael Joseph, 1996).

Dorothy Laird, *The Queen Mother* (London: Hodder & Stoughton, 1966).

Elizabeth Longford, *The Queen Mother* (London: Weidenfeld & Nicolson, 1981).

Penelope Mortimer, *Queen Elizabeth: A Life of the Queen Mother* (London: Penguin, 1986).